Mexico and Mexicans in the Making of the United States

History, Culture, and Society Series
Center for Mexican American Studies (CMAS)
University of Texas at Austin

Mexico and Mexicans in the Making of the United States

EDITED BY JOHN TUTINO

University of Texas Press ⟨⟩ Austin

Requests for permission to reproduce material from this work should be sent to:
    Permissions
    University of Texas Press
    P.O. Box 7819
    Austin, TX 78713-7819
    www.utexas.edu/utpress/about/bpermission.html

♾ The paper used in this book meets the minimum requirements of ANSI/NISO Z39.48-1992 (R1997) (Permanence of Paper).

Library of Congress Cataloging-in-Publication Data

Mexico and Mexicans in the making of the United States / edited by John Tutino.
        p.   cm. — (History, culture, and society series)
Includes bibliographical references and index.
ISBN 978-0-292-73718-1 (cloth : alk. paper) — ISBN 978-0-292-73719-8 (e-book)
    1. Mexican Americans—History.   2. Mexicans—United States—History.
3. United States—Foreign relations—Mexico.   4. Mexico—Foreign relations—United States.   I. Tutino, John, 1947-
    E184.M5M536   2012
    973′.046872—dc23

                                                    2011040168

For the extended and expanding
Campos and Delgado families of
New Braunfels, Kyle, and Austin, Texas:
they live the challenges and triumphs engaged here.

And for all the teachers in my
NEH Summer Seminars:
they taught me that Mexican and U.S. history are one.

Contents

Preface

This volume emerged from a long history linking the University of Texas at Austin (UT) and Georgetown University. José Limón and I were graduate students in Austin in the early 1970s. José created an innovative intellectual trajectory linking literature, folklore, and Mexican American studies and was already recruited to a lead role building the Center for Mexican American Studies. I followed a traditional path to Mexican and Latin American history. We knew of each other just a bit, connected by his assistant and my comadre, Rosalinda Delgado. Our paths diverged for years while I slowly grasped the importance of integrating U.S. and Mexican history—and in the process discovered the salient importance of José's work. Meanwhile, David Montejano, a sociologist, claimed leadership as the most innovative analyst of Mexicans in Texas history while teaching in the History Department in Austin.

I left Texas for a nomadic career. At St. Olaf College I had the pleasure of overseeing Andrew Isenberg's honors thesis—on indigenous peoples in Guatemala; it was a greater pleasure to invite him to join this project in recognition of his work on native peoples and the environment in the U.S. West.

As I settled at Georgetown in the early 1990s, my work became more transnational, crossing scholarly borders to trek north from Mexico into the United States. The teachers who joined the six National Endowment for the Humanities (NEH) Summer Seminars I led between 1990 and 2000 were a key stimulus to this project. They insisted that the histories of Mexico and the United States were inseparable—even as some NEH staffers resisted the notion.

Then Jane McAuliffe became dean of Georgetown College. The Americas Initiative that sponsored this project was her idea, and she put funds where her idea led. The goal was to cross national, ethnic, and disciplinary boundaries in innovative ways. She offered me the opportunity to lead the Initiative; I knew I was too busy as History Department chair, but the promise was too important to set aside. This volume emerged from the Initiative's first conference.

Jane has moved on to lead Bryn Mawr College; her vision marks this volume and much more that lives at Georgetown. Dean Chet Gillis has kept the Initiative alive in the face of economic constraints, demonstrating his commitment to the challenge of hemispheric understanding. The faculty community that continues to meet in monthly seminars to discuss texts in progress, crossing traditional borders and mixing disciplines, contributed to this volume in many ways. Our continuing Americas conferences keep us all creative.

From the beginning, the goal was a gathering of scholars to generate a volume. I had to invite José Limón and David Montejano—and Drew Isenberg, too. Then I asked myself who else had shaped my understanding in transforming ways and approached Ramón Gutiérrez, Shelley Streeby, and Devra Weber. Working with colleagues to recruit Katie Benton-Cohen to the Georgetown History Department introduced me to her work before it was published; we invited her to the conference and the volume before she got to the department. We are all illuminated by her youthful innovation. If I had an early idea, it was transformed in conversations among the participants and in learning from their texts.

Who should publish our volume? The obvious answer was the distinguished History, Culture, and Society Series published by the University of Texas Press. I proposed, José Limón facilitated, and Theresa May and two anonymous readers welcomed us with energy. While our project developed at the intersection of Georgetown and UT, many have moved on: David had already left for Berkeley when we began; José has just opened a new chapter at Notre Dame; Jane left for Bryn Mawr after the conference but before the book that presents the first published fruit of her vision. Katie and I remain at Georgetown; Theresa holds strong as a creative force at UT Press. The Texas-Georgetown link that stimulated this volume seems diasporic—perhaps a fitting foundation for studies of the inseparable history of Mexico and the United States.

Important assistance in making the Americas Initiative work has come from Kathleen Gallagher since the beginning. Stephen Levy produced the common bibliography and helped assemble the manuscript for publication. Bill Nelson made maps with skill and good cheer.

This edited volume really is a group project.

Mexico and Mexicans in the Making of the United States

Mexico and Mexicans Making U.S. History

JOHN TUTINO

The lives and rights of Mexicans living and working in the United States have been topics of discussion and debate since the 1840s. Recently, North American integration within an accelerating globalization of production and trade, work and culture has fixed political debates on "illegal" immigration. People from almost everywhere break U.S. border rules in search of work and new chances—for a few months, a few years, or a lifetime. Still, the largest numbers arrive from Mexico.

Political contenders and mainstream media fixate on Mexican migration "problems," Mexican labor "problems," even Mexican border security "problems." The fixation proved especially strong during the economic boom—or bubble—years of 2004-2008. For a time, the bubble burst, the boom gone, public talk about invasive Mexicans faded. Then, as the U.S. economy slowly revived, the 2010 election season saw the state of Arizona pass legislation that brought heated debates about Mexicans and migration back to the center of national attention. One searches in vain for parallel concern about the consequences for Mexican workers and families of the lack of work in the United States, the dearth of dollars in Mexican communities, and the impact of the U.S. crash on Mexicans' lives.

Migration is not the only focus of those who malign Mexico and Mexicans in U.S. public and political culture. The United States sustains an enormous demand for marijuana, cocaine, and other stimulants it defines as illegal drugs. That demand creates a vast market, and illegality makes it a rich, risky, and too often deadly market. A constitutionally protected market for guns in the United States supplies weapons that sustain both Mexican cartels and U.S. distributors in a transnational economy of deadly profitability. Still, U.S. culture proclaims and inflames a "Mexican" drug problem.

The rush to blame Mexico and Mexicans is not limited to migrants hired by U.S. employers and drug cartels that supply U.S. markets. The spring of 2009 brought another wave of worry about Mexican invasion—the H1N1 swine flu. Fortunately, the influenza proved more debilitating than deadly. Mexicans in Mexico suffered most—in disease, death, and daily restrictions. Still, U.S. media regaled a fearful public with visions of a deadly "Mexican" invader poised to kill susceptible "Americans" until it became likely that the virus had jumped from hogs to humans in a Mexican community where a U.S.-owned industrial slaughterhouse operated with few environmental and health safeguards. Then focus on the virus as another Mexican invader faded, giving way to a more constructive emphasis on global health in a globalizing world.

The flu became another episode of U.S. political and public culture constructing Mexico and Mexicans as others, as antagonists, as invaders—or worse. When scholars analyze the historical roles of Mexico and Mexicans in the United States, we too emphasize invasions and problematic migrations: the U.S. invasion of Mexico in the 1840s to claim vast territories, followed by rising waves of Mexican migration into regions of the United States that were once Mexican (and far beyond). Others emphasize exclusions: the denial of rights of property and citizenship to Mexicans in territories taken by the United States, despite the promises of the Treaty of Guadalupe Hidalgo; later Mexican migrants' exclusion from prosperity and political participation. There can be no doubt that invasions, migrations, and exclusions, historical and contemporary, matter to the linked histories of Mexico and the United States, and to Mexicans in the United States.

But they are not the whole of these histories. This volume aims to depart from established emphases and offer new perspectives on the historical and continuing roles of Mexico and Mexicans in making the United States. We seek to move beyond prevalent perceptions and debates, public and scholarly, grounded in an enduring but limited understanding of history. Most scholars presume that the nineteenth-century U.S. invasion that turned the Mexican North into the U.S. West led to a pervasive Anglo-American political, economic, and cultural dominance that left peoples of Hispanic ancestry a subordinated and often excluded underclass. Later migrations reinforced that subordination, leaving Anglo ways to persist and predominate. In that context, scholarship about Mexicans in the United States focuses on political exclusions, economic exploitations, ethnic differences, and assertions of rights.

There are essential and enduring truths in these understandings. The West was taken in a questionable war of conquest. Mexicans who suddenly became U.S. citizens were denied rights and pressed toward marginal economic roles. Through the twentieth century and into the twenty-first, migration from Mexico has remained essential to the settlement and development of the United States—West and East, rural and urban. And upon arrival, most migrants have faced relegation to a culturally alienated underclass. In that context, a struggle for rights has been inevitable and essential. It remains an essential focus of scholarly analysis.[1] How and why Mexican migrants—so desired by so many U.S. employers, from great corporations to families seeking maids and lawn workers—are constructed as alien invaders deserves equally careful study.

To promote a rethinking of current challenges, the chapters here aim to refocus historical understanding to emphasize the participation of Mexico and Mexicans in the foundation and development of the United States. We build upon studies of conquest-incorporation, migration-intrusion, and labor-exclusion (where many of our authors have made key contributions) to ask how early Hispanic foundations, decades of Mexican sovereignty, and their legacies in economic, political, and cultural interactions across sometimes shifting and always permeable borders led to ways arguably "Mexican" becoming incorporated into production and work, life and understanding in the United States. In our view, Mexico is not ultimately "other" to the United States; Mexicans are not "invaders" of the United States. Rather, Mexico and Mexicans have been and remain key participants (among many and diverse peoples) in the construction of the United States—our prosperity, our power in the world, our promise of inclusion, even our ways of segmentation and exclusion. Mexico and Mexicans are essential parts of "us," not an alien "them," despite the persistent insistence of so many of us in imagining an alien and invasive other.

U.S. history is opening to new perspectives. In *The Story of American Freedom*, Eric Foner brings the participations of women and African Americans and their struggles for equal inclusions to the center of the national narrative. Thomas Bender, in *A Nation among Nations*, sets the history of the United States in global context; he recognizes the importance of the 1840s war with Mexico in setting the vast boundaries and claiming the unparalleled resources that constituted a continental nation and set it on course to civil war before it could rise to global power.

Neither emphasizes the importance of Mexican foundations and Mexican American participation in making the United States. That is the goal of this volume.

We offer chapters that range from colonial times through the twentieth century and call for new appreciation of the constructive participations of Mexicans in shaping the United States. We offer differing emphases and interpretations, some converging, some raising new debates. We have discussed our common vision and our debates; here we share those conversations, hoping that wider discussions will lead to more inclusive understandings of Mexico and Mexicans in the historical formation and contemporary life of the United States.

The rest of the Introduction sketches the vision of Mexican foundations and participations in U.S. history that emerged from our studies. It proceeds by outlining our chapters, linking their themes, and adding discussions that aim to integrate the larger understanding we are approaching: a look at the U.S.-Mexican War of 1846–1848; a long section on migration and labor; a consideration of changing gender relations in the late twentieth century.

Hispanic Foundations and Indigenous Adaptations

Ways of life forged under Spanish rule set legacies that have endured, adapted, and expanded to shape the United States in important ways. We often forget that from the Carolinas to Florida and along the Gulf Coast, from New Orleans up the Mississippi to Saint Louis, and from Texas through New Mexico to California, most early and enduring contacts between Europeans and native peoples occurred under Spanish sovereignty. In 1776, the Spanish Empire ruled more of the current territory of the United States than did the British colonies that proclaimed themselves United States.[2] U.S. history recognizes the expansions that came with the acquisition of Florida from Spain, the purchase from France of vast Louisiana territories long ruled by Spain, and the taking of Texas, New Mexico, California, and more by war in the 1840s. Yet we presume that those acquisitions brought land and few people, opportunities but not legacies that endured.

My chapter, "Capitalist Foundations," explores how the dynamic commercial and expansive ways of Spanish North America shaped the Mexican North and the U.S. West. A colonial society grounded in mining,

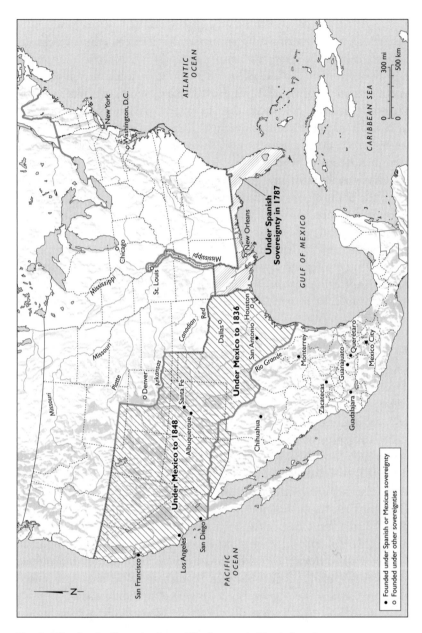

Map I.1. Overlapping Sovereignties and Settlements in North America

irrigated cultivation, and commercial grazing; forged by European, African, and Native American immigrants; and marked by ethnic amalgamations began in the sixteenth century around Querétaro and Zacatecas, now in north-central Mexico. By the early 1800s, it had driven north to encompass key regions of Texas, New Mexico, and California. I outline the creation of that colonial society, its pivotal role in early capitalism, its northward expansion, its incorporation into the United States, and how its legacies continue to shape regions once under Spanish and Mexican rule, and others far beyond.[3]

Silver was the most important commodity (and money) in the world in the eighteenth century and New Spain was the world's leading silver producer. From 1700 to 1780, output there increased four times over—and held at historical peak levels to 1810. A century of silver-driven dynamism sent commercial settlement deep into Texas, brought new economic activity into long-settled regions of New Mexico, and drove development up the California coast to San Francisco. Commercial ways and social relations shaped the Spanish Empire; they were especially dynamic as Spanish North America thrust northward in the eighteenth century.

The differences between Spanish and British foundations in North America emerged less from distinct European traditions than from Spanish priority in engaging the most densely settled and state-organized Amerindian societies and building an unprecedented silver economy. It was Spanish Americans who first encountered the state-based societies of Mesoamerica and the Andes, found mountains of silver at Potosí and Zacatecas, and connected American silver to Asian markets, in the process stimulating global trade and Spanish imperial power.

British colonists came later, confined to regions of independent and often resistant native peoples, never to find rich lodes of bullion. In New England they found religious and economic independence—and little profit. From the Chesapeake, across the Carolinas, and on Caribbean islands, slave plantations offered profits, always second to those of the silver economy. Priority, economic opportunity, and differing indigenous societies shaped differences between Spanish and British America more than did Catholicism, Puritanism, or other cultural differences.[4]

Spanish North America developed as a region of commercial and increasingly capitalist expansion that shaped the histories of both Mexico and the United States. The discovery of silver at Zacatecas, Guanajuato, and elsewhere north of the states and communities of Mesoamerica accelerated settlement and development from the 1550s. Chapter 1 explores the commercial dynamics, patriarchal hierarchies, and ethnic amalgamations at the center of that development as it drove north in the eighteenth century and after. It details how revolutionary conflicts within Mexico's war for independence, both beginning in 1810, undermined capitalist dynamism and northward expansion just as the nation began. And it outlines how the U.S.-Mexican War of the 1840s turned Mexico's North into the U.S. West, leading to an incorporation of Hispanic capitalism, beginning contests between contending ways of patriarchy and enduring encounters between Mexican ethnic amalgamations and U.S. racial polarities — all shaping the rise of the United States to continental hegemony.

The expansion of commercial ways and capitalist developments across North America, whether by Spanish mining and grazing driving northward or by Anglo-American prospectors and settlers trekking westward, were always shaped by encounters with Amerindians long on the land. Mythic visions emphasize Spanish incorporations of natives in missions and Anglo-American exclusions of Indians, often in wars of extermination. Missions and wars were common enough on frontiers where profit-seeking Europeans met natives struggling to adapt and survive in the face of grasping newcomers and deadly diseases. But mission subordination was but a part of Spanish relations with North American natives, and wars of exclusion ruled Anglo-Indian relations mostly toward the end of a long era of more complex interactions.

In "Between Mexico and the United States," Andrew Isenberg explores the challenges faced by the native peoples who first engaged the northward expansion of Spanish North America and then the westward thrust of the United States. He focuses on the active roles taken by natives during long periods that began when they first encountered Spanish North America in the seventeenth and eighteenth centuries and continued as they faced the full force of Anglo-American expansion in the last third of the nineteenth century. He emphasizes the transforming importance of independent peoples' adaptations of European livestock and technologies — and the later emergence of environmental challenges that undermined indigenous independence.[5]

Isenberg details how Navajos dealt with Spanish New Mexico to gain growing herds of sheep, become a pastoral society, and in time find fame as weavers. In the eighteenth century they profited from selling sheep, wool, and cloth south to mining communities in Chihuahua and beyond. He also shows how diverse peoples across the Great Plains between the Rockies and the Mississippi traded and raided to gain horses from New Mexico, becoming more skilled warriors and bison hunters in a Native American world that ruled the middle of the continent through the eighteenth century and into the nineteenth. Among independent indigenous peoples, contacts with Spanish North America allowed adaptations as pastoralists who found new strengths and stratifications that lasted more than a century. Adoption of European livestock and weapons brought better sustenance, new independence, and unprecedented political-military power.

Those adaptations enabled Comanches and other pastoral peoples to assert rising power when Mexican independence and the Bajío revolution undermined the economic dynamism of the silver economy and halted the historical expansion of Spanish North America. This was not unprecedented. In the 1680s, an alliance of Pueblos and pastoralists had ousted the Spanish from New Mexico at a time of decline in the silver economy. When the silver economy waned briefly around 1750, Apaches and others became more assertive. And after 1810, as Pekka Hamalainen and Brian DeLay detail, the first beneficiary of the demise of New Spain's power from Arizona through Texas was a newly expansive Comanche Empire. Its warriors raided deep into northern Mexico in the 1830s and 1840s.[6] This time, however, the collapse of silver capitalism as Mexico became a nation and the sharp assertion of indigenous power gave way to U.S. hegemony in a process marked by war against Mexico in the 1840s, a gold boom in California beginning in 1849, and a powerful development of mining, cultivation, and grazing in Colorado from the 1860s.

Isenberg emphasizes that the triumph of the United States was not the result of military power alone. The middle decades of the nineteenth century saw explosive grazing and bison hunting beyond the capacity of herd reproduction in fragile environments, undermining pastoral adaptations just as U.S. expansion energized. Ecological collapse pressed long-independent peoples to new adaptations, culminating not in exclusion but dependence. That transition, too, built on Spanish North American precedents. It began in California, where natives became pastoralists as mission residents while inland people took livestock to sustain independent ways. When Mexican liberals secularized the missions in the 1830s, most land went to commercial rancheros, leaving native neophytes to become dependent vaqueros—cowboys. Later, when gold boomed as the United States took power, ranchers employed native vaqueros to build a grazing economy to supply the mines, sustaining the "westward" expansion that replicated Spanish North America under U.S. rule.

In ways different in particulars but parallel in trajectory, Navajos, Comanches, and other peoples of the Plains saw pastoral adaptations collapse just as they faced a dynamically capitalist and militarized U.S. expansion after the Civil War. They, too, Isenberg emphasizes, were not simply exterminated or excluded. Many died from disease, others in war. But survivors remained and often faced life on reservations—Anglo-American versions of missions—where agents and preachers pressed natives to settle and lead Christian lives as dependent cultivators and workers. On the reservations and off, many found roles as cowboys and shepherds, persisting in pastoral ways, now laboring as dependents in a commercial economy, continuing a long sequence begun in Spanish North America and played out across the U.S. West.

War, Culture, and Commerce

In the 1820s, Mexico emerged from divisive wars for independence and began to face decades of political and social conflict as it struggled to become a nation. In the same years, the United States came out of the era of conflictive nation-making that began in 1776, saw political divisions and local rebellions in the 1780s and 1790s, almost brought dissolution in 1800, fought a war with Britain in 1812, and found resolution in the Missouri Compromise of 1820. The years from the 1820s through the 1840s seem times of trial for Mexico and of triumph for the United States—culminating in the war that transferred vast territories from the former to the latter.

Yet after that decisive contest for continental control, both nations faced deepening divisions that led to simultaneous civil wars in the 1860s. When we recognize the role of the war of the 1840s in making the United States a continental nation and limiting Mexico's potential expansion, and its importance in setting off deep and deadly conflicts in both nations in the 1860s, we begin to see that these were not separate histories of nation-making.[7] In important ways, the United States and Mexico became nations together from the 1820s through the 1860s.

To most U.S. scholars and citizens, the Civil War is the defining conflict of nineteenth-century U.S. history. The great war of North against South, of commercial-industrial prospects against slave traditions, ended slavery and gained national unity. It was a war fought mostly by people of European origins to determine the future of slaves of African ancestry and of relations between people color-coded as "races," black and white. What did Mexico and Mexicans have to do with the Civil War? Much more than is often recognized. Anglo-Americans settled Mexican Texas in the 1820s to gain the coastal plain for cotton and slavery. The bondage that defined the U.S. South had declined to insignificance by 1800 in New Spain, making abolition easy for Mexican nation-makers in 1829. Mexico's 1824 Constitution had emphasized state's rights, allowing Texans to ignore abolition for a time, but in the 1830s, Mexican leaders increasingly pressed Texans to respect national policy. Texans rebelled, claiming political independence to preserve slavery and expand the cotton economy.[8]

Mexico lacked the military power to prevent Texas' secession but would not recognize Texas independence. Struggling to prosper between a nation that would not let it leave and another not ready to defend it, in 1845, Texas sought entry into the United States. It would become a slave state bolstering the southern bloc. The southern border of Texas had always been the Nueces River, emptying into Corpus Christi Bay. But the Texans and their U.S. backers claimed the north bank of the Rio Grande. When Mexican troops crossed the Rio Grande to fortify its border at the Nueces, U.S. authorities proclaimed their territory invaded and began a war to confirm the annexation of Texas and take all the land through New Mexico to California.

Beginning in 1846, the U.S. military invaded Mexico by land and sea, taking Mexico City in September of 1847. The 1848 Treaty of Guadalupe Hidalgo, forced on an occupied nation, made the northern half of Mexico the western third of the United States. Before the battles began, Texas became a slave state, rich in cotton.[9] Californians found gold late in 1848— completing the trajectory of Spanish North American development in which mining drove the economy, irrigated agriculture supplied grains and other crops, and commercial grazing provided nearly everything else. California became a free state in 1850. The rest of the lands taken from Mexico reopened questions of the expansion of slavery and the national power of slaveholders. What once seemed settled in the Missouri Compromise of 1820 became unsettled, contentious, and ever more divisive, leading to the Civil War. The settlement of Mexican Texas as an extension of a southern U.S. economy built on cotton and slavery, the independence of Texas, the war with Mexico, and the taking of vast Mexican territories had everything to do with the coming of the U.S. Civil War, the most deadly and destructive conflict in the nineteenth-century Americas.[10]

Decades of conflict linking Mexico and the United States thus shaped— literally—the boundaries, politics, and economic prospects of both nations. During the same era, visions of Mexico, often debated yet always in play, became central to shaping U.S. political and popular cultures. In "Imagining Mexico in War and Romance," Shelley Streeby explores changing portrayals of Mexico and Mexicans in U.S. literary and visual cultures in this formative era.[11] She emphasizes three stages. The first began in the 1820s, when Pres. James Monroe's Doctrine proclaimed the emerging Mexican nation a sister republic, yet a republic that might require U.S. assistance and protection. The literature of the day, still mostly aimed at a literary few, echoed that view — with an emphasis on the importance of manly U.S. tutelage.

In the second stage, the 1830s and 1840s linked the two nations in escalating conflicts as Texas sought independence and then incorporation into the United States, leading to war from 1846 to 1848. Those in the United States opposed to the extension of slavery and territorial expansion, often northerners, pressed visions of Mexico as a sister republic even as they worried about its racially mixed peoples. Those who favored Texas independence and the 1840s war for territorial expansion, often southerners, increasingly saw Mexico as a failed republic, broken by racially mixed citizens and desperate for U.S. instruction — to be offered by manly Anglo men who would marry elite white Mexican women. As Streeby emphasizes, the 1840s saw the print revolution bring an explosion of popular literature just as attention focused on war with Mexico. Tales of battle and romance constructed U.S. superiority and Mexican failure, Yankee manhood and Mexican womanly dependence, Anglo-Saxon racial superiority and a Mexican inferiority rooted in an indigenous majority and excessive "racial" mixing.

Yet just over a decade after war appeared to decisively establish U.S. power and Mexican incapacity, the 1860s brought a third stage as both nations faced deadly civil war. Again, visions of Mexico were key parts of how USAmericans (as Streeby names them) understood themselves, their nation, and their conflicts. Again, portrayals were divided: southerners saw promise in Mexican conservatives and the brief empire of Maximilian of Hapsburg; northerners preferred the liberal Mexican republic led by Benito Juárez, yet they worried that as a Zapotec, he was too Indian to lead a modern nation. Once the North triumphed in the United States and Juárez and the liberals restored republican rule in Mexico, U.S. popular culture, now both literary and visual, increasingly focused on the brutality of the regime led by the "Indian" Juárez, its killing of Maximilian, thus its uncertain fitness to become a true American republic.

Romances continued to regale popular audiences with Mexico's womanly need for manly U.S. leadership. Such assertions of patriarchal superiority were more than metaphorical claims. The capitalist dynamism of Spanish North America had long been organized by patriarchy: powerful men ruled subordinate men, and men at every level ruled women—inevitably and rightfully. The expansive United States was no less patriarchal. To claim superiority over Mexico and Mexicans, U.S. Americans had to assert superior patriarchy. In the United States, that exalted Anglo patriarchy justified Anglo men's political and entrepreneurial power in newly incorporated territories. It also helped prepare the way—at least in Yankee minds—for an era in which U.S. tutelage came to Mexico mostly as capital investment that aimed to take profit while turning Mexican production to serve markets in the United States. The construction of a national culture, political and popular, focused on asserting U.S. manly superiority and the need of others, constructed as women and/or racial inferiors, to gain from U.S. instruction (and capital)—came during a half century of founding interaction with Mexico. The persistence of visions of Anglo manhood and Mexican womanly dependence is documented in José Limón's analysis in *American Encounters*, which explores literary and cinematic portrayals of Mexico and Mexicans in twentieth-century U.S. culture.

As Streeby emphasizes, the U.S. Civil War was pivotal to U.S. history, U.S. relations with Mexico, and the formation of a U.S. culture shaped in key ways by visions of Mexico and Mexicans. In "Mexican Merchants and Teamsters on the Texas Cotton Road," David Montejano reminds us that Mexicans participated in that conflict in ways beyond serving as imagined others in U.S. popular culture. Mexicans in Texas, the Rio Grande Valley, and the city of Monterrey became key actors in the Civil War, enabling the persistence of the cotton economy essential to Confederate independence. There is no hint that Mexican merchants and teamsters sympathized with plantation slavery. They, like many Anglo-Americans who went to once-Mexican lands in the 1850s, saw opportunities for profit and took them.

The war began in 1861, when Lincoln's government refused to accept southern secession (as Mexico had refused to recognize Texas' secession in 1836). To sustain its war for independence and slavery, the Confederacy needed cotton production and exports. But the Union blockaded southern ports, making exports difficult and uncertain. Into the breach stepped the merchants of Monterrey, Mexico. They built a profitable business buying cotton from Louisiana, Arkansas, and Texas—or "Mexicanizing" it for commission fees—shipping it by Mexican teamsters and carters across Texas and the Rio Grande, and exporting it at Matamoros or Bagdad on the Mexican side. Slave-made cotton reached markets, the Confederacy kept its key economic sector alive, and the fight for independence and slavery continued longer than it would have if the Union blockade had been more successful. (In addition, profits accumulated in Monterrey set that city on course to become the commercial and industrial capital of northern Mexico in the late nineteenth century.) If the Civil War was the quintessential U.S. conflict of the nineteenth century, Mexico and Mexicans were pivotal to its origins and to sustaining the Confederacy (not from idealism, but from purely capitalist goals) in a long fight finally lost.

The war that claimed vast lands from Mexico, the resulting westward expansion into territories first shaped by Spanish North American peoples and traditions, and then the war that ended slavery and set a reunified United States on course to capitalist industrialization combined to shape North American history in the nineteenth century, and beyond. Streeby and Montejano show that Mexico and Mexicans were key participants in the political, cultural, and economic conflicts and constructions that generated U.S. continental power. On a larger level, they show two deeply capitalist and patriarchal societies contesting continental rule—with Anglo-American patriarchs taking ever more power within North American capitalism on both sides of the border.

Labor and Liberation, Nation and Exclusion

The coming of U.S. sovereignty and political institutions along with growing numbers of "Anglo" merchants and settlers to lands once Mexican inevitably set off times of change. Too often we presume that rapid "Americanization" shaped the borderlands, drowning Mexican ways and peoples. Yet every careful analysis shows a more complex, interactive, adaptive history from Texas to California.[12] U.S. political institutions ruled, as did—in time—U.S. racial exclusions. But political leaders and their entrepreneurial allies repeatedly adopted Hispanic North American ways of mining, cultivation, and grazing, often taking over established enterprises by marrying Mexican heiresses, just as U.S. romance novels advised. Anglo-American entrepreneurs often continued profitable Hispanic ways of labor relations: advance payments still drew permanent workers; seasonal hands came from cultivating (and, later, urban) communities. Ethnic mixing persisted, newly challenged by U.S. ways of exclusion. In important ways, the borderlands remained Mexican even as they became important parts of the United States.[13]

Southern Arizona illustrates that process. It remained part of the Mexican state of Sonora after the U.S.-Mexican War, until Mexican financial straits (left by the war) and the U.S. desire for irrigable land and a rail route west led to the 1853 Gadsden Purchase. Katherine Benton-Cohen has detailed a century of history in Cochise County, from the 1840s, when the region mixed Mexican cultivators of mixed ancestry with independent natives, Apaches and others, through the railroad development and mining boom that made Tombstone famous in the 1880s and the labor conflict that put Bisbee at the center of U.S. national attention in 1917, leading to the region's emergence as a land divided between "Americans" and "Mexicans" in the 1930s.[14]

In "Making Mexicans and Americans in the Arizona Borderlands," Benton-Cohen explores three key moments in that history. In the early 1880s, agricultural settlements mixed diverse Mexicans with newcomers from the U.S. East and Europe. Together they built and maintained irrigation systems along rivers. Land, not ancestry or race, set primary social distinctions in early U.S. Arizona: Mexican men and women owned land, married each other and newcomers, and played leading roles in local affairs. Meanwhile, silver boomed at Tombstone, setting in motion violent conflicts over rule, profit, and labor—conflicts in which Mexican men were often desired workers and English-speaking cowboys a source of problematic violence for the mining industry. In all that, southern Arizona in the 1880s continued Spanish North American ways: the economy mixed mining, irrigated cultivation, and commercial grazing; society remained open to ethnic mixing; politics rewarded land and wealth—and patriarchy shaped everything.

Yet in the same decade, important changes were under way. Bisbee began as a copper town; its developers proclaimed it an "American camp," excluding the Chinese and limiting Mexicans to marginal work. U.S. racial exclusions challenged Hispanic amalgamations just as U.S. institutions of political participation might have offered real gains to Mexicans (who under the treaties that made Arizona part of the United States were "white" and citizens—if adult and male). Bisbee flourished economically, becoming a key copper mining center as the United States entered World War I in 1917. Employers there, mostly corporations based in the East, relegated Mexicans (and Italians and Serbs) to secondary labor and structural poverty. When they struck together, demanding equal work and pay as the nation mobilized for war, they faced the military, defeat, and deportation. The repression of that conflict consolidated the copper boomtown as a place for white Americans (managers and their charity-working wives, workers and their patriarchal families). In the early twentieth century, while Jim Crow hardened black-white racial lines in the South and war fueled xenophobic nationalism everywhere, "Mexican" and "American" (presumed to mean white and European) became divisive racial categories in Bisbee and across the Southwest.

In an epilogue, Benton-Cohen shows how New Deal programs consolidated new racial divisions during the depression of the 1930s. Relief programs confirmed the power of corporate mining; while white managers ruled the mines, their white wives ruled relief, entrenching patriarchal presumptions and racial claims that confirmed American rights and Mexican exclusions. In an economic structure in the tradition of Spanish North America, still patriarchal but ruled by U.S. corporations, Anglo-American racial exclusions prejudiced Mexicans' lives. Still, Benton-Cohen reminds us that away from the mines and the corporate power committed to racial division, some Arizonans kept traditions of ethnic fluidity alive.

Benton-Cohen's exploration of one important place, Cochise County, during the century after its incorporation into the United States emphasizes how the rise of U.S. corporate mining and a pivotal 1917 labor conflict led to a powerful racial binary dividing Mexicans from Americans. In "Keeping Community, Challenging Boundaries," Devra Weber explores the decades from 1900 to 1920 across a wider west, focusing on Mexican migrants and their roles in labor organizing.[15] The years around 1900 brought rapid development to the lands that remained the Mexican North and those that had become the U.S. West. Integrated by railroads and booming transnational markets, the borderlands drew migrants north to lay rails, to build cities, and to labor in mines, fields, and workshops—in both nations. Then the decade from 1910 to 1920 saw unprecedented conflicts on both sides of the border: revolution in Mexico; labor conflicts and mobilization for World War I in the United States.

Weber shows that migrants from Mexico were pivotal to building the western United States—and to organizing workers there. While corporate power drew Anglo-Americans and many European immigrants into a polar divide marking Mexicans as a racial other, people pressed to become Mexicans kept diverse identities. Many migrants from Mexico were indigenous—Mayos, Yaquis, and Opatas from as near as Sonora, Purépechas (Tarascans) from as far south as Michoacán. Many spoke native languages, knew Spanish, and learned English. Identities stayed grounded in ancestral communities as men worked in industrial mines; they joined and often led transnational and multicultural political and labor movements. Their lives reveal that diverse Mexicans contributed to building the U.S. West and to demanding fair remuneration and political participation for those who built it, refusing to become the singular other that corporate powers wanted and an emerging U.S. "national" culture asserted.

The ethnic mixing and adaptive identities long characteristic of Hispanic North America helped migrants from Mexico found, lead, and join the Industrial Workers of the World (IWW, or Wobblies). In cities and mining camps, along rail lines, and in commercial fields, diverse migrants from Mexico joined equally diverse workers from the U.S. East and Europe to demand fair treatment and better wages. They pressed for the rights of all workers—all men. They built new communities, made local gains, and forged traditions of struggle even while facing difficult, sometimes devastating, defeats, as at Bisbee in 1917. Perhaps reasserting the patriarchal traditions of Hispanic North America, they insisted that all workers were equally men.

Benton-Cohen and Weber focus on key years. As the twentieth century began, the economic ways of Hispanic North America endured across the Mexican North and the U.S. West, mixing mining, irrigated agriculture, and commercial grazing in a dynamic transnational capitalism. By 1900, people of Mexican ancestry were all but excluded from political power and mining entrepreneurship in the regions incorporated into the United States; a few prospered in agriculture and grazing. In that context, U.S. corporate power pressed alliances with Anglo-American and European workers to forge an American-Mexican split to bolster corporate rule, divide workers, and cut costs by paying Mexicans less. Mexicans were pronounced lesser men.

Meanwhile, workers of Mexican ancestry stayed open to ethnic interaction and joined communities of workers—all asserting rights as men. Their vision offered a road to ethnic openness, a road opened by diverse working men and blocked by powerful Anglo men and the women they empowered. After 1917, U.S. war-induced nationalism matched Mexican postrevolutionary nationalism to strengthen Mexican and American identities on both sides of the border. U.S.-style racial polarity appeared to trump Hispanic amalgamations in the 1920s, the depression of the 1930s, and into the wartime era of the 1940s and the Cold War that followed.

Continental Capitalism and Mexican Migration

Throughout the twentieth century, except during the depression of the 1930s, Mexicans came to the United States in rising waves, most to labor, many eventually to live. If from 1847 to 1900 Mexico and Mexicans shaped the United States primarily through enduring legacies of capitalist mining, commercial grazing, irrigated cultivation, and ethnic amalgamation, in the twentieth century those legacies were reinforced and sustained by the thousands, eventually millions, of Mexicans who came to work and live in lands once Mexican and far beyond. Mexican migration and Mexican laborers became pivotal to the North American experience after 1900. For good reasons, their coming has fixed the attention of scholars; for debatable reasons, their presence has elicited cultural controversy and political ire. Our studies suggest that migration and labor should be understood in the context of a North American capitalism increasingly integrated since the 1860s, changing debates about patriarchy, and enduring contests over ethnic amalgamations and racial polarities.

Migration remains the most intensely studied, discussed, and debated aspect of the relationship between Mexico and the United States. During the first half of the twentieth century, two landmark works shaped early conversations. In 1930, as depression hit, Mexican anthropologist Manuel Gamio published *The Life Story of the Mexican Immigrant*. He asked why so many had come to the United States during and after a Mexican revolution that mobilized nationalist rhetoric to promise social justice and popular welfare.[16] In 1949, U.S journalist and political activist Carey McWilliams offered *North from Mexico*, exploring the origins and importance of the bracero program negotiated by the U.S. and Mexican governments to bring Mexicans to work in the United States during World War II.

Subsequent scholars brought new complexities to understanding why so many Mexicans came to build and sustain the U.S. economy as it rose to global eminence. In *By the Sweat of Their Brow*, Mark Reisler details how Mexican migrants built railroads, mined silver and copper, and harvested crops across once-Mexican territories of the Southwest from 1900 to 1940—and how they moved beyond to sustain sugar beet farming and refining on plains from eastern Colorado to the Red River Valley of Minnesota and the Dakotas and settled city enclaves in Chicago and Saint Paul. In *Anglos and Mexicans in the Making of Texas*, David Montejano details how Mexican legacies and Mexican migrants were essential to building the Texas so prominent in the economy and politics of the twentieth-century United States. In *Dark Sweat, White Gold*, Devra Weber documents how the Mexican residents and migrants essential to California agribusiness struggled for work and rights during the depression. And Francisco Balderrama and Raymond Rodríguez detail the darker side of Mexicans' experience of the U.S. depression in *Decade of Betrayal*. While those who could struggled for rights and work, the majority faced welfare systems that made a ticket to the border the only relief available to Mexicans, including many children born U.S. citizens. The expulsions set up a legacy of resentment, leaving the United States little choice but to negotiate the bracero program, offering transport north, set pay, and basic rights to draw reluctant Mexicans north to labor in U.S. fields and factories during World War II.

Much of that migration has been explained by the changing particulars of Mexican history: an economic boom that concentrated land and minimized pay during the decades before 1910; the disruptive revolution of 1910–1920; the limits of reforms during the 1920s; the violence of the Cristero revolt in western Mexico after 1926. Even the repatriations of the depression years, pressed by local officials across the United States, are linked to the reforms of Mexican president Lázaro Cárdenas in the 1930s. His distribution of land to rural villagers and his protection of labor rights in emerging industries helped accommodate repatriated migrants. Was his expropriation of U.S. oil companies in 1938 in some small part a statement that if Mexicans could be pushed home, the Mexican nation could still assert its rights in Mexico?[17]

In that context, the apparently sudden shift from nationalizing oil in 1938 to mobilizing Mexican production and Mexican workers to sustain the United States in World War II seems diagnostic of the postrevolutionary regime's turn to the right in 1940. Yet when we recognize that the "radical" Cárdenas, who distributed land, favored labor, and nationalized oil, chose his "rightist" successor as president and remained in the cabinet as the minister of defense who coordinated support for the United States during the war, we begin to see that underlying continuities in Mexican politics, policies, and economic trajectories helped send Mexican migrants to the United States through the twentieth century. We should not be surprised, then, that the bracero program continued to deliver Mexicans to U.S. employers into the 1960s, and that when U.S. labor-rights advocates led a drive to end the program (insisting, rightly, that it exploited Mexicans and depressed U.S. wages), Mexicans kept coming.[18]

And they have kept coming, now to every region of the United States, to every aspect of our economy, through every era of politics in the United States and Mexico—in accelerating waves in times of boom, in lesser flows in years of decline. Much of this is detailed and analyzed in *Return to Aztlán*, the landmark study of Mexican migrants and migration in the later twentieth century by Douglas Massey and his binational team.[19] Cycles of politics and production, war and rebellion on both sides of the border helped time labor migration; they do not explain the underlying, enduring relationship that shaped life and migration in both nations from the 1860s.

Three intersecting and reinforcing historical processes ground the enduring role of Mexican migration in sustaining the United States and its economy. First, since the sixteenth century, European, Mesoamerican, and African migrants have moved north from regions around Mexico City and the Bajío seeking profit and work in an economy driven by silver and sustained by irrigated farming and commercial grazing. When the border moved south in 1848 (with a minor adjustment, also south, in 1853), neither the northward drive of Hispanic capitalism nor the migration of Mexicans stopped. The search for mines, grazing lands, and irrigable fields continued, as did the movement of peoples from regions of greater density (and limited resources) in central Mexico to zones of lesser density and vast resources (now in the United States). People moving north became immigrants by crossing a relocated border into a recently expanded United States.

In a second linked process, beginning in the late 1860s, that foundational northward expansion was reshaped by an accelerating integration of the U.S. and Mexican economies under the sway of U.S. capital. As the North won the Civil War and turned to westward expansion to build a national economy, Mexican liberals led by Benito Juárez emerged from wars against conservative foes, French occupation, and Maximilian's imagined empire to face debt, economic crisis, and limited territory for expansion. The great mining strikes of the nineteenth century that fueled and funded so much of the U.S. drive to the West were in California, Colorado, Arizona, and other lands taken from Mexico. Capital and economic stimulus concentrated in the United States; U.S. capitalists looked to "aid" Mexico by investing there. What else could a manly Yankee do?

To consolidate a national liberal regime, Juárez, his allies, and successors welcomed U.S. financiers to build railroads, revive mines, and stimulate trade, reenergizing Mexican economic growth and northward expansion. Profit concentrated among U.S. investors and allied Mexican elites; Mexico was drawn into a model of development that stimulated capitalist concentrations by emphasizing labor-saving technology. Such technology promoted profit and broadly (if imperfectly) shared welfare in a United States with ample resources (many taken from Mexico) and a limited population. In a Mexico left with unhealthful tropical lowlands, dense settlements, and limited resources in a rugged mountainous center, and a dry north constrained after 1848 by U.S. expansion, the same labor-saving ways promoted economic growth and capitalist concentration while they constrained opportunities for a struggling majority.

The nineteenth-century origins of the integration of the Mexican and U.S. economies under U.S. capital were documented long ago by David Pletcher in *Rails, Mines, and Progress*. John Hart details that integration's persistence and expansion in *Empire and Revolution*. Those who might let nationalist rhetoric convince them that the Revolution of 1910 derailed U.S. economic power in Mexico need only read the analysis of the Mexican economy from 1870 to 1929 by Stephen Haber and his colleagues.[20] They demonstrate that the economic trajectory of Mexico toward a capitalism shaped by U.S. investment and U.S. markets held strong from the 1880s to the crash of 1929. And what the depression slowed for a decade, World War II reaccelerated. From the 1940s to the North American Free Trade Agreement (NAFTA) in the 1990s, U.S. capital, markets, and labor-saving technologies have ruled an ever more integrated economy linking the United States and Mexico.

In the third key process, the integrated North American economy entered a new phase after World War II. Mexicans began to face explosive population growth, rapid urbanization, and a turn to industrial "green revolution" agriculture. None of those transformations were simply Mexican; all emerged from deepening North American integrations. Of course, the Mexican population explosion was essentially a Mexican process. Or was it? Growth began to accelerate in the 1930s and 1940s, when land and labor reforms gave rural and urban Mexicans incentives to have more children and better ways to feed them. But the explosive growth that fueled uncontained urbanization came as the U.S. pharmaceutical industry delivered to Mexicans in the 1950s the penicillin and other antibiotics invented in World War II. For more than a generation, Mexicans had more children and more children lived, an unquestioned good in families that brought unprecedented social challenges to the nation. Meanwhile, in a little-recognized pharmaceutical exchange, the same industry developed in Mexico—from Mexican folk remedies based on roots and herbs— the birth control pills that enabled more comfortable U.S. middle-class families to control reproduction. The Mexican population soared while U.S. growth slowed.[21]

Meanwhile, international capital kept increasing its role in Mexico; both national and international firms knew that labor-saving technologies were the only way to compete and profit. During decades of national industrial development from the 1940s to the 1960s, the Mexican state promoted and Mexican entrepreneurs adopted labor-saving techniques;

they celebrated times of "miracle" growth in production—and repeatedly lamented that growth failed to generate employment sufficient to sustain a rapidly growing population. In agriculture, rural communities that in the 1930s and 1940s gained just enough land for sustenance, in the 1950s saw population growth drive intense cropping that led to soil exhaustion and erosion. Mexico's revolutionary agrarian reform could not feed burgeoning cities.

In response, the green revolution promoted in Mexico by the U.S. government and the Rockefeller Foundation enabled commercial growers to expand production of wheat and vegetables using tractors and hybrid seeds, chemical fertilizers, herbicides and pesticides—saving labor while feeding prosperous urban consumers. Early on, the new agriculture paid little heed to the majority of maize farmers and consumers, who continued to struggle while growing numbers migrated to Mexican cities and U.S. fields and factories.[22]

The scientific revolution in Mexican agriculture increased production of crops that fed urban Mexicans, especially the growing middle class. But it, too, was labor saving. As a result, both in the decades of the "Mexican Miracle," when economic growth was fabled, and after 1970, when crises mounted, Mexicans' participation in the integrated North American economy generated population growth (finally slowing in the 1990s) and mass poverty marked by unemployment, informality, marginal lives—and continuing migration to the United States. Then in the 1990s, NAFTA opened Mexico to maize and wheat raised by subsidized farmers in the United States, shifting cultivation on Mexico's green revolution fields (with irrigation and industrial inputs) to tomatoes, strawberries, and other vegetables and fruits for comfortable U.S. consumers. As the twenty-first century began, rural Mexico ceased to produce sustenance or labor for Mexicans. It became instead a domain of migrant labor recruitment for transnational agribusiness.[23]

While Mexico adopted the capital-intensive, labor-saving ways promoted by the prophets of development, Mexicans faced population explosion, proliferating unemployment, marginal lives, and incentives to migrate to the United States, from which most advice and capital came to Mexico, to which so much profit, produce, and labor made in Mexico went. During the first half of the twentieth century most migrants came from Guanajuato, Michoacán, Jalisco, and regions north, continuing flows that have marked Hispanic North America for centuries. With the collapse of community agriculture in the Mesoamerican heartland from Mexico City southward beginning in the 1970s, migration began to accelerate from indigenous communities there. In the United States, this seemed a new development. The numbers of indigenous migrants did grow, and indigenous identities held strong in U.S. cities from Los Angeles to New York.[24] Still, as Devra Weber shows, there were always indigenous people among migrants.

When population growth and land erosion undermined village cultivation across central and southern Mexico after 1970, men turned to migrant labor, often in Mexico City, increasingly in fields across northwest Mexico and in the United States. They sought cash earnings to supplement or replace cultivation, to sustain family and community life. Mixing cultivation and day labor was an old response to land shortages and falling yields in Mexico. But, historically, men labored seasonally at nearby commercial estates, holding their roles—patriarchal roles—in family and community life. In the second half of the twentieth century, access to seasonal labor and cash required long treks north; the search for earnings to sustain patriarchy, family, and community took men out of families and communities for months, often years. Families and communities might be sustained, but patriarchal ways faced new strains. Mesoamerican villages became places of women and children for most of every year, then home to assertive men in annual visits during winter holidays. Family and community sustenance became transnational; patriarchy became transnational, in difficult, dependent, and insecure ways.

While villagers struggled to adapt, North American agribusiness and other sectors gained minimally paid, insecure, and temporary workers— easily hired and easily fired. Over the course of the twentieth century, Mexico generated a growing population, provided for its upbringing and education (within its limited means), and sent waves of desperate hands to labor for low wages in fields and factories, public works and private enterprise, family homes and neighborhood restaurants across the United States. Then, when age inhibited labor or a downturn cut employment, many Mexicans (who often have paid into U.S. Social Security, but who, as "illegals," cannot collect it) returned home to families and communities that struggled to sustain them. Businesses in the United States gain low-cost workers available to labor when necessary, providing a "flexible" work force that helps drive all incomes "racing to the bottom." Mexican communities struggle to survive—and to negotiate new ways of community, family, and patriarchy.

Over decades (and despite downturns) the U.S. economy has prospered and profited, the U.S. majority has struggled to hang on to middle-class ways, a favored minority of Mexicans in Mexico has also prospered, a larger minority there has struggled to claim and hold middle-class lives—and the Mexican majority has grappled with widening insecurity and deepening poverty on both sides of the border. In a self-reinforcing relationship, North American businesses continue to find advantage in hiring desperate Mexicans, and Mexicans continue to see migration as one of the few opportunities open to them in lives shaped by declining opportunities and desperate insecurity. The result is transnational symbiotic exploitation. The U.S. economy is dependent on Mexican workers to maximize profit in a globalizing world; Mexicans live dependent on minimally paid and structurally insecure labor that sustains the U.S. economy, and subsidizes the prosperity of its beneficiaries. That mutual dependence has become a symbiosis; the deep inequality between those who prosper and those who struggle to sustain families and communities makes that symbiosis exploitative. It has set in as an enduring relationship of structural inequity. In that, too, Mexicans have made—and continue to make—the United States and North America.

While migrant flows and symbiotic exploitations expanded through the late twentieth century and into the twenty-first, debates about Mexican migration and labor in the United States persist and periodically escalate. Defenders of U.S. labor fought to end the bracero program in 1964, yet migrants kept coming. César Chavez led a fight for decent wages and lives for California farmworkers, mostly Mexican Americans—and migrants kept coming.[25] After much debate, the late 1980s brought openings to citizenship for migrants already in the United States and aimed to limit new arrivals—and migrants kept coming. NAFTA promised development in Mexico that would hold Mexicans at home, but industry went to China—and Mexicans kept coming north. After 2000, migrants still welcomed by U.S. employers were denounced as illegal aliens; they were harassed and maligned in every way—and they have kept coming.

A pattern emerges: U.S employers, large and small, seek Mexican migrants for work that is seasonal or insecure, poorly paid, and without benefits. U.S. political culture, left and right, constructs the same migrants as a problem: exploited workers in the 1960s, illegal invaders after 2000. The mix is close to perfect for U.S. employers. They gain essential workers for little cost, workers always constrained, often threatened, and normally unable to press for rights or fair pay. It is a relationship we debate and lament, for some because it exploits Mexicans, for others because it threatens Americans. Yet it is a relationship that remains fundamental to the profitable prosperity of the U.S. economy and to the survival, however marginal, of growing numbers of Mexicans. It is a relationship that will continue, drawing Mexican migrants to harvest crops, build cities and suburbs, making and remaking the United States.

Can their work become less exploitative? Might a guest worker program bring labor to U.S. employers and limit exploitation of Mexicans? Or would it just solidify an underclass of Mexicans, essential to the United States, but denied any opening to the promise of American life? In the face of continuing challenges, many Mexicans drawn north to work have stayed; many of their children have built middle-class lives. Despite obstacles, they contribute to U.S. politics and to the American promise of inclusion.

Middle-Class Integrations, Ethnic Amalgamations

While Mexican migration continues to sustain U.S. production, profits, and middle-class lives, Mexican migrants and their Mexican American descendants contribute more than labor. José Limón's chapter, "Transnational Triangulation," reminds us that while scholarly studies and political debates about Mexicans in the United States have focused on migration and labor—most scholars in analytical celebration, many political voices in adamant condemnation—Mexican Americans have been joining the U.S. middle class. Given problems of definition and counting, certainty is impossible, but Limón argues plausibly that a majority of U.S.-born Mexican Americans claimed such roles and identities by the 1990s. And the rise of the Mexican American middle class, like the reacceleration of migration to labor, began during World War II.

Hundreds of thousands of Mexicans and Mexican Americans fought in the U.S. military, facing combat and dying in record numbers. Limón adds that important numbers who did not (or could not) enlist worked at the military bases that proliferated along the border. For those who joined, fought, and lived, their service sustained expectations of equal citizenship; the GI Bill promised postwar opportunities. For many who worked at the bases, the Cold War offered jobs that opened middle-class horizons. Meanwhile, Héctor García, a Mexican American veteran and physician from Corpus Christi, Texas, took the lead in demanding rights (starting with a soldier's burial), founding the American GI Forum, an organization that built on wartime roles and mobilized middle-class leadership to promote Mexican American political rights and economic opportunities, facilitating the ascent to middle-class lives.[26]

As Limón details, by the late twentieth century, while so many Anglos worried about Mexican immigrant invasions, growing numbers of U.S. citizens of Mexican ancestry joined the U.S. middle class. They found roles in the military and as base workers, as teachers, lawyers, and medical providers, as professionals in national, state, and local governments, as middle managers and skilled workers in diverse businesses, and as middling merchants and insurance agents. In all that, the long history of Mexican migration led to a classically celebrated outcome: ascent into a middle class claimed as the essence of "America." In that, too, Mexicans made the United States.

Limón also probes relations between migrants who still come in large numbers (and seem threatening to so many) and the children and grandchildren of their predecessors now settled in a middle-class life. For other immigrant groups, notably, the also-Catholic Irish, Italians, and Quebecois, the rise to middle-class life came mostly after the end of strong migration flows (due to restrictions set in 1924). Mexicans have sustained the longest and strongest migration to the United States during the twentieth century, thanks to exemption from the 1924 restrictions and continuing strong demand for their labor. Only in the case of Mexicans and Mexican Americans has the rise of a middle class come while migration held strong—and faced escalating debates.

Some analysts have worried that Mexican American rights organizations have been too middle class, as Limón notes. After a time of radicalism in the 1960s, they have not been as strident as some critics had hoped.[27] Limón concludes that the Mexican American middle class has not only attended to its own interests in diverse political ways, but has worked, and will continue to work, against the attacks on immigrants that have too often come as blunt assaults on Mexican origins, culture, and character. He argues that a growing Mexican American middle class will remain a progressive force, defending immigrants (if not every opening to immigration), keeping Mexicans and Mexican Americans linked as constructive participants in North American society as they become the core of the Hispanic majority within an emerging "minority-majority."[28]

While Limón focuses here on the rise of the Mexican American middle class, his earlier exploration in *American Encounters* emphasized that patriarchal gender relations were key to the understandings and misunderstandings that linked Mexicans and Anglo-Americans throughout the twentieth century. In recent decades, while Mexican Americans have claimed middle-class lives, they have also lived debates about patriarchal privileges and women's rights. Our historical studies show both Mexican and Anglo-American ways as deeply patriarchal. In nineteenth-century cultural debates, U.S. writers and readers asserted a superior Yankee patriarchy to justify war in the 1840s, postwar rule in newly acquired lands, and investment in Mexico after 1867. In early-twentieth-century labor conflicts managers imagined and aimed to implement a superior white patriarchy. Through the nineteenth and into the twentieth century, Mexican and U.S. social relations and cultural constructions shared presumptions of patriarchy, contesting power by debating patriarchal superiority.

After World War II, patriarchy faced challenges. In the United States and Mexico, women found openings in education and opportunities to take on middle-class professions and other employment. Yet patriarchy has been slow to recede at the heights of corporate and government power while many powerful, middling, working, and marginalized men have resented and resisted erosions of patriarchal prerogatives and presumptions. Simultaneously, U.S. public culture has imagined Mexican and Mexican American ways as uniquely patriarchal, marked by a deep and destructive machismo. It has proven an easy cultural slide from portraying Mexican men on both sides of the border as failed patriarchs to reimagining them as exceptionally, often violently, patriarchal. Studies that challenge such portrayals, such as Matthew Gutmann's *The Meanings of Macho* and Robert Smith's *Mexican New York*, do not shake public constructions.

As its long-pivotal role in orchestrating capitalist social relations faces new challenges, patriarchy remains at the center of transnational cultural constructions and debates. In *American Encounters*, Limón saw a new openness to Mexico and Mexicans in the 1950s—within unchallenged patriarchal visions. He showed how influential Mexican analysts sustained a view of Mexican men as dangerously patriarchal into the 1960s. In a work written in the 1930s but available in English only in the 1960s, Samuel Ramos portrayed Mexicans as living by a culture of inferiority that generated explosive violence.[29] Ramos surely meant and U.S. readers easily read that Mexican men were too often violent. Octavio Paz, in his classic *The Labyrinth of Solitude*, also published in English in the 1960s, transposed the portrayal of the threateningly violent Mexican male across the border into the United States in his much-debated and often-lamented vision of the pachuco.

Such offerings from Mexican intellectuals eased U.S. adoption of a view of Mexican and Mexican American men as destructively macho. Limón saw that African American men also faced construction in white America as threateningly patriarchal. A preliminary conclusion suggests that as women challenged patriarchy by demanding equal rights and opportunities, and as globalizing capitalism welcomed women to labor, middle management, and diverse professions, public portrayals of patriarchy found negative hues and shifted to malign racially or ethnically "other" men locked near the bottom of the social scale.

The cultural reconstruction of patriarchy reflected and reinforced social changes linked to the accelerating integration of the North American economy in a globalizing world. For decades, young Mexican men migrated to labor in the United States, seasonally, temporarily, or permanently, in large part because they lacked economic opportunities in home communities. Neither cultivation nor available employment allowed growing numbers in Mexican villages and urban barrios to claim traditional roles as patriarchal providers. Often, men took on migrant labor in attempts to reclaim the patriarchy undermined at home. Yet migration took them far from family and community, opening new roles for women and limiting patriarchy—unless and until the young man came home with the dollars to buy a truck or a taxi, set up a store, gain a piece of land, and reclaim patriarchal ways. Mexican communities lived cycles of departure and return—departure stimulated by economic challenges to patriarchy; absence creating new spaces for women; return bringing reassertions of patriarchy and uncertain negotiations.[30]

Parallel challenges emerged among many who migrated, stayed in the United States, formed Mexican American families, and joined the middle class. In *El dilema del retorno* (The uncertainty of going home), Víctor Espinosa details the history of a family that migrated from a town in Guanajuato to Los Angeles, California. The father led the way, becoming a skilled craftsman in a furniture factory, always aiming to hold the role of patriarchal provider. He dreamed of returning to Guanajuato, building a house on the plaza, and becoming a leader of civic, religious, and family life. His wife, from the same community, took advantage of openings allowed women in late-twentieth-century Los Angeles to start a taquería; their son joined the business, and they developed a small chain of restaurants. A daughter found success in school and in ice skating competitions, even competing in Europe. Was this the Mexican American middle-class dream? In many ways, yes, yet the father longed to live out his last years as a patriarch in Mexico. For him, that would define and demonstrate success as a migrant—as a Mexican man. Mother and daughter resisted; they aimed to retain the openings allowed by U.S. middle-class ways. The son was torn. In the end, the father built his house on the plaza and claimed local office; most of the family spent most of every year in Los Angeles, allowing the aging patriarch to imagine himself patriarch while the family lived middle class in California.

Have some Mexican and Mexican American men facing poverty, insecurity at work, and challenges to patriarchy at home and in the larger societies of North America become assertively, sometimes violently, patriarchal? Yes. So have others facing such displacement. Among working men, fated to labor in subordination, their only compensation low wages and presumptions of patriarchy, threats to patriarchy have led to violent assertions. Parallel challenges to patriarchy led to rising violence within families and communities around 1900, and then turned outward in revolutionary assertions, driving Mexico's social conflagrations of 1910.[31]

The key point is that violence in defense of patriarchy is not Mexican; it is a socially structured and culturally constructed response of men, Mexican and others, to threats to ways of life long laborious, increasingly insecure, and newly threatening to patriarchal prerogatives—the only advantage in lives of laboring subordination. We need to see diverse men's reassertions of patriarchy in the context of the rapidly changing world of globalizing North American capitalism. We need to explore Anglo-American constructions of Mexican patriarchy, of machismo, in the same context.

North American women, including Mexicans and Mexican Americans, increasingly seek middle-class lives and the openings of education, profession, and political participation they enable; Mexican and Mexican American men seek similar lives and openings and often cling to patriarchal presumptions. Their resistance is too often "explained" by a machismo rooted in Mexico. Yet resistance to the limits of patriarchy inherent in openings to middle-class and working women can be found across a broader "Anglo-American" society that is creating new opportunities for women in times of shrinking opportunities for all. Limón's emphasis on the rise of the Mexican American middle class, in the context of his earlier exploration of changing gender constructions, points to a need to explore debates about patriarchy among transnational and multicultural middle (and other) classes on both sides of the border. If patriarchy was pivotal to organizing the capitalist ways of Hispanic North America and to the cultural visions that justified its incorporation into an integrated North America under Anglo-American hegemony, we must analyze carefully the challenges to patriarchy now debated in families and communities across neighboring nations as they fuse in a globalizing world.[32]

In our concluding chapter, Ramón Gutiérrez explores an important aspect of that fusion: the historical Mexican and Mexican American openness to ethnic amalgamation, to mestizaje. Ethnic mixing was a key and enduring characteristic of Spanish and Mexican North America. Shelley

Streeby reveals early Anglo-American literary condemnation of such amalgamations. Katherine Benton-Cohen and Devra Weber show how ethnic/racial integrations were both challenged and reshaped by escalating racial polarizations in the early twentieth century and found ways to endure in families and communities (if unrecognized by mainstream Anglo-American culture). Were Mexican American mobilizations during World War II facilitated by that openness? Did the readiness to mix help the emergence of the Mexican American middle class and promote the search for rights to join the U.S. "mainstream" after the war?

Gutiérrez argues in Chapter 8 that an enduring Mexican American openness to amalgamations, rooted in New Mexico and other borderlands regions, remains an important and viable alternative to powerful Anglo-American traditions of racially constructed polarities. He identifies and characterizes three "transnations" with distinct social and racial tendencies that define a North America no longer contained by national boundaries. An Atlantic-Caribbean transnation was shaped historically within the United States by a sharp black-white divide; it has been challenged by the inclusion of Caribbean peoples accustomed to more graded characterizations, but polarities hold strong. In contrast, a MexAmerican transnation developed deep and enduring traditions of amalgamation, of mestizaje, even as it faced pressures toward polarizing dualities that made Mexican a racial other within the United States. A third transnation, a northwestern Ecotopia, extending into Canada with links to Asia, grapples with polarities of white and black coming from the Atlantic Seaboard as they meet the diverse racial-ethnic practices of Asian immigrants.

Integrating historical, anthropological, and survey information, Gutiérrez explores the deep roots and enduring persistence of racial dualities along the Atlantic-Caribbean Seaboard. He focuses in depth on MexAmerica, documenting the tradition of mestizaje and the recent imposition of polarizing visions that aims to make Mexican not white and akin to black, a racial other shaped by racial mixing. And he emphasizes the need for comparative study of how the coming of Asians with distinct ways of national-ethnic-racial definition may reinforce or alter the powerful polarities that shape life across the United States.

Gutiérrez documents the enduring openness to amalgamations among Hispanic peoples in New Mexico and elsewhere. He wonders if their practices and perceptions will ground a mode of resistant adaptation to dominant polarities—or perhaps reshape North America as it globalizes, incorporates diverse new immigrants, and sees Mexicans and other Hispanic peoples move from the old Southwest and urban enclaves elsewhere to populate ever more of the continent. Could mestizaje, broadly defined, be America's future? A good historian, Gutiérrez asks the question—and leaves us to ponder the answer.[33]

Our chapters suggest that the option of Anglo-Mexican mestizaje has always been open. After all, from the formative decades of the nineteenth century, U.S. literary and popular culture imagined manly Yankees marrying Mexican women—unions promoted as a way to liberate Mexico and Mexicans. When in the twentieth century, Anglo-Americans pressed Mexicans to live as a racial other, José Limón shows that visions of manly Anglos in sexual relations with Mexican women held strong. He emphasizes that in cinematic portrayals of Texas, ranging from *Giant* in the 1950s to *Lone Star* in the 1990s, openings to mixing persisted.[34] Notably, the racial othering of Mexicans came simultaneously with the deepening of Jim Crow impositions on African Americans in the early twentieth century. The new opening to ethnic mixing (within an enduring patriarchy) evidenced by Giant, came with the rise of the African American civil rights movement. And the construction of visions of assaultive patriarchy to characterize both Mexican American and African American men in the 1960s and after came as both communities pressed economic and civil rights—and as the movement for women's rights challenged patriarchy. Reflecting on that history, it is worth asking why mainstream U.S. culture so long constructed sexual relations between blacks and whites as taboo, while sex between Anglo men and Mexican women was seen as inevitable, a sign of Anglo superiority.

It is essential to emphasize that mestizaje has rarely challenged structural inequalities. It has worked historically to integrate enduring differences, opening power to people of diverse origins, constructing the less favored as equally mixed. In contrast, U.S. polarities sharpen divisions structured in power, illuminating inequities, sometimes facilitating challenges.[35] An inclusive Mexican tradition of "ethnic" mestizaje thus contests a divisive U.S. commitment to racial polarities as ways to organize inequalities and political participations in an ever more diverse U.S. society facing rapid incorporation into a globalizing world. Can mestizaje migrate from being a core part of Mexican society and a debated aspect of Anglo-Mexican relations to shaping a more inclusive, less polarizing North America? The proliferation of marriages and other relationships crossing black/white boundaries and their rising social and cultural acceptance suggest that a historically "Mexican" opening to mestizaje increasingly characterizes U.S. ways.

We need only look at the White House to see the potential. A second thought reminds us that mestizaje will be contested. To a scholar of Mexico based in Washington, D.C., yet with long experience in Mexico and Texas (and Massachusetts and Minnesota), it was easy for me to conclude that Barack Obama ran for president as an American mestizo—son of a Kenyan father and a white midwestern mother, raised by white midwestern grandparents, educated in Indonesia and Hawaii and at Harvard. His marriage to an African American woman added to the mix. He campaigned as a mestizo, emphasizing white and African ancestries, aiming to broaden his appeal to whites and blacks—and perhaps to Mexicans for whom mixing has been a norm. Is Barack Obama the first mestizo president of the United States?

Perhaps, but on inauguration day, the media, many African Americans, and many others exploded in celebration of the first black president of the United States. He has quipped that "I was black before I was elected president." He announced that he checked off African American, and only African American, on the 2010 census form. Is he being drawn into eastern Atlantic polarities and away from his mestizo roots? Loud and sometimes angry voices contest Obama's presidency, even his right to be president. Some perceive that resistance as inflamed by opposition to a black serving as president. Could it equally reflect discomfort with the mestizaje that shaped his life? For the moment, the Obama presidency and the resistance to it confirm that the tension between amalgamation and polarity holds strong.

Mexicans continue to come and mix; blacks and whites and Asians and others also mix. The future of North American ethnic-racial-national identities and relations remains open and uncertain. Culminating in Gutiérrez' chapter, our studies suggest that the Mexican North American tradition of amalgamation, of mestizaje, holds strong. It remains a contender, an alternative to racial polarities, ready to help shape the future of North America.

Inseparable Histories

This volume offers chapters by scholars with diverse visions to emphasize that New Spain, Mexico, and Mexicans have been involved in every aspect of making the United States: capitalist foundations, Indian relations, literary and cultural traditions, the Civil War, southwestern settlements, migration and labor, the rise of the middle class, and the enduring challenge of "race" relations. Three themes dominate. The first is that the early commercial ways of Spanish and Mexican North America set foundations in mining, irrigated agriculture, and commercial grazing that were fundamentally capitalist before they were incorporated into the United States—and they were incorporated into the United States, shaping not only regions once Mexican but lands far beyond. Hispanic capitalism is the great unrecognized Mexican legacy shaping U.S. history. It remains unrecognized because Hispanic ways of mining, irrigated farming, and commercial grazing, and the labor relations embedded in them, were taken over by "Anglo-Americans"—by marriage, by purchase, by legislation, by theft—who were committed to their own superiority and loathe to recognize the deeply Mexican ways that sustained their power.

The second legacy, equally rooted in the ways of Spanish and Mexican North America, also compatible with prevailing Anglo-American ways, is patriarchy. Hispanic North American capitalism was structured and integrated by patriarchy. So were southern U.S. plantation ways and the commercial society of the U.S. North. When they met to dispute continental power in the nineteenth century, Anglo-Americans eagerly adopted Hispanic capitalism and justified it by proclaiming a superior Yankee patriarchy, a patriarchy mobilized to marginalize Mexicans in an economy they labored to sustain. Then after World War II Anglo-Americans reimagined patriarchy as a negative characteristic of Mexicans, as machismo—after Mexicans fought in World War II, demanded civil rights, and joined the U.S. middle class. Throughout, patriarchy remains a pivotal, debated, and changing aspect of Mexicans' participations in making the United States.

The third legacy of Hispanic North America developed within the history shaped by capitalism and patriarchy: ethnic amalgamation, mestizaje, forged diverse identities that changed over generations, reflected wealth and power more than ancestry, and shaped the commercial-patriarchal ways of Spanish and Mexican North America from the sixteenth through the nineteenth centuries. Yet while Anglo-Americans were quick to adopt Hispanic capitalism and to engage patriarchy by arguing they were better and stronger patriarchs, they resisted and often denigrated Mexicans' social amalgamation. When lands once Mexican were taken into the United States, their Hispanic Mexican and indigenous residents faced the polarizing assertions of powerful Anglo-Americans who imagined themselves white and privileged whiteness. In an enduring contradiction, Anglo-Americans worked to adopt the economic ways of Hispanic capitalism, to assert themselves as more patriarchal than Mexican patriarchs, while resisting the amalgamations that defined Hispanic ways.

Through the first half of the twentieth century, Anglo corporate and political power ruled the economy of the Southwest and built a polar culture in which white Americans ruled and constructed Mexicans as a racial other. Yet among Mexicans, diversities and amalgamations continued—if rarely recognized outside their families and communities. As Mexicans have continued to come to labor and to live in larger numbers, to settle across regions never under Mexican rule, and to become by far the largest part of the largest "minority" in the United States, their children have become middle class. They seek to prosper in a capitalist world, they join in continuing debates about old patriarchal ways and emerging women's rights and opportunities—and they remain open to amalgamations. By their lives and in their politics, Mexican Americans offer an example in contrast to the racializing polarities that have long challenged the American dream.

The North American capitalism rooted in important part in Hispanic traditions holds entrenched in a trajectory of globalization that will surely endure—and inevitably change. The challenge of constructing a postpatriarchal society persists. And the Mexican alternative of ethnic amalgamation remains a potentially liberating alternative to the polarizing ways of Anglo-American racial dualities. That people who brought the United States key ways to capitalist power, who continue to come to labor within that capitalist economy, who work to forge families and communities on routes toward middle-class lives, who join in the challenges of addressing patriarchal inequities, and who offer a liberating option of ethnic mixing—that such Mexican peoples are marked and maligned as alien others in a society they built and continue to build would be mystifying if it were not so divisive, debilitating, and destructive.

Notes

1. The classic analysis from this perspective is Rodolfo Acuña's *Occupied America* (Englewood Cliffs, N.J.: Prentice Hall, 2010).

2. David Weber, *The Spanish Frontier in North America* (New Haven: Yale University Press, 1992), offers a comprehensive analysis of the early Spanish presence.

3. The chapter builds upon my book *Making a New World* (Durham, N.C.: Duke University Press, 2011), focusing on implications for U.S. history.

4. Building upon *Making a New World*, this vision contrasts with the emphasis

on distinct Spanish and British religious and political cultures emphasized in J. H. Elliott's *Atlantic Empires* (New Haven: Yale University Press, 2006). It easily coincides with the perspectives in Jorge Cañizares-Esguerra's *Puritan Conquistadores* (Stanford: Stanford University Press, 2006), which emphasizes shared Spanish and British visions of native Americans.

5. Isenberg builds on his own fundamental studies in *The Destruction of the Bison* (New York: Cambridge University Press, 2001) and *Mining California* (New York: Hill and Wang, 2006).

6. Pekka Hämäläinen, *The Comanche Empire* (New Haven: Yale University Press, 2009); Brian DeLay, *The War of a Thousand Deserts* (New Haven: Yale University Press, 2009).

7. On the former Mexican territories and the origins of the Civil War, see John Ashworth, *Slavery, Capitalism, and Politics in the Antebellum Republic* (Cambridge: Cambridge University Press, 1995).

8. On slavery and Texas independence, see Randolph Campbell, *An Empire for Slavery* (Baton Rouge: Louisiana State University Press, 1989); Paul Lack, *The Texas Revolutionary Experience* (College Station: Texas A&M University Press, 1992). For an important study of early Texas, see Raúl Ramos, *Beyond the Alamo* (Chapel Hill: University of North Carolina Press, 2008).

9. See Andrés Reséndez, *Changing National Identities at the Frontier* (Cambridge: Cambridge University Press, 2006); Richard Griswald del Castillo, *The Treaty of Guadalupe Hidalgo* (Norman: University of Oklahoma Press, 1992).

10. Michael Morrison, *Slavery and the American West* (Chapel Hill: University of North Carolina Press, 1999); Michael Holt, *The Fate of Their Country* (New York: Hill and Wang, 2005).

11. Streeby extends the analysis offered in *American Sensations* (Berkeley: University of California Press, 2002).

12. See Leonard Pitt's *Decline of the Californios* (Berkeley: University of California Press, 1999); Albert Camarillo's *Chicanos in a Changing Society* (Cambridge: Harvard University Press, 1996); David Montejano's *Anglos and Mexicans in the Making of Texas, 1836–1986* (Austin: University of Texas Press, 1986); Katherine Benton-Cohen's *Borderline Americans* (Cambridge: Harvard University Press, 2009).

13. See Howard Lamar, *The Far Southwest, 1846–1912* (Albuquerque: University of New Mexico Press, 2000); Montejano, *Anglos and Mexicans*.

14. See *Borderline Americans* and its intersections with different yet reinforcing transnational perspectives in Samuel Truett, *Fugitive Landscapes* (New Haven: Yale University Press, 2006).

15. Weber turns, thus, to the decades before the California labor conflicts she explores in *Dark Sweat, White Gold* (New York: Oxford University Press, 1994).

16. Manuel Gamio, *The Life Story of the Mexican Immigrant* (New York: Dover Publications, 1972).

17. The best analysis of Cardenismo, especially in its relations with the United States, is Adolfo Gilly, *El Cardenismo* (Mexico City: Cal y Arena, 1993).

18. While we await an in-depth analysis of the *bracero* program, perhaps the best introduction and overview is the compilation assembled in Jorge Durand, ed., *Braceros* (Mexico City: Miguel Ángel Porrúa, 2007).

19. For follow-up, see Massey et al., *Beyond Smoke and Mirrors* (Albany, N.Y.: Russell Sage Foundation, 2003).

20. Stephen Haber, Armando Razo, and Noel Maurer, *The Politics of Property Rights* (Cambridge: Cambridge University Press, 2003).

21. See Gary Gereffi, *The Mexican Pharmaceutical Industry* (Durham, N.C.: Duke University Press, 1983); Gabriela Soto Laveaga, *Jungle Laboratories* (Durham, N.C.: Duke University Press, 2009).

22. Cynthia Hewitt de Alcántara, *Modernizing Mexican Agriculture* (Geneva: United Nations, 1976).

23. See Angus Wright, *The Death of Ramón González* (Austin: University of Texas Press, 1990); Michael Kearney, *Reconceptualizing the Peasantry* (Boulder, Colo.: Westview Press, 1996).

24. See, for example, Robert Smith, *Mexican New York* (Berkeley: University of California Press, 2005).

25. On Chávez and the farmworkers, see Miriam Pawel, *The Union of Their Dreams* (New York: Bloomsbury Press, 2009).

26. See Patrick Carroll, *Felix Longoria's Wake* (Austin: University of Texas Press, 2003).

27. For a study of early radicalism leading to middle-class participation, see David Montejano, *Quixote's Soldiers* (Austin: University of Texas Press, 2010).

28. On relations between Mexican Americans and Mexican migration, the classic study is David Gutiérrez, *Walls and Mirrors* (Berkeley: University of California Press, 1995). For a new analysis that largely supports Limón's view, see Tomás Jiménez, *Replenished Ethnicity* (Berkeley: University of California Press, 2010).

29. Samuel Ramos, *Profile of Man and Culture in Mexico* (Austin: University of Texas Press, 1962).

30. For case studies, see Luis González y González, *San José de Gracia* (Austin: University of Texas Press, 1982); Wright, *The Death of Ramón González*.

31. John Tutino, "The Revolution in Mexican Independence," *Hispanic American Historical Review* 78, no. 3 (1998): 367–418; and idem, "From Involution to Revolution in Mexico," *History Compass* 6, no. 3 (May 2008): 796–842.

32. The basis for such analysis is emerging in a proliferation of studies of women in migration and Mexican American families and communities. See, for example, Pierrette Hondagneu-Sotelo, *Gendered Transitions* (Berkeley: University of California Press, 1994); idem, ed., *Gender and U.S. Immigration* (Berkeley: University of California Press, 2003); and Vicki Ruiz, *Out of the Shadows* (New York: Oxford University Press, 1998).

33. Gutiérrez, who sets gender at the center of North American history in *When Jesus Came the Corn Mothers Went Away* (Stanford: Stanford University Press, 1991), knows such analyses will focus on changing gender relations.

34. All this is explored in Limón, *American Encounters*.

35. That sharp delineations facilitate oppositions was made clear long ago in Carl Degler's classic analysis of slavery and race in Brazil and the United States, *Neither Black nor White* (New York: MacMillan, 1971).

CHAPTER 1

Capitalist Foundations: Spanish North America, Mexico, and the United States

JOHN TUTINO

Capitalist globalization began in the sixteenth century when Chinese demand for silver stimulated silver production in recently conquered Spanish America. That pivotal link generated trades that spanned the globe and energized production in Europe, the Americas, and Asia. New Spain, the colonial predecessor of Mexico and of regions extending into the U.S. Southwest, played a pivotal role in those founding developments. Its silver economy stimulated global trade and drove commercial settlement north, reaching New Mexico before the British began to settle North America after 1600. From the sixteenth to the eighteenth centuries, vast regions now in the United States forged colonial foundations in a Spanish Empire that promoted mining, commercial ways, and global trades.

Thus began a drive toward capitalism that began in New Spain and later flourished in the United States. The history of North America cannot be understood without recognizing the roots of capitalism in New Spain and their enduring legacies across the continent.

When the coastal colonies of British North America declared themselves united states in 1776, the Gulf Coast and everything west of the Mississippi remained under Spanish rule or home to independent natives. Between the constitution that founded the nation in 1787 and the Civil War that ended slavery and set national unity in 1865, key episodes of nation making brought lands and people under Spanish sovereignty into an expansive United States: Louisiana and its hinterland by purchase in 1803; Texas, New Mexico, and California by war in 1846–1848. In the process, the Anglo-American nation incorporated much of the capitalism and culture of Spanish North America.

Too often, histories focus on triumphant "American" expansionism, or on Anglo domination and Hispanic and indigenous victimization. Those

contrasting views share the presumption that the legacies of Spanish colonial foundations were few and soon faded within the United States. A
quaint language of cowboy life (*vaqueros*, lassos, rodeos) and exotic mission ruins (do we all long for San Juan Capistrano?) might remain, but
the United States was and is something different: dynamic, commercial,
and expansive. As a result—rightly in the view of some; wrongly insist
others—Mexicans became subordinates in once-native lands. When other
Mexicans came in waves of migration after 1900, they were greeted as
outsiders in a nation that would not recognize a long history of shared
foundations.

There is historical reality in visions of expansion, Anglo rule, Hispanic
subordination, and Mexican migrants arriving to live as alien others.
Still, across regions originally forged within Spanish and then Mexican
(together, Hispanic) North America, colonial foundations under Spanish
sovereignty left legacies that shaped—and continue to shape—the United
States. Most notably, a powerful variant of capitalism began in northern
New Spain, to later mark much of the West in the United States. It began
in the sixteenth century when the silver mines of Guanajuato and Zacatecas and the trading, cultivating, and grazing region around Querétaro and
Celaya (the Bajío) combined to stimulate global trade and drive commercial settlement northward. In the late eighteenth century, regions from
San Antonio through Santa Fe to San Francisco were tied into a colonial
order generating mining wealth while sustained by irrigated cultivation
and commercial grazing. Later Anglo expansionists eagerly adopted all
that—by invasion, by coercion, and often by marrying the daughters of
Hispanic entrepreneurs.

Spanish North America also left a legacy of cultural amalgamation.
Diverse migrants from Europe, Mesoamerica, and Africa mixed to forge
new Hispanic amalgams. A few became rich from mining and trade; more
claimed lands to develop commercial estates; most labored in mines or
fields or herded cattle and sheep across open plateaus. Along frontiers
driving northward, missions aimed to make independent natives into
Christian subordinates, available to labor in the commercial economy.
In long historical processes, identities changed. By the late eighteenth
century, people of entrepreneurial success and political importance were
nearly always Spanish—whatever their ancestry. Many mine workers and
cowboys were proudly mulatto. Cultivators in estate communities and at
missions were *indios* in the eyes of landlords and clergy; many remained
Otomí, Tarahumara, Tepehuan, or Yaqui in home communities. Independent natives built identities as Apaches or Comanches, while "*bárbaros*"

in the eyes of Spanish officials and entrepreneurs. Ancestry was complex and hard to trace.

A first reflection might suggest that the expansive United States adopted the commercial ways of Spanish North America but rejected its cultural amalgamations. A second thought leads us to consider how the incorporation of Spanish North America accelerated the commercial dynamism of the United States—and left an example of ethnic flexibility as an alternative to prevailing ways of separation and exclusion.

The vision proposed here builds on the understanding offered in David Weber's classic studies of the U.S. Southwest under Spanish and Mexican rule. He details emerging societies based on grazing and mission communities, building irrigation where possible, caught up in trade and conflict with independent native peoples. He emphasizes, however, Spanish and Mexican policy initiatives that aimed to shape distant frontiers, and repeatedly failed.

My analysis frames New Spain's northern frontiers as extensions of the commercial societies that developed over centuries from Querétaro and Guanajuato to Zacatecas and San Luis Potosí, on to Parral, Sonora, and Chihuahua—and beyond. There, Spanish North America was founded and shaped by silver and the commercial ways it fueled; regime plans and mission goals always adapted more than they ruled. The dynamic commercial society forged there drove north to set foundations of entrepreneurial production and amalgamating ethnic relations in frontier regions that later became U.S. borderlands. As Howard Lamar details in his classic study of politics in the territories taken into the Anglo-American nation in 1848, new rulers and forward-looking investors repeatedly worked to maintain the mining and property codes of Spanish and Mexican North America. My analysis sets Weber's frontiers in the context of the long history of Spanish North America, builds on Lamar's understanding that Anglo-American entrepreneurs saw opportunity in Hispanic commercial ways, and extends David Montejano's emphasis that Anglos and Mexicans joined in conflict and confluence to make Texas—and the United States.[1]

The first section emphasizes that New World capitalism began in New Spain; it outlines North American colonial foundations by emphasizing four primary variants: Spanish Mesoamerica, where Spaniards ruled enduring Mesoamerican communities; Spanish North America, where commercial dynamism and cultural amalgamation drove northward; plantation North America, where export crops raised by African slaves shaped racially polarized societies; and European North America, where English, French, and other settlers cut timber, tilled the soil, fished, and traded—

excluding native peoples while trading with them. The rest of the study sketches a history of New Spain focused on Spanish North America, tracing its economic dynamism and northward expansion, then exploring the crisis that came with Mexico's wars for independence beginning in 1810. It concludes by emphasizing how the United States–Mexico war of the 1840s incorporated vast lands and key legacies of Hispanic North America into the United States, accelerating the Anglo-American nation's drive to continental and global hegemony. An epilogue sketches the enduring legacies of Hispanic capitalism in twentieth-century North America.

Capitalism and Colonial Formations

When the Genoese mariner Christopher Columbus, sailing under Castilian sovereignty, hit upon the outer islands of the Caribbean in 1492, the American continent blocked a voyage aimed to accelerate European trade with Asia. For half a century, Castilians and others focused on exploring lands they did not know, conquering states that ruled densely settled regions in Mesoamerica and the Andes, always searching for ways to pay for the enterprise and generate profits. Their conquests were enabled by the delivery of smallpox and other diseases that devastated New World populations and debilitated their states and economies. Around 1550, the conquest was consolidating and a Spanish regime forming—while accelerating depopulation left ever fewer people to produce, labor, pay tributes, and become Christian. The prospects of Europeans' first American colonies were uncertain.

Yet in a few fateful years, the American enterprise revived. In the 1540s, colonials found mountains of silver at Potosí in the Andes and Zacatecas in northern New Spain. In the 1550s, soaring Chinese demand created premium prices for the metal now decreed the only money and medium to pay taxes in the world's largest economy.[2] Spain's Americas— then the only Americas outside the coastal settlements of Portuguese Brazil—turned to the construction (better, the reconstruction) of colonial societies aiming to maximize silver production.

That meant engaging diverse indigenous societies in distinct geographic environments and reorienting them to the extent possible into foundations for silver mining, commercial enterprises, and enduring colonial societies, societies that would benefit European regimes, entrepreneurs, and settlers by accelerating global trade. Because indigenous societies differed, American geographies varied, and Europeans came at different times, the economic potential and social organizations of New World colonies differed in important ways.

North America emerged from histories grounded in indigenous precedents and reshaped by colonial encounters that brought Europeans and Africans to the Americas to participate (in unequal ways) in accelerating global trade. The key to an integrated history of North America is to take indigenous precedents seriously, to examine economic prospects and colonial societies and cultures carefully, and to understand modern nations as emerging from all that in complex ways.

New Spain came first. It began with the conquest of the Mexica (Aztec) regime in the 1520s and the subsequent subordination of the other states of Mesoamerica. Early on, Spaniards adapted to, built upon, and transformed Mesoamerican institutions. *Encomiendas* granted European conquerors rights to collect tribute goods and use seasonal labor services from the people of Mesoamerican *altepetl* (city states). They allowed Spaniards to benefit from indigenous ways of production and rule. Yet from the start, smallpox and other Old World diseases drove down native populations, shrinking the tribute goods and labor available to newcomers struggling to rule a world new to them. After 1540, with population plummeting and economic prospects uncertain, the Spanish future in North America was tenuous.

Then, in 1546, Spaniards guided by native allies found mountains of silver at Zacatecas, far north of Mexico City. As Chinese demand soared, Spanish America built an economy focused on silver. By 1600, about two-thirds of the precious metal passed east to Europe, where it stimulated production and trade that extended through the Islamic world of the Middle East and South Asia, eventually reaching China to be exchanged for silks, spices, and other goods. The other third sailed west from Acapulco to Manila, where Chinese merchants gathered to trade spices, silks, and other things precious for silver. The result was an early commercial capitalism in which silver mined in Spain's Americas drove growing trades linking Europe and China. Globalization was under way by 1600, with Spanish America a pivotal participant.

Silver revived economic prospects in New Spain while smallpox continued to devastate native populations. Rich deposits at Taxco and Pachuca, near Mexico City in the heartland of Mesoamerica, and others located to the north at Zacatecas and Guanajuato spurred local development and global commerce. Colonial elites gained unprecedented riches, and the imperial treasury took soaring revenues as mining stimulated commercial cultivation and textile production focused on growing

Spanish cities and towns. Still, colonial development took different paths in Mesoamerica, where indigenous state traditions and cultivating communities shaped colonial ways, and in the North—where sparse peoples without states gave way (not without resistance) to new commercial ways.

Around Mexico City and across regions south and east, where indigenous states had ruled cultivating communities for centuries before Europeans arrived, the regime congregated and reconstituted surviving communities as *repúblicas de indios* (indigenous republics), giving Spanish legal form to Mesoamerican rights and landed domains. Meanwhile, disease and depopulation forced change while Christian proselytization pressed cultural adaptations. Still, Mesoamerican legacies held strong in regions historically shaped by Mesoamerican states, institutions, and cultures. To the end of the colonial era, centuries of engagement with a European regime, Christian beliefs, and global trades built upon Mesoamerican communities and traditions, shaping a society best described as Spanish Mesoamerica.

Where the silver economy flourished near enduring Mesoamerican communities, cities like Mexico City, Puebla, and Valladolid (now Morelia) became pivots of a commercial complex of mines, estates, and industries sustained by the production and labor of communities organized as indigenous republics. Between 1570 and 1630, as population hit its nadir, surviving native cultivators were congregated in communities granted lands to ensure their sustenance; as the silver economy boomed and labor demands soared, villagers were pressed to wage work by a regime-sanctioned labor draft, the *repartimiento*. Men in native communities labored in nearby commercial fields, urban construction, and other projects. Most went twice a year for a week; the rest of the time they worked family lands and pursued crafts in their communities, sustaining themselves and selling in local markets. As population stabilized around 1630, the draft ended in the face of local recalcitrance—but the labor link tying landed villagers to the commercial economy was set, a characteristic of Spanish Mesoamerica that endured for centuries.

Farther south, silver mines proved scarce, mining's commercial stimulus weak. Commercial life was limited to cochineal, an indigenous dye made by Mixtec families in Oaxaca, plus the provision of foodstuffs and cloth to small Spanish towns. Among Oaxaca's Zapotecs and the Mayas of Yucatán, Chiapas, and Guatemala, native notables ruled relatively autonomous indigenous republics that retained lands that sustained most families through the colonial centuries. In the more commercial regions around Mexico City and across less dynamic zones to the south, communities grounded in the Mesoamerican past remained the foundation of colonial life for centuries. Landlords and merchants profited as they could, more near Mexico City, less to the south. Their entrepreneurial goals and profits were limited by the rights and lands granted native republics. The regime maintained stability by focusing on judicial mediation of disputes between colonials and communities, and between communities. Spanish Mesoamerica developed by grafting commercial capitalism onto an enduring base of Mesoamerican communities.[3]

North of Mesoamerica, the stimulus of silver proved stronger—and indigenous ways were different. The colonial society that developed there after 1550 was thoroughly commercial. Around 1500, the basin now called the Bajío, stretching west from Querétaro toward Guadalajara, was a contested frontier. The Mexicas and a competing Tarascan state pressed north but faced the adamant resistance of the state-free hunters, gatherers, and cultivators the Mexicas maligned as Chichimecas—sons of dogs. After Spaniards conquered the Mesoamerican states and found silver to the north at Zacatecas (and then in the Bajío at Guanajuato), Chichimecas equally fought Spanish colonization. The stimulus of silver mixed with Chichimeca resistance to make Spanish North America a place of persistent conflicts and frontier wars, contests mediated by missions and repeatedly ended by smallpox's devastation of native peoples. Amid conflicts that began in the Bajío after 1550 and continued far to the north after 1750, Spanish North America developed as a commercially expansive society that produced most of the silver that shaped New Spain and its global trade.

Lacking Mesoamerican traditions, except as brought north by migrants, indigenous republics were scarce in the North. The dynamism of silver and the weakness of community legacies made New Spain's North the most commercial region of the Americas from the sixteenth century on. Mesoamericans, Europeans, and Africans came, faced resistant Chichimecas and others, all meeting and mixing in a society that during three centuries expanded to shape broad regions including New Mexico, Texas, and California. Colonial life focused on mining, irrigated cultivation, and commercial grazing. A search for profit orchestrated commercial social relations. As Chichimecas and independent peoples to the north died, fled to the margins, or passed through missions to find lives of laboring subordination, almost everything in Spanish North America was new.

New Spain thus generated two distinct social formations: Spanish Mesoamerica remained grounded in enduring indigenous communities reconstituted as indigenous republics, producing silver for global trade by mobilizing the work and produce of indigenous peoples first focused on their own sustenance; Spanish North America developed as a fully commercial, ethnically amalgamating, geographically expansive society mixing people from across the Atlantic world, producing even more silver for global trade as it drove north into the continent. Together they formed New Spain—economically dynamic, ethnically complex, and remarkably stable to the end of the eighteenth century. Mexico began in 1821 as an attempt to fuse the contrasting societies of New Spain into one nation, just as the stimulus of silver collapsed.[4]

The global importance of New Spain and the Spanish Andes, their stimulus of soaring trades, and their continuing delivery of unprecedented revenues to the Spanish monarchy were set by 1600. The sixteenth-century enterprises that forged a global Hapsburg Empire of sovereignty, production, and trade (including Portugal and its domains in Brazil, Africa, and Asia from 1580 to 1640) radically altered global dynamics. If other Europeans were to compete for power and the wealth of trade, they had to join the rush to expansion. The Dutch, forged in revolt against Hapsburg rule, took the lead by assaulting Portuguese possessions in Asia and later in Brazil. The British (and soon the French) turned to the Americas. It is important to recognize that they came late. The Spanish had set the model, generating silver and trade by mobilizing the peoples of Andean and Mesoamerican states facing depopulation and disorganization. The British, relegated to regions Spaniards had explored and left aside, found no silver and people deeply resistant to mobilization for newcomers' profit. The result, after a century of experiment, was a British North America fundamentally different from New Spain, yet also divided into distinct southern and northern societies.

To understand the development of mainland British America, it is essential to recognize the stimulus of global trade as demonstrated by the precedents set in Spanish America. It is equally essential to recognize that the Anglo-American colonization driven by those precedents was shaped on the ground in North America by encounters with indigenous peoples fundamentally different from those with state traditions early incorporated in the Spanish project.[5]

In the sixteenth century, North American native peoples lived in diverse societies shaped in part by historical interactions with Mesoamerican states and peoples. At Cahokia and across the Mississippi basin, Mesoamerican influences marked city-states built around temple platforms and sustained by cultivating villagers. Mesoamerican maize was the dominant staple across eastern woodlands as far north as Massachusetts.

Still, when Europeans first crossed the lands north of Mesoamerica in the sixteenth century, states were few and in decline—a trajectory accelerated by smallpox and other new diseases. As the seventeenth century began, most peoples north of Mesoamerica lived free of states and other structures of concentrated power and enduring inequity. They mixed cultivation with hunting, fishing, and gathering in societies of local independence and relative equality, especially when compared with the state powers and hierarchical ways of Mesoamericans and Europeans.

Spaniards surveyed North America during the sixteenth century. They established early missions in the Southeast, calling natives to lives of Christian dependence. Some came and stayed; many visited, tried European tools and beliefs, adapted what they found useful, and returned to home villages. Others resisted. In the process, smallpox spread and made clear the liabilities of life among Europeans. Without mines to stimulate commercial settlement, the decline of native populations set the demise of Spain's southeastern missions. Native survivors were left with immunities and lessons that led many to resist when other Europeans came later. Farther north, coastal North America saw only the visits of British, French, and other fishermen—again bringing contacts, lessons, and diseases—until settlement began after 1600.

With Spain entrenched in the Andes, Mesoamerica, and mining regions stretching north, European latecomers were left to focus on the Caribbean and Atlantic shores. Early encounters with Spaniards and the diseases they brought had all but emptied the islands of native peoples. There, first in Barbados, later in Jamaica, Saint Domingue, and elsewhere, the British and French built sugar and slave plantation colonies modeled on the success of Portuguese Brazil. Sugar and slavery proved second only to silver as ways to colonial wealth and stimuli to commodity and (in)human trades. They shaped Brazil and the Caribbean for centuries.[6]

When Britons engaged the coastal peoples of North America, they found communities mixing cultivation, fishing, and hunting without traditions of life under state rule. John Smith and others searched for gold and silver but found no rich mines along the Atlantic Seaboard. Nor did sugar flourish on the mainland, leaving exports to secondary crops like tobacco, rice, and indigo on southern coasts, fish, furs, timber, and grain in the North.

Near the sea and inland, indigenous people resisted incorporation as dependent producers. From the start, natives and Europeans viewed each other as "others." Early on they traded furs and native captives for European tools and weapons. Later, British settlers shifted to focus on cultivation for sustenance and export. Again, contact brought diseases that devastated native populations. Most Britons saw indigenous survivors as obstacles to personal prospects and colonial development. Natives were pressed inland, often eliminated when they resisted. Indigenous precedents and European responses shaped British America even as natives faced exclusion from colonial life.[7]

Native legacies of independence and resistance were broadly parallel along the northern and southern coasts of North America. It was differing potentials for export production on lands cleared of natives that shaped distinct southern and northern ways under British rule. From Brazil through the Caribbean and up the coast to the Chesapeake, the growth of export plantations in the eighteenth century consolidated colonies (under diverse European sovereignty) grounded in African slavery. To the north (extending into French Canada), plantation crops did not flourish, slavery was limited, and production for sustenance and export depended on families and small enterprises. In southern British America slavery shaped production, social relations, racial visions, and cultural adaptations; to the north, the limited role of plantations and slavery led to more homogeneous colonial societies, more integrated internally by market dynamics. There, social relations and cultural conversations developed primarily among immigrant Europeans.

The contrasting colonial ways of Spanish Mesoamerica and North America shaped New Spain and left fundamental challenges to making Mexico a nation—helping make the era from 1810 to 1930 a time of enduring political and social conflict. The contrasting trajectories of southern and northern British America, with their inevitable variants and interpenetrations, mark the history of the United States, culminating in a devastating Civil War and leaving enduring legacies of racial polarization.[8] This chapter recognizes all that—and argues that Hispanic North America set a third colonial foundation equally essential to understanding the United States.

This vision of four primary colonial social formations shaping North America emphasizes the fundamental importance of social relations of production. So does the history of Hispanic North America that follows. The ways people work to engage the environment, to produce the necessities of life, and to generate the wealth that sustains those who profit and rule combine to structure societies for the majority of their inhabitants. The ways people understand and debate the legitimacy of the relationships and inequities grounded in production shape the cultures of most peoples and communities in powerful ways. In any society, prevailing ways of production link everyday issues of work, family, and belief to larger structures of environment, population, production, regime, and ideology. In the colonial Americas, social relations of production developed at the intersection of local traditions, Atlantic empires, and global trade.[9]

Founding Capitalism in the Americas:
Spanish North America, 1550–1700

When Europeans arrived in the Americas, the great river they would name for Santiago marked a frontier between Mesoamerica, with its cultivating communities and contending states, and the dispersed, state-free peoples who inhabited the fertile basin lands of the Bajío and the dry plateau country reaching north. Earlier, Mesoamerican states had reached to Zacatecas and beyond; its cities had traded with peoples in the Upper Rio Grande Valley and the Mississippi Basin. But the domain of states receded south during the centuries before 1500, leaving the Bajío and the arid lands to the north without states, inhabited by mobile hunters and gatherers, others who mixed hunting, gathering, and shifting cultivation, and scattered communities of cultivators where the environment allowed.[10]

In the aftermath of the Spanish conquest of Tenochtitlan, the Mexica capital, Otomí peoples long subject to Mexica power drove north into the Bajío. Led by Otomí lords and accompanied by a few Franciscans, they founded Querétaro in the 1530s and settled the rich lands east and west along the Lerma River.[11] When expeditions farther north found silver at Zacatecas in the 1540s, the agricultural zone built by the Otomies around Querétaro was set to sustain mining and grazing enterprises farther north. Silver connected Zacatecas and Querétaro to expanding European and world trade. It drew a rush of settlement after 1550: Europeans, African slaves, diverse Mesoamericans, and their mixed offspring came in search of riches for a few, opportunities for the many, and work for the bound. From the beginning, Spanish North America was globally linked, commercially defined, and settled by migrants from across the Atlantic world. It was a colonial order thrusting northward in constant engagement and often in conflict with stateless native peoples.

As Chinese demand and Zacatecan mines kept the stimulus of silver strong, after 1550, the regime sanctioned a line of settlements between the Otomí foundations around Querétaro and the northern mining center. San Miguel el Grande, San Felipe, León, and Aguascalientes asserted

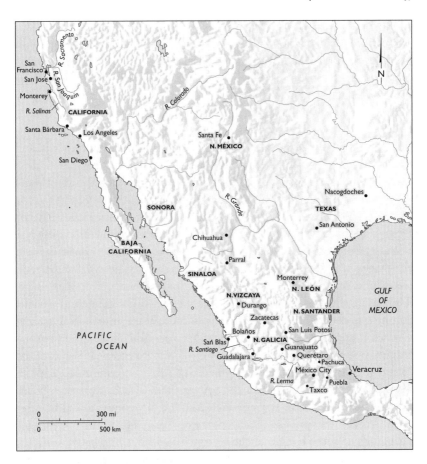

Map 1.1. Spanish North America

European dominion on the road to Zacatecas. New towns promoted cultivation where irrigation allowed; grazing estates spread across the country. Chichimecas saw their lands invaded by entrepreneurial and laboring migrants; livestock trampled resources essential to native survival. In response, Chichimecas began to hunt European livestock and gather crops, tools, and textiles. Atlantic invasion brought threat and opportunity: if cattle and sheep invaded Chichimeca lands, Chichimecas would hunt cattle and sheep; if crops took over rich bottomlands, they would gather crops; if horses, metal tools, and weapons gave Europeans mobility and power, Chichimecas would gather horses, tools, and weapons.[12]

Europeans and Mesoamericans saw such gathering, adaptation, and experimentation as assault and theft. They answered with war. From the

1550s to the 1590s, Chichimeca wars made Spanish North America a place of endemic violence. Spaniards and Otomies based at Querétaro fought together to stop, or at least to contain, the attacks of Chichimecas fighting to survive amid the new ways of Spanish North America. Military victory proved elusive, but smallpox and other imported diseases pummeled native peoples, Otomí and Chichimeca alike.

Viceroy Luis de Velasco II sanctioned a negotiated peace in the 1590s. Surviving Chichimecas were settled in villages; allocated lands, tools, and livestock; and taught by friars to live as Christian cultivators. Such missions became and long remained key institutions seeking to subordinate stateless peoples within Spanish North America.[13]

After 1600, the foundations of Spanish North America consolidated from Querétaro to Zacatecas. Mining boomed with new discoveries at San Luis Potosí. Otomí Querétaro flourished as a center of Spanish trade and textile production surrounded by irrigated fields. Celaya, San Miguel, León, and other towns grew as smaller Spanish replicas of Querétaro. The result was a complex regional economy: silver generated dreams and profits and fueled global trade; commercial cultivators and grazers claimed lesser but steadier profits by supplying mining centers and urban markets; merchants in Mexico City, Querétaro, and Zacatecas profited by integrating the entire system—financing mines to accumulate capital, investing in commercial estates to secure their wealth. Regime officials were most interested in revenues and peace. They concentrated in cities and towns, as did most clergy, except the few assigned to mission communities, often on the fringes of the region.[14]

Communities were everywhere in Spanish North America: mining communities, urban communities, estate communities, and, on the frontiers, mission communities. But outside of major cities and towns organized by Spanish councils (and Querétaro, the leading city of the Bajío, which remained a native republic ruled by an Otomí council deep into the seventeenth century), in Spanish North America most settlements lacked the community lands and republican councils that grounded the autonomies of Mesoamerican villages to the south. Missions were designed to be temporary, ruled by clergy while native neophytes learned Christian deference and laboring dependence. Native residents had no claim to the land, no right to self-rule. A few Tlaxcalan and other transplanted Mesoamerican communities did gain lands and local rule, as did the early Otomí settlements along the southern margins of the Bajío; they held rights and landed autonomy denied to most across Spanish North America.

The mining camps and estate communities where most northerners lived and worked beginning in the late sixteenth century had no rights to lands and no self-rule; few had resident clergy. They were company towns ruled by the enterprises that employed their residents. Managers reporting to mine operators or landed entrepreneurs were key intermediaries. Commercial goals orchestrated everything from work to family life; hierarchies of patriarchal dependence extended from the powerful to the working poor.[15] Rich and powerful entrepreneurs, often close to regime officials, ruled mining, trade, and estates. They employed managers, always men, who engaged many more men as mine workers, herders, and cultivators—some as salaried employees (often obligated workers receiving advance salaries and food rations in exchange for promises to labor), others as tenants.

Along hierarchies of patriarchal inequality, powerful men gave dependent men opportunities to serve and work, sometimes to prosper, usually to survive. Dependent men gained the means to assert patriarchal rights in subordinate families—to claim that they sustained wives and children (who always worked in the households men presumed to rule). Dependent men acquiesced in labor service, gaining access to land and salaries, reinforcing household rule while negotiating with wives and neighbors over how well they "provided." Enterprises reinforced household patriarchy to gain workers for an expanding commercial economy. Shared commitments to patriarchy stabilized unequal, often exploitative, relations linking entrepreneurs and workers, blunting the potential for conflict between the few who ruled and took profit and the many men who worked to sustain families they expected to rule.[16]

During founding decades and long after, the relations of patriarchal dependence that organized northern communities allowed most men and families enough sustenance and security to attract migrants from Spanish Mesoamerica to the south. Northern mines and estates developed amid historically sparse populations, conditions that endured in the face of the resistance of native inhabitants. Mines had to offer high wages and often ore shares to entice men to take the deadly risks of labor underground.[17] Estates had to offer security and sustenance to gain and hold families of tenants, cultivators, and stock herders.

Northern entrepreneurs also brought African slaves to labor in mining camps, on grazing estates, and as household servants, especially before 1650. But in the commercially dynamic and ethnically complex society of the Bajío, slaves repeatedly found ways to freedom: by flight; by slave men producing free children with indigenous women; by slave mothers giving babies to free families to raise as their own. In the long run, slavery proved more a means of forced migration than forced labor in the Bajío and Spanish North America. Slaves' offspring mixed into a larger, ethnically amalgamating population. A few became landholders; many more lived as mine workers and herdsmen, tenant farmers and rural laborers. In time, a prosperous minority claimed Spanish status. Mine workers often asserted mulatto identities. At rural estates others of African ancestry merged with immigrant Mesoamericans in communities of *indios* (a category of colonial subordination only slowly becoming an ethnic identity) in the late seventeenth century. The *vaquero* (buckaroo, cowboy) of Spanish North America was almost always a mulatto, a Spanish speaker mixing African and indigenous ancestry.[18] Across northern New Spain, social relations were driven by commercial goals, shaped by labor scarcities, and orchestrated by patriarchal hierarchies reaching from the pinnacle of power to the producing poor. Ethnic relations and identities proved fluid and changing.

As the foundations of Spanish North America consolidated from the Bajío to Zacatecas, its commercial ways drove northward. Early advances led to uncertain outposts, extending as far as New Mexico, where the upper Rio Grande met the Rockies. In the 1630s, rich silver strikes set Parral (now in southern Chihuahua) as the northern anchor of mining and trade. Commercial estates spread across the countryside there, building irrigation for cultivation along streams, setting livestock to graze everywhere. Independent natives again faced hard choices: resist, retreat, or try life in missions that offered Christianity, laboring dependence, and unprecedented contagion.[19] In fits and starts, the search for silver always leading, with commercial development quick to follow and missions ready to force and accommodate indigenous adjustments, the northward thrust of Spanish America continued through the seventeenth century and into the eighteenth, focused on upland plateaus from the Bajío to New Mexico.[20]

During the early 1600s, Hapsburg rulers based at Madrid integrated vast domains across Europe, the Americas, Africa, and Asia to forge the first globalization.[21] New Spain was a key participant, generating silver and wealth in two different colonial societies. In Spanish Mesoamerica, Europeans seeking silver, profit, and power encountered powerful states, conquered them, and built a colonial society grounded in enduring landed communities. After 1550, the intersection of silver discoveries and disease-driven depopulation there led to a commercial economy grafted upon self-governing landed indigenous republics; social relations revolved around mediations between Spanish power and native communities. The majority retained indigenous languages and ethnic identities in times of depopulation and long after. During three centuries, Spanish Mesoamerica divided sharply between Spaniards and ethnically diverse indigenous peoples. Hispanic life was commercial, focused on profiting from mining and the commercial estates that sustained mines and cities—all linked to a global economy. Indigenous villagers retained landed autonomy, produced first for family sustenance and local markets, and forged native Christian cultures focused on community integration. Patriarchy ruled there, too, organizing life among Spanish elites and within native families and communities, but it divided into separate hierarchies, one organizing Spanish cities, the other integrating native communities. In the economically dynamic basins near Mexico City, the two sectors of Spanish Mesoamerica were linked by villagers' provision of foodstuffs to city markets and seasonal labor at commercial estates, and by judicial mediations—forging an enduring stability after 1600.[22]

In Spanish North America, Europeans seeking silver, profit, and power encountered natives without states, mostly sparse and mobile peoples hunting, gathering, and cultivating across arid plateau country stretching far to the north. There Europeans did not conquer, they colonized. They built a new society settled by peoples from across the Atlantic world, a society defined by commercial goals, organized in communities denied autonomy, orchestrated by patriarchy, and defined by dependence. Peoples of diverse origins met and mixed in commercial communities; slaves of African ancestry found routes to freedom (yet rarely escaped laboring dependence); ethnic boundaries proved porous; identities were fluid and subject to change. By the late seventeenth century, nearly everyone spoke Spanish. Hierarchies of patriarchy reached from powerful elites to working families. All the while, Spanish North America drove north in constant conflict with independent peoples.[23]

Those contrasting colonial orders combined to form the Viceroyalty of New Spain. They shared a political capital in Mexico City, an institutional church closely linked to the regime, and an overarching system of finance and trade ruled by the merchant-financiers of Mexico City, who funded mines and invested in lands both near the capital and across the North.

Still, Spanish Mesoamerica and Spanish North America differed in fundamental ways. The North was a more ethnically mixed, linguistically Spanish, fully commercial society—and more expansive than Spanish Mesoamerica. Patriarchy integrated everything.[24] The regime pursued revenues by promoting silver production and related commercial enterprises. Missions aimed to pacify Chichimecas, Tarahumaras, Yaquis, and others, pressing them to become dependent producers in commercial enterprises. Courts and clergy were sparse on the ground across the North. Life there revolved around promoting, profiting from, and, for the majority, laboring in an expanding commercial society that fueled global trade, filled regime coffers—and consolidated patriarchy.

Silver Booms and Northward Accelerations: Spanish North America in the Eighteenth Century

The eighteenth century brought a new wave of silver bonanzas and northward expansion to Spanish North America. After a lull that began in the 1640s and deepened in the 1680s, from 1700, Chinese demand for silver soared again, driving up prices and production.[25] Meanwhile, the eighteenth century saw population in Europe and the Americas, linked commercially for two centuries, grow simultaneously for the first time, tripling or more in many regions. Together they stimulated a new transatlantic combination of commercial dynamism and population pressure, stimulating economic expansion, escalating conflicts, and social polarization.[26] As Euro-Atlantic production and trade grew, demand for silver expanded—drawing more of the commodity that was money, thus potentially capital, from China to Europe. When the price of silver fell around 1750 in Asia, Europeans accelerated their competition for New Spain's output. Thus began a shift from the multicentered dynamism of early capitalism toward a European dominance marked by British ascendance. New Spain's silver remained pivotal to the global economy through decades of transition. Production concentrated in Zacatecas, Guanajuato, and regions north, doubling from 1700 to 1750, and again from 1760 to 1780, to hold near peak levels past 1800. Throughout, New Spain's mines stimulated European war, trade, and industry.

In Europe, silver flowed toward France and England, strengthening production, trade, and regime revenues in the powers locked in competition for European and Atlantic dominance. Spain struggled to stay a contender as trades and revenues grounded in its colonies passed through to fortify its neighbors. Precisely because its empire generated pivotal wealth, Spain remained a participant in Atlantic wars. Regions around Barcelona lived an early industrial transformation after 1770. Still, the eighteenth-century boom in New Spain mostly fortified power and industry in France and Britain. The European prosperity driven by silver and Atlantic trade was the context of the rationalizing assertions of Enlightenment thinkers. Striving to control home production and global trades, Europeans forged beliefs that posited reason as the base of their "rightful" drives toward power and profitable production—and explained the "inferiority" of those they aimed to rule in the Americas, Asia, and beyond.[27]

The same boom drove continuing economic dynamism and northward expansion in New Spain. Mining, profits, and regime revenues soared at Guanajuato, Zacatecas, and elsewhere; farther north, settlement consolidated at San Antonio in Texas, intensified around Santa Fe in New Mexico, and drove up the coast of California to San Francisco. With boom came challenges. Communities in Spanish Mesoamerica faced new pressures on lands and local rule. Producing families in Spanish North America, especially in the Bajío, faced declining earnings, rising rents, and threats to patriarchy. Social tensions deepened; cultural conflicts escalated. Yet economic expansion and social stability held, interrupted only by sporadic conflicts and a wave of uprisings quickly contained in the 1760s—followed by new decades of economic boom and northward expansion that lasted past 1800.

New Spain remained pivotal to global production and trade through a century of transforming change. Its population tripled from about two million to nearly six million; most still lived in the Mesoamerican communities of the Center and South; growth was more rapid in the North. Silver production rose from five million pesos annually around 1700 to ten million pesos at mid-century, to average over twenty million pesos yearly from 1775 to 1800, fueling colonial production, northward settlement, and Atlantic and global trade.[28] Across New Spain, wealth concentrated while communities faced population pressures. Still, Mesoamerican and North American communities faced economic boom and new exploitations in contrasting ways.

In Spanish Mesoamerica, mining boomed before 1750 at Taxco, later at Real del Monte near Pachuca. In Spanish North America, silver revived first at Zacatecas and in far Chihuahua, then at Guanajuato and across San Luis Potosí.

Mine workers did not fare so well. Taxco and Real del Monte tried to reenergize Mesoamerican traditions of drafting workers from nearby villages; few came and disputes proliferated. Across New Spain and especially in the North, most eighteenth-century mine workers were mestizos and mulattoes, men of mixed origins paid high wages, food rations, and ore shares for doing dangerous work that drove the world economy. Mine operators faced rising costs and growing populations; keen to profit, they tried to cut wages and rations and eliminate ore shares. They set off conflicts that peaked in 1766 and 1767, focused on work grievances at Real del Monte and on regime demands and new taxes at Guanajuato and San Luis Potosí. Committed first to the revenues mining generated, authorities mediated a resolution at Real del Monte and repressed riotous workers at Guanajuato and San Luis Potosí.[29] Then Bourbon reformers made concessions to entrepreneurs and mediated labor relations just enough to sustain production, profits, and regime revenues. The effort succeeded; New Spain's mines yielded silver near historical peaks into the nineteenth century.

In Mesoamerican regions around Mexico City, the silver boom fueled urban expansion and commercial development; combined with population growth, they drove rising demand for food, cloth, and other goods. Still, near the capital the persistence of native republics and the continuing mediation of courts and clergy limited and contained conflicts. As rising populations struggled to live on limited lands in native republics, commercial estates expanded production and recruited growing numbers of seasonal hands among men and boys in nearby communities. Growers profited and villagers gained earnings to supplement limited cultivation, sustaining families, communities, and men's patriarchal claims.

Historical ties linking landed villages and commercial growers in the core of Spanish Mesoamerica became symbiotic exploitations. Estates and communities were bound together in ways that were simultaneously symbiotic and exploitative: villagers' labor became essential to landlords' profits and to the survival of families and communities facing growing populations with limited land. And symbiotic exploitation, backed by judicial mediation when conflicts arose, stabilized social inequities around Mexico City: village men "needed" the work that exploited them if they were to lead families struggling to survive. Commercial estates profited, communities endured, and patriarchy held in the Mesoamerican core. The economy grew, villagers lived deepening exploitations, and stability held to 1800 and after.[30]

Eighteenth-century commercial dynamism and social pressures struck the communities of Spanish North America in different ways. In the Bajío, mining boomed at Guanajuato, driving a strong regional economy. Across surrounding basins, estates expanded irrigation to raise wheat, fruits, and vegetables for prosperous cities and towns. They shifted maize to marginal uplands, where poor tenants planted former pastures and faced declining yields. Families long drawn to estates by chances to rent land, gain secure employment, and claim food rations faced escalating pressures. Wages held steady at best while prices rose and rations declined; rents increased, and those who could not pay faced eviction. Some took on new rentals in marginal uplands, clearing fields only to face collapsing yields. Families in estate communities, long dependent, faced new insecurities. In a commercial society integrated by hierarchies of patriarchy, laboring men struggled to provide for families—the social cement and cultural legitimation of their patriarchal claims. With poverty deepening, security vanishing, and patriarchy threatened, grievances escalated. Still, stability held as long as the economy grew and the regime ruled.[31]

North of the Bajío, in contrast, eighteenth-century silver expansion and population growth reconsolidated family security and patriarchy, reinforcing the colonial order. Mining centers in Zacatecas and San Luis Potosí lived times of boom and bust—but silver always boomed somewhere. Administrative and commercial cities grew; fertile enclaves at Aguascalientes and Río Verde developed irrigated estates with growing resident communities. Migration accelerated, but north of the Bajío it rarely kept pace with a growing demand for working families. Mine workers still gained ample pay and ore shares. Estates still provided wages, credit, rations, and tenancies to draw settlers. Beyond the Bajío, northern estates offered lives of dependent security orchestrated by patriarchy into the nineteenth century.[32]

Beyond Zacatecas and San Luis Potosí, Spanish North America drove north. Drawn by mining strikes in Chihuahua and the foothills of Sonora (and every strike stoked dreams of the next find farther on), by opportunities to develop estates to supply new mines, by hopes for land independent of estate monopolies, and by quests for Spanish status among people of mixed ancestry, entrepreneurs seeking mines or lands, men and families seeking work or a plot to plant, and many others trekked north. As always, expansion was limited by natives who preferred autonomy while engaging commercial ways: they hunted and gathered livestock and produce; they took or traded for horses and guns; they sought alliances against indigenous enemies; they tried mission life to sample Christianity and cultivation at the cost of dependence and disease—and they periodically turned to violence when they saw advantage or nothing went their way.

Despite that continuing resistance, the eighteenth century brought Spanish North America and its commercial, ethnically fluid, and deeply patriarchal ways to broad areas later taken into the United States. Early in the century, the establishment of French New Orleans drew Spanish settlement to San Antonio, with mission extensions reaching northeast to Nacogdoches. With the transfer of Louisiana to Spain in 1765, the east Texas frontier was less contested. Tejas in the east, Comanches to the west, and other natives took advantage of trade rivalries to solidify independence. San Antonio set the northeastern extension of Spanish North America; it was a place of trade, crafts, and irrigated cultivation surrounded by *ranchos* grazing cattle across vast spaces and by independent Amerindians.

As always, native peoples found threat and opportunity, experimented with mission life while hunting Spanish livestock, mixing conflict and adaptation while their numbers plummeted. As the eighteenth century ended, San Antonio centered a grazing economy that extended from the Rio Grande to Corpus Christi Bay; coastal Karankawas tried mission ways at least seasonally; Comanches negotiated and Apaches fought to remain independent in the interior; Tejas and others near Louisiana planted, traded, and did diplomacy with real strength.

Meanwhile, the economy of Spanish North America reached north to incorporate New Mexico. There Spaniards had long struggled to rule Pueblo communities in a replica of Spanish Mesoamerica; simultaneously, Spaniards and Pueblos traded and fought with nomadic Apaches, independent Navajos, and others on a frontier of conflictive contacts. When eighteenth-century silver production stimulated settlement and development in Chihuahua just south, livestock and textiles from New Mexico found markets there, accelerating commercial life among Hispanic settlers, Pueblo communities, and sheep-grazing, cloth-making Navajos—tying all to Spanish North America. The decline of mining at Chihuahua around 1750 curtailed that trade and set Apaches, Comanches, and others to seek gains in a new time of warfare. After 1770, new commercial dynamism stimulated an alliance with Comanches and escalated conflicts with Apaches. At the oldest of frontier outposts, commercial expansion stimulated production and trade—and changing alliances and conflicts with independent peoples.

Spanish North America pressed its last northward thrust along the California coast, beginning at San Diego in 1769 and reaching San Francisco in 1776. By 1800, there were towns and presidios at San Diego, Los Angeles, Santa Barbara, San Jose, San Francisco—and a capital at Monterey. The men who founded the Spanish council at Los Angeles were entrepreneurial migrants who left mulatto status and ancestors behind. Missions again aimed to settle and Christianize native peoples while *ranchos* expanded grazing all around. Both used indigenous labor to raise crops and livestock for towns and presidios and to supply ships opening new Asia trade. British vessels stopped regularly in the 1790s; ships from the young United States came after 1800. The last frontier of Spanish North America found an opening to the Pacific, while settlers searched for mines (that proved scarce in coastal ranges). Town dwellers opened irrigated fields; *ranchos* expanded grazing farther out; missions drew natives to commercial lives, pressed Christianity, and consoled in the face of death caused by disease. By 1800, native Californians were vanishing, replaced by the commercial ways, diverse people, and proliferating livestock of Spanish North America.[33]

In the Bajío, where Spanish North America began, the eighteenth-century boom stimulated profits and revenues and provoked deep social dislocations that challenged patriarchy. In the mining and grazing zones just north, the same era generated commercial opportunities along with social security that reinforced patriarchy.

Meanwhile, commercial expansion drove far into the continent. As documented by *alcabala* sales tax revenues, commercial production grew apace with population in the Bajío, more rapidly around Zacatecas, San Luis Potosí, Durango, and Chihuahua, and surged explosively in newly incorporated regions along the coasts and in the far north.[34]

While silver and commercial development drove northward, Bourbon reformers aimed to increase regime power and revenues, stimulating sporadic social conflicts and deepening cultural polarization. Officials, aiming to sustain Spanish power against a rising British challenge, promoted mining and trade. They pressed administrative powers and tax collections and limited the roles and riches of the church. In the 1750s, reformers began to remove Franciscans from rural parishes, replacing them with diocesan priests subject to regime oversight. In the 1760s, officials built monopolies to take new revenue from tobacco and playing cards, popular "necessities" in sometimes rich and always raucous mining towns. At the same time, officials pressed workers into militias, building resentments when deployments in deadly lowlands looked imminent. In 1766 and 1767, resistance exploded among mine workers at Real del Monte, Guanajuato, and San Luis Potosí. Rioters resisted taxes, monopolies, and militia service; they defended the Jesuits when a royal order of expulsion came amid escalating conflicts.

Insubordination in the heartland of the silver economy faced swift repression. Then officials negotiated. They could not strengthen Spanish power by destabilizing New Spain, the chief support of that power.[35]

The popular resistance that challenged regime power and colonial entrepreneurs in key regions of New Spain began at the same time as the movement to resist British rule in coastal North America. The causes were parallel, the consequences, contrasting. The Seven Years' War of 1756 to 1763 saw Britain gain French Canada and threaten Spanish Havana; in 1765, France ceded Louisiana and the western Mississippi basin to Spain. After the war, all the Atlantic powers faced debts from conflicts that brought Britain small gains and left Spain in control of New Spain's silver—and vast new lands.

Both empires pressed colonials for new revenues to pay the cost of war, the cost of keeping them colonial. People in coastal British America and in the Bajío and nearby New Spain rose in resistance. But in British America, resistance persisted for more than a decade; merchant and planter elites joined with discontented artisans and farmers in conflicts that led to an unprecedented independence proclaimed in 1776 and gained in 1783.

In New Spain, resistance came mostly from mine workers, urban artisans, and a few rural communities. Rebellious crowds were neither led nor backed by leading entrepreneurs, who joined regime officials to crush the risings and sustain the profits and revenues of the silver economy. The key difference: the coastal colonies of British North America were marginally profitable to colonial elites and costly to British rulers; neither saw gain in paying the costs of colonial rule; Spanish North America remained hugely profitable to colonial entrepreneurs and generated revenues essential to the Spanish regime—keeping both committed to colonial rule.[36]

After crushing the risings of 1767, reformers demanded less and negotiated more in the silver economy. They shifted reform demands to religious culture, promoting enlightenment and the diffusion of Spanish among indigenous peoples. Clerics saw popular festivals as "primitive"; they labeled community rituals calling for help from the Virgin "superstitious." The regime and its clergy railed against cultural autonomies just as social dislocations proliferated in the Bajío, the heart of the silver economy. From the 1770s on, commercial boom mixed with population growth to generate social polarization there while cultural tensions escalated. Social pressures deepened, but while economic dynamism held, so did social stability.[37]

The silver economy carried on, sustaining New Spain and driving Atlantic wars and trade into the nineteenth century. Spanish Mesoamerica and North America remained distinct colonial societies integrated by the power of Mexico City—the political capital and commercial pivot of both. Everywhere, diverse peoples faced, negotiated, and adapted to the silver boom, commercial expansion, Bourbon reforms, and pressures toward enlightened religion. Amid opportunities for the entrepreneurial few and deepening pressures on working majorities, both of New Spain's colonial orders held. The commercial ways of Spanish North America drove deep into the continent, drawing migrants northward and pressing uncertain natives into mission encounters.

Bajío Insurgency, Mexican Independence, and the Transformation of North America, 1800–1845

War engulfed the Atlantic world beginning in the 1790s. For a quarter century, industrializing Britain fought revolutionary and Napoleonic France for European and Atlantic dominance. Spain's transatlantic domains were drawn into those wars for many reasons—including the importance of New Spain's silver to wartime treasuries and the global economy. The people of New Spain, already negotiating social pressures heightened by population growth, faced new demands and escalating uncertainties. Blockades alternated with years of open trade. Imposed autarky, when silver could not leave but cloth makers enjoyed local monopolies, gave way to open markets, when silver flowed to Europe and industrial textiles flooded Mexico. The Bourbons demanded rising exactions from rich entrepreneurs. Tax collectors pressed hard on natives and mulattoes. People across New Spain paid for wars that brought only disruptions. Still, elites remained wealthy, Mesoamerican communities negotiated to hold autonomy, and northern workers and tenants struggled to sustain dependent families. The regime mediated, negotiated—and the colonial order held into the nineteenth century.[38]

It broke in 1808, when Napoleon invaded Spain, captured the monarchy, and imposed his brother as José I. It was a great gamble, in part set off by the urge to claim control of Spain's colonial trade and revenues in the aftermath of the French loss of the wealth of Saint Domingue in the Haitian revolution. The gamble did not pay off. Across Spain, people responded with popular insurgencies called *guerrillas* (little wars), then by juntas asserting popular sovereignty, leading to a Cortes (Parliament) that wrote a liberal constitution at Cádiz in 1812, a charter that aimed to contest French rule and hold the empire together. Napoleon broke centuries of legitimate monarchical rule, provoking unprecedented crisis and creativity across Spain and New Spain.[39]

In the richest of colonies, political jockeying began in Mexico City in 1808 and continued into 1810, when provincial men in the Bajío, frustrated in efforts to join in the reconstitution of imperial sovereignty, set off a mass insurgency led by Father Miguel Hidalgo. Debates about sovereignty led to a popular rising that challenged everything in a decapitated empire. Hidalgo mobilized men from Bajío estates, Guanajuato mines, and native villages in nearby Michoacán and around Guadalajara. Insurgency began where Mesoamerica met the Bajío, the foundation of Spanish North America, the heart of the silver economy. During four explosive months, the rising drew up to eighty thousand rebels. But it was little planned, often divided, and poorly armed. Colonial elites again dropped political spats to oppose a threat from below. Troops backed by militias from San Luis Potosí crushed Hidalgo's insurgency early in 1811.[40]

What followed set a new course for North America in the context of a changing world. Hidalgo and key allies were captured and executed, but Ignacio López Rayón, José María Morelos, and others retreated to isolated strongholds and pressed political movements backed by guerrilla armies demanding American sovereignty. Meanwhile, men from rural communities who had risen with Hidalgo went home to drive regional insurgencies from the Bajío to Guadalajara. They denied regime power and estate property for years. The silver mines at Guanajuato, the engines of eighteenth-century boom, struggled to operate with guerrillas all around. Other risings followed, notably just northeast of the capital in the dry zone of Otomí communities and pulque estates from the Mezquital through Apan. Most resisted regime power into 1815; Bajío insurgents held out until 1820.[41]

Popular insurgencies amid political conflicts made war for independence a revolutionary confrontation. Sovereignty, social relations, production, and cultural constructions were all in play. Revolutionary outcomes followed. While rebel leaders and ideologues fought toward political independence, insurgent communities demanded autonomy in family production and local culture. In the Bajío, they ended commercial cultivation, breaking estate lands into family *ranchos*. When rebels there finally negotiated pacification between 1818 and 1820, most recognized estate property only when landlords agreed that production would stay the province of family *ranchos*. Insurgent communities thus ended the commercial ways that had threatened their security and challenged patriarchy during the late eighteenth-century boom. They entrenched family production in *ranchero* communities living as tenants on estate lands. Bajío families claimed new autonomies, and important minorities of women emerged as prosperous *rancheras*. Patriarchy, too, was renegotiated in newly autonomous Bajío communities.[42]

Insurgency proved limited across Spanish Mesoamerica. Still, communities there fortified autonomy by asserting political rights during the war for independence. The Cádiz Constitution of 1812 promised municipal autonomy and electoral participation to loyal communities. From 1812 to 1814, and again in 1820, old indigenous republics latched onto new political rights granted by the Cádiz charter to reinforce historical autonomies—while they blocked other liberal programs, notably, the privatization of community lands.[43] Mesoamerican communities proved adept at adapting liberalism when it came as a program to preserve Spanish rule in New Spain. They embraced the promise of political sovereignty and claimed rights to local militias while they blunted assaults on landed autonomies.[44]

While elites fought over independence and popular communities pursued autonomy, the conflicts of 1810–1820 undermined the silver economy, which had shaped New Spain and the world economy for centuries. The insurgency separated the economies of Spanish Mesoamerica and North America. Neither silver nor livestock traveled safely from the North to Mexico City while insurgents ruled the Bajío. Silver production plummeted, disrupted by war and curtailed by lack of investment; it all but ended at Guanajuato when the great Valenciana mines flooded in 1820. Silver produced north of the Bajío entered trade via newly opened ports on the Gulf and Pacific coasts. Ores mined and refined near Mexico City paid for counterinsurgency wars. Patterns of trade and profit shifted radically: Mexico City effectively ruled only its environs and regions south; the North broke into zones seeking new ways to engage the world. The silver economy that had integrated New Spain and stimulated global capitalism was gone.

Insurgency finally ended in the Bajío in 1820, leaving the commercial engine of Spanish North America to start an uncertain reconstruction. A year later, a coalition of elites and military commanders, most having fought against independence and popular insurgents, proclaimed a Mexican monarchy, just as the economy that made New Spain rich and pivotally important in the world faced collapse. Thus began the attempt to make a nation of the two colonial societies of New Spain. In 1824, the imagined monarchy gave way to a federal republic. Decades of political conflict followed: monarchists fought republicans; centralists fought federalists; conservatives fought liberals—with no enduring resolution before the 1870s. Slow and uncertain attempts to revive mining mixed with debates about whether to industrialize or focus on export production. Diverse projects aimed to forge the social ways of Spanish Mesoamerica and

North America into one nation ruled by singular laws. It was a recipe for enduring conflict.

In the new nation, still more imagined than real, every faction proclaimed a commitment to popular sovereignty; many identified as republicans or liberals. They followed precedents set by Bourbon reformers and Cádiz liberals, aiming to transform Mexico's peoples and the religious cultures forged under Spanish rule.

They faced an enduring dilemma. Most liberals saw native republics as regimes of privilege, their community landholdings as brakes on economic life. Most villagers remained committed to life in landed republics, and across Mesoamerican Mexico they formed a majority of the people who had just been proclaimed sovereign. In diverse ways, new leaders sought policies that would assert liberal principles—and keep indigenous communities acquiescent, at work, and paying taxes. Villagers responded creatively, embracing offers of electoral participation, opposing attacks on community lands and local autonomy. An uneasy social peace held amid political conflicts through the 1820s and 1830s.

In Mexican North America, early national projects engaged very different communities. Families working tenant *ranchos* built during insurgency or claimed in its disruptive aftermath easily shared liberal visions of a society of small producers. Still, liberals' unwavering defense of property rights gave tenants little chance to become proprietors. And liberal programs to limit the property and power of the church often seemed attacks on religion in deeply religious northern communities. Seeking to bring liberal programs to a still-imagined nation, to homogenize diverse regional societies, liberals deepened the differences dividing Mesoamerican and North American Mexico. Legitimacy was constantly negotiated and never certain. To men who imagined a singular state and society, ways of governing that accepted the autonomy of indigenous communities and recognized that different regions could sustain distinct ways of life, production, rule, and worship seemed pernicious legacies of Spanish rule—and no way to make a nation.[45]

Meanwhile, political conflicts and a broken commercial economy helped communities press for autonomy. Across Mesoamerica, where villagers remained the base of rural life and production, a key source of taxes, and the primary workers at struggling estates, landlords lamented insubordination while managers complained of recalcitrant hands demanding premium wages. In the Bajío, estate tenants maintained family production and deeply religious cultures. Across the sparsely settled zones stretching north, tenant *ranchos* proliferated while commercial life slowly revived. Mesoamerican communities reinforced old autonomies and claimed new political participation. Northern estates long shaped by commercial production and patriarchal labor relations became communities of entrenched tenants; men and a few women there gained new autonomy in family production, though most lived on estate lands. In regions long peripheral to the colonial economy—highland Michoacán and Jalisco, the rugged Huasteca east of San Luis Potosí, coastal zones extending into Texas and California—new settlers established independent *ranchos* and *ranchero* communities with deeply religious cultures. In diverse ways, the early national decades brought enduring autonomy to Mesoamerican communities and new independence to estate tenants and *rancheros* across Mexican North America.[46]

Meanwhile, the imagined national economy, without the dynamism of silver, fragmented. The separation of the Mesoamerican and northern economies begun during times of insurgency was reinforced by political federalism and the opening of northern ports at Tampico on the Gulf and San Blas on the Pacific. Mexico City no longer ruled the North financially or commercially; northerners traded directly with the rising economic powers of the Atlantic world.[47] The colonial regime and economy had integrated Mesoamerican and North American social formations. After independence, nation builders imagined a homogenizing unity, yet they lived new economic, political, and social fragmentations. With mining depressed, commercial cultivators faced capital shortages, weak markets, assertive workers, and stubborn tenants. For the first time, Mexican entrepreneurs sought foreign capital; national authorities took loans from abroad. Political federalism alternated with periods of central rule; public and private debt soared while economic fragmentation fueled commercial uncertainty—all facilitating popular autonomy, which further limited state consolidation and commercial dynamism.

Mining recovered slowly. Zacatecas saw little insurgency after 1810 and revived in the 1830s. Guanajuato came to life again in the 1840s, bringing national production near late-colonial levels. Meanwhile, Mexicans debated the challenge of industrialization. England had pioneered mechanized cloth production in the late eighteenth century and claimed economic hegemony across the Atlantic world in the wars of 1790–1815 while extending its commercial and imperial powers toward Asia. In the 1820s, British recognition was essential to be a nation in the Atlantic world; British financiers were key sources of loans to fledgling governments and of the capital and technology to revive flooded mines. British envoys used that leverage to open Mexican markets to industrial textiles.

Mexican cloth makers, mostly artisans recovering from a decade of strife, struggled. Late in the 1820s, they pressed for protection via the short-lived popular regime of Vicente Guerrero. The conservatives who ruled in the 1830s raised tariffs to fund the Banco de Avío, a development bank that promoted industrialization. Industry came early to Mexico, internalizing the industrial threat to artisan life. By the 1840s, mills expanded at Puebla, around Mexico City, and at Querétaro in the Bajío.[48]

The conflicts and transformations of the decades after 1810 radically altered the trajectory of Mexican North America. During the colonial era, ties to Mexico City were strong. Merchants there provided capital and links to world trade; the Spanish regime promoted mining and worked to stabilize the social relations essential to economic dynamism, funding the military and the missions to contain indigenous resistance. With independence, relations with Mexico City shifted to focus on a new politics that generated deep and enduring divisions. Across the North, financial capital had to be raised locally or recruited from abroad. Military forces depended on scarce local revenues. Without funds and facing liberal opposition, missions collapsed. Conflicts with indigenous peoples escalated. Comanches and other found new independence at Mexico's far northern frontiers.[49]

The globally linked northward dynamism that defined Spanish North America for centuries stalled. The Bajío, the historical foundation of that dynamism, was transformed by insurgency into a region of limited mining and family production in textiles and agriculture. Families there lived more independently; they controlled and kept more of what they made. As a result, the Bajío no longer generated the capital or goods to drive the economy northward.

Farther north, regional fragmentation ruled. When mining revived at Zacatecas in the 1830s, it served Zacatecas, not Mexico or Mexican North America. Elsewhere across the North, entrepreneurs and settlers sought opportunity as they could. They enjoyed direct access to the world economy, yet capital proved scarce and markets limited. They faced independent indigenous peoples ready to learn from, adapt to, and resist commercial ways while fragmented production and disputed state powers left provincial regimes with neither the resources to sustain missions nor forces to coerce compliance. Apaches, Comanches, Yaquis, and others asserted rising power—resistance in the eyes of frustrated nation builders. For decades after independence, northward expansion was stalled by economic fragmentation, political division, community autonomy, and escalating conflicts with independent peoples.

Still, the underlying dynamics of Mexican North America remained those forged under Spanish rule; a society driven by silver mining and sustained by commercial cultivation and grazing on large estates remained the norm. Social relations of production held as deeply commercial, still shaped by hierarchies of patriarchy that orchestrated tenancies and labor relations. The population remained a fluid mix of Europeans and others of Mesoamerican and African ancestry. Independent indigenous peoples still challenged the northward drive.

Insurgency and independence thus brought fundamental shifts within enduring orientations. Entrepreneurs struggled while working families found new autonomies. Political fragmentation and conflict mixed with economic fragmentation and uncertainty, all limiting elite powers and facilitating popular assertions. The Bajío adapted a new order based on mining and family cultivation; Zacatecas saw mining wealth as a source of regional power; provinces farther north claimed new independence while facing limited economic prospects and staunch native resistance. The northernmost zones of Mexican North America, meanwhile, engaged peoples and trades from the expansive United States in ways that proved both profitable and disruptive.

Anglo-American penetration of Hispanic North America accelerated after Mexico's independence. Mexican Texans seeking to promote commercial development at the northeastern fringe of the new nation welcomed Anglo-American settlers with land grants and political rights, provided they accepted Mexican sovereignty. The newcomers aimed to develop Texas' coastal plains for cotton cultivation with slave labor. Other less prosperous immigrants drove into the interior, setting off new conflicts with Comanches and other independent natives. When Mexico abolished slavery (long unimportant as a labor system there) in 1829, Texas struggled for an accommodation. Perhaps they could keep their slaves but import no more. Into the 1830s, such potential compromise proved unsatisfactory to Mexican leaders and Texas settlers, leading Anglo-Texans (and a few prosperous Mexicans) to rise to claim independence. The Texas revolution of 1835 saw migrants from the United States proclaim popular sovereignty to demand political independence—and to promote a regime of cotton and slavery. (The transnational and cross-cultural paradoxes of nineteenth-century liberalism are striking. Mexican liberals proclaimed freedom for slaves and dreamed of ending community autonomy; Mesoamerican communities took liberal political rights to defend corporate land and autonomy; Anglo-American migrants to Texas sought liberal republican rights to preserve slave property.)[50]

While Anglo-Americans settled Texas, fought a revolution for sovereignty and slavery, and struggled to sustain an independent republic into the 1840s, New Mexican officials and entrepreneurs saw the profit of trading to supply mines to the south in Mexico fade. Seeking new outlets for commerce, they welcomed Anglo-American traders via the Santa Fe Trail, linking the New Mexican economy to the United States while facing rising conflicts and changing trades with ever more assertive independent indigenous nations.[51]

The last region of North America settled under Spanish rule, California, drove up the coast after 1769, setting missions, presidios, towns, and *ranchos* from San Diego to San Francisco. Once again, Hispanic settlers and vast herds of livestock invaded indigenous societies struggling to adapt while facing deadly diseases. Missions and *ranchos* introduced commercial production that after 1800 supplied U.S. ships bound for Asia. Then Mexican independence isolated California from the nation to the south. Revenues that had sustained the missions disappeared just as natives faced accelerating depopulation and rising labor demands.

Mexican liberals knew the solution; they dissolved the missions in the 1830s. Native survivors were freed of mission rule—and denied rights to mission lands. Irrigated croplands and vast pastures were divided among those ready to develop commercial enterprises (*ranchos* in the Spanish North American tradition). Leading Hispanic Mexicans and a few Anglo-Americans and Europeans gained vast holdings. The northwestern outpost of Spanish North America shifted from mission rule to a more open commercial economy under Mexican sovereignty, while New England clipper ships called at California ports to buy provisions, hides, and sealskins for Asian trade.[52]

After Mexican independence, the frontiers of Hispanic North America disengaged from the regions to the south that earlier sustained their development. Meanwhile, emerging leaders in northern states and territories faced the disruptive conflicts of an early national politics focused on a distant Mexico City. Northerners dealt as they could, seeking new relations with the expansive United States while facing difficult, often conflictive, relations with mission residents and independent natives. In the process, they engaged the global economy in new ways: Texans turned directly to the Atlantic via cotton and slavery; New Mexicans traded via the Santa Fe Trail; Californians fueled the expanding Asian trades of New England mariners.

War, Conquest, and the U.S. Incorporation
of Hispanic North America

The 1840s proved a critical juncture in the history of North America. Mexicans began to surmount the conflicts and fragmentations of the postindependence years. Mining revived, new textile industries flourished, cultivation remained strong in Mesoamerican communities and among northern tenants and *rancheros*, while commercial estate production remained limited and profits uncertain. Moderate liberals and conservatives began new accommodations that might stabilize the political arena, though there was much to do and conflicts continued.

But just as Mexicans approached a national consolidation, the United States provoked a war to usurp vast territories of Mexican North America. Anglo Texans who had claimed independence in 1835 sought annexation to the United States a decade later; they were ready to relinquish sovereignty to preserve the cotton and slave economy—and to take control of the Rio Grande. Beyond Texas, the opportunities for U.S. commerce in New Mexico and California were enticing, at least to a prosperous and well-connected few. After decades of escalating Comanche and Kiowa assaults on northern Mexico, the war proved an unequal contest. The United States was seventy years an independent nation, with a burgeoning northern industrial society and a booming southern cotton and slave economy linked to British industrialization. Mexico was but twenty-five years a nation, still devising a regime and seeking a national economy (like the United States around 1800). Key battles were hard fought; in hindsight, the outcome was close to inevitable.[53]

The war between Mexico and the United States transformed the histories of Mexico, the United States, North America, and the world. The consequences for Mexico are well recognized. The war demonstrated that Mexican political actors had yet to forge a strong national state. They had failed to merge the divergent ways of Spanish Mesoamerica and North America into an integrated national economy and an imagined national culture. During the war, many provincial leaders worked first to strengthen regional power; many indigenous peoples fought not for the nation but for land and cultural autonomy. The loss of vast, valuable, but little-populated northern territories seemed a secondary concern to those focused on regional politics and community life.

After the war, Mexican polarities deepened. Radical liberals took power in the 1850s and pressed reforms that denied both the Catholic Church and Mesoamerican communities historical rights to corporate property.

Villagers resisted locally while the church backed a conservative war against the liberals and their reforms from 1858 to 1860. Liberal victory led to debts, French invasion in 1862, and Maximilian's French-backed experiment in monarchical liberalism from 1864 to 1867. The commercial economy was slow to revive; community autonomies persisted. The return of the liberal republic in 1867 led to a contested national consolidation aided by U.S. investment and resisted by Mesoamerican communities still struggling to slow land privatization.[54] Finally, in the 1870s, Porfirio Díaz began to solidify an authoritarian liberal regime that stabilized the Mexican polity by tying it economically to the United States. The war of the 1840s revived and lengthened Mexico's time of political conflict, commercial uncertainty, and social fragmentation.

It also transformed Mexico's place in the world. From the sixteenth century, New Spain had fed the global economy with silver. From 1700 to 1810, Spanish North America was an engine of global development. But the demise of Chinese demand, the rise of British industry, and the Bajío revolution that brought down the silver economy combined to leave a Mexican nation searching for a new role in the world. After the war with the United States and the loss of the northern territories, Mexicans increasingly engaged the world through the United States. When Mexico built railroads after 1870, U.S. investors owned the trunk lines driving north to the border. When silver revived, U.S. capital ruled. When Mexico developed copper, petroleum, and exports, U.S. entrepreneurs and markets predominated. While a Spanish colony, New Spain was a leading participant in global trades; as a new nation, Mexico faced war and invasion that accelerated its reconstruction as an economic dependent of the United States.

The consequences of the war for the United States were equally transforming. The taking of vast territories from Mexican North America reopened and intensified debates over the expansion of slavery—leading directly to the U.S. Civil War of 1860–1865.[55] Any comparison that presents Mexico as violently conflictive during the century after its independence and the United States as more peaceful and stable must consider the probability that the Civil War brought more death and destruction to the United States than long conflicts of nation building inflicted on Mexico.

Equally important yet less recognized, the taking of the regions from Texas to California incorporated Hispanic North America as a third historical tradition in the construction of the United States. Vast lands rich in resources enhanced the prospects for U.S. economic power. A modern United States without Texas, Colorado, and California is unimaginable. Yet most interpreters of U.S. history see the nation emerging from two colonial traditions: one grounded in the freedoms of commerce and community in the British colonial North; the other built on the plantation slavery and racial divisions of the British colonial South. They allied to claim independence in the 1780s, expanded in dynamic conflict for decades, fought the Civil War, and then continued under northern dominance, struggling to accelerate commercial development and to approximate ideals of political freedom while grappling with stubborn legacies of slavery and racism.[56]

The incorporation of the lands taken from Mexico in 1848 is usually seen as a conquest, taking territory while subordinating, even destroying, the people and traditions that remained from centuries of Spanish and Mexican rule. In oft-cited examples, the Treaty of Guadalupe Hidalgo promised U.S. citizenship and the preservation of historical land rights to residents of conquered territories. But Anglo racism limited Mexicans' political rights while Anglo entrepreneurs took Mexicans' lands by combinations of legal power, judicious marriages, and fraud.

All that is true, but it offers a limited vision. In fundamentally important and enduring ways, much of the society and culture, notably, the economic ways and ethnic amalgamations of Hispanic North America, persisted within states from Texas to California; in time they expanded to zones never under Spanish or Mexican rule. Hispanic North America set a third tradition in U.S. production, social relations, and cultural debates.

There is no doubt that in East Texas and Northern California, where Hispanic settlement was late and limited, and where early cotton planting and the gold rush quickly left Mexicans small minorities, they faced economic, political, and social exclusion.[57] But in South Texas, New Mexico, and coastal California, Mexicans remained numerically strong for decades. They negotiated political participation, often under leaders, both Mexican and Anglo-American, who utilized Mexican styles of patriarchal politics. When the Anglo-American rulers of regions claimed from Mexico wrote state constitutions and legal codes, they repeatedly aimed to keep the mining and land systems of Spanish North America—not to favor Mexican residents, but to facilitate Anglo-American entrepreneurs' ability to profit from established commercial ways focused on mining, irrigated cultivation, and large-scale grazing. As a result, nearly everywhere that Spanish and Mexican settlement had distributed land, when Anglo newcomers took them by means fair and nefarious, they used them to continue ways of production and labor relations grounded in the traditions of Spanish and Mexican North America.

The persistence and expansion of Hispanic North America within the United States after 1848 is highlighted by developments in three regions, one seared in the American imagination, the others less recognized. When the gold rush came to California in 1849, it completed an economic model begun under Spanish rule. Mining stimulated irrigated cultivation in the valleys and grazing across nearby uplands, often on large holdings granted under Spanish or Mexican law. Military conquest and U.S. politics ensured that Anglo-Americans (many married to Mexicans) reaped most of the profits as the last frontier of Spanish North America became the state of California.[58]

Less recognized—except in episodes of infamy at Tombstone and Bisbee—the regions that became southern Arizona's Cochise County by the Gadsden Purchase of 1853 also replicated Hispanic North America under U.S. rule. Assertive Apaches had kept Spanish and Mexican settlement limited and insecure before 1848. Promises of U.S. cavalry protection accelerated settlement from the 1850s. Silver mining at Tombstone and irrigated cultivation at Tres Alamos combined with grazing all around—developments accelerated in the 1880s with the completion of the Southern Pacific Railroad and the coming of copper mining at Bisbee. Early on, while still facing Apache resistance, the county continued Hispanic ways of ethnic amalgamation, including Anglo and black American immigrants. It took decades of conflict—notably, labor conflict at Bisbee—for Anglo-American racial exclusions to take hold after 1900.[59]

Finally, after the Civil War guaranteed U.S. national unity and transcontinental rails linked the mountain west to both coasts, Colorado—where the Rockies meet the high plains—produced another replica of Hispanic North America. Gold and then silver led the way. Irrigated cultivation sustained the mines and the burgeoning city of Denver. Beyond the limits of stream irrigation, vast grazing operations spread across the plains. Just north of the historical northern outpost of New Spain in New Mexico, Colorado was part of the lands taken from Mexico, but mostly home to independent natives before 1848. There, Anglo-American leaders re-created Spanish North America for their own profit, with Mexicans and New Mexicans participating primarily as tenants, workers, and cowboys.[60] Similar ways of development, with inevitable variations, shaped the later nineteenth century across Utah, Montana, Nevada, and Idaho.

While Hispanic North American ways spread northward into territories never effectively under Spanish or Mexican sovereignty, they held strong in the conquered territories we call the borderlands. From the King Ranch and the surrounding estates of South Texas, through the complex mix of large holdings, Hispanic communities, and Pueblo villages in New Mexico, to the vast commercial ranches that marked the cutting edge of agrarian capitalism in California, the continuities with the Hispanic North American past are striking to those willing to recognize them. Great landlords operating vast holdings for commercial profit shaped production and social relations. Where grazing ruled, resident dependents—often of Mexican ancestry—claimed wage advances and food rations in exchange for labor in social relations that operated as hierarchies of patriarchy. (The original "western" cowboys were often Spanish-speaking mulattoes; they left a legacy of independence and bravado and a language of work that lives on. Anglo-America celebrates their skill and independence—and imagines them as men of pale skin, rarely speaking Spanish.) Where commercial growers demanded seasonal laborers, they came from communities of small cultivators: in Texas from villages along the Rio Grande; in the highlands of New Mexico from Pueblo communities; in California from people recently out of missions and congregating in town barrios from Los Angeles to Santa Barbara to Monterey.

The mining and grazing economies of the mountain and intermountain West and the agrarian capitalism of Texas and California developed as extensions and adaptations of the commercial capitalism of Hispanic North America, newly taken over by Anglo-Americans as eager to claim the profits as to deny the Spanish and Mexican roots of the economies and societies they ruled. Anglo power adopted and adapted commercial production across newly claimed borderlands, promoting a society that integrated mining, grazing, and cultivation where water allowed. Meanwhile, the fluid mixing of diverse peoples that defined Hispanic North America continued to shape the culture of working communities, urban and rural, mixing that was both reinforced and challenged by new migrants from Mexico, the U.S. South, and Asia. Spanish North America became an enduring and inevitably changing part of the United States.[61]

A Glance at the Twentieth Century

The decades after 1870 were a time of transnational interpenetrations. Anglo-American investors built railroads tying Mexico to the United States and took control of Mexican silver mining (led by the Guggenheims' American Smelting and Refining Company—ASARCO), ruling key sectors of the still-vibrant economy of the Mexican North. Simultaneously, Anglo-American capitalists took over the promotion and expansion of Hispanic North America across the U.S. West. In Mexico, they cultivated ties with the authoritarian regime of Porfirio Díaz. In the United States, they found succor in the policies of federal and state governments. Despite separate polities, the Mexican North and the U.S. West—both built on Spanish North America—remained on a course of expansion and integration, now led by Anglo-American entrepreneurs with Mexican allies in business and government. Mexicans, some becoming Mexican Americans, worked everywhere.[62]

Everything seemed to change in 1910. Mexico lurched into revolution marked by an anti–United States nationalism that mixed uneasily with demands for autonomous landed communities (echoing Mesoamerican traditions). The United States intervened, occupying Veracruz in 1914, chasing Pancho Villa in 1916—all to limited effect—and then joined the great war that marked a new assertion of power in Europe. Mexico turned inward while the United States looked eastward; both promoted heightened nationalisms. The historical integration grounded in shared Hispanic North American foundations slowed, at least in national politics and nationalist rhetoric.

Still, the Mexican commercial economy deep in U.S. capital and oriented to U.S. markets held strong (except for a few years of intense revolutionary warfare) to 1929 and the Great Depression.[63] Disruptions caused by revolutionary wars and then the antistate, deeply Catholic Cristero revolt of the 1920s sent rising waves of migrants from Mexico to the United States, often from the Bajío and nearby areas. Mexican North Americans trekked north to work in U.S. border states founded as the northern frontier of Spanish North America.

If the revolution and its aftermath slowed capital flows from the United States to Mexico, the human integration of Mexican North America accelerated across national borders. Through the 1920s, Mexican North Americans harvested crops and built cities, dams, and irrigation systems across the U.S. West; many joined, even led, struggles to promote worker rights.[64]

The break came with the depression. The U.S. economy collapsed. Mexican migrants were regularly denied relief and sent "home," often with U.S.-born, U.S.-citizen children.[65] The Mexican economy weakened and faced the need to absorb migrants. While Franklin Roosevelt struggled to revive U.S. capitalism with state projects and new labor rights, Lázaro Cárdenas accelerated Mexican nationalism, backed radical labor rights, and completed a massive land reform that took from commercial estates across Mexico and gave to new communities called *ejidos*—rooted in Mesoamerican tradition yet ruled by an authoritarian, developmentalist, if populist, regime. Culminating in the 1938 Mexican nationalization of U.S. and British petroleum companies, the 1930s proved a decade of maximum separation.[66]

World War II returned the neighboring nations to their historical integration—with a new twist. During and after the war, growing numbers of men from indigenous communities in central and southern Mexico trekked north to labor across the United States. The grafting of a dynamic commercial economy (now in the United States) onto enduring landed communities, first through an organized labor draft, then by informal migrations, forged a twentieth-century re-creation of the symbiotic exploitation that historically had tied Mesoamerican communities to expanding capitalist production.

Mexico entered the 1940s having redistributed 50 percent of its arable land to *ejido* communities. Families with new lands ate better, produced and sustained more children, and sent only limited labor and foodstuffs to the wider society. Petroleum nationalization and then World War II slowed capital flows from the United States to a trickle. Still, the Mexican regime consolidated in the 1930s by agrarian, labor, and nationalist reforms still aimed to promote capitalist development, even to attract U.S. capital to key sectors (despite contrary rhetoric). To spur cultivation to sustain a growing population surging into cities and working in new industries, officials invited U.S. scientists backed by the Rockefeller Foundation to come to Mexico and create what came to be known as the "green revolution." Wheat cultivation with hybrid seeds, chemical fertilizers and pesticides, mechanization, and irrigation favored north Mexican commercial cultivation, while Mesoamerican communities with *ejido* lands mostly raised and ate maize. The "revolutionary" government (led by former president, now defense minister, Lázaro Cárdenas) joined the United States in World War II, sending a small force to the Philippines and turning Mexico's economy to do all it could to support wartime mobilization.[67]

The negotiation of a transnational labor draft was pivotal. As the United States sent men to war and drew women to factories, many farm fields and building sites faced labor shortages. Mexicans were not quick to fill the void. Many had recently gained land in *ejido* communities; most remembered the expulsion of Mexicans in the early 1930s, when the depression cut U.S. labor demand. So the two governments negotiated a labor treaty, creating the draft known as the *bracero* program. Mexicans were recruited at home, paid for transportation, promised a minimum of wages and working conditions, and paid to return at the end of the contract.[68]

That wartime innovation revived a Spanish Mesoamerican tradition. In the 1570s, when depopulation led to the congregation of a shrinking native population into landed republics while the silver economy created growing demand for labor at mines, cities, and estates, the colonial regime organized the *repartimiento* draft to send men from rural communities to work seasonally in the commercial economy. The *bracero* program of the 1940s was a binational draft drawing workers from recently landed Mexican communities to work in a growing North American economy. Distances were longer; treks lasted a year or more. Still, Mexican villagers were drawn to temporary labor sustaining global capitalism—in war and after.

The colonial *repartimiento* ended in the dynamic regions of Mesoamerica around Mexico City in the 1630s, but the labor relations it forged persisted for centuries, tying landed villages and commercial cultivators together in symbiotic exploitations. The *bracero* draft persisted from the 1940s to 1964; it finally ended long after the war by the combined opposition of U.S. organized labor and outcries against state-sponsored labor exploitation on both sides of the border. Again, however, the relationship in which workers based in landed communities (by the 1950s facing population growth and land shortages) provided seasonal labor to commercial enterprises persisted long after the draft ended. U.S. employers—commercial cultivators, construction and landscape contractors, meat processors, and many others—came to depend on new relations of symbiotic exploitation tying them to communities across Mexico.

Since World War II, U.S. employers have relied on Mexican villagers for the subsidies inherent in their poorly paid seasonal labors, while villagers rely on the same poorly paid and deeply insecure labor to sustain families, communities, and claims to patriarchy. This transnational symbiotic exploitation is both a legacy and an extension of social relations that stabilized dynamic exploitations in colonial Spanish Mesoamerica. Since the 1980s, growing numbers of Mexican Mesoamericans, many retaining indigenous identities, have joined the Mexican North Americans journeying to work in *el norte*.[69] Transnational symbiotic exploitation has helped to stabilize the dynamic exploitations that shape North America under U.S. hegemony.

Reflections from 2010

Long before NAFTA, foundations in Spanish North America shaped shared legacies and integrated histories across what became the Mexican North and the U.S. West. Commercial production on a grand scale linking mining, irrigated cultivation, and grazing defined key regions of both nations, even as the coming of U.S rule brought new political ways and unprecedented cultural conflicts as Hispanic ethnic amalgamations tested Anglo-American racial divisions. More recently, the twentieth century accelerated labor migrations that forged a transnational symbiotic exploitation linking U.S. capitalism and Mexican communities—Mesoamerican and North American. The dynamism of the United States as it led the globalization of the world economy in the second half of the twentieth century was shaped by Spanish North American legacies and sustained in essential ways by growing numbers of workers brought north in the transnational expansion of the symbiotic exploitation that long shaped Spanish Mesoamerica. The histories of the United States and Mexico are inextricably linked.

Yet those who rule and many who struggle to work for a bit of comfort, or just to survive, in both nations persistently see mostly separation and difference. Since the late twentieth century, in a turn reminiscent of the depression years, many in the United States increasingly construct Mexicans as aliens, intruders responsible for problems rather than producing members of transnational communities who sustain a continental economy in a globalizing world. When the U.S. economy all but collapsed in 2008 and 2009, jobs became scarce. Mexican workers seemed expendable; many returned to home communities facing even deeper economic difficulties. For a time, the rhetoric that constructs Mexicans as intrusive aliens and casts prejudice on Mexican Americans becoming middle-class citizens as others quieted a bit. By 2010, with the U.S. economy reviving and politics polarizing, angry anti-Mexican rhetoric soared again.

Still, the shared foundations of the Mexican North and the U.S. West in Spanish North America persist to shape common legacies of production and social relations. U.S. capital continues to dominate economic life in Mexico, and the United States still relies on growing numbers of Mexicans in expanding relations of symbiotic exploitation. In the twenty-first century, there are no national economies; national societies seem uncertain and changing constructs; national cultures are hard to find or define. Still, national polities and polarizing nationalist political cultures fuel perceptions that too many Mexicans come to the United States.

While the historical integration of Mexico and the United States accelerated after 1950, a fundamental change occurred. For decades beginning during World War II, the United States and its employers sought ways to draw Mexicans to work in the United States, first via the *bracero* draft, then via diverse informal incentives. Now the goal of many in the United States is to limit migration to work, and especially to live. As populations have grown in the United States and soared in Mexico, and as high-tech labor-saving ways of production proliferate, a shortage of labor has turned into a surplus of immigrants. U.S. employers still seek Mexican workers; they are paid little and easily fired. Many U.S. citizens facing insecurity and job loss press to curtail Mexican migration, a goal inflamed by more than a few politicians. No resolution is in sight, but an emerging consensus argues that people must remain citizens and long-term residents of their home nations, while a new labor draft (or a permit system) might recruit just enough temporary workers for key businesses, and then send them home.

The result would lock the United States and Mexico into symbiotic exploitation, the symbiosis serving U.S. employers and the middle class, the exploitation falling on Mexicans locked for life in a dependent economy ruled by U.S. capital, many surviving by working for low wages far from home, treated as alien others. Such an outcome would serve U.S. businesses well, providing continued access to inexpensive workers in Mexico and the United States, workers constrained by growing numbers and entrenched poverty in Mexico and by temporary status or "illegality" in the United States. Benefits to Mexicans—beyond minimal survival—would be few. U.S. citizens of Mexican ancestry, however rapidly they claim middle-class lives, would continue to face negative reflections grounded in the limits and prejudices imposed on Mexicans in the United States, whether as "guest workers" or "illegals." The working majority in the United States would face limits on their earnings imposed by a segmented labor system (there can be no labor market in a permit system). Any political or labor organization aiming to organize across borders to promote shared benefits would be inhibited by the division of the integrated North American economy into separate national polities, and by the persistence of ethnic and economic divisions within them.

It is time to recognize the shared foundations and continuing integrations that link New Spain, Mexico, and the United States. New Spain was built by the stimulus of silver and global trade as its diverse indigenous societies faced devastating depopulations. For centuries, Spain's pivotal North American colony was an engine of early globalization, while Spanish Mesoamerica and Spanish North America forged distinct New World societies. Mexico emerged from a war for independence that was also a revolutionary upheaval in the Bajío, where New Spain's two societies met. After independence, the nation grappled with the challenge of integrating contrasting social orders while the silver economy collapsed.

The United States first developed at the intersection of two historical traditions: the commercial ways and mostly European peoples of a colonial North becoming industrial and the plantation ways and racial polarization of a slave South charging west. The war of 1846–1848 incorporated Spanish North America—its mining, irrigated cultivation, and commercial grazing, its Mexican people and ethnic amalgamations—into the United States, setting off the war that ended U.S. slavery, set northern industrial dominance, and accelerated a westward expansion that built on Hispanic North American precedents.

Since then, the histories of Mexico and the United States have been inseparable, even as their states have promoted nationalist cultures that proclaim fundamental differences. If we look beyond the assertive nationalisms of Mexicans who fairly resent U.S. conquest and subsequent dominations and of Anglo-Americans who insistently see everything they have as created by themselves, the historical trajectories of the indigenous peoples, colonial encounters, and modern nations of North America become more complex, more interactive, and more understandable. We are not long separate and ultimately different peoples struggling to merge; we are peoples emerging from long interactions, struggling with the separating claims of nations and nationalisms—in a world shaped by globalizations that began in important ways in New Spain and Hispanic North America. If we aim to understand that complex history, and especially if we hope to promote shared justice as it continues, we must begin to see the integrations that define its trajectory—and ask why so many cling to visions asserting separation and difference.

Notes

1. Weber's *The Mexican Frontier, 1821–1846* (Albuquerque: University of New Mexico Press, 1982), *The Spanish Frontier in North America*, and *Bárbaros* (New Haven: Yale University Press, 2006) are all essential to this analysis. Lamar's *The Far Southwest, 1846–1912* remains pivotal to knowing the politics that incorporated the Mexican North into the United States. Montejano's *Anglos and Mexicans* in many ways began the study of Mexican legacies and peoples as integral to the United States.

2. Dennis Flynn and Arturo Giráldez, "Born with a 'Silver Spoon,'" *Journal of World History* 6, no. 2 (1995): 201–221.

3. Guillermo Bonfil-Batalla's *México Profundo* (Mexico City: Grijalbo, 1994; trans., *México Profundo: Reclaiming a Civilization* [Austin: University of Texas Press, Institute of Latin American Studies, 1996]) and Enrique Florescano's *Etnia, estado y nación* (Mexico City: Taurus, 1997) are brilliant and influential examples of this enduring tradition. For the *repartimiento* draft, see Charles Gibson, *The Aztecs under Spanish Rule* (Stanford: Stanford University Press, 1964). On how villages sustained commercial life through the colonial era, see John Tutino, "Urban Power and Agrarian Society: Mexico City and Its Hinterland in the Colonial Era," in *La ciudad, el campo y la frontera en la historia de México* (Mexico City: Universidad Nacional Autónoma de México, 1992). On the maintenance of community traditions in different ways in Oaxaca and Yucatán, see the opening chapters of Karen Caplan, *Indigenous Liberalisms* (Stanford: Stanford University Press, 2009). On judicial mediation and rule across Spanish Mesoamerica, see Brian Owensby, *Empire of Law and Indian Justice in Colonial Mexico* (Stanford: Stanford University Press, 2008).

4. This vision of Spanish North America and the larger analysis of this essay builds upon Tutino, *Making a New World*.

5. Eric Foner's *The Story of American Freedom* offers a brilliant and influential example of this persistent tradition. Richard White's *The Middle Ground* (Cambridge: Cambridge University Press, 1991) began the transition. Daniel Richter's *Facing East from Indian Country* (Cambridge: Harvard University Press, 2001) helps bring indigenous foundations back toward the center of the history of British North America, a work reinforced by Alan Gallay, *The Indian Slave Trade* (New Haven: Yale University Press, 2003), and Juliana Barr, *Peace Came in the Form of a Woman* (Chapel Hill: University of North Carolina Press, 2007).

6. Among many important works, see Richard Dunn, *Sugar and Slaves* (Chapel Hill: University of North Carolina Press, 1972), and Stuart Schwartz, ed., *Tropical Babylons* (Chapel Hill: University of North Carolina Press, 2004).

7. Richter, *Facing East*, synthesizes and cites a growing literature on early indigenous-British relations.

8. For two important yet different views (among many), see John McCusker and Russell Menard, *The Economy of British America, 1607–1789* (Chapel Hill: University of North Carolina Press, 1985), and Jack Greene, *Pursuits of Happiness* (Chapel Hill: University of North Carolina Press, 1988).

9. A more detailed discussion of this approach is in the introduction to Tutino, *Making a New World*.

10. Alfredo López Austin and Leonardo López Luján, *El pasado indígena* (Mexico City: Fondo de Cultura Económica, 2001).

11. On early Bajío settlement, see David Charles Wright Carr, *La conquista del Bajío y los orígenes de San Miguel de Allende* (Mexico City: Fondo de Cultura Económica, 1998).

12. Peter Bakewell, *Silver Mining and Society in Colonial Mexico* (Cambridge: Cambridge University Press, 1971); Philip Powell, *La guerra chichimeca, 1550–1600* (Mexico City: Fondo de Cultura Económica, 1994).

13. The pacification and the shift to missions are detailed in Philip Powell, *Mexico's Miguel Caldera* (Tucson: University of Arizona Press, 1977).

14. This general characterization reflects the arguments presented in Tutino, *Making a New World*.

15. My view of the centrality of patriarchy is detailed in ibid. It is grounded in Steve Stern, *The Secret History of Gender* (Chapel Hill: University of North Carolina Press, 1995), and previewed in Tutino, "The Revolution in Mexican Independence," *Hispanic American Historical Review* 78, no. 3 (1998): 367–418.

16. Again, my dependence on Stern, *Secret History*, is clear. See also Ana María Alonso, *Thread of Blood* (Tucson: University of Arizona Press, 1995).

17. The classic statement of this is in Bakewell, *Silver Mining and Society*.

18. See María Guevara Sanginés, *Guanajuato diverso* (Guanajuato: Ediciones La Rana, 2001); Tutino, *Making a New World*.

19. Robert West, *The Mining Community in Northern New Spain* (Berkeley: University of California Press, 1949); Michael Swann, *Tierra Adentro* (Boulder: Westview Press, 1982); Susan Deeds, *Defiance and Deference in Mexico's Colonial North* (Austin: University of Texas Press, 2003).

20. New Mexico developed as a frontier anomaly, where a small Spanish elite ruled indigenous communities that did gain rights to land and self-rule as indigenous communities—the roots of the modern Pueblos. Thus the far north of Spanish North America included a region more like Spanish Mesoamerica in local organization (thus the name New Mexico) yet notably engaged in both conflicts and exchanges with independent indigenous peoples just beyond. See Ramón Gutiérrez, *When Jesus Came*; James Brooks, *Captives and Cousins* (Chapel Hill: University of North Carolina Press, 2002).

21. On the centrality of the Spanish Empire to globalization, see Henry Kamen, *Empire* (New York: HarperCollins, 2003); and Stanley and Barbara Stein, *Silver, War, and Trade* (Baltimore: Johns Hopkins University Press, 2000).

22. On patriarchy in Spanish Mesoamerica, see Stern, *Secret History*; on enduring stability, see William Taylor, *Drinking, Homicide, and Rebellion in Colonial Mexican Villages* (Stanford: Stanford University Press, 1979).

23. Again, this reflects Tutino, *Making a New World*; Guevara Sanginés, *Guanajuato diverso*.

24. Perhaps the clearest illustration of this distinction comes from two studies by Cheryl English Martin. In *Rural Society in Colonial Morelos* (Albuquerque: University of New Mexico Press, 1985), she analyzes a key region of Spanish Mesoamerica by focusing on the relations between estates and communities. In *Governance and Society in Colonial Mexico* (Stanford: Stanford University Press, 1996), she analyzes a key region of Spanish North America with a focus on patriarchy.

25. Dennis Flynn and Arturo Giráldez, "Cycles of Silver," *Journal of World History* 13, no. 2 (2002): 391–427.

26. David Hackett Fischer, *The Great Wave* (New York: Oxford University Press, 1996).

27. The dual face of the Enlightenment is demonstrated in many studies; for an analysis focused on Spanish America, see D. A. Brading, *The First America* (Cambridge: Cambridge University Press, 1991).

28. D. A. Brading, *Miners and Merchants in Bourbon Mexico, 1763–1810* (Cambridge: Cambridge University Press, 1971).

29. Ibid.; Laura Pérez Rosales, *Minería y sociedad en Taxco durante el siglo XVIII*

(Mexico City: Universidad Iberoamericana, 1996); Doris Ladd, *The Making of a Strike* (Lincoln: University of Nebraska Press, 1988); and Felipe Castro Gutiérrez, *Nueva ley y nuevo rey* (Zamora: Colegio de Michoacán, 1996).

30. I develop this argument most generally in *From Insurrection to Revolution in Mexico*.

31. Ibid.; idem, "Revolution in Mexican Independence."

32. Tutino, "Life and Labor on North Mexican Haciendas"; idem, *From Insurrection to Revolution*.

33. On Texas, see Jesús F. de la Teja, *San Antonio de Béjar* (Albuquerque: University of New Mexico Press, 1995); Robert Ricklis, *The Karankawa Indians of Texas* (Austin: University of Texas Press, 1996); and most recently and brilliantly, Barr, *Peace Came in the Form of a Woman*. On New Mexico, see Ramón Gutiérrez, *When Jesus Came*; and Brooks, *Captives and Cousins*. On Sonora, note Cynthia Radding, *Wandering Peoples* (Durham, N.C.: Duke University Press, 1997). The essential synthesis on California is Martha Ortega Soto, *Alta California* (Mexico City: Universidad Autónoma Metropolitana, 2001), now complemented in depth by Steven Hackel, *Children of Coyote, Missionaries of Saint Francis* (Chapel Hill: University of North Carolina Press, 2005). On early Los Angeles, see Antonio Ríos-Bustamente, *Los Angeles* (Mexico City: Instituto Nacional de Antropología e Historia, 1991).

34. The *alcabala* yields are calculated and analyzed in Appendix D in Tutino, *Making a New World*.

35. Castro Gutiérrez, *Nueva ley y nuevo rey*; José de Gálvez, *Informe sobre las rebeliones populares de 1767* (Mexico City: Universidad Nacional Autónoma de México, 1990); Felipe Castro Gutiérrez, *Movimientos populares en Nueva España, 1766–67* (Mexico City: Universidad Nacional Autónoma de México, 1990).

36. I develop this comparative perspective in chap. 4 of *Making a New World*. The British American side can be explored beginning by reading Edmund Morgan and Helen Morgan, *The Stamp Act Crisis* (Chapel Hill: University of North Carolina Press, 1995); Edward Countryman, *The American Revolution* (New York: Hill and Wang, 2003).

37. William Taylor, *Magistrates of the Sacred* (Stanford: Stanford University Press, 1996); Dorothy Tanck de Estrada, *Los pueblos de indios y la educación en la Nueva España* (Mexico City: El Colegio de México, 1999); Gerardo Lara Cisneros, *El cristianismo en el espejo indígena* (Mexico City: Archivo General de la Nación, 2002).

38. Carlos Marichal, *La bancarrota del virreinato* (Mexico City: Fondo de Cultura Económica, 1999).

39. François-Xavier Guerra, *Modernidades e independencias* (Mexico City: Fondo de Cultura Económica, 1993).

40. Hugh Hamill, *The Hidalgo Revolt* (Gainesville: University of Florida Press, 1966); Carlos Herrejón Peredo, *Hidalgo* (Mexico City: Secretaría de Educación Pública, 1986).

41. Brian Hamnett, *Roots of Insurgency* (Cambridge: Cambridge University Press, 1986); Tutino, "Buscando independencias populares," in José Antonio Serrano and Marta Terán, eds., *El tiempo de las independencias en la América Española* (Zamora: El Colegio de Michoacán, 2002); Eric Van Young, *The Other Rebellion*

(Stanford: Stanford University Press, 2003); and Juan Ortiz Escamilla, *Guerra y gobierno* (Seville: Universidad de Sevilla, 1997).

42. Tutino, "The Revolution in Mexican Independence."

43. See Antonio Annino, "El Jano bifronte," in Leticia Reina and Elisa Servín, eds., *Crisis, reforma y revolución* (Mexico City: Taurus, 2002). For regional case studies: Terry Rugeley, *Yucatan's Maya Peasantry and the Origins of the Caste War* (Austin: University of Texas Press, 1996); Claudia Guarisco, *Los indios del valle de México y la construcción de una nueva sociabilidad política, 1770–1835* (Zinacatepec: El Colegio Mexiquense, 2003). For a national vision, see Alfredo Ávila, *En nombre de la nación* (Mexico City: Taurus, 2002).

44. Van Young, *Other Rebellion*.

45. For perspectives on the politics of conflict and nation building, see Fernando Escalante Gonzalbo, *Ciudadanos imaginarios* (Mexico City: El Colegio de México, 1992); Timothy Anna, *Forging Mexico, 1821–1835* (Lincoln: University of Nebraska Press, 1998); Florencia Mallon, *Peasant and Nation* (Berkeley: University of California Press, 1995); and Peter Guardino, *In the Time of Liberty* (Durham, N.C.: Duke University Press, 2005).

46. On Bajío tenants, see Tutino, "Revolution in Mexican Independence"; on Michoacán *rancheros*, Luis González, *Pueblo en vilo* (Mexico City: El Colegio de México, 1968); on Texas, Andrés Tijerina, *Tejanos and Texas under the Mexican Flag, 1821–1836* (College Station: Texas A&M University Press, 1994); and on California, Ortega Soto, *Alta California*.

47. Araceli Ibarra Bellón, *El comercio y el poder en México, 1821–1864* (Mexico City: Fondo de Cultura Económica, 1998).

48. Peter Guardino, *Peasants, Politics, and the Formation of the Mexican National State* (Stanford: Stanford University Press, 1996); Robert Potash, *El Banco de Avío de México* (Mexico City: Fondo de Cultura Económica, 1959); Walther Berneker, *De agiotistas a empresarios: En torno a la temprana industrialización mexicana, siglo XIX* (Mexico City: Universidad Iberoamericana, 1992); Aurora Gómez-Galvariato, ed., *La industria textil en México* (Mexico City: Instituto Mora, 1999).

49. On California, see Ortega, *Alta California*; on New Mexico, R. Gutiérrez, *When Jesus Came*, and Brooks, *Captives and Cousins*.

50. Campbell, *An Empire for Slavery*; Lack, *The Texas Revolutionary Experience*.

51. Andrés Reséndez, *Changing National Identities at the Frontier* (Cambridge: Cambridge University Press, 2004, 2006).

52. Ortega Soto, *Alta California*, and Hackel, *Children of Coyote*.

53. On native raids, see Hämäläinen, *Comanche Empire*; Delay, *War of a Thousand Deserts*. On the politics of the war in Mexico, see Josefina Vázquez, ed., *México al tiempo de su guerra con Estados Unidos, 1846–1848* (Mexico City: Fondo de Cultura Económica, 1997). On popular mobilizations, Tutino, *From Insurrection to Revolution*; Reed, *The Caste War of Yucatán* (Stanford: Stanford University Press, 2002); Leticia Reina, "The Sierra Gorda Peasant Rebellion, 1847–1850," in Katz, *Riot, Rebellion, and Revolution*, 269–294; Luis Granados, *Sueñan las piedras* (Mexico City: Ediciones Era, 2003).

54. Resistance is summarized in Tutino, *From Insurrection to Revolution*. The key role of U.S. interests in the liberal consolidation is detailed in Hart, *Empire and Revolution*.

55. The importance of the Mexican War and the territories taken to the origins of the Civil War is clearly recognized by scholars of those crucial times. See, for example, Michael Holt, *The Rise and Fall of the American Whig Party* (New York: Oxford University Press, 1999); Ashworth, *Slavery, Capitalism, and Politics*; and Streeby, *American Sensations*. That role is less emphasized in most larger historical interpretations.

56. Foner, *The Story of American Freedom*, offers such a synthesis.

57. On the cotton regions of Texas, see Neil Foley, *The White Scourge* (Berkeley: University of California Press, 1997); on gold rush California, see Susan Johnson, *Roaring Camp* (New York: Norton, 2000).

58. S. Johnson, *Roaring Camp*; Isenberg, *Mining California*; and John Walton, *Storied Land* (Berkeley: University of California Press, 2003).

59. This synthesizes Benton-Cohen's *Borderline Americans* and her chapter in this volume.

60. This understanding of Colorado is based on George Vrtis, "The Colorado Front Range," PhD dissertation, Georgetown University, 2006. The large trends are easily seen in Patricia Nelson Limerick, *The Legacy of Conquest* (New York: Norton, 1987).

61. As I developed the notion of Spanish and Mexican North America as a distinct, dynamic commercial civilization, such an understanding of the U.S. West emerged clearly from reading Limerick, *Legacy of Conquest*, on the West in general; Montejano, *Anglos and Mexicans*, Foley, *White Scourge*, and Limón, *American Encounters*, on Texas; and Gilbert González, *Labor and Community* (Urbana: University of Illinois Press, 1994), and Weber, *Dark Sweat, White Gold* on California. It is worth pondering why U.S. scholars and Anglo-American culture have been more ready to recognize the Mexicanness of New Mexico. There, the persistence of Pueblo communities created a society more Mesoamerican, more alien, and more exotic, thus more acceptable as Mexican. The notion that there are Hispanic-Mexican legacies in the commercial ways we most celebrate, and in labor relations we promote yet lament, seems less acceptable.

62. This is clear in Hart, *Empire and Revolution*; David Pletcher's classic *Rails, Mines, and Progress*; and Limerick, *Legacy of Conquest*.

63. Haber, Razo, and Maurer, *The Politics of Property Rights*.

64. Reisler, *By the Sweat of Their Brow*; and Weber, *Dark Sweat, White Gold*.

65. Balderrama and Rodríguez, *Decade of Betrayal*.

66. On Cárdenas' reforms, see Nora Hamilton, *The Limits of State Autonomy* (Princeton: Princeton University Press, 1982); Gilly, *Cardenismo*.

67. On the World War II shift in Mexican policies, see Friedrich Katz, "International Wars, Mexico, and U.S. Hegemony," in Elisa Servín, Leticia Reina, and John Tutino, eds., *Cycles of Conflict, Centuries of Change* (Durham, N.C.: Duke University Press, 2007).

68. The classic analysis written just after the war remains McWilliams, *North from Mexico*.

69. Among the many studies of late-twentieth-century migration, see Massey et al., *Return to Aztlán*; Durand, *Más allá de la línea*; Kearney, *Reconceptualizing the Peasantry*; and Víctor Espinosa, *El dilema del retorno* (Zamora: El Colegio de Michoacán, 1998).

CHAPTER 2

Between Mexico and the United States: From *Indios* to Vaqueros in the Pastoral Borderlands

ANDREW C. ISENBERG

From the end of the sixteenth to the beginning of the nineteenth centuries, the northern frontier of New Spain comprised a broad expanse of western North America between the Gulf of Mexico and the Pacific Ocean. At its height in the late eighteenth century, New Spain's territory reached the northern Great Plains.

Spanish colonization brought sweeping changes to this region. Some of the most important of these changes were ecological: Old World microbes, plants, and animals transformed the environment well beyond the limits of Spanish settlement. Ecological change was not merely incidental to Spanish conquest: microbes decimated native populations, and the Old World crops and livestock that settlers introduced helped sustain their colonies.

Yet natives were not simply passive victims of the Spanish Conquest. The response of the region's native inhabitants to the Spanish ecological invasion was varied and, at times, decisive in its impact on the history of New Spain's northern frontier. Natives, particularly those whose continued control of their lands marked the limits of Spanish expansion, turned the Spanish ecological invasion to their own advantage by becoming pastoralists who controlled thousands of head of livestock. By the mid-nineteenth century, when the northern frontier of New Spain had become northern Mexico and the southwestern United States, both new republics faced indigenous people empowered by their control of Old World livestock.

There were two means by which natives became pastoralists on New Spain's northern frontier: first, as forced laborers in mission communities and on estates that grazed sheep and cattle; and second, as independent people who acquired sheep and horses (primarily through trade but sometimes by force). Historians have largely assumed that the former type, such as the Luiseños of Alta California, who tended cattle at Franciscan missions, characterized New Spain's "frontier of inclusion," which found a place for natives as laborers in the colonial hierarchy. Historians have categorized the latter type, such as the Comanches and other horse nomads of the Great Plains, as typical of a characteristically Anglo-American "frontier of exclusion."[1]

Yet on New Spain's northern frontier, neither the distinction between subordinated and autonomous native pastoralists nor that between incorporation and exclusion was ever so neat. In the seventeenth and eighteenth centuries, numerous natives who were forced to tend livestock for the Spanish threw off their masters to become autonomous pastoralists; the Yokuts of the California interior, who escaped the coastal missions to become equestrian hunters and herders and foiled Spanish efforts to subdue them, are a case in point.[2] In the middle and late nineteenth century, as Mexico and the United States sought to conquer the pastoral societies that the Spanish ecological invasion had helped to create, formerly autonomous pastoralists were reduced to tending livestock for Mexican and Anglo ranchers. Both Mexico and the United States pursued policies designed to reduce natives to dependent laborers in a grazing economy.

That grazing economy originated in the mid-eighteenth century, when livestock populations exploded on New Spain's northern frontier. In New Mexico, the few hundred sheep that Spanish settlers had introduced in the late sixteenth century had become three million by the early nineteenth century. By that time, horses, a few of which had diffused from New Mexico to the Great Plains beginning in the late seventeenth century, numbered roughly two million in the grasslands. Cattle had a later start than either sheep or horses, but by the early nineteenth century, the few hundred that Franciscan missionaries had brought with them in the late eighteenth century had grown to at least 100,000 in both Texas and Alta California. By the middle of the nineteenth century, there were over three million cattle in Texas and over one million in California.

Thousands of settlers thrived on these domesticated grazing animals. On the eve of the Texas rebellion against Mexico in 1835, pastoralism helped to support an estimated 14,000 settlers in California, 40,000 in Texas, and 70,000 in New Mexico.[3]

In one sense, the irruption of millions of domestic grazing animals in remote northern New Spain confirms historian Alfred Crosby's meta-narrative of European "ecological imperialism." According to Crosby, the invasion of European microbes, plants, and animals into the temperate

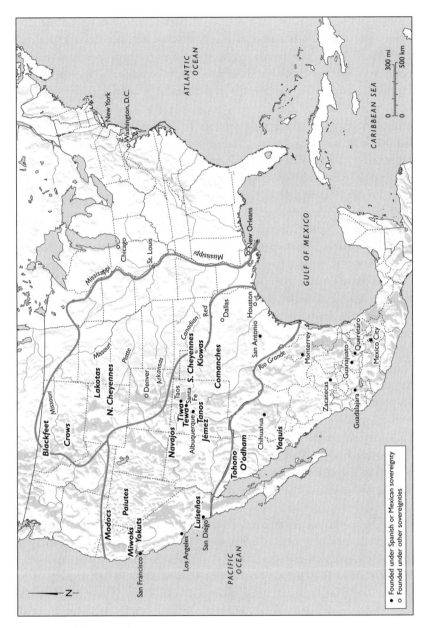

Map 2.1. Amerindians between Mexico and the United States

regions of the Americas, Australia, and New Zealand between the sixteenth and nineteenth centuries made those places into "neo-Europes." Old World diseases swept away natives, and European populations thrived upon the Old World plants and animals that "exploded"—to borrow the term of ecologist Charles Elton—in new environments. Crosby's important insight was that European might and technological advantage mattered less than the accident of ecology in accounting for the success of European imperial adventures. Indeed, the emergence of societies relying on grazing animals was typical of settlement in colonial North America: Spanish and English settlers introduced their livestock throughout the New World, and the fate of their colonies often depended on the success of their cattle and sheep.[4]

Yet on New Spain's northern frontier, not only colonists thrived on Old World livestock. Natives transformed their resource strategies and social structures to adapt to the introduction of domesticated European grazing animals. Some native groups—notably, the Navajos in New Mexico and the Lakotas, Comanches, and other nomads in the Great Plains—adapted so well to the exotic grazers that they dominated their regions into the second half of the nineteenth century, well after other native groups had succumbed to the power of Mexico or the United States. Northern New Spain was hardly a neo-Europe; on New Spain's northern frontier, not all natives were swept aside; those blessed by foresight, or merely by fortune, adapted themselves to the new realities of the European ecological and economic invasion of the Americas.

Native societies that organized their subsistence around livestock complicate Crosby's paradigm because a residue of bygone frontier historiography persists in his analysis: unlike the old frontier historians, he attributes the erasure of natives to ecological accident rather than to cultural inferiority, but like them he does not question that the natives were erased. The old understanding of the frontier that Crosby implicitly invokes was decidedly linear. It imposed a cultural linearity, imagining a line of difference between settlers and natives. Yet more problematic, his concept of frontier imposes a temporal linearity. The frontier was a place where a settler society transformed the land, making it progressively more modern and prosperous. Historical change on the frontier, according to this notion, was not only unidirectional but also foreordained.[5] Yet the emergence of native pastoral societies on New Spain's northern periphery confounds any sense of frontier linearity. Instead, the Hispanic North was a complex cultural and ecological borderland between natives and colonists. Just as colonists relied on livestock for the success of their settlements, natives acquired livestock to maintain their autonomy from colonial rule.[6]

Although their emergence was complex and unpredictable, there was a geographical logic to the rise of pastoral societies on the semiarid fringes of the Spanish North American empire. Pastoralism and livestock production often emerge on grasslands at a great remove from urban or mining centers; more intensive and profitable land uses such as orchards, dairy production, or the cultivation of grains occupy places closer to centers of population. Sheep grazing thus first took hold in the Mezquital Valley north of Mexico City in the sixteenth century before moving in stages toward Zacatecas, Durango, and, eventually, New Mexico.[7] Structurally, the economic function of pastoralism on New Spain's advancing northern frontier was the production of cheap animal products for urban centers.[8]

While the structural place of such societies followed a certain geographical logic, the explosion of populations of grazing animals on marginal lands proved to be difficult if not impossible first to contain, then to sustain. Irruptions of domesticated grazing animals in new environments are typically followed by abrupt population declines.[9] After explosive herd growth in the seventeenth and eighteenth centuries, by the middle of the nineteenth century, natives in New Mexico and the Great Plains witnessed the decline of their primary resources and the grazing lands upon which those animals subsisted. Like their ascent, the decline of these pastoral societies followed no predictable pattern. Yet in each region, natives adapted to the new economic and ecological realities as their grandparents had adapted to the European ecological invasion. Natives on what had once been Mexico's northern frontier found work as laborers—cowboys, shepherds, vaqueros—in a reconfigured landscape in which formerly common lands had been enclosed and livestock, once the resource of natives, had become the property of Euro-Americans.

Seen from a native perspective, the U.S. West—from the Mississippi River to the California coast—was not a neo-Europe ecologically transformed into a version of the Old World.[10] Rather, natives in the region adapted to the European ecological invasion, especially to the introduction of grazing animals, and endured—even thrived. Nor was it a frontier of exclusion, as frontier historians of the U.S. West would have it, where natives were erased. Instead, natives found a place in the region's ranching economy (though, like the peasants in many Mexican villages, in some notable cases they resorted to rural protest to secure that place). To put it bluntly, the region, much of which belonged formally to the Mexican state until the middle of the nineteenth century, belongs in a fundamental sense to Mexico's history of adaptive and enduring native communities.

I

The Upper Rio Grande Valley that Juan de Oñate and his followers entered in 1598 was in certain respects no different from the region today. An inverted "U" between the Jémez and Sangre de Cristo mountains, the valley ascends from approximately 1,200 meters in elevation near Albuquerque to 1,800 meters near Taos. A northward, fingerlike extension of the Sonoran Desert—naturalists call it the Upper Sonoran biome—the valley's annual average precipitation is a mere twenty-five centimeters.[11] To the northeast of the Rio Grande Valley, the San Juan Basin is drier still; there, the annual precipitation is between two and fifteen centimeters.

In most other respects, however, New Mexico in the late sixteenth century was a different world. Notably, the Upper Rio Grande Valley was home to an estimated thirty-four thousand native villagers. To take advantage of scarce water for their gardens of corn, beans, and squash, the pueblos of the Tiwas, Towas, Tewas, Tanos, and other groups were clustered along the Rio Grande; roughly 99 percent of the population thus occupied only 1 percent of what became the province of New Mexico. The villagers might have branched out along tributaries of the Rio Grande, but up-country natives—Apaches, Comanches, Utes, and the Navajos of the San Juan Basin—discouraged such expansion. The Navajos (or, as they called themselves, the Diné), though they sometimes raided the villages, were primarily hunters and gatherers who also raised crops (the term "Navajo" is derived from a Tewa word meaning "large arroyo with cultivated fields").[12]

The arrival of the Spanish transformed the subsistence strategies of both villagers and outliers in New Mexico. The natives of the pueblos not only added wheat, apples, and plums, among other Spanish agricultural imports, to their traditional crops,[13] more important, they began to raise goats, cattle, and—most significantly—sheep. The population of sheep, notably, the hardy Churro, which had evolved in adaptation to arid climates in the desert Middle East, rose sharply in the province of New Mexico in the seventeenth and eighteenth centuries. Oñate's followers and Franciscan friars had brought a few hundred sheep to the province. By 1757, there were 112,000 sheep in New Mexico. The eighteenth century saw an accelerating northward thrust of mining, settlement, and urban development in regions as close as Chihuahua. New Mexicans, including Spaniards and natives, responded by selling livestock and woolen cloth to markets south. Commercial grazing intensified, and by 1820, on the eve of Mexican independence, there were perhaps three million sheep in New Mexico.[14] Observers—from Gov. Fernando Chacón to the U.S. travelers Zebulon Pike and Josiah Gregg—estimated that the annual export of sheep from New Mexico south to Chihuahua in the early nineteenth century might have been 200,000 or more.[15] From Chihuahua, New Mexican sheep supplied the silver mines of Hidalgo del Parral and Batopilas.

By the mid-seventeenth century, however, it was not merely the villagers of the Upper Rio Grande Valley who raised sheep in colonial New Mexico. In 1669, in the midst of a decade-long drought and famine in New Mexico, the Navajos appropriated eight hundred sheep from the Ácoma pueblo. The Navajos' transition to sheep pastoralism was solidified in the wake of the Pueblo revolt of 1680, when the villagers rose up and temporarily drove the Spanish from the province. The Navajos took control of large numbers of sheep abandoned by the Spanish, who had fled south. A decade and a half later, when the Spanish returned to New Mexico in force, many of the inhabitants of the Jémez pueblo fled to the Navajo up-country, the Dinetah. Absorbed by the Navajos, the Jémez brought their sheep, and a century's worth of experience at sheep raising, with them.[16]

Where the drought-prone environment allowed, as in Canyon de Chelly and Canyon del Muerto, a few Navajo bands combined sheep raising with agriculture.[17] For most bands, however, sheep pastoralism rapidly assumed a central place in Navajo subsistence, displacing the combination of planting, gathering, and hunting that had stabilized Navajo subsistence by distributing it across a diversity of resources. Among these bands, pastoralism transformed Navajo society. Because the possession of a large flock became a measure of status, the dominance of sheep in Navajo society—or, rather, societies, as the Navajo were subdivided into autonomous clans—encouraged ambitious men to raid the pueblos for sheep. By the early eighteenth century, the Navajos regularly drove sheep away from the pueblos, although in order to avoid retribution they were careful to avoid taking from the Spanish flocks. Men who amassed large flocks came to dominate a Navajo society in which the possession of sheep was uneven.[18]

The social imperative to assemble large flocks encouraged overgrazing. Successful sheep raisers prevented potential competitors from challenging their dominance by occupying every available patch of scarce grazing lands. Sheep thus transformed not only the Diné but the Dinetah. By the 1720s, the Navajo flocks numbered perhaps 11,000, roughly the maximum number of animals the San Juan Basin could support. The Navajos began to expand south and east in search of pastures for their flocks; by the 1730s, some Navajos grazed their flocks within twenty-five kilometers of the Jémez pueblo.[19]

The Rio Grande Valley was yet more crowded with sheep than the San Luis Basin. New Mexico's sheep were concentrated around Albuquerque; as early as the 1730s, petitioners noted that the pastures around Albuquerque were overgrazed. The overgrazing and trampling of grasslands opened the meadows to invasive plants such as juniper.[20] In upland regions where the Navajos grazed their flocks during the summer, overgrazing transformed open Ponderosa pine and mixed conifer forests to dense, fire-prone thickets of Douglas fir.[21] Moreover, concentrations of sheep likely contributed to the rapid erosion of hillsides known as gullying, gully erosion, or arroyo cutting.[22]

Despite these environmental costs, sheep pastoralism initially facilitated Navajo subsistence.[23] However, the advantages that sheep pastoralism offered the Navajos came at a strategic price. As their subsistence became increasingly dependent on sheep and they edged ever further into the Rio Grande Valley in search of forage, the Navajos, once the scourge of the pueblos, themselves became vulnerable to attack. By the 1820s and 1830s, Mexican settlers were moving into the Dinetah. The settlers had come to the Upper Rio Grande Valley following a smallpox epidemic in 1780 that had halved the population of the pueblos; by 1793, two-thirds of the inhabitants of the valley were Spanish-speaking settlers from the south.[24] After independence, the settlers were supported by the Mexican army; between 1822 and the onset of the Mexican-American War in 1846, Mexican forces mounted an extensive, ongoing campaign against the Navajos. By capturing or destroying thousands of sheep, Mexico forced the Navajos to withdraw from the Rio Grande Valley back into the highlands.[25]

When the United States conquered New Mexico in 1846, it adopted the Mexican strategy of decimating sheep flocks in order to pacify the Navajos. Kit Carson's infamous campaign against the Navajos in 1863 and 1864 borrowed heavily from the tactics of the Mexican army three decades earlier: he, too, destroyed or captured thousands of Navajo sheep to force the natives to submit. Indeed, Carson's troops engaged the Navajos themselves only infrequently, as the natives steadily retreated in the face of his pursuit. The targets of Carson's campaign were Navajo sheep: the day following the announcement by Carson's commander of a one-dollar bounty on every Navajo sheep captured, one of Carson's officers together with thirty men rounded up a flock of one thousand. The Utes employed by Carson as scouts and auxiliaries captured far greater numbers—as many as seventeen thousand by one estimate—which they added to their own flocks. Faced with starvation following the loss of their flocks, thousands of Navajos surrendered in the spring of 1864.[26]

The fate of the Navajos was predictive of that of other societies in the Hispanic North that adapted to Old World grazing animals. Initially, as the animals provided a ready supply of meat, the natives' autonomy and power grew. Yet a singular dependence on their primary resource made them vulnerable. Livestock made an easy target for enemies such as Carson; moreover, the growth of the flocks eventually outstripped the available forage. Sheep raising, the basis of the Navajos' power in the seventeenth and eighteenth centuries, became a strategic weakness by the middle of the nineteenth century, a vulnerability which both Mexico and the United States exploited.

A similar arc—the adoption of European livestock first enabling native autonomy and then hastening Euro-American conquest—characterized the Great Plains to the north and east of New Mexico. When the natives of the pueblos temporarily threw off the rule of the Spanish in 1680, they not only accelerated the Navajos' adoption of sheep pastoralism, the rebels of the pueblos also took possession of Spanish horses. Within decades, a thriving trade in horses emerged between New Mexico and the seminomadic natives of the Great Plains. By the middle of the eighteenth century, tens of thousands of horses had diffused to native groups in the farthest reaches of the northern Great Plains. By the beginning of the nineteenth century, there were perhaps two million horses in the Great Plains, concentrated primarily in the southern grasslands.[27]

Like much of New Mexico, the Great Plains is a semiarid grassland that slopes gradually from fifteen hundred meters in elevation at the foot of the Rocky Mountains to six hundred meters at the banks of the Missouri River. The average annual precipitation of the vast grassland is a mere sixty centimeters; most of the region receives less than forty centimeters. Averages mean little in the grasslands, however; the region's precipitation is prone to significant fluctuation. Prolonged droughts—some lasting ten years or more—have occurred during the last several centuries.[28]

In the Great Plains, invading horses competed for forage with another large grazing animal, the bison. Although enthusiastic observers once estimated that 75 million to 100 million bison once inhabited the grass-lands, more sober estimates of carrying capacity have reduced the esti-mate of the historical Great Plains bison population to a maximum of be-tween 24 million and 27 million.[29] That bison population was constantly in flux. The unpredictable impact of fire, wolf predation, blizzards, and, most important, drought periodically caused the numbers of bison to de-cline precipitously.[30]

Much as sheep revolutionized the subsistence of natives of New Mexico, the horse transformed the Arapahoes, Assiniboines, Atsinas, Blackfeet, Cheyennes, Comanches, Crows, Kiowas, and Lakotas. These societies had subsisted on the fringes of the plains in the late seventeenth century. They had relied primarily on hunting and gathering (and, in some cases, farming) in the regions outside the grasslands while travel-ing seasonally to the plains to hunt bison on foot. The introduction of the horse so facilitated bison hunting that these seasonal migrants to the Great Plains abandoned their reliance on a diversity of resources and re-invented themselves as equestrian nomads.[31]

In New Mexico, the Navajos' adoption of sheep pastoralism encour-aged raiding; the transition to horse nomadism in the plains engendered a similar social revolution. Because the acquisition of horses was crucial to the success of the nomads' new resource strategy, like sheep raiders among the Navajos accomplished horse raiders climbed to positions of status in the plains societies.[32] Horse raising—and horse raiding—was particularly important in the southern Great Plains, where bison were fewer but where horses thrived in a moderate winter climate. The Coman-ches, Kiowas, southern Cheyennes, and southern Arapahoes raided Coa-huila, Durango, and Chihuahua and sold the horses they appropriated there to bison hunters to the north. By the 1840s, they had found new customers: Euro-American overland immigrants.[33]

Just as sheep pastoralism among the Navajos created disparities of wealth and encouraged raiding, horse nomadism in the Great Plains atomized native societies. To find sufficient pasturage for their horses and to hunt bison divided into small grazing groups, the nomadic societies splintered into small foraging bands for the majority of the year. The divi-sions of the nomads militated against stable or authoritative social organi-zations. The nomadic groups warred against competing groups for access to the best hunting territories. Factions within groups sometimes battled one another; in the south-central plains, for instance, the Cheyennes en-dured a bitter factional split in the 1830s.[34]

As in New Mexico, exotic grazing animals transformed not only native societies but also the environment. Just as the Navajos came to have a singular reliance on sheep, the Lakotas, Cheyennes, and others became, after their adoption of the horse, year-round inhabitants of the Great Plains who subsisted primarily on the bison. Together with inherent environmental pressures on the herds, these new nomadic societies contributed to a sharp downturn in the bison population in the middle decades of the nineteenth century. The popular stereotype of the historical equestrian nomads imagines them living in harmony with the bison: hunting only when necessary and wasting no parts of their kills. Yet nomadic bison hunting was not a tested, time-honored resource strategy. Like sheep pastoralism in New Mexico, it was an experiment in response to the ecological changes created by the European ecological invasion of America.[35]

The sixty thousand or so nomads of the plains probably killed half a million bison annually for subsistence and trade with other natives. The northern plains nomads traded bison meat and robes for corn at the Mandan and Hidatsa villages on the upper Missouri River, while the southern plains nomads traveled to the New Mexican pueblos for trade. An annual harvest of half a million bison was likely close to what the natural increase of the bison population could sustain.

Beginning in the second third of the nineteenth century, the nomadic societies increased their harvest of the bison when they began to supply annually over 100,000 bison skins to U.S. merchants who ascended the Missouri River from Saint Louis in steamboats. Like the shepherds of New Mexico, the mounted hunters of the plains had become producers of animal products for distant urban markets. Their pressure on the bison—combined with a mid-century drought and the degradation of a large swath of the central plains by overland immigrants bound for California and Oregon—decimated the herds. As quickly as the commerce in bison robes emerged, it collapsed: by the end of the 1850s, the number of robes shipped down the Missouri River had fallen by half.[36]

In the last third of the nineteenth century, the inherent precariousness of the nomads' subsistence based on the bison facilitated Euro-Americans' ability to wrest control of the plains from them. Between October 1867, and April 1868—a few years after Kit Carson's campaign against the Navajos—a special U.S. Indian Peace Commission negotiated a series of treaties with several nomadic societies of the Great Plains. Gen. William Tecumseh Sherman, a member of the Peace Commission, wrote to his brother, John Sherman, a U.S. senator from Ohio, on June 17,

1868, that "the commission for present peace had to concede a right to hunt buffaloes as long as they last, and this may lead to collisions, but it will not be long before all the buffaloes are extinct."[37] The language of the treaties Sherman helped to negotiate was temporizing: the Indians "yet reserve the right to hunt . . . so long as the buffalo range . . . in such numbers as to justify the chase." Sherman was ultimately proved correct: by 1883, Anglo hide hunters—who as the leading edge of American industrial expansion into the plains were armed with powerful rifles and connected by rail to urban markets—had driven the bison nearly to extinction, while the horse nomads had submitted to the reservation system.[38]

Across New Spain's eighteenth-century northern frontier, populations of grazing animals had exploded. By the mid-nineteenth century, the irruption of sheep and horse populations had created significant environmental consequences: in New Mexico, the environment had been degraded; in the Great Plains, the rise of the horse came at the expense of the bison. The consequences for the societies that had organized their subsistence around these animals were dire. In the eighteenth century, natives such as the Navajos and Comanches had adapted to the European ecological invasion so successfully that for generations they maintained their autonomy in the face of the Spanish, Mexican, and American forces sent to subdue them.[39]

By the middle of the nineteenth century, however, overdependence on sheep and horse pastoralism, a dependence in part stimulated by Mexican demand for sheep and cloth and by U.S. markets for bison robes, was the undoing of the pastoralists. Large flocks of sheep overgrazed the Dinetah and proved an easy target for Mexican and American adversaries. In the Great Plains, horses so facilitated bison hunting that the natives became singularly dependent on the declining bison herds, a vulnerability the United States did not fail to exploit. In each instance, the collapse of animal populations immediately and necessarily preceded the submission of the natives to the reservation system.

II

The explosive growth of grazing animal populations in the eighteenth century created thousands of herders and hunters across the northern frontier of New Spain. In the wake of the collapse of sheep and bison populations, native herders and hunters did not disappear. Instead, they adapted to new ecological and economic realities, becoming wage workers in the pastoral economy. The reservation system actively encouraged the incorporation of natives as laborers.

While Mexican historians have long recognized the importance of native laborers in the livestock economies of the New World, seeing Indians as cowboys is a relatively new development in the history of the U.S. West.[40] Historians' long-standing interpretation of the United States' conquest of its western frontier has emphasized that while Americans' desire for natives' land was acute, neither settlers nor the state had more than a passing interest in drawing on natives as a source of labor. As Howard Lamar and Leonard Thompson wrote in 1981, in contrast to South Africa, where the demand for indigenous labor was high, "Indians came to have no practical function in the white world, a view that helps explain why Indians were constantly removed from the paths of white advance."[41] By 1985, Lamar had retreated somewhat from this view. Drawing on the work of historian Albert Hurtado, he noted that, particularly in California, miners and ranchers relied on the labor of natives.[42] Still, for most historians, the idea that Euro-American settlers relied on native labor — whether coerced through force or enticed with wages — remained exceptional.[43]

Yet on a frontier of settlement where labor was scarce, it was hardly exceptional to rely on native labor. The incorporation of natives as laborers was the dominant tradition in Spanish North America, and it persisted there and in regions beyond when the Mexican North became the U.S. West. Nowhere was this more apparent than in the vast cattle empire of coastal Southern California, a semiarid grassland like the Upper Rio Grande Valley and the Great Plains.[44] By 1773, California missionaries had introduced 205 head of cattle. Like invading Old World animal and plant species throughout the New World, the cattle population exploded. By 1805, the missions held 95,000 cattle and 130,000 sheep. Natives outside the missions, notably the Miwoks and Yokuts, also adopted livestock in uncounted numbers.[45] The cattle quickly transformed the vegetation of the coastal grasslands. California bunchgrasses, though highly nutritious, cling to the soil by slender and shallow roots and thus cannot withstand heavy trampling and grazing. Rapidly expanding cattle herds destroyed drought-resistant native grasses, while Old World grasses invaded and flourished in the disturbed environment.[46]

Mexico's secularization of the California missions in 1833 transferred control of most Southern California cattle not to former mission neophytes but to the rancheros, the powerful men who controlled the great agricultural estates of Mexican California. While in nineteenth-century

Mexico, a "rancho" was a modest, middle-sector, commercially oriented farm or ranch, the Southern California ranchos are better understood as haciendas, grand estates whose owners constituted the rural elite.[47]

By the end of the 1830s, California rancheros had developed a version of the grazing-export economies of New Mexico and the Great Plains. The rancheros sustained themselves by selling cattle hides and tallow to British and U.S. merchant vessels. The industry was provincial California's largest economic sector. Between 1826 and 1848, California exported an estimated six million hides. The work of tending to the cattle and producing hides fell to vaqueros, principally the descendants of local natives such as the Luiseños who had been Hispanized at the missions. In 1834, as many as 30,000 native dependent laborers tended the cattle of Southern California.[48]

The ranchos' production of beef rather than hides and tallow expanded significantly following the discovery of gold in the Sierra Nevada foothills in 1848. Gold production, like silver mining in New Spain since the sixteenth century, stimulated farming and ranching enterprises that relied on native labor.[49] The demand for beef in the gold country gave the rancheros what the hide and tallow market had only minimally provided: a market for their cattle. Rancheros reoriented their production from hides and tallow to beef. Like the shepherds of New Mexico, whose fortunes had depended on the provision of meat to the silver mines to the south, the rancheros became peripheral producers of meat in an economy dominated by mining. Between 1852 and 1859, the number of cattle in California more than doubled, from just under 450,000 to over 1.1 million.[50] By the end of the 1850s, not only were there more cattle in California than any other single domesticated species, there were nearly three times more cattle than people.

At that moment, when California's grazing lands were most heavily stocked—indeed, perhaps overstocked—a series of environmental catastrophes beset the region: flood, pestilence, and, most disastrously, drought. Floods in the winter of 1861–1862 washed away grasses on Los Angeles-area ranchos; the winter that followed was one of the driest in California's history: only eight centimeters of rain fell in Southern California in the winter of 1862–1863, well below the average annual precipitation in Los Angeles of thirty-eight centimeters. Moreover, cattle in the summer of 1863 competed with another species for remaining grasses: that summer, grasshoppers swept into the coastal grasslands, concentrating in the San Fernando Valley and at Anaheim.[51] Rain might have restored the forage, but the winter of 1863–1864 was as dry as the previous season: only eight centimeters of rain fell in San Diego in the winter of 1863–1864.[52]

Throughout the state on the eve of the drought, there were approximately 3 million horses, cattle, and sheep. Of those, an estimated 800,000 died. Most of the losses were in Southern California, where some counties, such as Los Angeles, lost between two-thirds and three-quarters of their cattle. In the wake of the drought, the deeply indebted rancheros were forced to dispose of their lands to Anglo settlers to satisfy their creditors. While historians of the U.S. West have tended to see aridity as an obstacle to Anglo settlement, in Southern California, drought was the underlying cause for the control of the land passing from Mexicans to Anglos.[53]

Despite the collapse of the Southern California cattle population, native vaqueros persisted into the early twentieth century. In San Diego County, Luiseños were regularly employed as vaqueros in the late nineteenth century, as they had been since secularization. As San Diego's livestock industry shifted from cattle to sheep (California's sheep population rose from half a million in 1859 to four million in 1873), Luiseños were increasingly employed as shepherds, earning 50 or 75 cents a day in the pastures.[54]

When the United States took California from Mexico in 1848, federal authorities made plain their desire to see natives continue as laborers for local estates. The federal Indian agent for Southern California, Benjamin Wilson, and his subagent for San Diego County, Cave Johnson Couts, were both Tennesseans who had married into Hispanic ranchero families. Explicitly comparing the native laborers of California to the African American slaves of their home state, Wilson and Couts bound over natives convicted of vagrancy or other petty crimes to service on local estates, a practice also common in Texas, northern Mexico, and, later, the post–Civil War U.S. South.[55]

In the decade following the war, the California system that, as Wilson put it, "encourage[d] them [the natives] to labor," became national policy.[56] Between the end of the Civil War and the middle of the 1870s, virtually every treaty negotiated between the United States and natives of the North American West anticipated the integration of the natives into the Euro-American economy as agricultural laborers and provided for the construction on reservations of blacksmith shops, carpenter's shops, wagon and plough makers' shops, sawmills, flour mills, and, most significantly, manual labor schools.[57] U.S. treaty makers envisioned reservations where the natives made up a pool of dependant laborers—

a vision that resembled, in many respects, the bygone Spanish missions. That vision moved beyond mere resemblance beginning in 1869, when the U.S. government delegated the administration of vocational training on reservations to Protestant missionaries.[58]

The United States' flirtation with a mission system was brief; by the mid-1870s, it had shifted toward a policy of privatization of native labor; that shift occurred simultaneously with Mexico's effort to disaggregate native communities, distribute commonly held lands among individuals, and assimilate natives as agricultural laborers. Mexican privatization proceeded in spasms. Some efforts preceded and immediately followed independence; there was a spate of privatizations following the Ley Lerdo (a privatization law championed by the finance minister, Miguel Lerdo de Tejada) of 1856 and the liberal Constitution of 1857; but then they dropped off during decades of civil war and French occupation until the ascension of Pres. Porfirio Díaz in 1876. Privatization reflected Mexican liberals' desire to reduce the property holdings of corporate bodies—the church and native communities—and commercialize the economy.[59] In perhaps the most extreme instance, the Mexican government forced the Yaquis of Sonora from their villages, divided their rich and often irrigated lands into estates, and sold those Yaquis who resisted into forced labor on plantations in Yucatán.[60]

Yet Mexican natives and peasants were not merely victims of state power in the nineteenth century. In many places, notably, the Bajío, where the commercial mining, cultivating, and grazing economy of Spanish North America had begun, they won modest but measurable successes against privatization, as thousands of families claimed tenant ranchos on former commercial estates. Elsewhere, where indigenous communities retained common lands, persistent resistance to privatization delayed implementation to the late nineteenth century and in some cases prevented its completion before the onset of revolution in 1910. Yet even without the formal implementation of privatization, as indigenous populations grew, large numbers of men and boys came to labor seasonally in commercial agriculture to sustain their families.[61]

In the United States, the proletarianization of native labor was particularly rapid in gold rush California.[62] Farmers in California, where large-scale, mechanized farms emerged early, drew heavily on native labor.[63]

The reliance on native agricultural labor persisted in California to the end of the nineteenth century. By 1879, the natives of the Round Valley Reservation in California's Mendocino County worked seasonally in the fields of neighboring Anglo farmers. The natives—not only field-workers but also carpenters and blacksmiths—earned such high wages working for off-reservation employers that reservation authorities were forced to raise wages for reservation work.[64] A similar reliance on native labor prevailed across the Sierra Nevada in Mormon settlements, where Paiute men and women worked as household laborers and field hands.[65] As early as 1855, a Utah Indian agent, Garland Hurt, noted that the Paiutes were "employed by the settlers of the Carson Valley as herdsmen and laborers on their farms."[66]

Hurt's observation that the Paiutes worked as "herdsmen" is significant. While natives labored in numerous trades, they often found themselves employed as keepers and processors of grazing animals. In some cases, they tended to the very species they or their parents had once herded when they had been members of autonomous pastoral societies. The Tohono O'odham, inhabitants of the Sonoran Desert on both sides of the Mexico-U.S. border, are a case in point: in the late eighteenth century, they had acquired horses and gradually shifted from hunting feral cattle that had escaped from Sonoran missions to herding them; by the end of the nineteenth century, they were employed as vaqueros by both Mexican and American ranchers.[67]

The equestrian nomads of the Great Plains made a rapid transition from hunting bison to herding cattle. Members of the two largest Lakota reservations—Pine Ridge and Rosebud—worked as cowboys on numerous ranches in the Dakotas and Nebraska. By the end of the nineteenth century, the Fourth of July rodeos on the Rosebud reservation were drawing thousands of spectators to observe native cowboys engage in bronco busting and steer riding. (Similarly, native rodeos on western Apache reservations were thriving by the 1880s.) Like Anglo cowboys who put their own brand on motherless calves, Lakota cowboys began running their own stock in the late nineteenth century. By 1902, there were thirty-one thousand head of cattle belonging to the members of the Pine Ridge Reservation; there were approximately twenty-five thousand head on the Rosebud Reservation.[68] Other native cowboys became ranchers as well: by the end of the First World War, the Tohono O'odham grazed thirty thousand cattle on their reservation in Arizona. Likewise, until their reservations were appropriated by the federal government in the early twentieth century, the Kiowas, Comanches, and Kiowa-Apaches of southern Oklahoma raised large numbers of cattle.[69]

While the Cheyennes, Tohono O'odham, and other native cowboys eventually became ranchers, native cowboys were not welcomed into the western U.S. ranching economy without incident. Some natives who sought to retain possession of some of their lands while also working for wages—in other words, those who like the indigenous inhabitants of the Mexican Bajío resisted full proletarianization—encountered the full force of U.S. authorities bent on enclosing commonly held native lands. Enclosure was ordinarily accomplished through the courts, as in southern Oklahoma, where the federal government seized the Kiowas' and Comanches' reservation with its extensive grazing lands.[70] Yet the enclosure of U.S. reservations, like the privatization of many Mexican indigenous communities, sometimes sparked violence—most notably in northeastern California in 1872, where ranchers controlled over twenty thousand head of cattle.[71]

In the sparsely populated plateau in northeastern California, local natives, the Modocs (who in the eighteenth and early nineteenth centuries had played a peripheral part in the rise of grazing animals in North America, shuttling New Mexican horses from the Great Basin to the Columbia Plateau), found employment driving teams, mowing hay, riding fences, and retrieving stray cattle. All was well, it seemed, until the outbreak of the so-called Modoc War in late 1872.

The violence between Modocs and the United States—a series of events that briefly captured the attention of North Americans—should be understood within the context of the proletarianization of Modoc labor. Long before 1872, the Modoc combatants had been integrated into the local ranching economy. The Modocs ran afoul of U.S. policy because they stayed in their traditional homeland in California, in close proximity to employment as ranch hands, rather than removing to a federally assigned reservation in Oregon. While U.S. authorities wanted to remove the Modocs to Oregon, the Modocs had the support of prominent Anglo settlers as well as Newton Booth, the governor of California, who petitioned federal authorities to allow them to remain in northeastern California because of their utility as laborers.[72] Indeed, when the Modoc uprising had been pacified by the summer of 1873, local ranchers hoped to restore the status quo ante, with Modocs available for hire as ranch hands and domestic servants, a relationship that paralleled ties between native villagers and commercial farmers and ranchers across Mexico. Several ranchers wrote to the secretary of the interior in 1873 that the remaining Modocs were "useful farm hands capable of and fully competent intellectually to trade for and take care of themselves." They asked the secretary to assign the defeated Modocs to the care of a rancher who was also the former sheriff of Siskiyou County.[73]

In one sense, the Modocs in the 1870s epitomized the direction of change for natives across the broad region that had once been the Mexican North: having lost their land, and their independent control over grazing animals, they had become wage laborers in economies centered around commercial livestock production. The Modocs' revolt belongs in the context of rural revolts across nineteenth-century Mexico. Like native villagers there, the Modocs' resort to violence is best understood as a social revolt, an effort to renegotiate their status to remain both small producers and wage laborers in a ranching economy. They sought to remain in proximity to their employment opportunities as ranch hands and to slow the pace of enclosure by retaining control of the small plots of land that remained to them. In the context of the nineteenth-century U.S. West, the Modocs' resort to violence resembled the actions of Mexicanos who resisted the loss of their land following the American annexation of New Mexico, or the Anglo homesteaders and small ranchers who battled railroad and ranching interests in conflicts that included the Southern Pacific Railroad's dispute with Mussel Slough settlers between 1878 and 1882, the Texas Fence Cutters' War of 1883–1884, and the Johnson County War in Wyoming in 1892.[74]

In another sense, however, the Modocs were an anomaly within the United States. The spasm of violence in 1872–1873 occurred because they calculated that, faced with exile on a reservation in Oregon, they had few options left to them. For the most part, however, natives in what was Mexico's North and became the U.S. Southwest were everywhere adaptive in the face of change. Contrary to a popular (and sometimes scholarly) stereotype of natives clinging to ageless, premodern traditions and fighting to defend them, the indigenous inhabitants of the region rapidly adapted to ecological change in the eighteenth century, becoming shepherds and horse nomads. When groups such as the Navajos and Comanches battled U.S. and Mexican forces, they fought to defend the adaptations they had made to pastoralism.

By the middle of the nineteenth century, when both sheepherding and horse nomadism had become unsustainable, natives faced an influx of powerful entrepreneurs backed by prodevelopment states. Some natives resisted incorporation into a commercial economy, but most adapted as before by shifting into wage work. The Modocs resorted to violence in 1872 not to preserve their precontact traditions but to protect the adaptations they had made to the Anglo ranching economy.

A profound irony permeates these adaptations. Exotic Old World grazing animals—one of the key elements of the European ecological invasion of the Americas—first empowered and then disempowered natives of the Hispanic North. In the eighteenth century, grazing animals were the means for native societies to maintain their autonomy and to assert their power. The Navajos, Lakotas, Comanches, Modocs, and others capitalized upon the opportunities offered them by European grazing animals to become some of the most enduring native societies in the United States. They resisted U.S. forces longer and more successfully than other native groups. Yet in the nineteenth century, when sheepherding and horse nomadism collapsed, the care of the same exotic grazing animals became a means by which native laborers were integrated into an expanding Euro-American economy.

Notes

1. See W. J. Eccles, "The Frontiers of New France," in George Wolfskill and Stanley Palmer, eds., *Essays on Frontiers in World History* (College Station: Texas A&M University Press, 1983).

2. For the Yokuts, see Albert L. Hurtado, *Indian Survival on the California Frontier* (New Haven: Yale University Press, 1988), 34–36.

3. For sheep in colonial New Mexico, see Melissa Savage and Thomas W. Sweetnam, "Early 19th-Century Fire Decline Following Sheep Pasturing in a Navajo Ponderosa Pine Forest," *Ecology* 71 (December 1990): 2374–2378; for the diffusion of horses from New Mexico to the Great Plains, see Isenberg, *The Destruction of the Bison*, 33–44; for the expansion of cattle northward into Texas and California, see Terry Jordan, *North American Cattle-Ranching Frontiers* (Albuquerque: University of New Mexico Press, 1993); for the human population of California in the 1830s, see Isenberg, *Mining California*, 23; for Texas, see Clyde A. Milner II, "National Initiatives," in Milner, Carol A. O'Connor, and Martha Sandweiss, eds., *The Oxford History of the American West* (New York: Oxford University Press, 1994), 164; for New Mexico, see Allan G. Bogue, "An Agricultural Empire," in Milner, O'Connor, and Sandweiss, eds., *The Oxford History of the American West*, 282; for an overview of New Spain's northern provinces, see David Weber, *The Spanish Frontier*.

4. Alfred W. Crosby, *Ecological Imperialism* (New York: Cambridge University Press, 1986); Charles Elton, *The Ecology of Invasions by Plants and Animals* (London: Chapman and Hall, 1958). Many scholars have amplified Crosby's insights, including Jared Diamond, *Guns, Germs, and Steel* (New York: Norton, 1997). Many of Crosby's insights about epidemic disease were anticipated by William McNeill, *Plagues and Peoples* (New York: Anchor, 1976). For the dependence of American colonies on domesticated animals, see Crosby, *The Columbian Exchange* (Westport, Conn.: Greenwood, 1972); Virginia DeJohn Anderson, *Creatures of Empire* (New York: Oxford University Press, 2004).

5. See Frederick Jackson Turner, "The Significance of the Frontier in American History," *American Historical Association Annual Report* (1893): 199–227; see also Ray Allen Billington, "The American Frontier Thesis," *Huntington Library*

Quarterly 23 (May 1960): 201–216. Historians of the U.S. West have worked diligently in recent years to reconceive of the frontier as a place of cultural borrowings and interpenetrations. See Patricia Nelson Limerick, Clyde A. Milner II, and Charles E. Rankin, eds., *Trails* (Lawrence: University Press of Kansas, 1991); Stephen Aron, "Lessons in Conquest," *Pacific Historical Review* 63 (1994): 125–147. Historians of Latin America have also reimagined frontiers as places where lines of contact were permeable and where change was unpredictable and multidirectional. See Donna Guy and Thomas E. Sheridan, eds., *Contested Ground* (Tucson: University of Arizona Press, 1998); David Weber, The *Spanish Frontier*; see also Charles Hennessy, *The Frontier in Latin American History* (Albuquerque: University of New Mexico Press), 1978.

6. I use the term "borderland" to indicate a place of ongoing encounters between natives and colonists in which neither natives nor newcomers exercised a determinative power. In such places, permissive cultural interactions prevailed. For examples of scholarship that explore such places—using such terms as "middle ground," "frontier," "backcountry," and "borderland," see White, *The Middle Ground*; Andrew R. L. Cayton, ed., *Contact Points* (Chapel Hill: University of North Carolina Press, 1998); Eric Hinderaker and Peter C. Mancall, eds., *At the Edge of Empire* (Baltimore: Johns Hopkins University Press, 2003); Isenberg, "'To See Inside of an Indian,'" in Kenneth Mills and Anthony Grafton, eds., *Conversion* (Rochester, N.Y.: University of Rochester Press, 2003).

7. See Tutino, *From Insurrection to Revolution*; Elinor G. K. Melville, *A Plague of Sheep* (New York: Cambridge University Press, 1997).

8. This "central place theory" inspires much of the framework of William Cronon, *Nature's Metropolis* (New York: Norton, 1991), as well as the notion of the "mine–ranch settlement complex" in R. West, *The Mining Community in Northern New Spain*, 7.

9. Melville, *A Plague of Sheep*, 6–9, 154.

10. For a native perspective on the history of British North America, see Richter, *Facing East*.

11. Robert MacCameron, "Environmental Change in Colonial New Mexico," *Environmental History Review* 18 (1994): 17–39; William deBuys, *Enchantment and Exploitation* (Albuquerque: University of New Mexico Press, 1985), 3–6.

12. MacCameron, "Environmental Change in Colonial New Mexico," 17–25. For the Navajos, see Brooks, *Captives and Cousins*, 84, 90.

13. For Old World crops in northern Mexico, see William W. Dunmire, *Gardens of New Spain* (Austin: University of Texas Press, 2004).

14. Savage and Sweetnam, "Early 19th-Century Fire Decline," 2374–2378; David Weber, *The Spanish Frontier*, 310; MacCameron, "Environmental Change in Colonial New Mexico." For the Bourbon reforms of the eighteenth century that reoriented New Mexico's agricultural production toward export, see Ramón Gutiérrez, *When Jesus Came*, 318–327.

15. See William Denevan, "Livestock Numbers in Nineteenth-Century New Mexico, and the Problem of Gullying in the Southwest," *Annals of the Association of American Geographers* 57 (December 1967): 696–697.

16. See Edward H. Spicer, *Cycles of Conquest* (Tucson: University of Arizona Press, 1962), 210–213.

17. Tracy J. Andrews, "Ecological and Historical Perspectives on Navajo Land Use and Settlement Patterns in Canyons de Chelly and del Muerto," *Journal of Anthropological Research* 47 (Spring 1991): 39–67.

18. Gary Witherspoon, "Sheep in Navajo Culture and Social Organization," *American Anthropologist* 75 (October 1973): 1441–1447; Brooks, *Captives and Cousins*, 91.

19. Bailey, *If You Take My Sheep*, 78–87.

20. Thomas N. Johnsen, "One-Seed Juniper Invasion of Northern Arizona Grasslands," *Ecological Monographs* 32 (Summer 1962): 187–207.

21. Before the Navajos began to graze their sheep in the up-country, relatively frequent, low-temperature fires had kept the forests open and sunny. As increasing numbers of sheep nibbled grasses down to the ground, however, they enabled larger numbers of saplings to thrive; what had once been open forests dominated by Ponderosa pines became dense, shady thickets of Douglas fir—a tree that is disease-prone and susceptible to fire but that grows well in the shade. In the transformed up-country, fire became less frequent but, when it burned, it was catastrophic. See Savage and Sweetnam, "Early 19th-Century Fire Decline," 2374–2378; A. Joy Belsky and Dana M. Blumenthal, "Effects of Livestock Grazing on Stand Dynamics and Soils in Upland Forests of the Interior West," *Conservation Biology* 11 (April 1997): 315–327. For a similar transformation of a forest in Oregon from ponderosa pine to Douglas fir, see Nancy Langston, *Forest Dreams, Forest Nightmares* (Seattle: University of Washington Press, 1995).

22. Denevan, "Livestock Numbers," 691–703. The precipitating causes of gullying are complex and include both drought and high-intensity summer rainfall. But the causes are not merely climatic; overgrazing contributes to the problem of gullying by leaving hillsides more vulnerable to erosion. Environmental historian Richard White devotes the last third of *The Roots of Dependency* (Lincoln: University of Nebraska Press, 1983), to a defense of twentieth-century Navajo shepherds against the charge that their sheep herds were responsible for gullying. For overgrazing in the eighteenth century, see MacCameron, "Environmental Change in Colonial New Mexico."

23. Savage and Sweetnam, "Early 19th-Century Fire Decline."

24. Marc Simmons, "New Mexico's Smallpox Epidemic of 1780–81," *New Mexico Historical Review* 41 (October 1966): 319–326.

25. Bailey, *If You Take My Sheep*, 152–161; Clifford E. Trafzer, *The Kit Carson Campaign* (Norman: University of Oklahoma Press, 1982), 17–24. See also Brian DeLay, *War of a Thousand Deserts* (New Haven: Yale University Press, 2008).

26. For the bounty on sheep, see Brig. Gen. James H. Carleton to Col. Christopher Carson, August 18, 1863; also Carson to Capt. Benjamin C. Cutler, August 19, 1863. One Navajo leader claimed that the Utes had captured 17,000 sheep; see Capt. Joseph Bernay to Cutler, April 7, 1864. For the impoverishment of the Navajo, see Capt. Asa B. Carey to Cutler, February 14, 1864. All in Lawrence C. Kelly, ed., *Navajo Roundup* (Boulder, Colo.: Pruett, 1970). For the strategy of forcing the Navajos into surrender through the capture or destruction of livestock, see Tom Dunlay, *Kit Carson and the Indians* (Lincoln: University of Nebraska Press, 2000), 270–273; Isenberg, *Destruction of the Bison*, 128–129. See also Spicer, *Cycles of Conquest*, 215–220.

27. Isenberg, *Destruction of the Bison*, 39–44.

28. Friedrich Kraenzel, *The Great Plains in Transition* (Norman: University of Oklahoma Press, 1955), 17–23.

29. See Isenberg, *Destruction of the Bison*, 21–30; Dan Flores, "Bison Ecology and Bison Diplomacy," *Journal of American History* 78 (September 1991): 465–485.

30. Tom D. Dillehay, "Late Quaternary Bison Population Changes in the Southern Plains," *Plains Anthropologist* 19 (August 1974): 180–196.

31. For a more detailed description of the creation of the plains nomads, see Isenberg, *Destruction of the Bison*, 31–62.

32. See Alan Klein, "The Political Economy of Gender," in Patricia Albers and Beatrice Medicine, eds., *The Hidden Half* (Washington, D.C.: University Press of America, 1983); Bernard Mishkin, *Rank and Warfare among the Plains Indians* (Lincoln: University of Nebraska Press, 1992), 54–55.

33. Isenberg, *Destruction of the Bison*, 100, 119–120.

34. For warfare in the plains to gain control of hunting territory, see Richard White, "The Winning of the West," *Journal of American History* 65 (September 1978): 319–343. In 1768, according to a Lakota pictographic calendar, the two divisions of the Lakotas fought a civil war against a third division; see Martha Warren Beckwith, "Mythology of the Oglala Sioux," *Journal of American Folklore* 43 (October–December 1930): 339–442. For the Cheyennes in the 1830s, see Donald J. Berthrong, *The Southern Cheyennes* (Norman: University of Oklahoma Press, 1963), 82; E. Adamson Hoebel, *The Cheyennes* (Fort Worth, Tex.: Holt, Rinehart, and Winston, 1978), 113–114.

35. Unlike the Navajos, the horse nomads of the plains derived their subsistence primarily from hunting rather than herding. The nomads were unlike most foraging groups, which derived 80 percent or more of their subsistence from gathering a variety of plants. Rather, they relied primarily on hunting a single species. Ecological anthropologists have argued that large mammal hunting is the least reliable of resource strategies owing to the unpredictability of game movements and population dynamics. For those same reasons, the strategy can also be exceptionally wasteful. See Richard B. Lee, "What Hunters Do for a Living, or, How to Make Out on Scarce Resources," in Lee and Irven DeVore, eds., *Man the Hunter* (Chicago: Aldine, 1968); Tim Ingold, *Hunters, Pastoralists, and Ranchers* (Cambridge: Cambridge University Press, 1980), 69–75.

36. See Isenberg, *Destruction of the Bison*, 106–109; Elliott West, *The Way to the West* (Albuquerque: University of New Mexico Press, 1997).

37. Rachel Thorndike Sherman, ed., *The Sherman Letters* (New York: Scribner's, 1894). See also Isenberg, "The Wild and the Tamed: Indians, Euroamericans, and the Destruction of the Bison," in Mary Henninger-Voss, ed., *Animals in Human Histories* (Rochester, N.Y.: University of Rochester Press, 2002).

38. Isenberg, *Destruction of the Bison*, 123–163.

39. See Richard W. Slatta, "Spanish Colonial Military Strategy and Ideology," and Kristine L. Jones, "Comparative Raiding Economies: North and South," both in Guy and Sheridan, eds., *Contested Ground*.

40. As an indication of the importance of native labor in Mexico, historian Frans J. Schryer quotes a nineteenth-century estate owner in San Luis Potosí as saying, "He who has more Indians is the richest"; see Schryer, *Ethnicity and Class*

Conflict in Rural Mexico (Princeton: Princeton University Press, 1990), 116. For Indians as *vaqueros* in Mexico, see also Jordan, *North American Cattle—Ranching Frontiers*, 132.

41. Howard Lamar and Leonard Thompson, "The North American and Southern African Frontiers," in *The Frontier in History* (New Haven: Yale University Press, 1981), 33. See also James Gump, *The Dust Rose Like Smoke* (Lincoln: University of Nebraska Press, 1994), 138: "Despite the similarities in the Sioux and Zulu experiences—civil war, partition, and national disintegration—key differences clearly emerge. Economically, the Sioux were marginalized by their encounter with the United States, made 'useless' to the economic growth of the country. A defeated Zululand, on the other hand, transformed itself into a reservoir of cheap labor." David M. Emmons, "Constructed Province," *Western Historical Quarterly* 25 (1994): 437–459, and Cardell Jacobsen, "Internal Colonialism and Native Americans," *Social Science Quarterly* 65 (March 1984): 158-171, concur that natives were unimportant as wage workers.

42. Lamar, "From Bondage to Contract," in Stephen Hahn and Jonathan Prude, eds., *The Countryside in the Age of Capitalist Transformation* (Chapel Hill: University of North Carolina Press, 1985).

43. Those exceptions include Hurtado, "California Indians and the Workaday West," *California History* (1990): 2–11; John Walton, *Western Times and Water Wars* (Berkeley: University of California Press, 1992); Alice Littlefield and Martha Knack, eds., *Native Americans and Wage Labor* (Norman: University of Oklahoma Press, 1996); Robert B. Campbell, "Newlands, Old Lands," *Pacific Historical Review* 71 (May 2002): 203–238; Eric V. Meeks, "The Tohono O'Odham, Wage Labor, and Resistant Adaptation, 1900–1930," *Western Historical Quarterly* 30 (Winter 1999): 449–473.

44. Precipitation in Southern California, as in the interior grasslands, was slight and seasonal. Los Angeles receives only thirty-eight centimeters of annual precipitation and San Diego only twenty-five centimeters, almost all of which falls between November and April. Yet the actual annual precipitation fluctuates considerably. Drought years are interspersed with flood years. For grasslands, see Paul Sears, *Lands beyond the Forest* (Englewood Cliffs, N.J.: Prentice—Hall, 1969); Lauren Brown, *Grasslands* (New York: Knopf, 1985). For rainfall in Los Angeles, see Mike Davis, *Ecology of Fear* (New York: Vintage, 1998), 10–14. For the California grasslands, see Elna Bakker, *An Island Called California* (Berkeley: University of California Press, 1984), 350–351; Allan A. Schoenherr, *A Natural History of California* (Berkeley: University of California Press, 1992), 39, 315–317, 341–432. For drought in Southern California, see Crane S. Miller and Richard S. Hyslop, *California* (Mountain View, Calif.: Mayfield Publishing, 1983), 75–77. For precipitation in Southern California, see C. E. Grunsky Monthly Rainfall Records, William Hammond Hall Papers, California State Archives, Sacramento.

45. Hurtado, *Indian Survival*, 34–36.

46. See Hazel Adele Pulling, "A History of California's Range-Cattle Industry, 1770-1912," PhD dissertation, University of Southern California, 1944, 201; Steven Hackel, "Land, Labor, and Production," in Ramón A. Gutiérrez and Richard J. Orsi, eds., *Contested Eden* (Berkeley: University of California Press, 1998); Jordan, *North American Cattle-Ranching Frontiers*, 163.

47. For haciendas, see Magnus Mörner, "The Spanish American Hacienda," *Hispanic American Historical Review* 53 (May 1973): 183–216. For Mexican *ranchos*, see Frans J. Schryer, "A Ranchero Economy in Northeastern Hidalgo, 1880–1920," *Hispanic American Historical Review* 59 (August 1979): 418–443. For the development of the California *ranchos*, see David Hornbeck, "Land Tenure and Rancho Expansion in Alta California, 1784–1846," *Journal of Historical Geography* 4 (1978): 371–390.

48. A smaller number of California natives controlled plots of land and a small number of livestock; see Hackel, *Children of Coyote*. For California *vaqueros*, see Isenberg, *Mining California*, 103–113. François Chevalier maintains that the rodeo "was inspired by a form of Indian hunt"; see *Land in Society in Colonial Mexico* (Berkeley: University of California Press, 1963). A similar ranching economy emerged in nineteenth-century Venezuela to produce beef for markets in Cuba; see J. S. Otto and N. E. Anderson, "Cattle Ranching in the Venezuelan Llanos and the Florida Flatwoods," *Comparative Studies in Society and History* 28 (October 1986): 672–683.

49. See Bakewell, *Silver Mining and Society*.

50. "Transactions of the Agricultural Society of the State of California," *Appendix to the Journal of the Senate of the Eleventh Session of the Legislature of the State of California* (Sacramento: C. T. Botts, 1860), 344–345.

51. "Grasshoppers," *Los Angeles Star* (June 6, 1863).

52. Grunsky Rainfall Records, Hall Papers, California State Archives.

53. Some historians have attributed the loss of Mexican control over California estates to the work of the U.S. Land Commission; see Camarillo, *Chicanos in a Changing Society*; Richard Griswold del Castillo, *The Los Angeles Barrio, 1850–1890* (Berkeley: University of California Press, 1979). Yet while the Land Commission alienated considerable amounts of land in Northern California, to the south it left Mexican land grants largely intact; it was not until the drought of 1862–1864 that Mexican *rancheros* were forced to dispose of their estates; see Paul Wallace Gates, *California Ranchos and Farms, 1846–1862* (Madison: State Historical Society of Wisconsin, 1967), 15. Camarillo has argued that even when the Land Commission confirmed title, American squatters overran estates. Squatters were less common in Southern California than to the north, however, and many *ranchero* families, such as the de la Guerras of Santa Barbara, successfully transformed squatters into tenants. See Gates, *Land and Law in California* (Ames: Iowa State University Press, 1991), 158. Other historians have argued that Mexican *ranchero* families lost control of their land through intermarriage with American immigrants; see Pitt, *Decline of the Californios*. Yet most American immigrants to Southern California, including Abel Stearns, Cave Couts, Benjamin Wilson, and Alfred Robinson, were absorbed into Mexican culture, albeit the culture of the elite landowners. They also spent considerable sums helping their cash-poor in-laws maintain control of their lands; see Isenberg, *Mining California*, 103–120. Indeed, as in Texas, some *rancheros* shrewdly sought out American sons-in-law precisely to help them maintain their estates. For the Tejanos, see Montejano, *Anglos and Mexicans*, 36–37.

54. Richard L. Carrico and Florence C. Shipek, "Indian Labor in San Diego County, 1850–1900," in Littlefield and Knack, eds., *Native Americans and Wage Labor*.

55. See Isenberg, *Mining California*, 120–121. Labor systems on ranches in Latin America varied from wage labor in Argentina to peonage in California to slavery in Paraguay. See Jon Hoyt Williams, "Black Labor and State Ranches," *Journal of Negro History* 62 (October 1977): 378–789; Ricardo D. Salvatore, "Modes of Labor Control in Cattle-Ranching Economies," *Journal of Economic History* 51 (June 1991): 441–451; Silvio R. Duncan and John Markoff, "Civilization and Barbarism," *Comparative Studies in Society and History* 20 (October 1978): 602.

56. Benjamin Wilson to Cave J. Couts, June 13, 1853, Benjamin Davis Wilson Collection, Huntington Library, San Marino, California.

57. See Robert A. Trennert, "Educating Indian Girls at Non–Reservation Boarding Schools, 1878–1920," *Western Historical Quarterly* 13 (July 1982): 271–290.

58. See Henry E. Fritz, *The Movement for Indian Assimilation, 1860–1890* (Philadelphia: University of Pennsylvania Press, 1963), 56–86.

59. See John Tutino, "From Involution to Revolution in Mexico," *History Compass* 6 (May 2008): 796–842; idem, *From Insurrection to Revolution in Mexico*, 258–263; R. David Edmunds, "Native Americans and the United States, Canada, and Mexico," in Philip J. Deloria and Neal Salisbury, eds., *A Companion to Native American History* (Malden, Mass.: Blackwell, 2002).

60. See Jennie Purnell, "With All Due Respect," *Latin American Research Review* 34 (1999): 85–121; Robert H. Holden, "Priorities of the State in the Survey of the Public Lands in Mexico, 1876–1911," *Hispanic American Historical Review* 70 (November 1990): 579–608; Evelyn Hu—DeHart, *Yaqui Resistance and Survival* (Madison: University of Wisconsin Press, 1984); Cynthia Radding, *Wandering Peoples* (Durham: Duke University Press, 1997).

61. Tutino, "The Revolution in Mexican Independence; idem, "From Involution to Revolution in Mexico."

62. Albert L. Hurtado, *Intimate Frontiers* (Albuquerque: University of New Mexico Press, 1999), 75–81; idem, *Indian Survival*, 169–192.

63. John Bidwell, an early settler in Chico, became something of a labor contractor for other large estate owners; see J. H. Dye to Bidwell, September 12, 1854; and A. H. Stout to Bidwell, April 9, 1852, John Bidwell Collection, California State Library, Sacramento.

64. Todd Benson, "The Consequences of Reservation Life," *Pacific Historical Review* 60 (May 1991): 221–244.

65. Martha C. Knack, "Nineteenth-Century Great Basin Indian Wage Labor," in Littlefield and Knack, *Native Americans and Wage Labor*, 144–176.

66. Hurt, cited in Campbell, "Newlands, Old Lands," 212.

67. See Richard White, "Animals and Enterprise," in Milner, O'Connor, and Sandweiss, eds., *Oxford History of the American West*; and Dan Robinett, "Tohono O'odham Range History," *Rangelands* 12 (December 1990): 296–300.

68. Peter Iverson, *When Indians Became Cowboys* (Norman: University of Oklahoma Press, 1994), 70–79. For the Apaches, see Ben Chavis, "All–Indian Rodeo," *Wicazo Sa Review* 9 (Spring 1993): 4–11.

69. Robinett, "Tohono O'odham," 298; William T. Hagan, "Adjusting to the Opening of the Kiowa, Comanche, and Kiowa–Apache Reservation," in Peter Iverson, ed., *The Plains Indians of the Twentieth Century* (Norman: University of Oklahoma Press, 1985).

70. Those authorities were, in effect, extending to the U.S. West the process of enclosure that had started in Europe two centuries earlier. Enclosure meant forcing peasants (in Europe) or natives (in the Americas) into ceding their control over common lands; enclosing those lands into privately held estates where agricultural commodities could be efficiently produced; and reducing the now-landless to wage laborers. For an overview of enclosure, see Keith Wrightson, *Earthly Necessities* (New Haven: Yale University Press, 2000), 209-212; Michael Turner, *Enclosures in Britain, 1750-1830* (London: Macmillan, 1984), 11-15; Gilbert Slater, *The English Peasantry and the Enclosure of Common Fields* (London: Constable, 1907); Edward C. K. Gonner, *Common Land and Inclosure* (London: Macmillan, 1912), vi; Arthur H. Johnson, *The Disappearance of the Small Landowner* (London: Oxford University Press, 1963); Harold Perkin, *Origins of Modern English Society* (London: Ark, 1969), 124-133; J. A. Yelling, *Common Field and Enclosure in England, 1450-1850* (London: Macmillan, 1977); G. E. Mingay, *Parliamentary Enclosure in England* (London: Longman, 1997). Generally critical of the process of enclosure are J. L. Hammond and B. Hammond, *The Village Labourer, 1760-1832* (London: Longman's, 1912), 331-332; J. M. Neeson, *Commoners* (Cambridge: Cambridge University Press, 1993); Robert C. Allen, *Enclosure and the Yeoman* (London: Clarendon, 1992); and, especially, E. P. Thompson, *The Making of the English Working Class* (New York: Vintage, 1963), 219.

71. Stephen Powers, "A Pony Ride on Pit River," *Overland Monthly* 13 (October 1874): 347. By the end of the nineteenth century, sixty thousand sheep and forty thousand cattle grazed in northeastern California; see Thomas P. Vale, "Forest Changes in the Warner Mountains, California," *Annals of the Association of American Geographers* 67 (March 1977): 28-45.

72. E. Steele, A. M. Rosborough, to Commanding Officer at Fort Klamath, August 28, 1865, in Hagen, *Modoc War*, 1-2, Bancroft Library, University of California, Berkeley; Newton Booth to U.S. War Department, January 1, 1873, Military Department, Adjutant General, Indian War Papers, California State Archives, Sacramento.

73. Elisha Steele, William H. Morgan, John A. Fairchild, and H. Wallace Atwell to Columbus Delano, July 30, 1873, in Francis S. Landrum, ed., *Guardhouse, Gallows, and Graves* (Klamath Falls, Ore.: Klamath County Museum, 1988).

74. For New Mexico, see Robert J. Rosenbaum, *Mexicano Resistance in the Southwest* (Dallas, Tex.: Southern Methodist University Press, 1998); María E. Montoya, *Translating Property* (Berkeley: University of California Press, 2002). For Anglo settlers' conflicts with ranchers and railroad companies, see Richard Maxwell Brown, "Violence," in Milner et al., eds., *Oxford History of the American West*.

CHAPTER 3

Imagining Mexico in Love and War: Nineteenth-Century U.S. Literature and Visual Culture

SHELLEY STREEBY

After Mexico became independent in 1821 and established itself as a republic in 1824, the project of imagining and building the nation began. During these years, the United States, which had survived the War of 1812, began a second period of nation building focused on southwestward expansion, slavery, and managing the divisions between North and South. These two nation building projects were not separate. The dramatic expansion of the United States after 1820 came with the vast territories taken by war from Mexico in the 1840s. The debates over the expansion of slavery that culminated in the U.S. Civil War in the 1860s were intensified by the challenge of incorporating new territory into an already precarious and unstable union. The stories of nation-making in Mexico and the United States from 1820 to 1875 were thus inextricably linked and full of conflict.

Those links and conflicts were important in the world of culture as well as in the spheres of diplomacy, war, and politics. The U.S.-Mexico War of the 1840s coincided with the print revolution in the United States. The mass-circulation newspapers, story papers, dime novels, and other popular literature of the period provide ample evidence of Mexico's important role in early U.S. literary and cultural history. In the 1850s and 1860s, an emergent U.S. mass culture took up and transformed the ideas, genres, and conventions that proliferated in response to the U.S.-Mexico War; their legacies are still evident today in cultural forms such as the western and the race melodrama, as well as in ways of thinking about race, law, land, labor, citizenship, and national belonging that are rooted in the nineteenth century. Although most studies of U.S. literary and cultural history focus on transatlantic links between England and the United States, since the 1990s a growing body of scholarship has elaborated on the significance of Spain, New Spain, and Mexico. In what follows, I build on this work to emphasize the importance of looking south to Mexico and the Americas as well as east to Europe when analyzing the origins, early history, and multiple legacies of American literature. I also suggest that literature and culture were both indispensable tools and sites of contestation in nineteenth-century nation-building projects.

This chapter surveys the literary and cultural visions of Mexico produced in the United States in response to three periods of military conflict in Mexico: first, the war against Spain that began in 1810 and ended in 1821 with the emergence of Mexico as a nation; second, the Texas war for independence of 1835-1836 and the U.S.-Mexico War of 1846-1848, which together expanded U.S. national territory, diminished Mexico's, and radically transformed the relationships between the two nations; and, finally, the 1858-1861 War of Reform and the 1862-1867 French intervention in Mexico, a period of ongoing wars in Mexico that overlapped with the U.S. Civil War. Although it is sometimes suggested that during these years the United States turned inward in response to its own national trauma, I argue that debates about national divisions, race, labor, property, government, and empire were shaped by comparisons between the United States and Mexico in literature and culture.

The three periods present different conjunctions of culture and politics. On the cultural front, each moment is quite distinct: the first period predates the emergence of popular literature and mass culture in the United States, which came in the late 1830s and 1840s in the wake of improvements in print technology and the development of extensive transportation and communications networks. In the 1820s, then, access to print was relatively limited, and a republican conception of the literary privileged polite literature that aimed to serve a public function by teaching elite and educated readers to become virtuous citizens.[1]

During the era of U.S. expansion into Mexico, however, new and diverse kinds of literature and culture flourished and reached more people than ever before, as newspapers, story papers, and popular novels appealed to broader, cross-class constituencies. They quickly incorporated visions of Mexico and Mexicans into new forms of popular entertainment. Photography was also invented in the 1840s, and dozens of daguerreotypes survive from the U.S.-Mexico War era. Although photographs would not be directly incorporated into newspapers and other periodicals until after the half-tone process was invented in the 1880s, illustrators used them as the base for lithographs and other images reproduced in newspapers, story papers, and cheap pamphlet novels during the era of expansion into

Mexican territories. By the 1850s and 1860s, such illustrations were seen on full-color dime novel covers, in new illustrated weeklies, and in many other publications.

There are at least two notable trends, then, within the literary and cultural history that I am compressing here: the proliferation over time of diverse forms of literature and culture that reached both larger and more specialized audiences within an increasingly stratified literary and cultural field; and the increasing presence and importance of illustrations, photographs, and other images as part of that field. Both of these trends significantly shaped visions of Mexico in nineteenth-century U.S. literature and culture.

In each of the three eras, different configurations of international relations and sex/gender relations, as well as changing debates about slavery, labor, race, and republicanism in the Americas, also informed the diverse U.S. literary and cultural genres that addressed issues of nation- and empire-building in Mexico and the United States. In the 1820s, U.S. observers often viewed Mexican independence as an achievement that paralleled the U.S. revolutionary break with England. Still, the 1823 Monroe Doctrine also revealed how a U.S. discourse of revolutionary exceptionalism and hemispheric solidarity could transform into a legitimation of U.S. imperial aspirations and hierarchical inter-American relations.

During the 1830s and 1840s, as U.S. soldiers participated in wars fought against Mexico and as the United States annexed former Mexican territories, many of the war's opponents insisted that the United States was a republic, not an empire, and imagined Mexico as a sister republic. The war's promoters, on the other hand, formulated theories of Anglo-Saxon racial superiority and U.S. Manifest Destiny to support conceptions of Mexico as a racially heterogeneous, failed nation that could only benefit from U.S. intervention.[2]

Later, as the crisis over slavery deepened in the United States during the 1850s and Civil War divided the nation in the 1860s, Mexico's War of Reform and the French intervention that followed continued to provoke interest in the United States. Northerners sympathized and sometimes forged affiliations with liberal/republican forces in Mexico. Southerners, on the other hand, had ties to the conservative/royalist coalition there, including business connections that moved cotton exports through Mexican ports. In the U.S. literature and culture of this period, comparisons are often made between different forms of property, sites of production, and labor in Mexico and the United States. Southern plantation slavery and northern factories using free white labor are compared to Mexican haciendas using labor relations U.S. observers imagined as peonage, a state somewhere in between slavery and freedom.

Issues of race and republican rule were also important. Benito Juárez, Mexico's liberal president from 1858 to 1872, was by birth a Zapotec—an Indian in U.S. understandings of the time. His rule in times of conflict and consolidation raised questions about the ability of nonwhites to participate in republican government and provoked comparisons between Indian policies in the United States and Mexico.

In all three periods, questions of hemispheric relations, nation building, and issues of race, labor, and empire were mapped onto narratives of gender and sexuality. The two nations were often compared to fathers, mothers, brothers, or sisters as they were allegorized through the increasingly popular genre of international romance. These gendered and sexed ways of understanding relationships between races and nations are still with us, as José Limón's analysis in *American Encounters* of the twentieth century details. Today, many U.S. political leaders, cultural producers, and citizens continue to imagine U.S.-Mexico relations through narratives of family, heterosexual reproduction, and/or perverse sexuality.

New Nations and Old Empires

In his message to Congress on December 2, 1823, Pres. James Monroe made his famous declaration that "the American continents, by the free and independent condition which they have assumed and maintain, are henceforth not to be considered as subjects for future colonization by any European powers." Welcoming as "our Southern brethren" the new nations that were emerging in the wars of independence fought against Spain, Monroe warned European powers that they could not "extend their political system to any portion of either continent without endangering our peace and happiness." His declaration came at a time ripe for hemispheric republican solidarity. The young United States had fended off Britain's attempt to reassert power by sacking Washington and invading New Orleans in the War of 1812. Mexico was newly independent and writing the constitution that would make it a federal republic in 1824. Simón Bolívar was entering the final battles that would end Spanish rule in Andean South America the same year.

Yet as Gretchen Murphy has noted, Monroe's defense of a fraternal, hemispheric republicanism defined in opposition to European empires was haunted by "unspoken contradictions: most obviously, Indian removal and slavery, signs of colonialism and tyranny within the democracies of the New World, and also by the idea often expressed in the United States that Americans south of its borders were racially incapable of democratic self-rule." Monroe's remarks also helped to introduce a slippage between "anticolonial revolution and imperialist domination" that has recurred in the rhetoric of U.S. foreign policy since the 1820s.[3]

In another message to Congress earlier in 1823, Monroe had observed that "the revolutionary movement in the Spanish provinces in this hemisphere attracted the attention and excited the sympathy of our fellow-citizens from its commencement," adding that "this feeling was natural and honorable to them, from causes which need not be communicated to you."[4] Monroe suggested that, because of their own history of anticolonial revolution, U.S. citizens felt a "natural" sympathy for revolutionists in other parts of the Americas; he justified his recognition of Mexico and the other new nations by invoking the republican belief that a people who established independence by overthrowing tyranny deserved freedom. Yet even as Monroe formally recognized these nations as independent entities on the basis of their victories in wars against Spain, the brief comments later formalized as the Monroe Doctrine suggested a notion of hemispheric intimacy and connectedness that would, in the years to come, frequently be invoked as a justification for U.S. intervention in the Americas.

While Monroe envisioned Mexico and the other new nations in the Americas as brothers, many of the literary and cultural works that focused on Mexico at war throughout the nineteenth century imagined that nation as a woman in need of protection from rapacious men. In the seduction novels of the eighteenth century, libertines threaten heroines such as Pamela, Clarissa, and Charlotte Temple; in the increasingly ubiquitous international race romance genre of the nineteenth century, powerful Spanish and Mexican men disrespect the principle of consent and try to rape or force marriage on elite Mexican women, who stand in for the Mexican nation. In seduction novels and in international race romances, a political rhetoric of republicanism that raises questions about force, consent, virtue, tyranny, nation, and empire converged with stories of seduction, rape, and marriage; the conventions of the latter mediate the concerns of the former.[5] The national romances of Latin America analyzed by Doris Sommer represent one form of this melodramatic formula, translating political issues into questions about gender, sex, and family. In doing so, they respond to anxieties about the relationships among class and ethnic groups within each nation and struggle to construct a collective feeling of nationhood after divisive wars for independence.[6]

In U.S. English-language novels, international race romances with Mexican settings often feature a U.S. hero who models patriotism, manly republican virtue, and independence for Mexicans, and who becomes romantically involved with an elite Mexican woman. This romantic matrix, with its emphasis on the U.S. hero's rescue of the Mexican woman and his struggle to protect her from Mexican libertines and tyrants, raises larger questions about the relationship between Mexico and the United States, and about the role of the United States in the hemisphere, that resonate with the contradictions of the political relationships engendered by the Monroe Doctrine.

One of the earliest examples of an English-language, international race romance about Mexico's relationship to the United States is Timothy Flint's massive two-volume *Francis Berrian; or, The Mexican Patriot* (1826). Flint was a Massachusetts native and Harvard graduate who became a Congregationalist minister, a missionary in the Mississippi River Valley, an editor of literary magazines in Cincinnati and New York, and the author of several books, including *Indian Wars of the West* (1833) and *The Biographical Memoir of Daniel Boone* (1833), both of which appeared in multiple editions over the course of the nineteenth century.[7]

While the novel includes many of the conventions and character types that would later appear in the popular literature of U.S. expansion, it was directed at a more elite audience, partly because of the material, institutional, and technological conditions that shaped the literary field in the 1820s. Access to print and authorship was largely restricted to elites, although there were some important exceptions; a wide audience of artisan and working-class readers did not yet exist. Exemplifying a republican conception of letters and literature, Flint's novel aims to instruct and improve his readers even as he turns to what has been characterized as a "silky milky" story of international romance in order to teach lessons and raise questions about political virtue, patriotism, New World republicanisms, and the political relationships between the United States and Mexico (I, 230).

Like many of the novels of the U.S. revolutionary and early national era, *Francis Berrian* is a hybrid text that incorporates several genres. It is one of the earliest examples of the "Yankee in Mexico" literature that emerged in relation to other Yankee vernacular types in the poetry, drama, travel narratives, and novels of the period. The Yankee in Mexico narrative would later be taken up in U.S.-Mexico War opponent James Russell Lowell's *Biglow Papers* and then by poet, dime novelist, and working-class advocate A.J.H. Duganne, among others.

Flint's novel begins as a travel narrative in which a Yankee on his way to the "remote regions of the Southwest on the Spanish frontier" (I, 5) is captivated by the "extraordinary beauty of person" (I, 6) whom he observes in another traveler on the steamship, a wealthy young man whose "countenance wore the tinge of a summer sun" (I, 7). This "magnetic" (I, 5) figure turns out to be the eponymous hero, another native son of Puritan Massachusetts, who takes over the story for hundreds of pages in a picaresque narrative about his adventures in Mexico, where he lives among Comanche Indians, saves a rich Mexican woman named Martha from her captivity, teaches English in her father's royalist household, and then joins rebellious Mexican patriots, fights with them, and saves the heroine twice more from a rapacious Mexican royalist and soldier who wants to force her to marry him.

As he travels throughout Mexico, the hero encounters characters of different classes, races, regions, and nations; he speculates about Mexicans as a people and about their "slavery" under Spanish "tyranny" and wonders whether they are capable of asserting their national independence or whether their newly won liberty will degenerate into licentiousness and anarchy. In this section and in the parts that follow, the novel alternates between romance and scenes of war and political intrigue, connecting the erotic and the familial to the political. Although the novel betrays anxieties about the romance genre, which it identifies as a characteristically Spanish literary form, the narrator ultimately defends the genre against those who view it as immoral, unnerving, and liable to make readers "unfit for the severer and more important duties of life" by arguing that it is an important antidote to the U.S. tendency to focus on "the mere mercenary details of existence" (I, 12).

This defense of the romance implicitly continues in the next part of the narrative, which takes the form of an epistolary novel and consists of letters from Martha to an intimate female friend about her struggle to resist the rapacious royalist, her romance with and marriage to the Yankee hero, and the latter's heroism as part of the "patriot" army. Although the epistolary form was esteemed in the early national period for its ability to model the exemplary, virtuous interiority of the letter writer, and although the narrator justifies the inclusion of the letters on the grounds that they are "exact transcripts of the mind of Martha," more than anything they serve to aggrandize the Yankee's revolutionary manhood. In Martha's account, Berrian is the true leader of the Mexican patriots' successful revolution. The Yankee "really originated every measure, and his counsels eventually prevailed upon every point in question" (I, 227).

The narrative point of view switches back to the steamship interlocu-tor and the Yankee hero at the end. The latter closes the novel by empha-sizing his happiness with his Mexican wife, their plans to live in both the United States and Mexico, and his pride in their two-year-old son, who can "scold" his parents "in two languages" (II, 260). Although romances and marriages between U.S. men and elite Mexican women would be common in the popular novels of the U.S.-Mexico War era, Flint's earlier novel is unusual in imagining a bilingual child of such a union, as well as in its emphasis on both Mexico and the United States as a future home for the couple. U.S. male republican power rules, yet a bilingual transnational future remains an open possibility.

In many ways, this novel manifests the sympathy for New World revo-lutions which Monroe claimed, in his March 1823 message to Congress, had been "excited" in U.S. citizens. The hero identifies his "fortunes," after all, "with the patriots," whose "cause" he "joined" and whose "efforts at emancipating the great Mexican republic," as he puts it, were "con-summated in the ultimate and successful accomplishment of a revolution, which has wrested this great and fair portion of the American hemisphere from a miserable and blighting despotism" (II, 244). The hero's remark that "there seems to be an instinctive feeling, antecedent to reason, which causes, that every human being, born in our hemisphere inherits a feeling of independence, and a love of liberty, as his birthright" (I, 266), identi-fies a common, hemispheric feeling precisely with anticolonial sentiments and thereby participates in a project of hemispheric solidarity to which Monroe's messages to Congress also contributed.

This delineation of a hemispheric, anticolonial structure of politics and feeling, however, coexisted with a belief in U.S. superiority and inter-American hierarchies. For Flint (and presumably many readers), the Yankee hero epitomized Mexican patriotism and revolutionary man-hood to the relative exclusion of Mexican freedom fighters. Frequent ob-servations about the racial heterogeneity of Mexico's people and espe-cially about the degraded nature of Mexico's lower classes reveal anxieties about that nation's republican future on the part of those who believed in Anglo-Saxon superiority. The gendered power dynamics that figured the United States as a man and Mexico as a woman worked to naturalize U.S. dominance and Mexican subordination. The plot repeatedly turns on the heroine's vulnerability to different kinds of threats and on the hero's un-canny ability to rescue her when no one else can protect her, suggesting that the United States may need to step in to rescue Mexico from both external and internal tyranny and despotism. Thus, even though the novel ultimately, like Monroe, champions Mexico's revolution as a successful war against Spanish tyranny, it also imagines a role for the United States in Mexico that could easily slide from anticolonial solidarity to intervention and control.

While Timothy Flint's novel about Mexican independence registers the impact that anticolonial revolutions in the Americas had on U.S. literature of the early national period, Boston was not the only publishing center and New England was not the only region that contributed to U.S. debates about hemispheric republicanisms, new nations, and old empires. In the 1820s, Philadelphia was one of the U.S. cities (New York and New Orleans were the others) where émigrés from other parts of the Americas published literature in support of anticolonial movements in their homelands. In 1826, the same year that Flint's *Francis Berrian* appeared, the William Stavely Publishing House of Philadelphia issued a Spanish-language novel, *Jicoténcal*, a story published anonymously. It was probably written by one or more of the Cuban émigrés involved in the production of *El Habanero*, a literary and political magazine connected to the struggle for Cuban independence, also published by Stavely. Questions about the authorship of the novel have never been completely resolved, but most of the available evidence suggests that the novel is the product of what Anna Brickhouse calls a "coalitional authorship" among those responsible for *El Habanero*. Brickhouse suggests that writers for this magazine made up "a transnational collectivity that ensured its progress from exilic manuscript to printed book."[8]

This novel about the Spanish Conquest, the fall of the Aztec Empire, and the demise of the indigenous republics that are "buried under its ruins" offers a very different response to Mexico's wars of independence from those offered in the Monroe Doctrine and in Flint's Yankee in Mexico novel.[9] By reconstructing an ancient Mexico where republicanism flourished, the author(s) of *Jicoténcal* imagine a long history of republicanism in the Americas that precedes the U.S. experiment; thus the United States is displaced as the founder and inevitable model for the anticolonial revolution in Cuba that the authors hope to inspire through a literary focus on Mexico.

Jicoténcal is also part of a larger effort by Creoles (Americans of Spanish descent) in the late eighteenth and early nineteenth centuries to rescue and sometimes to reconstruct the indigenous past in order to establish the legitimacy of emerging nations, as Enrique Florescano and others have shown.[10] In the novel written in Philadelphia by Cubans about Mexico, the eponymous hero becomes a model for the Creole patriots because of his exemplary virtue, manifested especially in his willingness to subdue his passions and sacrifice his private interests for the good of the republic. The novel finds in a remote past all of the elements of republicanism that anticolonial Creoles hoped to consolidate in the present, including civil societies, patriotism, public spirit, and independence. Meanwhile, Hernán Cortés and his men become "half-savage barbarians" whose "invasions" (7) disrupt the civil ways of indigenous republics and pit indigenous peoples against each other, leading to a tragic conclusion: Spanish conquest and the execution of Jicoténcal. The Cuban Creole authors thus draw on the language of republicanism to identify their own struggles for independence with indigenous peoples' struggles against Cortés and other Spanish invaders.

The Spanish-language novel's vision of Mexico is more expansive than the one we have observed in that other U.S. novel of 1826 focused on that new nation, the English-language *Francis Berrian*. There, Flint's Yankee describes the Comanche Indians among whom he briefly dwells with a mixture of sympathy and condescension. Still, the captivity genre through which the narrator tells the story of his rescue of Martha, "the proud daughter of the white people," establishes boundaries between whites and nonwhites, between civilized people and savages. In *Jicoténcal*, on the other hand, it is the Spanish who are savages, while indigenous people provide the political and historical foundations for anticolonial struggles and republican government in the Americas.

Thus from the early years of anticolonial struggle and nation building, novelists writing in Spanish in the United States offered counternarratives to the stories of race and empire told in English by Anglo-Americans. At other times, however, writers in both Spanish and English would imagine bonds between "civilized" Spanish and Anglo empire-builders forged at the expense of "savage" Indians.

The authors of *Jicoténcal* also grafted debates about empire and republicanism in the Americas onto narratives of gender and sexuality, so that questions about war, tyranny, citizenship, patriotism, and political virtue translated into stories of desire, romance, force, consent, and sexual virtue. Flint's Mexican heroine, as we have seen, mostly serves to cast the Yankee hero in a heroic light. In *Jicoténcal*, in contrast, the indigenous hero's beloved is the "beautiful American" Teutila (19), an eloquent and exemplary figure who is besieged by the licentious Cortés and other Spaniards yet retains her virtue and independence on account of her "valiant and constant resistance" (79). She also plays an important part in the tragic ending, when she tries to kill Cortés to avenge Jicoténcal's execution. Although her attempt to repel the Spanish invader fails and the demise of the republic and the fall of the Aztec Empire ensue, she represents a powerful alternative to the elite, white, and compliant Mexican heroines imagined by Flint and other authors of English-language international romances about Mexico.

In looking to Mexico's past for historical precursors to their own struggle against Spain, however, the Cuban Creoles evaded the dramatic differences between their own favored position and the subordination faced by Mexico's indigenous peoples (and growing numbers of African slaves in Cuba) as they wrote. They thus sidestepped the question of their hierarchical relationships to the indigenous and enslaved peoples of their own era. When Flint represented contemporary Indians in Mexico, he identified them with a troubling racial heterogeneity that contrasts sharply with the elite Martha's whiteness and eligibility for international romance. The Cuban émigrés in Philadelphia avoided addressing the challenges of ethnic and racial power that shaped Mexico and Cuba during these years. We can only wonder whether and how readers in Mexico and Cuba responded to these novels, especially since in the nineteenth century Mexico became a nation and Cuba did not.

In the decades after *Francis Berrian* and *Jicoténcal* appeared, many English-language narratives about the Spanish conquest of Mexico were published in the United States, including Robert Montgomery Bird's *Calavar; or, the Knight of the Conquest* (1834) and *The Infidel; or, the Fall of Mexico* (1835). Jesse Alemán suggests that in the gothic histories of Spanish conquest published in the United States in this period, Mexico is situated as the United States' "uncanny, imperial other": the conquest narratives exhumed Mexico's lost potential as a civilized, indigenous New World nation in order to contrast this glorious past with Mexico's present, fallen, status as a "perverse," or failed, nation. In this way, Alemán argues, Bird "assimilates Mexico's past and rearticulates its Anglo-American hemispheric story in a literary act that sets the stage for the United States' continental colonization of the Americas."[11] What the Cuban authors of the Spanish-language *Jicoténcal* saw as a living model, the English-language authors of conquest narratives offered as proof of Mexican failure—and an opening to intervention. The mix of solidarity and subordination that coexisted in Monroe's doctrine was thereby mobilized, more and more, as a justification for empire.

This is true of the most famous and influential English-language narrative of conquest, W. H. Prescott's *History of the Conquest of Mexico* (1843). Prescott opposed the annexation of Texas and the U.S.-Mexico

War; still, U.S. soldiers who read his history imagined they were following in the footsteps of Cortés and his men. The book joined and inspired a host of other prewar conquest narratives that imagined an emergent U.S. empire in relation to the Aztec and Spanish empires, including Charles Averill's *Aztec Revelations* (1839), Edward Maturin's *Montezuma, the Last of the Aztecs: A Romance* (1845), and J. H. Ingraham's *Montezuma the Serf; or, the Revolt of the Mexitili* (1845). With the war under way, several U.S.-Mexico War novels also incorporated musings on Mexico's past into stories about the ongoing conflict, visions that reappeared in a number of the early dime novels of the 1860s and 1870s.

U.S. literary and cultural narratives about Mexico that appeared after the 1830s, however, departed from earlier paradigms in a few significant ways, even as the translation of questions about race, nation, and empire into narratives of gender and sexuality remained a constant. First, the print revolution allowed more popular literature to emerge in the 1840s; much of it tried to appeal to a broader, cross-class audience rather than to elites implicitly defined in sharp contrast to other classes. Second, as Texas independence and the U.S.-Mexico War brought U.S. expansion into Mexico, enthusiasm for Mexico's independence waned, fracturing along lines that roughly corresponded to the authors' inclination to support or oppose U.S. empire. And visions of the Spanish Conquest, the Aztec Empire, and the indigenous republics were reframed by newly influential scientific racisms and theories of Anglo-Saxon racial superiority, reinforced by the enduring Black Legend, which continued to construct the Anglo-American expansions as liberating and the Spanish Empire as uniquely evil.

Ingraham's *Montezuma the Serf*, which was published the year before the U.S.-Mexico War began, is both a harbinger of the new and a reminder of older ways of imagining Mexico. Issued by the Williams Brothers, one of the most prolific publishers of popular novelettes (as well as the story papers *Uncle Sam* and *The Flag of the Free*), *Montezuma the Serf* almost completely disregards earlier histories of the fall of the Aztec Empire in order to tell a fanciful story about the "slave" Montezuma's romance with the princess Eylla. Ingraham's Montezuma is the son of a poor net maker, making him a stand-in for the artisan and working-class readers that made up an increasingly large part of the audience for popular literature.

Throughout the novel, Ingraham champions the "citizens" who make up the virtuous, hard-working, artisan class to which Montezuma and his family belong, who persevere despite being "hourly exposed to the domineering whims and idle passions of the nobles, as well as the absolute will of the empire" (10). Spanish conquerors and empire builders are nowhere to be found in this novel; instead, the Aztec Empire is divided into classes that resemble emerging class divisions in the United States, where an artisan republic was being pressured and transformed by early industrialization. Montezuma becomes involved in a revolutionary plot that aims to place "this million in the possession of their natural rights" (25), notably including the right to feel that their "wives and daughters" belong to them rather than to "the licentious nobles" (26).

Ingraham divides Mexicans into a tyrannical class of sexually rapacious nobles and a virtuous, proto-republican artisan class. He does not racialize these divisions among indigenous people, however. Rather, he imaginatively identifies the anti-imperial struggles of the indigenous artisans with the class struggles of his own era in ways that may remind us of the appropriation of an indigenous past in *Jicoténcal*. At the same time, Ingraham posits the existence of another subordinated group in Mexico, made up of the noble's "swarthy," black-haired "household servants," who have been "brought from distant provinces" and "are of a different race than the Mexicans" (26). Ingraham notably does not include this class of black servants, who resemble the slaves of the United States, in the dreams of freedom he attributes to the subordinated Mexican majority.

Before the outbreak of war in 1846 reshaped U.S. visions of Mexico, Aztec Mexico could serve as a mythical place to model desired visions of social transformation for exiled Cubans writing in Spanish in Philadelphia and for an author writing in English in New York and seeking a working-class audience. Both visions avoided the problem of African slavery. But war soon made U.S. writers focus on contemporary Mexico, and the war's aftermath of territorial expansion made the challenge of chattel slavery unavoidable.

U.S. Empire and the Emergence of Mass Culture

That sharpening of focus began with the Texas fight for independence from Mexico beginning in 1835. In the pamphlet novelette *The Female Warrior: An Interesting Narrative of the Sufferings and Singular and Surprising Adventures of Miss Leonora Siddons*, wars in the Texas borderlands provide the occasion for the liberation of a slave as well as for the inversion of normative gender roles. Issued in New York by the prolific publisher of cheap crime and adventure novels, E. E. and G. Barclay, the novel aimed to profit from a new interest in Texas as a site of imperial adventure, from its 1836 declaration of independence through 1845, the year the U.S. annexation of Texas led to a bigger war with Mexico. During these years, a host of narratives about Texas appeared, including Joseph Field's *Three Years in Texas* (1836), Anthony Ganhil's *Mexico versus Texas* (1838), and James Dallam's *The Lone Star* (1845).

The Female Warrior merges the genres of the seduction novel and the female picaresque. The heroine, a native of Mobile, Alabama, moves to Galveston, Texas, with her father after he loses his savings in the Panic of 1837; she decides to cross-dress and join the Texas army when her father is killed defending his "adopted country."[12] She experiences a series of military adventures while dressed as a man but ends up being captured by Mexicans and imprisoned in Mexico City. There she is besieged by the "tyrant" Santa Anna (18), who offers to save her life if she becomes his mistress. Ultimately, she escapes from captivity and manages to return to Galveston and finally to Alabama, from where she narrates the story of her "adventures, trials, and sufferings" (19) in hopes that her readers "may never undergo the like calamities" (19).

Crucial to the heroine's transformation into "another being," however, is the intervention of Mary, "a black servant, who had lived in our family in more prosperous days, and who insisted on accompanying us" (1). Mary hopes to travel with the heroine Siddons and even procures men's clothes for her, but before Siddons leaves to join Sam Houston's army she tells Mary that "henceforth" she is "her own mistress" (6), freeing her slave as she liberates herself from the constraints of her gender role. In this way, the narrative registers the controversy over slavery in the borderland spaces of Texas: Mexico had banned slavery in 1829, which made it potentially a sanctuary for escaped slaves and would have ended settlement by southern slaveholders settling new lands for cotton cultivation. But Texas claimed an exemption, and U.S. southerners, like the fictional Siddons family, continued to colonize Texas with cotton and slaves. When a new Mexican national regime pressed abolition on Texas in 1835, Anglo Texas turned to independence, and slavery remained at the center of a decade of conflict between Mexico, Texas, and the latter's U.S. backers. Eventually, the United States would add Texas to the republic as a large slave state in 1845—and more war would soon follow.

Even though the southerner Siddons frees her slave at the outset of her adventures, *The Female Warrior*'s position on slavery is ambiguous; Mary is also represented as a loyal slave who would prefer to stay with her mistress, recalling the happy slaves of southern plantation fiction. The pamphlet is an early example of the mass-produced texts that the publishers marketed in many different parts of the United States, including the South; it aimed to appeal to diverse constituencies, including pro- and antislavery factions, a strategy that conforms to the broader political strategy of compromising over slavery to preserve the union. Such strategies became less effective at resolving political and regional divisions in the era of U.S. empire building, however, when the annexation of vast lands forced the question of whether slavery would extend those territories.

It is perhaps not surprising, then, that much of the literature written by authors who opposed the annexation of Texas and the U.S.-Mexico War of 1848–1848 focuses on the slavery question. In his essay "Resistance to Civil Government" (1849), for instance, Henry David Thoreau connects struggles over slavery to the U.S. invasion of Mexico as he calls on his readers to "do justice to the slave and to Mexico, *cost what it may*" (68, emphasis in original). James Russell Lowell also made the debate over slavery central to the satirical series of Yankee dialect poems about the war that make up *The Biglow Papers* (1848). And in *Sermons of War* (1847), Boston Unitarian clergyman Theodore Parker argued that "prostrate Mexico" had been "robbed" in order that "America may have more slaves" (73). In all these ways, these northern writers insisted that the extension of slavery was at the heart of the debates over the U.S.-Mexico War.

In his journalistic pieces written during the war, Frederick Douglass similarly linked James K. Polk's and the Democrats' dreams of empire to their plans "to perpetuate the enslavement of the colored people of this country" (1848); he also drew on the gendered discourses of hemispheric republicanism that had been popular in an earlier era as he denounced the "present disgraceful, cruel, and iniquitous war with our sister republic." The popular sentimental author Grace Greenwood (Sara J. Clarke) joined Douglass in conjoining an antislavery argument to a discourse of hemispheric republicanism in her short story "The Volunteer," where the war is characterized as "a most unholy war against a sister Republic" that is being fought "for the extension and perpetuation of human slavery." And in the labor and land reform press of the day, the yoking together of antislavery arguments with the ideal of a hemispheric republicanism was common in antiwar articles and other literature.

Indeed, even the popular war romances that proliferated during these years often linked the U.S.-Mexico War to slavery's extension. Dozens of war novelettes were published in the late 1840s, often before or after they were serialized in one of the popular story papers of the era, such as *The Flag of Our Union, The Star Spangled Banner*, and *Uncle Sam*. Story papers claimed audiences of forty thousand or more during the war years, and even U.S. soldiers in Mexico read them. Juxtaposing excerpts from novels with news items and editorials, they were an important part of an emerging mass culture. Most story papers tried to maintain the appearance of neutrality on the important political issues of the day in order to appeal to the widest possible audience; but from 1846 to 1848, the goal of neutrality frequently conflicted with the desire to capitalize on interest in the war. Some of the authors of popular story paper fiction, such as Ned Buntline and George Lippard, edited their own story papers and actively participated in white working-class political culture: Buntline advocated a nativist, proslavery agenda, while Lippard opposed nativism and slavery and championed an uneasy combination of land reform and empire building that he associated with radical democracy.

Lippard, who, like Buntline, was one of the most popular authors of the nineteenth century, wrote two U.S.-Mexico War romances, *Legends of Mexico* and *'Bel of Prairie Eden*. The latter is an uncharacteristically bleak novelette that begins on the prairies of Texas, where a "broken bank director" from Philadelphia, Jacob Grywin, has established a small colony of white workers, German immigrants, and slaves.[13] The novel portrays the Grywin family as cursed because the father cheated the widows and orphans who had savings in his bank in Philadelphia, and because he brought slaves to the U.S./Mexico borderlands, an area that Lippard hoped would instead provide land for landless white working families in the East. Grywin's daughter, 'Bel, is drugged with opium and seduced by a Mexican officer who kills her father and younger brother; the remaining Grywin son, John, seduces the Mexican officer's sister, Isora, and ultimately has him killed, although Isora never finds out about the murder. By the end of the novel, John has fallen in love with Isora, only to learn the meaning of the word "remorse" when Isora dies pining away for her lost brother. This tragic complex of international romances suggests that the war engendered dangerous passions that undermined the ostensibly democratic project of "liberating" Texas and Mexico, even as it implies that John, called "Juan" by the end of the novel, has perhaps become racially contaminated because of his participation in the war, his proximity to Mexicans, and especially his love for Isora.

Lippard's earlier, less pessimistic, novel, *Legends of Mexico*, provides stronger evidence of how republicanism was wedded to U.S. empire dur-

ing the war years. Misquoting Thomas Paine as he connects the U.S.-
Mexico War to the U.S. Revolutionary War on the novel's title page,
Lippard contends that "we fight not to enslave, nor for conquest; but
to make room upon the earth for honest men to live in." In this way,
Legends of Mexico appeals to a utopian vision of land reform and disavows
U.S. interests in slavery and conquest. Still, the specters of capitalism and
slavery that haunt the Grywin family in *'Bel of Prairie Eden* and the discourses of racial hierarchy that saturate both novels suggest that the mid-
nineteenth-century project of linking empire to democracy and freedom
remained troubled by doubts and contradictions.

Many of these contradictions emerge in the dozens of popular international race romances serialized in story papers and published separately as
cheap novelettes during the late 1840s. Despite their fanciful plots, many
of the narratives incorporated news of battles and other representations
of war from the penny press into their stories, resulting in hybrid narratives, part melodrama and part popular history. As Robert Johannsen and
others have observed, the U.S.-Mexico War was the first in which war cor-
respondents were widely used and the first that "people were exposed to
on an almost daily basis" through the penny press.[14]

It is not surprising then, that popular novelists such as Lippard and
Buntline refer to war heroes, Mexican officers, and important battles in
their war romances. Buntline foregrounds this double focus on romance
and popular history in the title and subtitle of his war novel, *Magdalena
the Beautiful Mexican Maid: A Story of Buena Vista* (1847), which, as the
narrator observes at the outset, "carries its own history along with it."[15]
Buntline makes officers and soldiers such as Gen. Zachary Taylor, Capt.
Charles May, Capt. Braxton Bragg, and other notable participants in the
war into characters in his novelette; the Battle of Buena Vista, which took
place on February 23, 1847, provides the backdrop for a tragic ending. At
the same time, Buntline invents two characters, Charley Brackett and the
eponymous Magdalena, who anchor his international romance: Brackett is a Texan whose mother was "Castillian" (26) and whose "Spanish
blood" makes him the perfect choice to be deployed by Taylor as a spy in
Mexico; Magdalena is the beautiful daughter of a Spanish *hacendado* who
is dangerously in debt to the villain, another rapacious Mexican officer.
Brackett and Magdalena fall in love, but all three of the main characters—
Mexican villain, Tejano hero, and Mexican heroine—die at Buena Vista,
a conclusion which reveals some of the anxieties about the war, international romance, and the annexation of Mexico that pervade many of these
novelettes.

Indeed, these international romances end badly as often as they result in marriage. Even when they unite their U.S. soldier-heroes with elite Mexican heroines, they tend to repeatedly and nervously mark the heroine's whiteness by contrasting it with the ubiquity of Mexico's nonwhite people, usually represented in disparaging ways. These plot conventions suggest how discourses of Anglo-Saxon racial superiority mixed with, reshaped, and limited ideas about hemispheric republicanism during the time of U.S. expansion into Mexico.

Popular novelettes about the U.S.-Mexico War also reveal how new visual technologies combined with the print revolution to produce new images of Mexico during these years. When Buntline introduces readers to a character modeled on Zachary Taylor in the first chapter of *Magdalena*, for instance, he observes that the officer, whose "person is seen lithographed at every shop window in the country, scarce needs a description" (25). The newly ubiquitous lithographs, as well as the daguerreotypes that began to appear in this era, inspired John Frost's *Pictorial History of Mexico and the Mexican War* (1848), while engravings and woodcuts representing U.S. officers, Mexican scenes, and important battles were reproduced in newspapers and story papers. Images were often based on newspaper accounts of battles or eyewitness sketches at the scene, but they generally eschewed realist strategies for representing war. Instead, they frequently drew on the conventions of historical painting to depict U.S. soldiers as virtuous patriots whose sacrifices ensured the triumph of republican values, an outcome that was visually identified with U.S. victory in the war.[16]

There were, however, a few exceptions, notably, an 1847 Currier lithograph entitled "The Night after the Battle—Burying the Dead." While many 1840s efforts to memorialize the war dead focused on burial sites and grave markers, Currier's lithograph disturbs dominant sentimental codes for representing death by showing bodies strewn across the landscape, raising the distressing possibility that some bodies would never be recovered and never properly put to rest.[17] A few of the lithographs produced after the bombardment of Veracruz and the intense house-to-house fighting in Monterrey also depict dead and wounded bodies as well as the material devastation caused by war. An 1850 Mexican lithograph closely resembles one of the same scene produced in the United States in 1846, but has a different title: "Heroic Defense of the City of Monterey" rather than "Third Day of the Siege of Monterey." These images emphasize death and loss rather than patriotic transcendence and the invasion of a Mexican "homeland" rather than the extension of republican freedoms. In a war that divided USAmericans, visual culture offered republican patriotic honor to those who celebrated it and wars and devastation to those who lamented it.

While the very first war photographs date from the U.S.-Mexico War era, they did not circulate widely and never became an important part of the war's popular culture: the daguerreotypes were small, with dimensions of only a few inches, and were difficult to see unless they were physically close to the viewer. They were usually presented in a case or a frame and were unique, one-of-a-kind mementos since there was no negative and because they were difficult to reproduce unless copied by a lithographer or engraver. The two sets of daguerreotypes that have survived, likely taken by the same unknown person, do not show action, due to the long exposure times required and the limits of the technology. Instead, they mostly offer portraits, views of buildings and other Mexican scenes that the daguerreotypist likely sold to soldiers and others passing through occupied northern Mexico.

A daguerreotype of Lt. Abner Doubleday, the inventor of baseball, with unidentified Mexican people is unusual because it was taken in the street rather than in the controlled environment of the studio, where most portraits were taken (often with the heads of the sitters held stationary by clamps). The photographer strayed from emerging conventions of portrait photography as he tried to capitalize on current events and produce memorable views of Mexico and the war. He (or someone else) also used the street as a backdrop in a daguerreotype of Brig. Gen. John Ellis Wool and his staff on horses, posing for the several minutes that would be required for the daguerreotypist to record this trace of the presence of the U.S. Army in the streets of Saltillo. This daguerreotype and three other views of U.S. troops in the street are as close as the *archive* comes to directly representing the military conflict that brought the soldiers to Mexico.[18] Photography's impact on visions of war remained limited. It could not yet capture the complexity of war, let alone honor its victims and victors or report its horrors.

Spanish-language sources and other texts by people of Mexican origin also had limited impact on U.S. understanding of the conflict that reshaped North America. Mexican voices were rarely recorded until long after the conflicts. On the struggles over Texas in the 1830s, Timothy Matovina's anthology, *The Alamo Remembered: Tejano Accounts and Perspectives*, contains valuable material, including several published accounts.[19] But it is revealing that the earliest ones date from 1858 and 1860, and most were published in the early twentieth century. On the period of the U.S.-Mexico War, Genaro Padilla and Rosaura Sánchez have written impressive studies of the *testimonios* solicited from Californios (Mexican Californians) in the 1870s by agents of Hubert Howe Bancroft, who generally relegated their accounts to footnotes or disagreed with their interpretations in his massive *History of California*.[20] Mexican perspectives were not welcomed in the United States during the wars for expansion and remained marginalized long after and still too often today.

Spanish-language newspapers, however, sometimes offered alternative visions of U.S. expansionism and republicanism in the war era. Kirsten Silva Gruesz has shown that the newspaper *La Patria* (1845–1861) was one of "the five largest-circulation papers" in New Orleans in 1850 and had sales agents in Florida, Cuba, and Mexico. It described the war as an invasion and focused on "the contradiction between the theory of U.S. republicanism and the practice of U.S. interventionism."[21] Many Spanish-language readers were surely receptive. And Ramón Alcaraz' *Apuntes para la historia de la guerra entre México y los Estados Unidos* (1848) was translated into English and published in New York in 1850 under the title *The Other Side*. It focused on exposing the same contradictions as its authors argued that the era of U.S. expansion, which USAmericans depicted as "one of light," was, "notwithstanding, the same as the former—one of *force and violence*" (32, emphasis in original). Did the publisher of the English translation imagine an audience of northern readers increasingly concerned as conflicts over slavery and its extension escalated in the wake of the "triumphant" expansion into Mexican lands?

Civil Wars: Labor, Race, and Republicanism in Dime Novels and Illustrated Newspapers

As the crisis over slavery intensified in the United States during the 1850s and then as civil war divided the nation in the early 1860s, Mexico was embroiled in its own political conflicts and civil wars. The War of Reform began in 1858 with a coup of conservative elites who refused to recognize the reformist Constitution of 1857. They went on to fight a long war against liberals led by Benito Juárez, whose government was recognized by the United States in 1859.

Liberal victory in 1860 did not bring easy consolidation. Conservatives continued to resist the Juárez government, which faced financial crisis. In July of 1861, it suspended foreign debt payments for two years. The decision was controversial and reversed in December of that year. But France under Napoleon III had already drawn Britain and Spain into a pact of intervention, aiming to force Mexico to pay. When by March of 1862 it became clear that France planned more than debt collection, Spain and Britain withdrew. But France continued the intervention, marching inland to face defeat by liberal forces at Puebla on May 5, 1862 (Cinco de Mayo). The battle only delayed the French advance, for reinforcements from Europe allowed the capture of Mexico City in 1863 and the imposition of the Austrian Archduke Maximilian as emperor of Mexico in 1864.

Although U.S. officials objected and invoked the Monroe Doctrine, the Civil War prevented the union from doing much about the European invasion of Mexico. After the northern victory in 1865, the United States did deploy fifty thousand troops to the U.S./Mexico border, did provide arms to Juárez' liberal forces, and did devise a naval blockade at Veracruz to stop France from landing more troops and supplies. Lincoln's secretary of state, William Seward, wanted France out of Mexico, so made loans and provided other support to sustain Juarez' forces.

Still, after the Civil War, various parties in the United States disagreed over whether Mexico was capable of republican self-government. Although some USAmericans again imagined Mexico as a sister republic in need of protection, the racial Anglo-Saxonism fortified by the U.S.-Mexico War persisted and limited transnational sympathy and solidarity.

In the U.S. South, moreover, many defeated Confederates fled to Maximilian's Mexico in hope of restoring a version of the world they had lost; white southerners who remained in the United States often embraced the idea of Maximilian's Mexican Empire.[22] During and after the simultaneous civil wars, Mexico continued to provoke popular interest in the United States, as northerners and southerners sympathized and sometimes forged affiliations with republican and royalist forces in Mexico.

Beyond war and politics, in the literature and culture of this period, comparisons were often made among different forms of property, sites of production (the plantation, the hacienda, and the factory), and labor (slavery, peonage, and free white labor) in Mexico and the United States. Debates about race and republicanism also persisted in both the U.S. South and the North. Northern dime novels and illustrated newspapers repeatedly raised the specter of a Mexican Indian "savagery" that was at odds with republican virtue and that might, it was strongly suggested, make Mexico fail as a nation. These northern anxieties were powerfully evident in representations of the execution of Maximilian that appeared in *Frank Leslie's Illustrated Newspaper* and *Harper's Weekly*.

The first of Beadle's famous series of dime novels appeared in June of

1860, less than a year before the U.S. Civil War began. From the beginning, Mexico was an important setting for this new form of popular literature. One of the first novels Beadle and Company published was William
Jared Hall's *The Slave Sculptor; or, The Prophetess of the Secret Chamber:
A Tale of Mexico at the Period of the Conquest* (1860), which was reprinted
three times in the decades that followed. Written by a judge from Ohio
who also wrote short stories about Mexico and the South for the popular press, the novel tries to capitalize on the popular interest in the Conquest period inspired by W. H. Prescott's best-selling history, also issued
in multiple editions over the course of the nineteenth century. The very
first sentence asserts this purpose, as Hall suggests that "no period of this
continent's history, is of deeper interest to the American people, than that
of the Aztec race" (9) before and during the Spanish conquest of Mexico.
Midway through the novel, just before inserting a long quotation from
Prescott, he confesses that he is "indebted" to Prescott's "elaborate and
classic works on the Conquest" for "many of the incidents presented in
these pages" (67).

Like Ingraham more than a decade earlier, Hall takes great liberties
with both popular and official histories as he focuses on the "slaves" of
the Aztec Empire. He singles out for sympathy a former slave girl, Mazina, whose skin is "clear and white," exhibiting not "one tinge of the
dusky, cinnamon hue, peculiar to the features of the aborigines" (11).
When Mazina's former master tries to make her marry his son, she re-
fuses to consent, and a struggle ensues over whether she will be forced to
do so. The conflict is represented through the codes of the seduction and
rape-revenge subgenre of the national and transnational race romances so
ubiquitous during the U.S.-Mexico War era. Mazina is a key character in
the novel, along with the former slave Maxtla; his "dress was that usually
worn by the laboring class, showing clearly the outlines of his muscular
frame" (12). While Mazina's dress and body connect her to a white laboring class, Maxtla is a great sculptor whose talent allows him to purchase
his freedom. Hall repeatedly emphasizes the whiteness of both Mazina
and Maxtla, who are "unlike those with whom" they "are surrounded"
(13), and in the end it is revealed that both Mazina and Maxtla are Spaniards who were sold into slavery in Mexico after a shipwreck.

In telling the story, Hall targets the sympathies of the mostly northern
white working-class readers who made up a substantial part of the dime
novel's audience. By offering two white slaves as points of identification,
moreover, the romance rearticulates and transforms the white egalitarianism and Anglo-Saxon racism that had been popularized during the U.S.-

Mexico War years. Although Spaniards are described as "off-white" in much of nineteenth-century popular literature, in this early dime novel the whiteness of the slaves of European descent is emphasized, and it is significant that Mazina and Maxtla marry each other rather than persons of another race or another nation.[23] In the end, they live in a large palace near Mexico City, along with Meztli, a slave girl and "strange child of the Aztecs," whose "skin was much lighter than usual" (15) and who promises to be Maxtla's slave for life if he saves her from being offered as a human sacrifice.

In the novel's last paragraph, Hall reveals that Meztli has remained "faithful to her pledge" (100) and that "the kind-hearted Aztec was far from being a slave in a family of her friends," for the couple's children called her "Aunt Mezzi." Here, Hall imagines a household that includes a slave who is one of the family, reproducing apologetic visions of happy slaves in a popular novel aimed at northern readers and published just before the U.S. Civil War began—a time when many northerners were open to compromise with the South over slavery in hope of keeping the union together and averting war. The first dime novel about Mexico thus turned to a remote past to imagine a history reshaped to address an uncertain present in order to appeal to a white, northern, working-class audience.

On the other hand, the second dime novel focused on Mexico, *The Peon Prince; or, the Yankee Knight Errant, a Tale of Modern Mexico* (1861), revisits the recent history of the U.S.-Mexico War. The notorious poet, land reformer, and popular novelist A.J.H. Duganne wrote *The Peon Prince*, which takes place just before the U.S.-Mexico War began, as well as its sequel, *Putnam Pomfret's War; or, a Vermonter's Adventures in Mexico* (1861). These novels are part of a large body of popular U.S.-Mexico War literature that was produced or reprinted as the Civil War began, including John Frost's *Pictorial History of Mexico and the Mexican War* (1848, 1862), Lippincott's *The Mexican War and Its Heroes* (1848, 1860), George Ballentine's personal narrative of the war (1862), and Brantz Mayer's *Mexico: Aztec, Spanish, and Republican* (1850).

Although Duganne's focus on an earlier era of war between neighboring nations may seem like an evasion of the civil wars taking place in the United States and Mexico, contemporary debates over race, labor, land, and nation- and empire building shape his plots. The hero of Duganne's novel is a Yankee named Putnam Pomfret, an "offshoot of that great Anglo-Saxon stock, whose footsteps track the paths of empire" (20). By making one of his protagonists a Yankee, Duganne adapted a regional type long popular in the theater and cheap fiction, including the story paper romances set during the U.S.-Mexico War. But although successful or blocked romances between USAmerican men and Mexican women are at the heart of many of the sensational story paper novelettes produced during the war, in this novel international homosocial bonding is more important than international heterosexual romance, as Duganne imagines the heroic collaboration of the Yankee, the Indian "peon prince" Zumozin, the Mexican Creole soldier Nunez, and an honest priest, Padre Herrata.

Instead of marrying his Yankee to the elite Mexican heroine, Inez, however, Duganne weds her to the Mexican soldier Nunez. International romances imagine an increasingly intimate relationship between the United States and Mexico, a possibility less desirable and less possible for the United States after the South seceded and years of bloody and destructive civil war ensued. Thus, rather than envisioning the United States taking over in Mexico, Duganne invents a republican coalition, no doubt inspired by Benito Juárez' forces, composed of Indian leaders and liberal factions within the army and the church which are friendly to the United States. In these novels, Duganne compares plantation slavery, hacienda peonage, factory labor in ways that echo and participate in the debates of his Civil War era. Bondage is everywhere a problem; freedom, everywhere the goal.

The new illustrated newspapers of the era, including *Frank Leslie's Illustrated Newspaper* and *Harper's Weekly*, more directly addressed issues raised by the war in Mexico and the French occupation that ensued. Harper's editorial perspective on U.S. relations with Mexico was similar to Duganne's in many ways: both echoed a northern republican worldview, though Duganne's version of this was more radical, with more emphasis on land and labor reform. In 1865, a *Harper's* writer worried over the French occupation of Mexico and defended the Monroe Doctrine, but insisted that "nobody, except an enemy of this country, wishes to see it hurled into another war at present." Another editorial on "Mexican policy" published the same year suggested that "a hint is as good as a kick, and produces the same result with much less friction." And a year later, the paper affirmed the "natural right" of the Mexican people to "domestic and Republican freedom" and warned that "no foreign State can rightfully interfere in such trials . . . on the ground of a desire to correct them." According to this logic, the reasons the French should leave Mexico were the same reasons the United States should not get involved.

On August 3, 1867, the year France withdrew its forces from Mexico, *Harper's* continued to insist that "Mexico should be left to work out her

own destiny" and that if the United States intervened it would be hypo-
critically and "deliberately repeating the rôle of France in occupying and
controlling the country." The same article revealed U.S. anxieties about
race and republican government in Mexico, however, since the writer
called Mexico "a chaotic country" and expressed doubts about Juárez'
ability to govern. This editor claimed "that Maximilian would have given
it a better government than can now be hoped for—that Juarez is merely
a partisan leader and will be opposed by others of the same kind—that
Maximilian's execution was a brutal blunder and crime—that Mexicans
are ferocious and incapable half-breeds, and that all these late horrors
would not have happened had General Scott remained in Mexico." Still,
he insisted that "Mexico has the same right to manage herself as she
pleases, so far as we are concerned, that we have ourselves—until Mexico
invades our rights or threatens our safety, when we may, of course, defend
ourselves." Thus *Harper's* repudiated U.S. empire building in Mexico out
of fear that the United States was not in any position to act successfully
in the wake of the Civil War. It should be apparent that this position was
quite compatible with the racially hierarchical republicanism and anxieties about incorporating Mexico or Mexicans that surface in Duganne's
novels, which is not surprising since these ways of thinking were one of
the persistent legacies of the popular literature of the U.S.-Mexico War
period.

As the 1867 *Harper's* quotation suggests, these anxieties became especially explicit in the wake of Maximilian's execution. That year, *Harper's*
published several illustrations documenting the French occupation and
its demise, including two on the front page of the August 10, 1867, issue:
one offered a view of Querétaro, Mexico, the city where Maximilian died,
while the other reconstructed the scene just before the June 19 execution,
as Maximilian and two of his generals faced two priests as well as the
firing squad about to execute them while a coffin ominously waited in the
foreground.

Many photographs of Maximilian and the French occupation exist;
both Mexican and foreign photographers were at work by this time producing cartes de visite, relatively small and inexpensive photographs
printed on thicker paper that purchasers could turn into narrative se-
quences in albums or exchange among themselves. One of Matthew
Brady's photographers, Andrew Burgess, who had also photographed the
U.S. Civil War, worked in Mexico at this time; he made a portrait of
Benito Juárez that circulated widely and served as the basis for one of

Harper's 1867 illustrations. Several studios issued hundreds of cartes de visite of Maximilian and his wife, Carlota, and Maximilian even hired his own photographer, Julio María y Campo. No photograph of the moment of execution remains, although in the wake of Maximilian's death one photographer re-created the scene by superimposing portraits of the executed men on an image of the execution site.[24]

While *Harper's* published a lithograph based on eyewitness accounts and sketches of the execution, *Leslie's Illustrated Newspaper* instead published portraits of Maximilian and Juárez, as well as a front-page drawing of the "sombrero worn by Maximilian at the time of his death," a lithograph of his head taken "from a photograph immediately after death" during the coroner's inquest, an engraving of his body in a coffin "awaiting removal to Europe" (October 5, 1867), another illustration of sailors guarding his "effects" (October 26, 1867), and, finally, an image of the Austrian yacht that carried his body from Mexico back to Europe. Such portrayals responded to the victory of Mexican liberals led by the Zapotec, thus Indian, Juárez, which were imagined as brutality inflicted by an uncivilized savage on a white European.

In Leslie's paper, especially, the racial hierarchies of popular U.S.-Mexico War literature persisted to block, shadow, and circumscribe expressions of hemispheric republican sympathies. In a front-page story published in the June 20, 1867, issue, for instance, just a day after the execution, the author anxiously observed that three weeks had elapsed since Maximilian's capture and wondered whether the prisoners had indeed been shot, as early reports suggested, by what the paper characterized as "a gang who can scarcely be restrained from the worst excesses of the most savage Indians." Calling Juárez the "semi-barbarous victor" of Mexico's war, the writer wished that "our protégé had behaved a little less like a savage than he has" and looked forward to a day when the Mexican people "will call on the United States to protect them against themselves," for "then and only then," he pompously concluded, "will dawn the day of the true regeneration of Mexico." Attributions of a "bloodthirsty nature," barbarity, and savagery to "Mexican Indians," so familiar to readers of popular U.S. conquest and imperial adventure literature, were thereby mobilized to attack the legitimacy of Juárez' government, or indeed of any government in which Indians participated, and to suggest that the United States should take the place of France in Mexico. The execution of Maximilian and the ensuing publication of lithographs, cartes de visite, and other images of this moment thus provided an occasion for popular illustrated papers such as *Leslie's* to promote U.S. empire in Mexico by adapting U.S.-Mexico War–era articulations of race and republican government to disparage Mexican efforts at nation building.[25]

By 1874, the wide circulation of images, popular histories, and other accounts of Maximilian in Mexico, including his execution, even inspired a Beadle's dime novel, *John Emerald's The Crested Serpent; or, the White Tiger of the Tropics* (1874), which is set "during the short reign of Maximilian" (9). Instead of making Maximilian a central character, however, Emerald imagines a villainous Frenchman, Arnaud Boussard, the titular white tiger, who, out of "excitement and adventure, remained with the army of Maximilian" (16) even after Napoleon withdrew French troops from Mexico. The symbolic center of the narrative is Paula Vallejo, the "pure Castilian white" daughter of a wealthy north Mexican *hacendado*, Jose, a liberal "patriot" who "love(s) republican Mexico" (11). Emerald gives the Vallejos the privileged position in this postwar international romance, suggesting a sympathy for Mexican nation building and hemispheric republicanism. But the novel also manifests anxieties about race and Mexican republicanism, anxieties that are precariously contained through the romantic racialism and white egalitarianism it imagines, binding together Mexican characters of different classes and races even as it unites Mexicans and USAmericans.

One of the main projects of the novel is to idealize hierarchical relationships between elite white Mexicans and nonelite Mexican Indians, so that Indians are integrated into the Mexican nation but in subordinate roles dependent upon the noblesse oblige of the elite landowning class. After Boussard lynches her father, Paula vows to avenge his death and immediately teams with Humfredo, an Indian servant who swears by his "Aztec blood" and "the love I bore my master" that he will be "unswervingly faithful" to Paula (17). Humfredo resembles the happy slaves in U.S. southern plantation novels, whose virtues are demonstrated by a willingness to sacrifice themselves for the comfort and safety of a master class whose superiority they instinctively recognize.

Paula's success in saving her nation hinges, in addition, on her willingness to make common cause with Mexican Indians. To advance their plot, Humfredo takes Paula to visit his mother, Marta, a priestess presiding over Aztec ceremonies at the chamber of the crested serpent, a huge monster that appears and crushes enemies at crucial times. Marta tells Paula that if she is to succeed in avenging her father's death and saving her nation, she must become a "daughter of the Aztecs" (14) by letting the serpent wind itself around her. After participating in the ritual, Paula dresses as a man and stains her face and hands brown in order to more effectively fight all "invaders and usurpers, for love of country and for revenge" (25).

In the end, after Paula, Humfredo, Marta, and their allies lure Boussard to the secret chamber, he is dispatched by the serpent. Immediately afterward, in a magnanimous act of individual land reform, Paula nobly offers her hacienda to Marta and Humfredo, who go there to live and thereafter "can count their cattle and horses by thousands." In this way, Emerald offers a fantasy solution to the persistent struggles over land, labor, race, and republican government in Mexico and the United States, one that romanticizes continuing, hierarchical power relations between whites and nonwhites even as it struggles to envision a different, post–civil war(s) future.

Paula is able to give her hacienda to her Indian allies only because she has another place of her own, an unusual "building of architectural elegance and superior mechanical finish" overlooking Mexico City, which she shares with her new American husband, Steager, a man "born to the saddle and warlike deeds" (28) who is now fighting with the Mexican liberals. At a critical moment, Steager impersonates an artist who has come to Mexico to "sketch scenes of the encampment of the greatest soldier of the Imperial army" (75), thereby alluding to the artists, newspapermen, and others who came to Mexico to document the French occupation. In the end, although the novel mobilizes sympathy on behalf of the Mexican liberals who resist the French, Emerald weds his heroine to Steager rather than to Hernando Vidal, a staunch Mexican liberal who "hated the Imperial government with the same bitterness as herself" (27), or any other Mexican hero.

The novel's fantasy solution thereby echoes the endings of so many U.S.-Mexico War–era story paper novelettes. Although the novel's final line lauds Mexican men who "live and die in the service of Republican Mexico," Paula Vallejo is finally "wooed and won" by a U.S. soldier who takes her away to live in "ease and plenty" (101).

In these ways, *The Crested Serpent* combines hemispheric republican solidarity and an anticolonial alliance in nation building with a romantic vision shaped by racism and fantasies of trans-American desire. Like a large body of U.S. popular literature that preceded it, the novel suggests how readily the U.S. embrace of the Monroe Doctrine and hemispheric intimacy could slide into coercion and control, and how egalitarianism available only to whites limited U.S. visions of a republican and democratic future in the Americas.

As Mexico became independent in the 1820s, U.S. political and literary culture promised solidarity against colonial rule. When a Texas war for independence to promote slavery in the 1830s culminated in a U.S. war against Mexico to annex Texas, its slave society, and all the lands from Texas to California in the 1840s, U.S. political and popular cultural visions divided sharply. Promoters of the expansion of the nation and of slavery saw heroic liberations; opponents of both lamented the use of violence to expand territory and slavery as an assault on republicanism in both Mexico and the United States. When conflicts over the expansion of slavery into territories taken from Mexico led to civil war in the 1860s, U.S. political, popular, and visual cultures again divided. While Mexicans faced their own civil war and French occupation, northerners imagined alliances with Mexico's liberals, yet worried that the Indian Juárez was their leader. Southerners, on the other hand, saw promise in Maximilian's empire. When the South fell in 1865, followed by Maximilian's defeat and death in 1867, northern victors worried that Mexican liberals led by a barbaric Indian could not possibly forge an effective republic. The only solution: Yankee tutelage.

These debates resonate in political tracts, elite novels, popular literature, and visual culture. Perhaps most powerfully, they resonated with the growing audience of U.S. readers who consumed romances in which manly Yankees wooed, won, and saved Mexican women—elite, white Mexican women. These novels taught the lesson that Mexican men were not ready to be manly heroes; indigenous Mexicans required the leadership of Yankee men as well as the intercession of elite white Mexican women with the wisdom to become wives of manly Yankees. The United States was white, male, republican, and powerful—all good. On the other hand, Mexico was mixed and too often indigenous, essentially female, incapable of republicanism, and thus fated to subordination. None of this was good for Mexicans, but was quite promising for a United States entering an era of capitalist expansion. The long-contested process of constructing a U.S. image of Mexico also helped build a powerful self-image for white USAmericans: they rightfully ruled at home, in territories taken from Mexico, and would rule in Mexico and elsewhere when opportunities emerged. Thus did conflicts in and against Mexico decisively shape and transform U.S. literature, culture, politics, and society during pivotal decades of nation building.

Notes

1. On republican conceptions of the literary, see Michael Warner, *Letters of the Republic* (Cambridge: Harvard University Press, 1992).

2. See Reginald Horsman, *Race and Manifest Destiny* (Cambridge: Harvard University Press, 1981).

3. Gretchen Murphy, *Hemispheric Imaginings* (Durham, N.C.: Duke University Press, 2005), 5, 2-3.

4. Ibid., 180.

5. Streeby, *American Sensations*, 81-158.

6. Doris Sommer, *Foundational Fictions* (Berkeley: University of California Press, 1991).

7. Timothy Flint, *Francis Berrian; or, The Mexican Patriot* (Boston: Cummings, Hilliard, 1826); following page citations come from this work. Although in the 1840s and 1850s, Flint's later, shorter works would be reissued by publishers of popular literature, *Francis Berrian* was published in Boston in 1826 and another edition appeared in Philadelphia in 1834, just before the emergence of the cheap-literature industry that began to flourish in the 1840s. See Frederick S. Stimson, "'Francis Berrian,'" *Hispania* 42, no. 4 (1959): 511-516; and Andrea Tinnemeyer, "Enlightenment Ideology and the Crisis of Whiteness in Francis Berrian and Caballero," *Western American Literature* 35, no. 1 (Spring 2000): 21-32.

8. Anna Brickhouse, *Transamerican Literary Relations and the Nineteenth-Century Public Sphere* (Cambridge: Cambridge University Press, 2004), 51. See also Rodrigo Lazo, *Writing to Cuba* (Chapel Hill: University of North Carolina Press, 2005).

9. *Xicoténcatl* (Austin: University of Texas Press, 1999), 7; following page citations come from this work. The first, Spanish-language, version of the novel is *Jicoténcal* (Philadelphia: William Stavely, 1826).

10. Enrique Florescano, *National Narratives in Mexico* (Norman: University of Oklahoma Press, 2006), 220-260.

11. Jesse Alemán, "The Other Country," *American Literary History* 18, no. 3 (Fall 2006): 406-426.

12. "The Female Warrior," in Jesse Alemán and Shelley Streeby, eds., *Empire and the Literature of Sensation* (New Brunswick, N.J.: Rutgers University Press, 2007); following page citations come from this work.

13. "'Bel of Prairie Eden: A Romance of Mexico," in ibid.; following page citations come from this work.

14. Robert Johannsen, *To the Halls of the Montezumas* (New York: Oxford University Press, 1985), 16.

15. "Magdalena the Beautiful Mexican Maid," in Alemán and Streeby, *Empire and the Literature of Sensation*; following page citations come from this work.

16. According to art historian Rick Stewart, Currier, who produced more than seventy lithographs of the U.S.-Mexico War, "initiated the concept of 'rush stock,' cheaply printed lithographs that were generated quickly after an event to capitalize on its public interest"; see, "Artists and Printmakers of the Mexican War," in Martha A. Sandweiss, ed., *Eyewitness to War* (Fort Worth, Tex.: Amon Carter Museum, 1989). See also Johannsen, *To the Halls of the Montezumas*, 222-230.

17. For more on how photographs of untended dead bodies violated sentimental ideals during the U.S Civil War, see Franny Nudelman, *John Brown's Body* (Durham: University of North Carolina Press, 2004).

18. All of these daguerreotypes are reproduced and expertly analyzed in Sandweiss, ed., *Eyewitness to War*.

19. Timothy Matovina, *The Alamo Remembered* (University of Texas Press, 1995).

20. Genaro Padilla, *"My History, Not Yours"* (Madison: University of Wisconsin Press, 1993); Rosaura Sánchez, *Telling Identities* (Minneapolis: University of Minnesota Press, 1995).

21. Kirsten Silva Gruesz, *Ambassadors of Culture* (Princeton: Princeton University Press, 2002), 113, 115.

22. See Andrew Rolle, *The Lost Cause* (Norman: University of Oklahoma Press, 1992).

23. See María DeGuzmán, *Spain's Long Shadow* (Minneapolis: University of Minnesota Press, 2005).

24. See Jesse Lerner, "Imported Nationalism," *Evil Winter 5* (2001–2002); http://www.cabinetmagazine.org/issues/5/importednationalism.php, accessed 11/1/2009.

25. See Manet, *The Execution of Maximilian* (1867–1869); and in the United States, Henry Flint, *Mexico under Maximilian* (1867); Frederic Hall, *Life of Maximilian I, Late Emperor of Mexico, with a Sketch of the Empress Carlota* (1868); John Dagnall, *The Mexican; or, Love and Land. Founded on the Invasion of Maximilian* (1868).

CHAPTER 4

Mexican Merchants and Teamsters on the Texas Cotton Road, 1862–1865

DAVID MONTEJANO

Perhaps nothing speaks more pointedly to the general amnesia with regards to Mexico and Mexicans in the history of the United States than their omission from the expansive American Civil War literature. What mention has been made of Mexicans and Mexico has generally focused on border troubles and on Mexican and Texas Mexican military participation—in other words, on bandits and soldiers. Here I wish to focus on Mexican merchants and teamsters and describe the vital commercial role they played in sustaining the western Confederacy. At the most basic level, I want to introduce them as important but overlooked participants in the American Civil War. On a more abstract plane, this chapter suggests that the "Texas cotton road," in existence only for the duration of the Civil War, heralded the potential of the U.S.-Mexican borderlands as an emerging commercial corridor in a global economy.

Much has been written about the "blockade runners" of the eastern Confederacy, of the sleek ships running out of Mobile or Wilmington on their way to Havana or Nassau. Little has been written, however, about the blockade running carried out on lumbering ox carts in the western portion of the Confederate states, or what was called the Trans-Mississippi Department. Historians who specialize in nineteenth-century western history have some awareness of the cotton road that traversed Texas southward toward Mexico, but they have not examined the character of this trade nor have they ventured beyond the Texas-Mexican border. What I argue in this essay is that when the Union blockade threatened the economy of the trans-Mississippi Confederacy and the demand for soldiers depleted the population of eligible white men, Mexican merchants and teamsters in essence assumed much of the critical freighting operations for the region. They took those roles not from sympathy with the Confederacy or slavery but in pursuit of profit and good wages.

This signaled an abrupt change in Anglo-Mexican relations in Texas. Mexican merchants and teamsters had been excluded from the expanding cotton economy of mid-nineteenth-century Texas. Virulent anti-Mexican sentiment, especially in the form of vigilante attacks on Mexican cart trains, had driven many Mexicans from the mercantile and freighting trade by the time the state seceded in 1861. But beginning in 1863 until the end of the war, a veritable army of Mexican teamsters—perhaps as many as fifteen thousand—handled the import and export of goods vital to the functioning of the Trans-Mississippi Confederacy.

Given the history of conflictual relations between Mexicans and Anglos in Texas, the reliance of the western Confederacy on Mexican merchants and teamsters for freighting and marketing cotton points clearly to its increasingly desperate need for labor and revenue as the Civil War wore on. The recognition and encouragement of this Mexican presence by Confederate authorities stood in contrast to the indifferent or hostile posture of Texas state authorities during the previous decade.

On the Eve of the Civil War

Anglo-Mexican relations in Texas in the decade following the Mexican American War of 1846–1848 were expectedly antagonistic. In Central and Southeast Texas, where substantial numbers of Anglo and European immigrants had settled, entire Mexican communities were uprooted. Mexicans were driven from Austin in 1853 and again in 1855, from Seguin in 1854, from the counties of Matagorda and Colorado in 1856, and from Uvalde in 1857. An Anglo pioneer in the Victoria area voiced a common sentiment of the time: "White folks and Mexicans were never made to live together, anyhow, and the Mexicans had no business here. They were getting so impertinent, and were well protected by the laws, that the Americans would just have to get together and drive them all out of the country."[1]

Beyond the bitter resentments left from the Mexican War, a frequent justification was that Mexicans were encouraging slaves to escape to Mexico. In 1854, delegates from nine counties representing slavery interests had met in Gonzales to form vigilante committees to prevent the flight of slaves to Mexico. Frederick Olmsted, after his 1855 "saddle-trip" through Texas, described the subsequent expulsions of "lower-class" peons accused of being horse thieves and consorters in slave insurrection. One newspaper item collected by Olmsted tells the story of the period plainly:

> MATAGORDA. — The people of Matagorda County have held a Meeting and ordered every Mexican to leave the country. To strangers this may seem wrong, but we hold it to be perfectly Right and highly necessary, but a word of explanation should be given. In the first place, then, there are none but the lower class or "Peon" Mexicans in the county; secondly, they have no fixed domicile, but hang around the plantations, taking the likeliest negro girls for wives; and, thirdly, they often steal horses, and these girls, too, and endeavor to run them to Mexico. We should rather have anticipated an appeal to Lynch law, than the mild course which has been adopted.[2]

Even in San Antonio, the former capital of Texas, there was an attempt to drive away a large section of the Mexican population, but the plan failed because the Germans, who would have formed a major element of the proposed vigilante committee, refused to support these efforts. Nonetheless, by 1856, San Antonio had been half-deserted by its Mexican population. The government, the "money-capital," and much of the land base of the former Mexican elite were in the hands of the Anglo pioneers. Most of the mechanics and smaller shopkeepers were German, while the Mexicans appeared "to have almost no other business than that of carting goods." Nearly 60 percent of the Mexican work force, according to Olmsted, were cartmen.[3]

The Mexican cartmen, however, would suffer the same fate as the despised "peon" of Southeast Texas. During the summer and fall of 1857, Mexican teamsters who carted freight along the San Antonio–Goliad highway were attacked by masked bands. The troubles came to be known as the "Cart Wars." The assailants were believed to be Anglo teamsters who resented the competition from Mexicans. Despite seventy-five murders, civil authorities were unwilling to arrest the attackers. The raids proved successful, and Mexicans were effectively removed from the freight business between San Antonio and the Gulf Coast ports.[4]

Beyond the Nueces River, however, where the great majority of the population was Mexican, such direct assaults and efforts were frequently met with outright resistance. The most dramatic example is the uprising in 1859 led by Juan Cortina, a leading landowner angered by the "mistreatment" of Mexicans at the hands of the new Americans. Cortina's band of rancheros seized control of Brownsville and defeated a unit of Texas Rangers before being driven to the Mexican side of the Rio Grande.

Beyond the Anglo line of settlement, the new American authorities generally governed in concert with the old Mexican elite through what I have previously described as a "peace structure." Such an alliance was not necessarily an awkward one, for the landed Mexican elite and the southern planter elite shared a similar worldview regarding land and labor. In San Antonio and Laredo, this cultural affinity was marked by a few prominent marriages between young Mexican *hacendados* and southern belles. Santos Benavides of Laredo best symbolizes the alliance. Cortina, on the other hand, represents the aristocratic defender of the commoner.[5]

Thus, in Central and Southeast Texas, where considerable numbers of Mexicans and Anglos lived, the tragic aftermath one expects of war—recriminations, dispossession of land and belongings, violence, and revenge—was much in evidence in the 1850s. In deep South Texas, where the Anglo elite constituted a small and conspicuous presence, the new political order generally relied on an alliance with key members of the old Mexican elite.

Such was the setting on the eve of the American Civil War. Texas Mexicans were generally indifferent toward the Civil War. They had not been a party to the political debates surrounding secession nor did they have much sympathy for the Confederacy or the institution of slavery. When hostilities broke out, Mexicans generally claimed exemption from military service on the grounds that they were not U.S. citizens. Nonetheless, Jerry Thompson estimates that in Texas three thousand Mexicans served the Confederacy and nine hundred, the Union. Support for one side or another basically followed the political alignments established during the immediate annexation period. Santos Benavides of Laredo, an ally of the new Anglo-Texan political elite, defended the Rio Grande territory for the Confederacy, while "robber baron" Juan Cortina favored the Union and delighted in attacking the Texan-Confederate forces. But most Mexicans who enlisted on one side or the other, according to González Quiroga, did so for economic reasons. The promise of a monthly salary, a uniform, and a rifle was sufficient inducement for enlistment. Failure to live up to the salary promise often led to desertion, underscoring again the tenuous loyalties of Mexicans to either side of the conflict.[6]

Despite the indifference of the Mexican population to the American Civil War, the sudden transformation of the Rio Grande into the Confederacy's sole unimpeded link to world trade lured many to work for the trans-Mississippi Confederacy. The prospect of wages moved many small ranchers to become teamsters in the booming cotton trade, and the prospect of profit moved many Spanish Mexican merchants to become involved in organizing the trade. With the onset of the Civil War, Mexico and Mexicans became critical elements for the commerce of the trans-Mississippi Confederacy. As González Quiroga has noted, the northern Mexican states of Chihuahua, Coahuila, Nuevo León, Tamaulipas, Zacatecas, Durango, and San Luis Potosí provided the South with large quantities of hides, flour, salt, sugar, coffee, lead, powder, and rope.[7] Equally important, after the blockade of southern ports by the U.S. Navy, Mexico provided the only channel for southern trade with world markets. Thus, maintaining cordial relations with Mexico became an important concern to the Confederacy, providing some protection for Mexicans in Texas, especially for those engaged in carting goods for the Confederacy.

The Cotton Road and International Markets

Beginning in 1862, the second year of the Civil War, planters in East Texas, as well as in Louisiana and Arkansas, began to look westward, toward the Mexican border, to market their cotton. By this time, the port cities of the western Confederacy had either been captured or effectively blockaded by Union forces. Before the blockade, steamers on the Sabine and Red rivers had carried cotton to New Orleans, but New Orleans was blockaded early, in June 1861, and captured by Union forces in April 1862. The same situation confronted planters and merchants who had previously relied on the Brazos and Trinity rivers in East Texas to ferry cotton to Galveston. After Galveston's temporary capture in October 1862, the port city was not a viable option. For a time, shallow-draught ships, or lighters, were able to evade the naval blockade by using the barrier islands and navigating down the Laguna Madre, but that option, too, was closed after the temporary capture of Corpus Christi in late 1863. The Union navy, however, could not extend its blockade to the Rio Grande, an international river whose use by Mexico was protected by the Treaty of Guadalupe Hidalgo. Thus, the only secure trade route for planters, merchants, and Confederate officials of the Trans-Mississippi Department was westward over land to the Mexican border, and then down the Rio Bravo, on the Mexican side, to a port town called Bagdad, a few miles below Matamoros.

This tiny port had been named Bagdad because it had been used as a disembarkation point for a U.S. Army camel experiment during the 1850s. During the Civil War, it became, as James Irby puts it, "the backdoor" of the Confederacy. Barges and small steamers flying the Mexican flag would take the cotton "outside the bar," where ocean-going vessels flying under various European flags were anchored, waiting their turn to load or unload cargo. At the height of the cotton trade, as many as two hundred ships were anchored outside the bar. Planters, in other words, were not the only concerned parties looking for a reliable cotton outlet. Merchants from every Western European nation, as well as from New England, were anxious to have secure access to southern cotton. Bagdad became a "Babylon" boomtown, to cite one apt description, where French, Germans, Irish, Hungarians, English, Spaniards, and Mexicans used a mixture of foreign languages to communicate.[8]

The business papers of José San Román and Charles Stillman, two prominent merchants based in Brownsville-Matamoros, provide an invaluable view of this war-related trade. Inquiries and advice about the cotton trade dominate their papers.[9]

Charles Stillman, from a Connecticut mercantile family, had been a merchant in Matamoros and northern Mexico since 1828. In this contested frontier, Stillman had demonstrated an ability to trade with friend and foe alike, even while they were at war. He had greeted Taylor's invading army when it occupied Matamoros in 1846. His Civil War correspondence with his commercial agents in New York and New Orleans (and in Monterrey and Manchester) is a further testament to his studied political neutrality and mercantile instincts.

José San Román, a Spanish citizen, had settled in Matamoros in 1846 as a representative of a dry goods firm based in New Orleans. By the time of the Civil War, he was a well-established and prosperous commission merchant. San Román's exports were silver bullion, lead, sugar, tobacco, goatskins, liquor, and coffee. His imports were clothing and dry goods. When the blockade disrupted the lucrative New Orleans–Havana trade, the trade axis shifted westward to Matamoros-Havana and gave the commercial house of San Román newfound importance. With the onset of war, he left the clothing and dry goods business to concentrate on the cotton export trade. While Stillman's mercantile network was based primarily in Texas, San Román was a key merchant for the elites of northern Mexico and the Lower Rio Grande Valley.

As early as November 1861, the commercial house of San Román was informing its business network in northern Mexico about a new trade with Texas: "A new trade in all kinds of products is beginning to open on this border with the interior of Texas."[10] Lead, woolen goods, manufactured cotton goods, dry goods, medicine, and, of course, the ingredients to manufacture gunpowder were all items desired in Texas.

Of particular note for San Román and Stillman was the potentially lucrative investment in cotton. English, French, German, and Spanish mills—not to mention New England mills—were scrambling to find new sources of cotton. San Román, responding to a request from Barcelona, described the situation to merchant Antonio Costa of Havana as follows (July 1862): "I am aware of the kind of cotton that Barcelona needs; in this plaza there are no great quantities to sell and one has to buy what can be found . . . land transportation to the Texas interior is every day more costly, up to 7 cents per pound has been paid."[11]

Likewise, a typical inquiry (February 3, 1863) to Charles Stillman about trade in Brownsville-Matamoros reads as follows: "The object of my present communication is to ascertain . . . whether I should conclude to open a trade with your section of the country and make purchases there. If I could get the goods transported by Mexican carts to Victoria on the Guadalupe River—and cotton carted back from that point by the same means—what prices would I have to pay for freights to that point & back to Brownsville—"[12] The inquiry came from Nacogdoches in far East Texas.

For a few years, the commerce of the trans-Mississippi district with world markets would rest in the hands of commission merchants such as the Vance brothers, Jean Baptiste Lacoste, and John Twohig in San Antonio; John Leyendecker in Laredo; and San Román and Stillman in Brownsville-Matamoros. They would organize the trade circuits that gave rise to the cotton road.

The cotton road was not one road but consisted of all the routes that cotton followed on its way to Mexico for export. It was actually a network of rail lines, water routes, and land roads that reached inland as far as southern Arkansas and western Louisiana. From Jefferson, Texas, on the northern border with Louisiana, the distance to Brownsville was 600 or 700 miles, depending on the route. Poor road conditions and bad weather could make a one-way oxcart trip take as long as eleven months in one direction. One cart train that loaded at nearby Pittsburg, Texas, for example, left on September 1, 1862, and reached Brownsville on July 22, 1863.[13] The rail system was poorly developed and maintained and consisted primarily of a spiderlike configuration in the southeastern part of the state. Its longest segment, some 160 miles, linked Beaumont, near the Louisiana border, with Alleyton, the terminus of the Buffalo Bayou, Brazos and Colo-

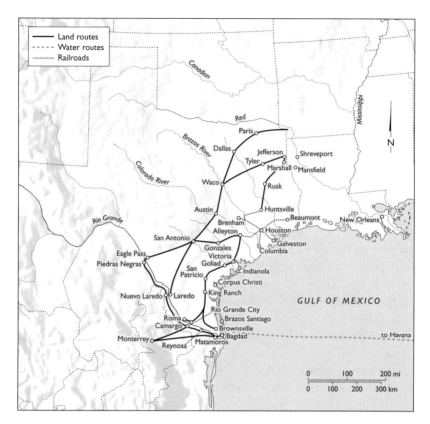

Map 4.1. The Texas Cotton Road

rado Railway (BBB&C). From Alleyton, the Mexican border lay some 300 miles away, or a few months distant by oxcart. How else to transport the cotton? With all water routes blocked, ox and mule cart trains were the only way.

The difficulties of this mode of freighting were many. Flooded rivers and roads, drought, shortages of rope and bagging material, and, most critically, shortages of animals and carts all bedeviled planters, cotton factors, and Confederate officials. Too much rain in East Texas had hampered cotton purchases, wrote Stillman's agent from Alleyton:

> We have had a great deal of rain within the last month which rendered it impossible to Travel about and I have done but little in the way of purchasing Cotton, but as soon as the weather will permit will use all my

exertions. . . . There is but little cot. on the Colorado for Sale and prices going up everyday. it is now worth 28 to 30c. I expect we will have to buy our cot. on Brazos River and take the chance of getting it over the Road to this place.[14]

Drought, on the other hand, also plagued South Texas. The same purchasing agent described the effects: "I did not send my Mexican back from San Patricio because it was as much as we could do to get to Mr. Belden Rancho there being no grape nor corn to be had in the whole route from San Anto. The consequence was that his horse gave out."[15] The drought of 1862–1864 was so severe that shallow-draught steamers stopped plying the lower Rio Grande between Roma and Matamoros.

War-related risks added to the woes of carting cotton. Threats of a "Yankee invasion" often forced planters and merchants to move cotton away from the coast as quickly as possible. When Brownsville fell into the hands of the federals in November 1863, the result was disastrous for those on the road from the King Ranch. Retreating Confederate troops burned all cotton on that leg of the cotton road. Supercargo George García, supervising a cotton train under contract to Stillman, penned an eloquent letter describing his circuitous journey up the Rio Grande, away from Brownsville:

Laredo, Texas Nov 25th 1863
Chas. Stillman Esq.
    Sir
Your cotton 77 bales have arrived at this place today and it was put across the river immediately. I contracted with your agent to haul it from where I received it to Brownsville, for 9c a pound. I arrived at Salt Lakes and there I was ordered with the loading to go to Davis Ranch, not finding any one authorized by you to receive it, I then drove up the Rio Grande and at the Sauce, Major Benavides ordered me to this place and would have burnt the cotton, if I had not left so soon. I drove very fast and on that account I lost some oxen. For such extra hauling I demand 6c additional per pound. I hope and trust you will come or send right off some one, to settle with me and receive your cotton it is on the other side well taken care of by me. I also charge you $1 per bale for cross it over the river.
    I remain yours,
George Garcia[16]

Mexico provided no refuge from military maneuvers. Indeed, crossing into Mexico meant crossing into another civil war, one that had raged
intermittently since 1858 between Juarista liberal republicans and anti-
Juarista conservatives and monarchists. At the invitation of the latter, the
French invaded in 1862 and installed Maximilian as emperor of Mexico in
1864. Matamoros and Bagdad experienced the vagaries of Mexican civil
war as they passed through different hands between 1862 and 1865. Juarista Juan Cortina, the feared robber baron of South Texas, had control
for a spell, as did the anti-Juarista royalists and their French allies.

Regardless of which side was in command, all recognized and encouraged the cotton trade. According to one source, trade with the Confederacy for a time accounted for two-thirds of Mexico's national income.
The revenues from the customhouses overcame ideological preferences
and made for enduring neutrality on the part of Mexican authorities. The
complex politics of the Mexican civil conflicts did not upset the flow of
cotton through Matamoros.[17]

Thus, in spite of many obstacles and risks, a great commerce sprang
up along the cotton road. Its major shipping points became boomtowns
with a highly diverse population. Thus, the population of Alleyton, in the
description of the Houston Tri-Weekly Telegraph, was "composed principally of Mexican teamsters, carts, teams, dogs, wives, cotton buyers,
cotton sellers, merchants, pedlars, speculators, foreigners, and soldiers."[18]
Alleyton as a shipping center became a miniature version of Bagdad, the
port at the receiving end.

So how much cotton was carted down the cotton road? A hurricane in
the late nineteenth century destroyed the municipal records of Matamoros, thus making a precise accounting based on import duties impossible.
An indication of the magnitude of this trade, however, can be seen by
the duties collected at the customhouses at Reynosa, Nuevo Laredo, and
Piedras Negras in 1863. According to the calculations of Robert Kerby,
these duties, amounting to some $175,000 per month, suggest that be-
tween 21,000 and 29,000 bales passed through these ports each month.[19]
In other words, at least 250,000 bales, and perhaps as many as 348,000,
crossed into Mexico through the customhouses above Matamoros in 1863.

Confirmation of the magnitude of the trade comes from Liverpool-
Manchester, England, the primary destination of southern cotton. The
quarterly reports of the Cotton Supply Reporter (1861–1866), an industry newspaper from Manchester, tabulate raw cotton imports according
to their point of origin.[20] If these reports are organized by year and ori-

Table 4.1. United Kingdom Raw Cotton Imports from North America, 1861–1866

	No. of Bales Shipped					
Shipped From	1861	1862	1863	1864	1865	1866
Southern U.S. ports	6,746,438	30,431	9,973	8,108	467,817	3,118,817
Bahamas & Turks Island	7	43,220	202,009	227,814	129,336	4,158
Atlantic Mexican ports	—	27,960	172,126	227,854	326,640	3,145
Total	6,746,445	101,611	384,108	463,776	923,793	3,126,120

Note: Selected ports only.
Source: *Cotton Supply Reporter* (Manchester, Eng.).

gin, one gets a sense of the volume of cotton flowing through Matamoros-Bagdad to England (see Table 4.1).

Table 4.1 demonstrates that for the southern ports, the sharp decline in cotton exports from 1861 to 1862, with recovery beginning in 1866, came with the interregnum of the Civil War. Between 1862 and 1865, southern cotton was squeezing past the northern blockade through the Bahamas and Mexico. At the height of this trade in 1864, over 400,000 bales arrived in England. The Bahamas, and Nassau in particular, was the destination of preference for the blockade runners of the Deep South. Mexico was the destination for cotton from the western Confederacy. What is striking is that the amount of cotton exported from Mexico between 1862 and 1865 surpassed that of the better-known Bahamas' trade by more than 150,000 bales. Once the war ended, exports from both points of blockade evasion collapsed.

The Making of "Mexican Cotton"

During the Civil War era, Mexico was not a cotton-growing country. "Mexican cotton" was southern cotton that had been sold to Mexican-based owners. It was, in other words, a legal definition based on respect for Mexico's neutrality. Neutrality meant that the hostilities of the Civil War were in a sense suspended on Mexican soil. Thus, one found a curious mix of people—soldiers, deserters, spies, consular officials, merchants, planters, northerners, southerners, Europeans, and, of course, Mexicans—commingling in the neutral ports along the Lower Rio Grande.

Respect for Mexico's neutrality also meant that the rules of the market regarding ownership and profit held sway over the war exigencies of North and South. But these rules were subject to military challenge. Political and military contemporaries from both the Union and the Confederacy were aware that there was no such thing as Mexican cotton except in a technically legal sense; authorities from both sides made repeated attempts to control the trade. For planters and merchants, "foreign" ownership surfaced as a protective strategy, however tenuous the protection.

On the Union side, the export of Mexican cotton was seen as a poorly disguised ruse. Admiral Farragut and his subordinates believed that the cotton was being shipped "without good faith transfer to Mexican ownership and was therefore subject to seizure for that reason, although the bills of lading, as certified by the American Consul at Matamoros, were in perfect order."[21] In early February 1862, a man of war, the U.S.S. Portsmouth, appeared off the mouth of the Rio Grande, creating "a panic in the market" and paralyzing the cotton trade. Two more U.S. steamers joined it, setting off rumors of a possible invasion. Then in a direct challenge to the suspect cotton trade, the U.S.S. Portsmouth seized the British steamship Labuan as it loaded Mexican cotton. The British consul based in Matamoros protested angrily to no avail. The Labuan and its cargo were sent to a federal prize court for adjudication. In a letter to the Avendaño brothers of New Orleans, commission merchants with an interest in the Matamoros trade, San Román noted that "the above-named Frigate has seized the English steamer that was carrying cotton and it is said has sent it to the north . . . there will be difficulties in this matter."[22]

The three U.S. warships effectively blockaded the river for a month before a warship from England and one from France appeared off the mouth. The Brownsville Flag reported that the British frigate Phaeton, commanded by Admiral Teatham and carrying fifty-six guns, and the French corvette Bertholet, commanded by Jonquieres, with six guns, eighty pounds rifled, had come on a "visit": "Admiral Teatham speaks in the most favorable terms of the South, and is evidently in sympathy with our revolution. . . . He denies being here, however, to take any part in the difficulty, or to do any thing with the blockade, but simply states his mission to be to keep the mouth of the Rio Grande open to the trade of the world, at all hazards. The English evidently do not intend to allow the paper blockade of the Yankees to extend itself to the ports of Mexico."[23] San Román believed that the situation would soon change, as he explained in a letter to his New York commercial agent, M. Echeverría and Company: "for the moment I am not ready to begin trading because of the many difficulties that currently present themselves on this frontier; outside the bar of the Mouth of the River we have some 18 boats loaded with merchandise and unloading them is difficult; also there are two steamships of war one English and the other French; it is believed that soon cotton can be exported."[24]

European gunboat diplomacy effectively ended the Union's attempt to extend the blockade to the Rio Grande. The Lincoln administration did not desire to engage in hostilities with the English or the French. The Labuan was later released by the prize court.

With the realization that the North would not block the export of cotton at Bagdad, a "cotton feast," in the apt description of Brownsville historian Harbert Davenport, began: "By October, 1862, all merchants in northern Mexico, including Texans and other foreigners, were joining in the cotton feast, buying Texas cotton in transit on the sandy roads of south Texas, wherever it could be found. . . . it could no longer be said, much less proved, that cotton moving through Matamoros and Bagdad was not Mexican owned."[25] Mexican merchants who had been shipping specie through Matamoros, Davenport later added, "began using portions of their capital to speculate in cotton."[26]

Perhaps more frustrating for Union navy commanders was the fact that the New York customhouse was clearing contraband-loaded vessels for Matamoros. One commander of the Eastern Gulf Blockading Squadron, after boarding a Matamoros-bound ship cleared from New York, wrote a letter of protest to secretary of the navy Gideon Welles about the "gross abuse of the privilege of a neutral port, and that by vessels under our own flag, sailing with regular clearances from our own customhouses." Hope of "crushing the rebellion," noted Lt. Comm. Joseph Couthouy, would "be utterly vain, so long as unlimited supplies are allowed to be poured from our Northern ports into the heart of the State, through the Rio Grande and Matamoros, which is but another name for Brownsville, there being hardly a firm of any note in the first city that has not a branch house in the latter also." Couthouy concluded his report in a tone of exasperation: "It may be that all this correspondence and trading with and consigning cargoes to so notorious a partisan of the rebels as Charles Stillman is perfectly legitimate, honorable, and eminently patriotic, but it still somewhere conflicts with my preconceived ideas of what should be regarded by every loyal citizen and honest man as illegal, dishonorable, and traitorous to the last degree."

Such reports prompted Secretary Welles to protest to treasury secretary Salmon P. Chase, in spring of 1863, to exert greater control over the issuance of clearances. Welles complained that there were about two hundred ships "having regular clearances from Northern ports off the mouth of the Rio Grande, waiting to discharge their cargoes and receive cotton." Welles urged Chase to curb the illicit trade.[27]

The Union army did attempt to stop the cotton trade when it occupied Brownsville in November 1863, but this merely forced the cotton road to cross into Mexico at Piedras Negras and Laredo. Laredo, as a contemporary witness put it, "suddenly sprang into prominence as the greatest cotton shipping point in the South. The Federals sent an expedition from Brownsville against this point, but Benavides with his regiment of cavalry, nearly all Mexicans—drove the enemy back, and the cotton trade continued in its increasing volume until the evacuation of Brownsville in 1864."[28]

Thus the export of cotton continued unabated as did northern commercial participation in it. After several months of occupation, the federal troops were withdrawn (in April 1864) in order to mount a military campaign along the Red River in northern Louisiana. The military objective remained the same: to disrupt the cotton trade of the trans-Mississippi Confederacy.

If U.S. naval officers were rankled by the presence of "dishonorable" northern merchants in the Bagdad trade, the Confederate military command was equally upset by the cotton speculators and planters who put profit above southern honor. The fact that southern cotton might find its way to New York was a minor concern compared to the problems the western Confederacy faced in attempting to procure cotton for export. Export of government-owned cotton was seen as the best and perhaps only way to secure funds for munitions and other war matériel. This strategy pitted military officials against speculators and cotton merchants, who easily outbid Confederate purchase offers, and it pitted them against planters who were not keen on accepting Confederate currency or certificates. This paralleled the difficulty the Union was having regulating the northern merchants, brokers, and politicians involved in the Matamoros trade.

Unlike their brethren east of the Mississippi, the growers of the Trans-Mississippi Department were reluctant to sell their cotton to the government for Confederate currency or certificates; many refused. The growers of the western Confederacy had the option of transporting their cotton to the Mexican border, where a specie market awaited them. Indeed, the specie market came to them as commission merchants traveled the plantations of East Texas looking to buy cotton. As Robert Kerby has noted, "private speculators, who were able to offer planters the highest prices for cotton, were rapidly cornering the stocks of cotton needed to barter for the goods. Without some sort of regulation, there was real danger that the speculators might succeed in monopolizing commerce with Mexico."[29]

As Confederate currency lost value, the predicament for the Confederate states became increasingly desperate. It was becoming "More & more difficult Evry day," as plantation owner Robert Clark explained to Stillman, "to buy property unless on a specie basis."[30] Moreover, rumors of possible "impressment" moved some Texas planters to seek foreign buyers. Thus, T. A. Jackson of Brenham petitioned San Román to claim Jackson's cotton: "If you can send me carts or wagons to carry two hundred Bales I would like for you to do so as it is impossible to get wagons here to carry cotton off. I have two hundred Bales here and I want you to claim it as there is such rumor here that the government will take all the cotton that is shipped to Mexico unless owned by some House in Mexico or some other foreign firm."[31]

To complicate matters, Texas authorities frequently contravened or weakened Confederate cotton policies. In 1862, the Legislature created a State Military Board whose mission was to equip state militia on the basis of cotton purchases and exports, thus entering the state into direct competition with Confederate purchasing agents. Governor Lubbock and later Governor Murrah also proved responsive to the pleas of planters for exemptions from Confederate policy.

Bureaucratic mismanagement, internal competition within the Trans-Mississippi Department, and inconsistent policies compounded the problems. A prime example surfaced in early 1863. Majors Simeon Hart and Charles Russell, quartermasters of San Antonio and Brownsville, respectively, had recommended tackling the transport problem by assembling cotton at San Antonio, Goliad, and Santa Gertrudis and permitting Mexican merchants to come for it. The plan was put into operation in January 1863, but the following month Gen. John B. Magruder, commanding officer of the District of Texas, issued regulations forbidding cotton export by anyone other than authorized government agents, thus effectively eliminating Mexican merchants from the trade. Magruder was reaffirming an earlier prohibition.

This elicited a strong protest from Gov. Santiago Vidaurri of Nuevo León on behalf of Mexican merchants. Vidaurri followed up by refusing to let Mexican carts cross over into Texas. The policy tempest was settled when the Confederate War Department issued an order forbidding interference with the cotton trade west of the Mississippi by the Confederate military command. According to Davenport, General Magruder and other Confederate officers resented the order, considering it "a sop to the speculators who had been buying Confederate cotton at high prices for cash." As a result, Magruder, not having any interest in guarding a speculative trade, basically left Brownsville unprotected.[32] The federal army would take Brownsville in November 1863 without encountering any resistance.

In Davenport's dismissive summary, the handling of the cotton trade illustrates "the progressive stupidity of the Confederate Government." The Confederate government looked to Matamoros for essential supplies but never developed a comprehensive plan for managing this trade. Instead, the Brownsville–Santa Gertrudis area was occupied "by an army of incompetent 'agents,' each of whom had authority to sell cotton and buy supplies, though destitute of business experience, common honesty, and ordinary good sense."[33]

The competing interests of growers, commission merchants, state politicians, and military officials made for a chaotic and ever-changing cotton market in the western Confederacy. Mexican interests also acted to counter any tight Confederate regulation of cotton export, much as English and French interests had acted to challenge the Union's seizure of "foreign-owned" cotton. Thus, domestic and international considerations allowed for the unrestricted flow of southern cotton as Mexican cotton. Foreign ownership protected southern cotton from Confederate confiscation on land and from Union confiscation at sea.

Mexican Merchants and the Cotton Trade

U.S. naval intelligence was correct that many Brownsville merchants had taken on a Mexican hue simply to evade any problem with the blockade. Confederate citizens and supporters involved in the export trade were under pressure to disguise their property interests. Some merchants, like "Connecticut Yankee" Charles Stillman, followed a sort of market neutrality and attempted to maintain trade with both North and South in spite of hostilities. Thus, shortly after the outbreak of war, Stillman was receiving advice from his business partner in New York that wool for army blankets would be in high demand. But the Matamoros trade was coming under scrutiny, so along with the market advice came a caution—that he ship goods "in name of some mesican or Foreigner":

New York August 28. 1861

    Friend Charley

We have just received word from the Costom house that they will clear our vessel. which is a relief to us I don't beleav they will clear any more. My opinion is you could not do so well aney whear [else] with your Wool. For all the Woolen manufacters are to [make?] for Government on coars goods & [Starr?] Blankets for the army . . . dont ship the Wool in your name ship it in name of some mesican or Foreigner. Be careful what you write for we are watched on all sides.[34]

Heeding this advice, Stillman began to use Jeremiah Galván and Santiago Yturria as fronts, or "cutouts," in order to disguise the nature of his transactions. A few months later, Mifflin Kenedy and Richard King, business partners of Stillman's, transferred ownership of their riverboats to Mexican registry. The three were heavily involved in *los algodones* (cotton), with King's rancho functioning as a depot for Confederate cotton during most of the war period. The new owners of the riverboats were Mexican friends of Stillman's, Kenedy's, and King's. This semiclandestine business of Stillman and associates hints at an intriguing tale about the triumph of the market over sectionalism and war. My focus here is on the so-called Mexican friends who made this possible.

The House of Yturria

The Mexican merchants, it turns out, were not simply front men. Jeremiah Galván and Santiago Yturria were successful merchants in their own right. One account estimates that Galván was taking in $150,000 in receipts per month; Yturria was doing even better. Strategically positioned as the British vice-consul in Matamoros, Galván facilitated the business affairs of his older brother Francisco. Bernardo, the youngest of the three Yturria brothers, was assigned to Houston to act as Francisco's agent. The Yturria brothers were a powerful mercantile clan in Brownsville-Matamoros. While supportive of their friend Carlos Stillman, they did not hesitate to become directly involved in the Texas cotton trade. The Yturria family memoir provides an interesting account of one of their commission merchants working from Alleyton, a major shipping point on the cotton road.[35] Rafael Alderete was Francisco Yturria's roving agent in 1862 and 1863, traveling throughout Central and East Texas, Arkansas, and western Louisiana, selling Yturria's merchandise and buying and shipping cotton to Matamoros. In April 1862, he was at Alleyton, bargaining for the best deals in a chaotic cotton market and keeping an eye out for a rumored Yankee invasion following the fall of New Orleans. The ensuing panic had moved planters to sell at bargain rates: "There would be nothing to lose because every day it will be cheaper, due as much to the lack of freighters as to the fear that it will be lost when it is seized by the enemy or [ordered] burnt [by Confederate officials]. The enemy is now able to come ashore whenever it wants . . . so all cotton near the shore is very exposed."[36] Six weeks later, in mid-July 1862, Alderete's warning had been realized. "Not only have [the Yankees] seized the boats that were arriving with cotton," he wrote, "but they have also come ashore and taken said item." Alderete was referring to the Union blockading the fleet off Galveston.[37]

Compounding the situation was competition with other merchants at Alleyton: "This has become a stopping place for peddlers, many coming from San Antonio with cloth, bagging, and Mexican rope and shoes and some other items." Alderete wanted to take Yturria's merchandise to Houston, where "we can get better prices than here. . . . But it is somewhat difficult to take and bring a load to Houston because of the poor condition of the railroad. Still, I hope to load up two or three cars when I put together the rest of our goods and by these same means bring the cotton which we have over there."[38]

Later, on the way back from Houston, the Yturria cotton "escaped a great fire on the railroad. Only our cotton was saved. The agent is a friend of mine, and he puts our cotton on the covered cars whenever he is able to."[39]

After a year of weathering such difficulties on the road, the pressure finally got to Alderete. In one of his final letters from the road, written May 27, 1863, from Columbus (across from Alleyton), Alderete bluntly tells Yturria that "life here is intolerable, and even more so considering that it is not in your best interest, given the rise of [prices for] cotton and freight. As for myself, I am quite convinced that, the economic advantages notwithstanding, all of this is not worth it. No amount of money can compensate for what I am suffering physically and emotionally."[40]

When Brownsville fell to the Union forces in November of 1863, momentarily slowing the cotton trade, Alderete left the commission business and returned to the Yturria home in Camargo.[41]

The House of San Román

Arguably the most prominent merchant of the "twin cities," overshadowing even the well-known figure of Charles Stillman, was José San Román. Although San Román and many of his associates were Spaniards, their base of operation in northern Mexico—as well as their Spanish culture—made them Mexican merchants whenever they crossed into the Texas interior. In Texas, Spaniards were often seen as high-class Mexicans, in part because many Mexican-born elite members claimed to be Spanish rather than Mexican. In a region that had changed hands four times in forty years—from Spain to Mexico (1821) to the Republic of Texas (1836) to the United States (1845) and then to the Confederacy (1861)—the question of citizenship was not likely to count as much as cultural identity or skin coloration. On this frontier, the distinction between "Hispanic" and "Mexican" was tenuous and at times irrelevant. In short, like the identity of Mexican cotton, the identity of the Mexican merchant was a construction of sorts.

San Román's mercantile network was quite extensive, with significant commercial relations throughout northern Mexico and Europe, with Monterrey, New Orleans, Havana, New York, Manchester, and London as key centers. M. Echeverría & Co. was San Román's agent in New York, Joseph Railton & Sons in Manchester. J. A. Bances and Genaro del Regato watched over San Román's interests in Havana. In Mexico, Hernández Hermanos of Monterrey and Somohano of Vera Cruz were important relationships. In fact, for the elites of northern Mexico and the Lower Rio Grande Valley, San Román was the pivotal merchant.[42]

After mid-1861, as cotton became the dominant export item of his business, his contacts in Texas expanded beyond the Lower Rio Grande Valley to Houston, Victoria, Brenham. The San Román papers of this period are filled with advice to Texas planters, as well as to his Mexican associates, that cotton was beginning to be exported through Matamoros to Europe. Also prominent in the San Román papers are inquiries or entreaties from Texas merchants and planters regarding carts and cartmen. The request of John Lang of Houston, who had 450 bales near the Colorado River, to gather the teams and drivers for their transport to the border, was commonplace.[43]

San Román had intended to begin shipping cotton to New York in February 1862, but the appearance of a U.S. frigate effectively stopped all shipping from Bagdad. When trading resumed in mid-1862, San Román, perhaps in a testing of the waters, at first shipped cotton to Liverpool via New York City. By the end of 1862, he was shipping Mexican cotton for sale on the New York market. San Román meticulously followed the letter of international law and secured any necessary diplomatic permission. His shipments to New York included the "certificado del U. S. Consul."[44]

Economic historian Mario Cerutti has compiled a list of San Román's cotton shipments for 1863, giving us an excellent idea of the scope of his international trade.[45] In that year, José San Román exported slightly more than 10,000 bales (10,469) under his insignia. The bulk of the cotton, some 7,000 bales, went to Havana, where it was stored and sold at a later date to the highest bidder. Slightly more than 3,000 bales were consigned to Liverpool. Slightly fewer than 300 bales were consigned to New York, and about 150 went to Barcelona. To put this in perspective, if all the cotton sent to Havana were later sold to Liverpool, then San Román would have had an ownership interest in fully 6 percent (10,469 of 172,126 bales) of all the Mexican cotton arriving in the United Kingdom in 1863. In short, San Román had an impressive share of the Bagdad export market.

What is clear is that San Román's northern Mexican mercantile network joined in the purchase of southern cotton and its resale as Mexican cotton. It was a potentially lucrative, if speculative, investment. It was worth taking a risk. As San Román noted in a letter to his New York agent, M. Echeverría, Don Bernardino García had spoken to him, "and he has told me that he is going to consign Cotton to you and that you shouldn't have any fear." Hernández Hermanos of Monterrey and Somohano of Vera Cruz were also regular investors in the cotton trade.[46]

The merchants of northern Mexico, as we have seen, did not limit their buying to the border. By early 1863, many were traveling to Alleyton and Columbus in Southeast Texas to purchase cotton directly from the planters. Commission merchant Joseph Kleiber wrote José San Román from Columbus, noting that "there are plenty parties here from Mexico who cannot or do not know how to get Cotton." Kleiber was trying to impress upon San Román that he, on the other hand, did know how to get cotton.[47] Kleiber, who also served as a government cotton agent, was well positioned to procure cotton and the required military permits. He was one among many influentials that San Román could call upon to deal with intransigent military officials.

Such a case arose in April 1863, when José Fernandes of Monterrey wrote from Alleyton, asking San Román to secure permission to cross the cotton to Mexico:

Señor D. José S. Román

Brownsville

   My Dear Sir

Included in this I remit to You two receipts one of 45 bales, and the other of 10, altogether 55 bales cotton, that on the 23rd past were carted from here [by] D. Margarito Martines and D. Francisco Gutierres . . . and I ask of You to inform Monterey about what you have delivered, recording the receipt that they carry so that I can pay them in Monterey and in case that I'm not there that it be done in my place by Messrs. D. José Palacio and Co who are already aware of this, as are the freighters. I have not been able to renew the permits given by General Bee.⁴⁸

Fernandes, who was having difficulty securing the required Confederate permits to take the cotton to Monterrey, ended his letter on an optimistic note: "because up to now it has been difficult, in this case You will see if you can pass them, and if not let them be by the edge of the river because some day they will pass."⁴⁹ Fernandes was convinced that "some day" the cotton would be allowed to cross.

Mexican Teamsters on the Cotton Road

Only two months after the first Battle of Bull Run, we begin to find commentaries in Texas newspapers about a "loose" and "floating" population of Mexicans engaged in the cotton trade or in various liberal bands fighting French imperial troops in northern Mexico. These wars—the American Civil War and the Mexican War against French Intervention—created severe labor shortages along the border; they simultaneously absorbed manpower for their armies while stimulating cross-border trade. Such trade required teamsters and teams of mules and wagons. The demand for teamsters and wagons was such that it created a scarcity of wagons in Monterrey (in November 1862) because many teamsters had gone to Texas. "The northward migration of freighters seeking higher earnings often reached levels that depleted labor supplies in Mexico," González Quiroga has noted.⁵⁰ Thus the generals and the merchants competed for the human and animal means of transportation.

Teamster wages in Texas reflected the scarcity of both manpower and teams. A sure sign of a labor shortage was a strike of "salt hands" in 1861 on Charles Stillman's Los Laureles Ranch. In September 1861, they demanded one dollar a day wages instead of the seventy-five cents they were receiving.[51] The ranch management was hopeful that lack of work would drive them back to work at fifty cents a day, but it was wishful thinking. Freighting paid more. Through the 1850s, drivers had been paid one dollar for carrying one hundred pounds one hundred miles. This rate remained in effect until 1861. By 1863, the rate had increased to between five and six dollars. In 1864, a freighter could earn between six hundred and fifteen hundred dollars, depending on the size of the wagon, for hauling cotton from San Antonio to Matamoros, nearly three hundred miles distant. Their services were so much in demand, in fact, that teamsters could negotiate advances and payment in specie rather than in Confederate money. Robert Clark wrote Stillman from Victoria, Texas, that "there is a great demand for Wagons at 7 cts specie. The tendency in prices is upward. Paper is out of the question with teamsters, they won't have it. In fact it may be said in general to be fast failing here as a medium of circulation except as far as the Government is Concerned."[52]

The invoices and letters in the Stillman and San Román papers make clear the complete dependence on Mexican teamsters for the transport of cotton. San Román and Stillman employed hundreds of Mexican freighters to haul goods on both sides of the border. A majority of Stillman's teamsters came from the Mexican towns along the Lower Rio Grande, whereas San Román drew most of his workers from the interior of Mexico, particularly from Tamaulipas and Nuevo León. Richard King and Mifflin Kenedy used their own ranch hands to cart cotton and supplies throughout the trans-Mississippi Confederacy. Prominent merchants in San Antonio such as the Vance brothers, Jean Baptiste Lacoste, and John Twohig would contract with other merchants or agents situated on the Rio Grande to recruit Mexican freighters and arrange other transportation needs. The firm of Attrill-Lacoste of San Antonio employed the services of John Leyendecker of Laredo. The house of Twohig had agents Friedrich Groos and Daniel Murphy in Piedras Negras and Monterrey, respectively.[53] Preliminary indications suggest that Mexican teamsters could be found all along the cotton road, at points as far away as Arkansas and Louisiana. Their presence became increasingly pronounced as the Civil War wore on.

By late 1862, in the words of Robert Kerby, the Confederate army "was fast running out of spare white men." Military commanders began to impress Negro laborers to prepare defense fortifications, freeing soldiers for combat duty. In early 1863, Texas and Arkansas enacted tough conscription laws and formed local "home guards" to enforce them.[54] And the

Confederate government revoked the exemption from military conscription that had been given to teamsters.

This exemption had meant that there was no shortage of youngsters and men wanting to be teamsters. As former teamster John Hunter recalled, "For these trains there was no dearth of teamsters before reaching Brownsville. That point once reached, many would escape into Mexico and the return trips were always short on drivers. The outbound trains had no difficulty securing teamsters. The Conscript law was in force and thousands preferred driving an ox team to service in the army. School teachers, college professors, society dudes became ox drivers."[55] The young John Hunter himself had taken advantage of the exemption to leave his North Texas home for the questionable security of neutral Matamoros.

As the American Civil War entered its third year, however, the exemption for teamsters was rescinded, and local authorities created home guards, made up of young boys and old men who were to enforce the tightened conscript regulations. The popular term for them, John Hunter recalled, was "heel flies," but these flies, with their police powers, could prove to be more than a nuisance.[56] The Fort Brown Flag noted with approval what could happen to those who flaunted the conscript law: "A Mexican who claimed to be neutral and refused to be conscripted was put in the guard house on Wednesday night. Not liking the quarters, he attempted to escape, when a musket ball settled the matter in short order. Death is a supreme remedy for neutrality."[57]

Any adult Mexican male living in or traveling through Texas in the last two years of the Civil War had to have proper papers, or *permisos*. This was particularly the case in the major towns along the Texas cotton road—Columbus, Clinton, Goliad, Beeville, San Patricio—and on the King Ranch, each of which had organized local home guards. The Mexicans working the oxcart trains were subject to searches and interrogation. What had given merchant Rafael Alderete considerable freedom to travel through East Texas was the fact that he himself was a captain in his local home guard.

At the same time that the Confederate States of American (CSA) ordered that conscripts would no longer be furloughed as teamsters, it issued a decree explicitly protecting Mexican teamsters. The CSA circular, issued January 31, 1863, read as follows:

VII. Mexicans, and other foreigners, bringing supplies into the county, will not be interfered with in any manner whatever but, on the contrary, it is hereby made the duty of every officer, or agent of the Govt. to afford them ample protection.

Such Mexicans, or foreigners, however, will only be employed in hauling cotton out of the country, by the Govt., or State of Tex, through their authorized agents, or by direct authority from these HeadQtrs., or by permits signed by Brigadier General Bee, or Major S. Hart.[58]

This CSA order not only sanctioned the employment of Mexican teamsters, an already existing reality, but also permitted merchants from northern Mexico to participate directly in the wartime commerce of Texas and the South. The decree, and the reality it recognized, was all the more striking because it represented a change in policy in the Anglo settlements of Central and East Texas. Many of the counties through which Mexican teamsters had to traverse—Matagorda, Colorado, Guadalupe, Travis— had passed ordinances in the mid-1850s expelling their "low class, peon" Mexican population from the area. Moreover, vigilante attacks against Mexican teamsters in 1857 had attempted to drive out Mexican competition from the freighting business between San Antonio and the Gulf Coast. Now in 1863 and 1864, the provision of local goods and the export of local cotton depended almost entirely on Mexican teamsters.

The extent of Mexican involvement in carting cotton? The huge ox-carts, with seven-foot-high wooden wheels, had beds approximately fifteen feet long and six feet wide. According to Frank Yturria, a scion of the Yturria mercantile clan, each cart could carry twenty bales, or about ten thousand pounds of cotton. The cotton trains consisted of ten to fifteen carts hauling the cotton of several planters or merchants. John Hunter, an erstwhile teamster, described trains of twenty-five wagons with loads of ten to twelve bales apiece.[59]

These large trains of ten or more carts were usually "long-distance" trains. The Stillman and San Román papers indicate that many cotton trains were "small"—four to six carts, or whatever was available—and rarely carted maximum loads. Considerations of speed and the availability of oxen or mule teams may have called for lesser loads. Distance was undoubtedly a factor as well.

If we extrapolate from my earlier count of cotton bales sent to the United Kingdom—again keeping in mind that much cotton went elsewhere—we can arrive at rough but suggestive estimates of the number of oxcarts that were used in *los algodones*. By creating a range of high and low estimates based on whether carts carried a maximum load of twenty bales

Table 4.2. Carts on Texas Cotton Road

	1862	1863	1864	1865	1866
			No. of bales		
U.K. imports (bales) from Mexican ports	27,960	172,126	227,854	326,640	3,145
Capacity			No. of Carts		
20 bales/cart	1,398	8,606	11,392	16,320	157
10 bales/cart	2,796	17,212	22,784	32,664	314

Source: Number of bales from Table 4.1. Cart numbers, author's calculations.

apiece or a lesser load of ten bales, we get a glimpse of what was an immense traffic flow (see Table 4.2).

If all cotton imported into the United Kingdom in 1863 had been carried by carts with a load of twenty bales, then more than eight thousand carts must have been put in service; in 1864, more than eleven thousand carts; and in 1865, more than sixteen thousand. If ten bales had been the average load, then in 1863, more than seventeen thousand carts had been used; in 1864, more than twenty-two thousand; and in 1865, more than thirty-two thousand. To put it another way, in 1865, somewhere between forty-five and ninety carts arrived in Brownsville-Matamoros on a daily basis. These numbers provide a conservative view of the great traffic that coursed back and forth from Alleyton to the Rio Grande.

These estimates of the number of carts also suggest the number of Mexican teamsters involved in the cotton trade. Beginning in 1863, the cartmen, with few exceptions, were Mexican; the heel flies made sure of that. Thus one can estimate that in 1863, between eight thousand and seventeen thousand Mexicans teamsters carted "trans-Mississippi" cotton to the Río Bravo, a range that increases in 1864 to eleven thousand and twenty-two thousand. In 1865, between sixteen thousand and thirty-two thousand Mexican teamsters may have carted southern cotton![60] These are admittedly surprising figures that merit further research.

The key assumption here is of one cart delivery per year. If the carts made two trips up and down the cotton road per year, then the above figures for both carts and teamsters would be reduced by half. On the other hand, since it was commonplace for teamsters to complete only one or two of the three legs of the cotton road, the above estimates might also undercount the number of teamsters and carts involved in freighting. San Antonio, Victoria-Goliad, and the King Ranch served as depositories and way stations where outbound wagon trains could drop off their cotton loads and return homeward with goods imported from Mexico, Europe, and New York, while inbound trains did the reverse. There was a circulation of teamsters and carts between the various legs of the cotton road that my estimates cannot adequately capture. One point should be clear, however: by the third year of the Civil War, Mexican teamsters were the backbone of the market system of the trans-Mississippi Confederacy.

A Concluding Note

The economic life of the trans-Mississippi Confederacy can hardly be understood without recognizing the critical role played by Mexico and Mexicans. The Mexican port of Bagdad at the mouth of the Rio Grande was the South's outlet to world markets during the Civil War. Foreign ownership of southern cotton—called Mexican cotton—afforded a veneer of protection from confiscations by either Confederate or Union forces. Mexican merchants in Texas and in northern Mexico were not simply front men, however; they were independent entrepreneurs who became indispensable factors in organizing the export of cotton and the import of goods. Indeed, it was their claim of ownership, along with the claims and interests of European merchants, that allowed Texas cotton to be exported in spite of the wartime blockade.

Even more critical was the veritable army of Mexican teamsters who hauled merchandise up and down the cotton road of Texas. In fact, as the Civil War wore on and labor became increasingly scarce, Mexican teamsters became the dominant freighting workforce of the western Confederacy. Given the conflictual relations between Anglos and Mexicans during the previous decade, the presence of an estimated fifteen thousand or so Mexican teamsters points to the increasingly desperate straits of the Confederacy after 1862. This was a case where economic and military needs subordinated, for a few years, the animosities between Anglo and Mexican in Texas.

After the defeat of the Confederacy, Charles Stillman would take his profits to New York and found National City Bank; José San Román and other Mexican cotton merchants took their capital and consolidated their trades in Monterrey—helping it become the capitalist powerhouse of the Mexican North. Most Mexican carters and teamsters faded from sight, struggling to find transport contracts or returning to their small ranches as railroads began to marginalize them on both sides of the border.

The Texas cotton road disappeared, but the strategic importance of the U.S.-Mexican borderlands as a commercial corridor, especially for commodities of questionable or suspect identity, had been established.

Notes

I wish to thank Miguel González Quiroga and John Tutino for their comments on an earlier draft.

1. Frederick Law Olmsted, *A Journey through Texas* (New York: Dix, Edwards & Co., 1857; reprint, Austin: University of Texas Press, 1978), 245.

2. Ibid., 502–503.

3. Ibid., 156–160, 169; see also Montejano, *Anglos and Mexicans*, 26–30; Miguel González Quiroga, "Mexicanos in Texas during the Civil War," in Emilio Zamora, Cynthia Orozco, and Rodolfo Rocha, eds., *Mexican Americans in Texas History* (Austin: Texas State Historical Association, 2000).

4. Montejano, *Anglos and Mexicans*, 29; also Arnoldo De León and Kenneth L. Stewart, *Tejanos and the Numbers Game* (Albuquerque: University of New Mexico Press, 1989), 33–34. Recent historiography questions the assertion that Mexicans were removed from the freight business between San Antonio and the Gulf Coast; see Larry Knight, "The Cart War: Defining American in San Antonio in the 1850s," *Southwestern Historical Quarterly* 109, no.3 (January 2006): 320.

5. Montejano, *Anglos and Mexicans*, 34–41.

6. Jerry Thompson, *Vaqueros in Blue and Gray* (Austin, Tex.: Presidial Press, 1976), 9–11; González Quiroga, "Mexicanos in Texas during the Civil War," 55–56.

7. González Quiroga, "Mexicanos in Texas during the Civil War," 54.

8. James A. Irby, *Backdoor at Bagdad* (El Paso: Texas Western Press, 1977), 5–7.

9. The Charles Stillman Papers are housed at Houghton Library, Harvard University, and the José San Román Papers are housed at the Briscoe Center for American History, University of Texas at Austin. Among these papers are ledgers with entries organized by cotton brand, name of seller, number of bales, prices, costs, and so on. These ledgers provided the inspiration, and solid departure point, for this project.

10. Letter from Simón Celaya, San Román's clerk, to [indecipherable], Monterrey, November 16, 1861, San Román Collection, Letter Press Book, September 30, 1861–May 29, 1862, 54. All translations are mine unless otherwise noted.

11. Letter, San Román to Antonio Costa, Havana, July 28, 1862, San Román Collection, Letter Press Book, June 1–November 11, 1862.

12. Letter from H. H. Edwards, Nacogdoches, February 3, 1863, Box 9, "Letters 1863," Stillman Papers.

13. John Warren Hunter, "The Fall of Brownsville on the Rio Grande, Novem-

ber 1863," typescript, n.d., "Notes on Rio Grande Valley" Folder, Harbert Davenport Papers, Lorenzo de Zavala State Library, Austin, Texas.

14. Letter from Josiah Turner, Alleyton, February 9, 1863, Box 9, "Letters
1863," Stillman Papers.

15. Turner, San Patricio (?), to J. H. Phelps, Houston, April 24, 1864, Box 10,
"Letters 1864," Stillman Papers.

16. A supercargo was the owner's agent, usually a trusted employee or merchant, who traveled with the valued merchandise. García's command of English,
exquisite penmanship, and exacting accounting suggest a formal education and a
mercantile background. García might have been a merchant from Victoria or San
Antonio (García to Stillman, Box 9, "1863" Folder, Stillman Papers).

17. See Frank Daniel Yturria, *The Patriarch* (Brownsville: University of Texas
at Brownsville, 2006), 75.

18. Tri-Weekly Telegraph (March 27, 1863), in Andrew Forest Muir Papers,
Folder 63.1, Woodsen Research Center, Rice University.

19. Robert L. Kerby, *Kirby Smith's Confederacy* (Tuscaloosa: University of Alabama Press, 1972), 168.

20. *Cotton Supply Reporter* (Manchester, Eng.), 1861–1866.

21. Letter from Harbert Davenport to Holland McCombs, June 26, 1953, "Los
Algodones" Folder, Box 2-23/214, Harbert Davenport Papers.

22. Letter from San Román to Avendano brothers, New Orleans, February 6,
1862, San Román Collection, Letter Press Book, September 30, 1861–May 29, 1862.

23. As reported in the Galveston Civilian-Extra (April 1, 1862), Andrew Forest
Muir Papers, Box 27, Folder 16.

24. San Román to Echeverría, New York, March [day indecipherable], 1862,
San Román Collection, Letter Press Book, September 30, 1861–May 29, 1862.

25. Letter from Davenport to McCombs, June 26, 1953, "Los Algodones"
Folder, Davenport Papers.

26. Letter from Davenport to McCombs, July 7, 1953, "Los Algodones" Folder,
Davenport Papers.

27. Report to Hon. Gideon Welles, Secretary of the Navy, from Lieutenant
Commander Couthouy, commanding U.S. bark Kingfisher, Key West, March 19,
1862, Official Records of the Union and Confederate Navies in the War of the
Rebellion (Washington, 1921), Series I, Vol. 17, pp. 191–192; letter from Secretary
of the Navy Gideon Welles to Secretary of the Treasury Salmon Chase, April 21,
1863, Series I, Vol. 17, p. 417.

28. John Warren Hunter, "The Fall of Brownsville on the Rio Grande, November 1863," typescript, n.d., "Notes on Rio Grande Valley" Folder, Harbert Davenport Papers.

29. Kerby adds that Confederate and Texas purchasing agents in Monterrey
and Matamoros also found that Mexican and European vendors were reluctant
to accept Confederate scrip or treasury warrants in payment. See Kirby Smith's
Confederacy, 168.

30. Letter from Robert Clark, Victoria, August 23, 1863, Box 9, "Letters 1863,"
Stillman Papers.

31. Jackson, noting that San Román's accounting left him short thirty-three
bales of the ninety-nine forwarded, asked if Captain Kenedy had sold some of

the cotton at King Ranch; Jackson to San Román, April 14, 1862, Letters to San Román, 1862, 1863, San Román Collection.

32. The new regulations issued by General Magruder (in April 1863), which a Confederate Cotton Bureau would oversee, called for a tithe of 10 percent of all cotton to support the war: letters from Harbert Davenport to Holland McCombs, July 21, July 24, 1863, "Los Algodones" Folder, Box 2-23/214, Harbert Davenport Papers.

33. The lack of trust in the competency of the local Confederate command was dramatically illustrated when the Matamoros cotton merchants offered to finance a military campaign to recapture Brownsville but only if commanded by Col. John Ford, whom they believed was an honest and skillful military officer: letters, Davenport to McCombs, June 29, July 3, 1863, "Los Algodones" Folder, Box 2-23/214, Harbert Davenport Papers.

34. James Smith to Charles Stillman, received September 30, answered October 4, 1863, Box 9, "Letters 1863," Stillman Papers.

35. Yturria, *The Patriarch*, 83–87.

36. Alderete to Francisco Yturria, May 28, 1862, in ibid., 85.

37. Alderete to Francisco Yturria, mid-July 1862, in ibid., 85.

38. Alderete to Francisco Yturria, February 13, 1863, in ibid., 86.

39. Alderete to Francisco Yturria, April 28, 1863, in ibid., 86.

40. Alderete to Francisco Yturria, May 27, 1863, in ibid., 86–87.

41. Ibid., 87.

42. For an excellent work on José San Román, see Mario Cerutti, *Propietarios, empresarios y empresa en el norte de México* (Mexico City: Siglo Veintiuno Editores, 2000).

43. Lang to San Román, February 19, 1863, San Román Collection, Letters to San Román, 1863.

44. Letters from San Román to M. Echeverría & Co., New York, October 12, October 27, 1862, San Román Collection, Letter Press Book, June 1–November 11, 1862.

45. Cerutti, *Propietarios, empresarios y empresa*, 180–185.

46. San Román to M. Echeverría & Co., New York, November 19, 1862, San Román Collection, Letter Press Book, November 1862–May 1863.

47. Joseph Kleiber, Columbus, to José San Román, April 12, 1863, San Román Collection, Letters to José San Román, 1863.

48. Fernandes, Alleyton, to San Román, April 10, 1863, San Román Collection, Letters to José San Román, 1863.

49. Ibid.

50. Many wagons had also been expropriated by the Mexican government for use in their resistance to the French invasion—still another reason why Mexican cartmen might want to go to Texas; see González-Quiroga, "Mexicanos in Texas during the Civil War," 58–59.

51. LeRoy P. Graf, "The Economic History of the Lower Rio Grande Valley, 1820–1875," PhD dissertation, Harvard University, 1942, 434.

52. Letter from Rbt. Clark, Victoria, Aug. 23, 1863, Stillman Papers; also see González-Quiroga, "Mexicanos in Texas during the Civil War," 60–61.

53. González Quiroga, "Mexicanos in Texas during the Civil War," 59–60. He

notes that of the twenty-seven cart drivers recruited by Groos in a six-month period (March–August of 1863), all but one were Mexican.

54. Kerby, *Kirby Smith's Confederacy*, 56–58.

55. John Warren Hunter, "The Fall of Brownsville on the Rio Grande, November 1863," typescript, n.d., "Notes on Rio Grande Valley" Folder, Harbert Davenport Papers.

56. Ibid.

57. *The San Antonio News*, August 27, 1863, reprinting items from the Fort Brown Flag, August 14, 1863.

58. See J. Z. Leyendecker Papers, Folder 1, Center for American History, University of Texas at Austin.

59. Yturria, *The Patriarch*, 73; Hunter, "The Fall of Brownsville," "Notes on Rio Grande Valley" Folder, Harbert Davenport Papers.

60. These estimates exclude the supercargo, cook, and wrangler who typically accompanied the large trains of ten carts or more. Teamsters on small trains generally took on these roles.

CHAPTER 5

Making Americans and Mexicans in the Arizona Borderlands

KATHERINE BENTON-COHEN

Midnight, July 12, 1917. In a remote mountain town near the Arizona-Mexico border, Sheriff Harry Wheeler quietly appointed as many as two thousand temporary deputies. Just before dawn, the gun-toting men emerged "as if by magic," as the front page of the *New York Times* reported the following day.[1] They swarmed the steep, narrow streets, rounding up well over a thousand residents who were suspected participants and sympathizers in a strike by the radical Industrial Workers of the World (known as the Wobblies) against the copper mines of the town of Bisbee, in Cochise County, Arizona.

The Wobblies—who welcomed workers of all skills, races, sexes, and nationalities—were among the nation's most vocal and hated antiwar activists. The first line of their union constitution begins, "The working class and the employing class have nothing in common." Wobblies had participated in many high-profile strikes and free-speech battles that year. In Bisbee, the union's most shocking demand was for a wage increase for surface workers—almost all of them of Mexican origin—to within fifty cents of what "white" miners underground made.

The majority of those rounded up on July 12 were young, single men. Ninety percent were immigrants, and a majority of these, Mexicans or Slavs. Under the hot July sun, the captives were marched at gunpoint through town, past the mines, to a baseball field two miles away. There, local residents watched as the deputies loaded their charges into twenty-three boxcars, to be shipped nearly two hundred miles to the middle of the New Mexico desert. An army camp in nearby Columbus, New Mexico, saved the deported men from thirst and starvation. The event captured national headlines and became known across the country as the Bisbee Deportation.

Pres. Woodrow Wilson was embarrassed into launching a federal investigation. Sheriff Wheeler told investigators that he was protecting his nation and doing his manly duty to save "white women" from "foreigners." It came down to asking himself, he explained, "Are you an American, or are you not?"[2]

Ninety years later, another Cochise County citizen posse grabbed national headlines. In the late 1990s, the U.S. Border Patrol stopped more undocumented migrants along the county's eighty-mile border than at any other section of the U.S.-Mexico boundary. In 2004, the Border Patrol made 235,648 apprehensions of undocumented immigrants in Cochise County, about double the county's entire permanent population. During the 2008–2010 economic downturn, apprehensions have fallen, but the Border Patrol—augmented in the twenty-first century by National Guard troops—has remained nearly ubiquitous, with about one agent in the county for every seven residents of present-day Bisbee.[3]

Unauthorized civilians patrolled the border, too, among them the Minutemen Civil Defense Corps, founded in 2004 in nearby Tombstone by newspaper publisher and gunfight reenactor Chris Simcox. The Minutemen say they oppose violence, but many carry arms. At least one has been convicted of murder.[4] Supporters of the Minutemen believe they are restoring the geographical border to the racial border it once was.

The truth, of course, is that the border as a racial line is a fiction, and always has been. A hundred years ago, people in the region belonged to what many people understood to be different "races" and fought for equal inclusion in the mining and agricultural communities of the Arizona border region. Ethnic Mexicans could be white, and Italians could fail to be. Rich and poor, immigrant and native, miner and farmer, manager and worker, man and woman—they all fought over how race would be defined and who would benefit from these definitions. The Minutemen's notoriety and today's racialized debates over immigration demonstrate that this is a history still vitally relevant.

This chapter traces the racial system that emerged in Cochise County, Arizona, from 1881 until the New Deal. Cochise County encompasses the southeastern corner of Arizona, bordering New Mexico and Mexico. The county was home to Geronimo and the Chiricahua Apaches, one of Arizona's most important ranching regions, the silver camp of Tombstone, and the industrial copper town of Bisbee. The county has inspired hundreds of popular histories and westerns (including a best-selling mystery series starring a woman sheriff). The confluence of the typical and the infamous or spectacular in Cochise County makes it particularly fertile ground for investigating the relationships between class, nation, region, and gender in formulating racial definitions.[5] Its history reminds us that the old black-white racial narrative fails to capture race's true complexity in the United States.

Sheriff Wheeler's question hints at this complexity: Who counts as an American? This question begs others: How did immigration from Europe, Mexico, and China shape the meanings of race? How did ideas about race vary over space and time? The persistent calls to be a man, or to protect women and children, make us ask: How did ideas about manhood and womanhood shape ideas about race? By examining these questions in the framework of Cochise County's history, we can learn a great deal about how "Mexican" and "white American" came to seem like opposing ideas to so many people in the early twentieth century.

My study of Cochise County depends on two central premises. The first is that to talk about racial divisions between Mexicans and whites in the U.S.-Mexico borderlands requires an understanding that these categories themselves have a history. "Mexican" was hardly a self-evident category. The *casta* distinctions of New Spain recognized gradations of ancestry and color, but the categories were already blurry in the North by the late eighteenth century and no longer legally recognized in Mexico after 1812.[6] Equally fluid—and never codified—was *calidad*, roughly, one's reputation, which was defined in reference to origin, skin color, class position, family reputation, and comportment. And in the United States, the Treaty of Guadalupe Hidalgo and the Gadsden Purchase, which offered U.S. citizenship to residents of the ceded territories, made Mexicans legally white. Yet over time, these meanings became increasingly invisible to "Anglos," a group who themselves inhabited an invented category. ("Anglo," a term that emerged by the 1930s, was the southwestern version of "white.") Because racial distinctions were largely regional, the Irish, for example, were safely white in the American West long before their status was secure farther east, the topic explored by Linda Gordon's study of the Arizona copper town of Clifton-Morenci.[7]

A deep historiography both informs and ignores questions about racial categories, class, and social position in the Southwest. Pioneering Chicano community studies of the 1970s and 1980s documented the importance of landownership and capitalist transformations in the reshaping of relations between Mexicans and Anglos.[8] Recent work has shown that conflict with native peoples shaped racial status among both Mexicans and Americans as well as the relations between them.[9] But most of these formative studies consider the division between Mexican and Anglo as a priori complete.[10] (David Montejano's fine book is called *Anglos and Mexicans in the Making of Texas, 1836–1986*, not *Making Anglos and Mexicans in Texas*.)

So more questions remain. Upon closer examination, the racial status of the people drawn to industrial mining and small business opportunities in the copper borderlands grows blurrier rather than clearer. If Mexicans were legally white yet not white, what were Serbian miners? What about Italian grocers? Always white? Sometimes? Why? How did the answers to these questions change over time, and why? Why in the post-9/11 world are so many Americans surprised that people from all over the world traverse our border with Mexico? This phenomenon is not new. A borderland that was a magnet for worldwide immigration—a tangled web of transcontinental, transatlantic, and transpacific crossings—became perceived as a literal and racial line in the sand, albeit one easily crossed.[11]

Since the late 1990s, many scholars have demonstrated how new immigrants and new scientific and social theories of race redefined whiteness. Much of the early literature focused on "new immigrants" in the Northeast and industrial Midwest like Italians, Eastern European Jews, and Slavs. Scholars of the American South have also conducted some searching investigations of what it meant to be white in the part of the country where race appears to be the most clear cut.[12]

Some historians have begun to assess the relationship of ethnic Mexicans to whiteness. Yet few examine the making of white Anglos—a category that explicitly excludes ethnic Mexicans—in the West.[13] This lacuna is surprising for any number of reasons, to name just one: the stereotype of remaking oneself on the frontier. What more thorough way to remake oneself than to go from being racially in-between to white? Two light-skinned African American friends of mine (both Louisiana Creoles) told me they had family members who passed as white. Both noticed that these folks passing as white always seemed to move to California, a place they saw as a site of racial as well as personal reinvention.[14]

California has garnered the most scholarly attention to the West's startling diversity. Studies about Mexicans, native peoples, Jews, Asians, and African Americans there have underscored California's uniqueness, not its typicality.[15]

Arizona is not California. In the 1850s, after California's gold rush boom, only a few thousand people lived in Arizona, which was still part of New Mexico territory and largely ignored by the Spanish, Mexicans, and Americans. So while California's history offers crucial insights, it cannot substitute for more sustained investigations of other parts of the U.S.-Mexico borderlands (also true for New Mexico, in its own way as sui generis as California).[16]

If my first goal is to take seriously the history of whiteness on the border, my second is to uncover the ways that women and gender are central to the history of race in the borderlands. People understand categories like gender and race reflexively and simultaneously, so a history of race or gender is necessarily both. Many scholars have explored how ideas about gender and sexuality—and, not least, how women themselves—shaped racial interactions and racial divisions in the borderlands. White women, both as symbols and as active agents, had surprising power to mold the racial worlds of possibilities in the American Southwest. And men have gender, too: any examination of gender in the American West has to reckon with what I have elsewhere called the racial hierarchy of manliness. As Susan L. Johnson has noted, no other "place has been so consistently identified" with white masculinity. What this meant in practice is that unwhiteness was often perceived as unmanly.[17]

Race, gender, place: all these combined in the reputation of Bisbee, Cochise County's largest city, as a "white man's camp." There, a nineteenth-century world of many "races"—Chinese, Apache, Mexican, Italian, Irish, Jewish—gave way, by the 1930s, to a strict racial border between Mexicans and white Americans (or Anglos).

Funneling several racial categories into just two happened in two ways: by removal and by redefinition. The first way, removal, applied to the two local populations whose roots were closest and farthest from Cochise County: the Chiricahua Apaches and the Chinese. In 1886, the federal government banished every Chiricahua Apache it could find to two dank army forts in Florida after the surrender of Geronimo. In the same years as the Apache Wars, local Chinese exclusion campaigns reduced the county's Chinese population dramatically, though not entirely. (Much as Cochise County's border became one of the busiest crossing points for undocumented migrants in the 1990s, so it was for Chinese immigrants a century earlier in the aftermath of the Chinese Exclusion Act of 1882, which barred all but a handful of elite Chinese from entry into the United States.)[18]

The removal of Apaches and Chinese made possible the transformation of other racial categories. A camaraderie among Mexicans and "Americans" bred by the dangers of the Apache Wars disappeared. Then Mexican workers replaced Chinese and Indians at the bottom of twinned racial and labor hierarchies.[19] After 1900, a copper boom ramped up the power of industrial mining operations to define labor relations and, with them, racial definitions. An older ranching and farming economy in which Mexicans could find economic autonomy and civic inclusion through landownership could not compete with the mining juggernaut and the powerful elites who oversaw it. In the early twentieth century, the arrival of new immigrants from over three dozen countries to work in the region's copper mines created new contention over who was white, even as it pushed Mexicans farther to the racial margins. Along the way, conceptions of manliness, family economies, and proper womanhood informed these debates and redefined whiteness.

The microhistory of the border region of Cochise County helps us understand the ways that the complexities of race in the American Southwest became funneled into the false binaries of racial ideas in the United States. Three key moments in Cochise County's history illustrate this narrowing of racial possibilities. The first is 1881, the year the county was created, and a time when diverse communities still harbored multiple racial possibilities. The second illustrative moment is 1917, the year of the Bisbee Deportation. In retrospect, that fateful year closed off the possibility of many racial futures for Cochise County, though that was not immediately clear. I conclude with a brief coda on 1934. The depression devastated southern Arizona's agricultural and mining economies, yet it did so in ways that increased the power of the biggest mining corporations. The New Deal gave local elites federal money to implement racially segregated programs, often administered by white women whose considerable gains had come at the expense of racial minorities. In the end, then, the binary of Mexican (regardless of nativity or citizenship) and white American became firmly entrenched at the expense of more fluid possibilities.

1881: Year of Possibilities

In 1881, Cochise County was carved from Tucson's Pima County to accommodate Tombstone's spectacular growth. In the new county, race relations could differ even over a few miles' distance. Three communities—the farm and ranch settlement of Tres Alamos, the silver boomtown of Tombstone, and the copper camp of Bisbee—demonstrated the diversity of ways of defining race and racial boundaries in the new county.

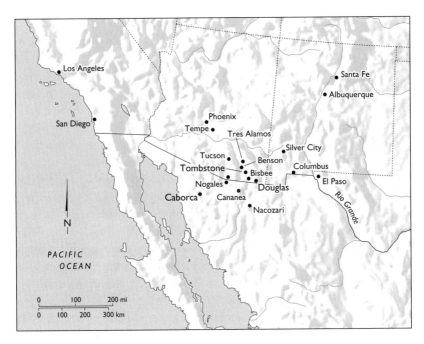

Map 5.1. The Arizona Borderlands

Tres Alamos

The oldest and least known of the three communities no longer exists: Tres Alamos, located along the San Pedro River in what became the northwestern corner of the county. As a place based on agriculture, here land-ownership and water rights—not race, national origin, or even sex—were the crucial status markers.[20] In Tres Alamos, connections between Mexicans and Euro-Americans were everywhere—in water rights agreements, shared school governance, intermarriage, and, especially, in the warfare against the Chiricahua Apaches that persisted until 1886. It was a place of irrigation, ethnic mixing, and substantial landownership by women—all traditions of Spanish North America.[21]

The Tres Alamos site, well-watered and fertile, had been inhabited intermittently for centuries by native peoples and Spanish settlers. It was abandoned during the Civil War, but in 1865, a few Mexicans and Euro-Americans from Tucson began resettling along the river, flanked by army troops to protect against the Chiricahua Apaches. By the early 1870s, close to two hundred people lived on small farms there and grew wheat, barley, maize, and beans.[22] In the 1870s and 1880s, Spanish-surnamed people constituted close to 25 percent of those who bought public land and 13 to 15 percent of those who filed successful homestead claims.[23] Other farmers included Euro-American migrants from places like Maine and Missouri, German immigrants, and at least two African Americans.

The life of Tres Alamos' first successful homesteader, Antonio Grijalba, illustrates how the culture and economy of Tres Alamos operated. Grijalba was the descendant of a prominent Tucson family dating to the Spanish era; he began his career as a merchant in Tucson. He was related to several other river landowners, also with roots in Tucson. In 1881, he kept about two hundred head of cattle and farmed seventy to one hundred acres of corn, beans, and grain. When he died in 1906, his real estate, water rights, livestock, and other investments were worth over $7,000, a sizable sum in the frontier West. Grijalba also traveled in cosmopolitan circles. He held accounts with two German immigrants, several German Jews, a Spanish-surnamed attorney in Bisbee, and a Chinese merchant married to a Mexican woman. He inhabited a complex and, for lack of a better word, integrated social world.[24]

These kinds of connections among Tres Alamos residents were evident from childhood through death. In 1875, local men of both Mexican and Anglo descent created one of Arizona's first school districts and a one-room school. Its children, school board members (including Grijalba), and teachers included both Mexicans and Americans. When Tres Alamos residents died, executors and examiners of both Mexican and American origin presided over their friends' and neighbors' probate proceedings.[25]

Nowhere was the complementarity and complexity of life in Tres Alamos more evident than in the use of water, the desert's most precious commodity. Tres Alamos' farmers, Grijalba included, pooled their resources to build the cooperative irrigation canals common to the Southwest known as *acequias*. Tres Alamos' first canal agreement, in 1866, was created by a Mexican American man and his Anglo son-in-law, two other Mexican Americans, an African American, a German immigrant, and an elderly Illinois native who was the wealthiest man in Arizona. A decade later, a Mexican American woman, María Ruiz, who was daughter to one owner and the widow of another, became via inheritance a farmer and owner of water rights alongside all these men.

Conflicts over water rights were endemic, but they did not divide by national origin. A descendant of the intermarried Ruiz-Montgomery family, for example, recalled that "Simon Madrid and [Thomas] Dunbar were our families' mortal enemies." Lawsuits over water (including a nasty case involving Grijalba) pitted neighbor against neighbor, but *not* Mexican against Anglo. Nor were these agreements—and disagreements—only among men. A Montgomery family descendant recalled, "I guess my great grandma [María Ruiz de Montgomery] threatened Dunbar to have him locked up for stealing her water."[26]

In Tres Alamos, the only important social division was between Apaches and everyone else. Before 1886, San Pedro farmers and traders frequently banded together as "unofficial militias" to defend their land from Apache raids. Schoolteacher Mary Bernard Aguirre remembered being awakened one morning by "a hoarse voice saying, 'Los indios, los indios'" at her window. Chiricahua Apaches had reportedly killed three men on a ranch six miles away.[27] In 1872, after another Apache raid on Tres Alamos, "a party of fourteen men mounted [their] animals" to follow the Indians' trail. One resident reported, "The little force of citizens was forced to retire with the loss of one of their companions killed—Ramón Altamirano."[28] In response, thirty-five men—native Mexicans and American migrants—teamed up and set out. After yet another raid, the same resident reported that "the people are saddling up to follow them . . . and will be on their trail in a few minutes."[29] It is safe to say that "the people" were both Mexican and Anglo.

While the people of the militias were men only, Mexican women played an important role in expanding Mexican families' landownership and forging ties with Euro-American settlers. Before 1900, 14 percent of Mexican American homesteaders were women. After 1900, this percentage increased to about one-third. Their actual numbers were small, but this was twice as high a proportion as that of women among Euro-Americans during their peak years of homesteading. Historians have overlooked Mexican American women homesteaders, but Arizona's civil law provisions protected married women's property rights,[30] and homesteading could expand family landholding. The law forbade married women from filing homestead claims, but single or widowed women could do so, then tie the knot and bring the land to the marriage.[31]

Women's land was usually connected to larger family landholdings, but they also held some control over their land and property. When landowner María Ruiz de Montgomery was widowed, she managed and farmed her land herself. "I don't know how long she has been cultivating," her son explained in 1889, "but a long time." She hired people to work the land she controlled, but this was standard practice for male "farmers," too.[32] Several Mexican women recorded and used their own cattle brands.[33]

Many Mexican women combined landownership with intermarriage. María Ruiz de Montgomery is one example. German immigrant William

Ohnesorgen married a Mexican woman, possibly another Ruiz, and members of the Dunbar and Soto families also intermarried.[34] In the 1870s, almost a quarter of all marriages in Pima County, which still included Tres Alamos, were between Anglos and people with Spanish surnames. Half of the prominent Americans who founded the Arizona Pioneers' Historical Society in 1885 had married Mexican women.[35]

Intermarriage does not create or imply racial, economic, or gender equality. Gender and race are relations of power, and marriage is rarely a partnership of equals.[36] Yet, as many scholars have shown, intermarriage *can* tell us something about the history of race in a region. Unlike in almost every other non-European ethnic group in the American West, marriage between Mexicans and Anglos has never been illegal.[37] It actually could not be because, legally, Mexicans were white. Former Mexican citizens in the acquired territory were guaranteed U.S. citizenship and property rights. In theory, this was guaranteed regardless of racial status such as mestizo, *indio*, or even *afromestizo*. Early Arizona law offered voting rights to "every white male citizen of the United States, and every white male citizen of Mexico" who had "elected to become" a U.S. citizen by right of the Treaty of Guadalupe Hidalgo or the Gadsden Purchase.[38] At least on paper, the category "Mexican" remained a national, rather than a racial, label.

But citizenship and suffrage rights are not coterminous (as woman suffrage advocates were busy reminding their fellow Americans). Even after the Fourteenth Amendment, loopholes restricted the voting rights of nonwhites. Western territories and states withheld voting rights from Mexicans by arguing they were mestizo, and thus partly if not wholly "Indian." In the twentieth century, Mexican Americans across the West resorted to the courts to prove their whiteness. In 1884, only 29 out of 2,836 registered voters in Cochise County were Mexican American.[39] They faced the double burden of proving whiteness and U.S. citizenship. Yet homesteaders represented the lion's share of those Mexican Americans on the voting rolls.[40]

Homesteaders were a self-selected group, comfortable claiming American citizenship and willing to have it scrutinized. For all its concern over the racial status of Mexicans, Arizona law failed to define whiteness — which meant that the assumption of someone's whiteness amounted to their actual possession of it. This was a decidedly Latin view of race.[41] Legal cases from around the country in the late nineteenth and early twentieth centuries demonstrate this "I know it when I see it" jurisprudence of race. Many of Arizona's Mexican American homesteaders belonged to families widely considered to be Spanish, and thus white. Perhaps they expected no trouble on this score, or maybe they thought that homesteading settled the matter. In fact, very few people of "pure" Spanish descent lived on the Arizona frontier, but *limpieza de sangre* (blood purity) was historically negotiable on New Spain's and Mexico's northern frontiers. Landowning often led to Spanish status.[42]

In 1881 Tres Alamos (and a handful of similar places across Arizona Territory), integration, cooperation, and family consolidation flourished among people of Mexican and European descent. Landownership, not "race," was the key component of status. Combining past tradition and present-day realities, the people of Tres Alamos created an integrated enclave that represented a possible, plausible future for southern Arizona. Yet their world was also fragile, for their delicate balance of cooperation and coexistence depended on a land-based economy and, ironically, the thing they most dreaded—Apache warfare. By 1881, huge changes to the region—the arrival of the Southern Pacific Railroad, the boom at Tombstone, the recommitment to destroying Apache autonomy—were shifting the lives of Tres Alamos residents.

Tombstone

In 1877, prospector Ed Schieffelin discovered silver at the place he dubbed Tombstone in response to critics who claimed he would find only his own grave. News of the lode traveled slowly at first. But by 1881, Tombstone had exploded into a rambunctious and bustling urban sprawl of perhaps ten thousand people. Prospectors from California and Nevada brought the racial mores of mining camps with them to Tombstone and supported a fervent, though unsuccessful, anti-Chinese campaign in 1880.

However, this campaign and other controversies were overshadowed by a gunfight on October 26, 1881, which pitted the Earp brothers and their friend "Doc" Holliday against the Clanton and McLaury brothers, part of a group known as the "Cowboys." This event, when scrubbed of dime-novel gore, turns out to be a remarkable episode in U.S.-Mexico relations. Unlike Tres Alamos, Tombstone was dominated by Euro-Americans. In contrast to their attitudes about the Chinese, however, many local residents demonstrated remarkable solidarity with their neighbors in Mexico victimized by the renegade Cowboys.

Tombstone was a typical polyglot mining camp. Almost half of its residents were born outside the United States. Yet, in spite of the renowned mining skills of Sonorans, in 1880, less than 1 percent of Tombstone's miners were Mexican. This hinted at discrimination, exacerbated by industrialization that rendered traditional Spanish-Mexican mining techniques obsolete.[43] Tombstone did remain closely tied to Mexico's mining industry as an ore-processing and supply depot, at a time when Pres. Porfirio Díaz was aggressively courting American business investment. As a result, in the 1880s, the border remained utterly permeable to the flow of both financial and human capital.[44]

This situation worked out nicely for businessmen, but also for criminals. The wide-open borderlands supported a band of "desperadoes and outlaws" conducting a "reign of terror" on both sides of the border, stealing cattle and horses, holding up stagecoaches, and murdering their mostly Mexican victims.[45] The American bandits were known as Cowboys, and they numbered anywhere from 30 to 380, depending on who was counting.[46] The Clantons and McLaurys were among their leaders, but these men had a respectable side, too, as Democratic activists and partisans of the local county sheriff, Johnny Behan.

The Earps, in contrast, were Republicans who opposed Behan (and to make matters worse, Wyatt Earp stole Behan's girlfriend), but most important for this chapter was the fact that this conflict became a national and diplomatic emergency. A firestorm erupted in Washington, D.C., over the Cowboys' raids into Mexico. Months before the shootout, Sonora's governor, Luis Torres, complained to U.S. federal officials that "our border is in continuous alarm,"[47] and warned that Mexican citizens "threaten to take matter into their own hands if they are not protected" by the United States government."[48]

A war of tit-for-tat between Cowboys and Mexicans had racked up several murders on both sides of the border. One of them, in the summer of 1881, involved the Clanton family. In retaliation for a Cowboy raid that killed four men, Newman "Old Man" Clanton (father of the OK Corral gunfighters) and six other men were ambushed during the night. Five men, including the Clanton patriarch, were killed. The shootings were likely committed by Sonoran soldiers retaliating for a recent altercation between the Cowboys and Mexican troops.[49]

Even before the incident at Guadalupe Canyon, complaints about Cowboy attacks on Mexicans were escalating. In June 1881, Arizona's U.S. attorney, C. B. Pomroy, warned the federal government that "citizens of the United States are constantly committing depredations of the most barbarous character" on Mexican citizens. If not stopped, these crimes and trespasses "may lead to an open rupture between that country and our own, at any time." Pomroy worried that the Cowboy raids would lead to "an international controversy, if not war."[50] The failure to use troops to put down the Cowboys, warned commanding general of the U.S. Army William Tecumseh Sherman, might leave the United States "compromised with our neighbor Mexico."[51] Another official called the Mexican government "very much incensed at our seeming neglect." Governor Torres implored U.S. officials "to act promptly" and placed three hundred Mexican troops on his side of the line.[52]

It was not a good time for a fight. After years of warfare and tense relations between Mexico and the United States, the ascension of the dictator Porfirio Díaz in 1876 had brought friendlier diplomacy and massive investments that high-ranking officials wanted to protect. The acting governor of Arizona warned the attorney general that if something was not done, "the cow-boy will come to control and 'run' that part of our Territory with terror and destruction and probably cause serious complications with our sister Republic Mexico, with which we are now in fullest peace."[53] The United States was indebted to Mexico's good graces, and both locals and officials knew it. Had these crimes "been inflicted upon our people by Mexicans," U.S. Attorney Pomroy admitted, it would have "aroused a whirlwind of indignation from the Rio Grande to the Gulf of California, and doubtless long ago led to an invasion of Mexican soil."[54]

Foreign investors wanted a border permeable to international capital, but not to Cowboy raiders. Arizona's chief U.S. marshal informed the U.S. attorney general that "raiding robbing and murdering on the border . . . is causing great injury to the business interests of our growing territory."[55] A Tucson newspaper editorial noted that "Sonora is rapidly filling up with Americans," but that violence threatened to erase the "advantages to be devised from co[m]mercial and social intercourse between the two countries."[56]

Local Euro-American residents expressed genuine sympathy for both Mexican citizens and their government. In February 1881, Tucson's Democratic paper implored readers to "let our Mexican neighbors understand that our people are determined to rid them and Arizona of these outlaws and they will be protected in following them across the line into our borders, and treating them in a summary manner."[57] The last comment appears to endorse Mexican authorities shooting down American Cowboys on U.S. soil!

In Tombstone, defenders of the Mexican attack on Clanton's party at Guadalupe Canyon were not hard to find. As Earp partisan George Parsons wrote in his diary, "This killing business by the Mexicans, in my mind, was perfectly justifiable, as it was in retaliation." Local journalist Clara Brown observed that, while no one was happy about "the great massacre," "the Mexicans were not the first to inaugurate the present unhappy state of affairs. . . . The Mexicans have lost a great deal of stock, and some of their countrymen have been murdered."[58]

The campaign against the Cowboys turns many stereotypes about western race relations and allegiances on their head. Vigilante justice in the West was often racially motivated and directed, just as it was in the American South.[59] Tombstone had its fair share of racial prejudice, yet here was a case where calls for vigilantism were directed against white Cowboys, whose attacks were mainly against Mexicans. At one point, federal authorities even considered using the army's Apache scouts to chase down the Cowboys. Using scouts, wrote one proponent, the Cowboys' "ranches can be entirely surrounded and the occupants captured, provided proper secrecy can be maintained."[60]

Indians chasing Cowboys with army approval? Military and civilian law enforcement scotched the plan after word of a renewed Apache War outbreak. In the end, it took Pres. Chester Arthur's threat of martial law and a rash of vigilante murders by the Earps and their sympathizers to put down the Cowboy threat.

Here is the backstory of the shootout at the OK Corral. In the early 1880s, American criminals—not Mexican immigrants—made the Arizona border a site of controversy and danger. General Sherman visited Tombstone in April 1882 and called for greater federal power to patrol the border, not because of illegal immigration (a concept that barely existed and was in reference to the Chinese), but because "the cowboys make use of the boundary line to escape pursuit first on the one side & then on the other."[61] Arizona governor Frederick Tritle pleaded for a "mounted border patrol" decades before the U.S. Border Patrol was officially established in 1925, but he wanted the men to chase American outlaws, not Mexican immigrants.[62] Many Americans in Tombstone sympathized with and saw as their allies those Mexicans caught in the Cowboys' cross fire.

Bisbee

Even as Tombstone residents were taking sides with Mexico against American Cowboys, the copper camp of Bisbee, twenty-five miles away, was securing a reputation as a "white man's camp." This was a term used across the West, with varied meanings.[63] Bisbee's version meant that no Chinese could live or work there and that Mexicans were restricted to the most menial mine labor and lowest pay. In 1881, the venerable New York brass trading firm of Phelps, Dodge & Co. purchased Bisbee's Copper Queen Mine, which became the company's first copper mine. The white man's camp ideology would define labor and race relations in Bisbee for sixty years, while the Copper Queen—which produced 40 percent of the state's copper and 12 percent of the nation's by the early twentieth century—would transform Phelps Dodge into one of the most powerful mining corporations in the world and a guiding force in Arizona's economy and government.[64]

In 1881, Bisbee was still a tiny camp of two hundred people, unimpressive compared to bustling Tombstone. Yet the smaller settlement was already a functional mining and smelter center reliant on wage labor. *Whose* wage labor, however, was a growing concern to the area's skilled miners, many of Cornish, Irish, and Welsh descent. Over half of Bisbee's two hundred residents were foreign-born, same as in Tombstone. Unlike Tres Alamos and Tombstone, though, as much as two-thirds of Bisbee's population was "Mexican" (including, of course, American citizens of Mexican descent).[65] Yet Bisbee's Mexican population did not enjoy the equanimity of class and social relations fostered in Tres Alamos, or the sympathies expressed by Tombstone residents for Mexicans across the border.

Local lore dates Bisbee's self-identification as a white man's camp to a meeting in the back of John "Pie" Allen's general store on Christmas Eve, 1880.[66] There local men worked up a district code—a social compact and set of laws to enforce "law and order." Similar legal codes, which were not bound by statute but were meant to "keep the peace" in rough mining camps, had originated in the mining regions of Cornwall (whence many of Bisbee's residents had come), but their technicalities also relied—without acknowledgment—on Spanish and Mexican legal traditions. These quasi-legal district codes also governed the gold diggings in California and the silver camps of Colorado, where they were often used to exclude Chinese and Latin American miners, in other words, to create white man's camps. Arizona's earliest-known white man's camp had an 1863 code that barred "Asiatics & Sonorians . . . from working this district."

Exclusionary pacts generally appeared in new settlements with no indigenous Mexican landowners and merchants. Where Mexican "pioneers" did exist, exceptions could be made. One code decreed that "no citizens of Mexico shall hold or work claims in this District except the boy Lorenzo Para who is one of the original discoverers." Lines of demarcation were not always clear, however: one group of miners who excluded Mexicans later added an amendment to their code decreeing that a three-man committee "shall decide who are & who are not Mexicans."[67] These variations underscored the permeability and local specificity of racial boundaries.

The code created at Pie Allen's store did not explicitly declare Bisbee to be a white man's camp, at least not in the public record. Yet from its earliest years Bisbee's reputation as a white man's camp enjoyed, as one local reporter explained, "unanimous unwritten consent."[68] Some people characterized Bisbee's anti-Chinese rule as a defense of women's work, "made for the protection of the widows from foreign countries who had made the mining camp their home. They were honorable and good people and had families of small children."[69] Since many—indeed, most—laundresses were Mexican, this rule could presumably protect Mexican women. When a Chinese man attempted to run a laundry in Bisbee, local residents reportedly burned a Chinese dummy in effigy; the man left.

Sex taboos also enforced anti-Chinese rules. Early Bisbee resident Juanita Tarin remembered some Chinese men being run out of town for doing "what they wanted" with a "white girl, a lady, it was a white lady." The "law found out and they were deported from here."[70] This rumor had a powerful meaning, regardless of its veracity.

The second rule of the white man's camp—more subtle than the anti-Chinese rule—proscribed Mexican men from working at the better-paying underground mining jobs. Mexican men were clustered in backbreaking and unrewarding surface work, and thus were known as "topmen." This work paid less than mining jobs underground. It was equally dirty and almost as dangerous, but it was less lucrative and less respected.

In addition to being segregated into Mexican jobs, Mexican men also earned lower pay even when they performed the same work as other men. A race-based wage scale, known as the dual-wage system, was common even in so-called Mexican camps like Clifton-Morenci, where Mexicans performed all but the supervisory work.[71] Copper Queen payrolls from 1885 (the earliest available) until the 1920s explicitly list Mexican and white wages separately,[72] even for the same job description. In 1885, a job wheeling adobe bricks, to name just one example, earned whites at the Copper Queen $2.25 a day, and Mexicans $1.50.[73]

One argument for the lower wages was that Mexicans were unskilled miners. As early as 1882, the foreman of the Copper Queen Mine claimed that Mexicans in Bisbee had no mining experience.[74] Such claims were an abrupt turnabout from the colonial and early U.S. periods, when Sonorans were prized for their mining skills. Lamented one Mexican observer in 1889, "Work for Mexicans is very scarce and pay is low. . . . What hope do we have living in a country where we are looked at with such prejudice, where justice isn't for us, and where we are treated as the lowest of the human race?"[75]

The rules of the white man's camp constituted a kind of ideology. They categorized jobs and wages by race, but in doing so they also structured local citizenship and hierarchy and values. The rules helped some people and harmed others, yet implied neutrality by invoking explanations that they reflected the natural order of things. As theorists Trevor Purvis and Alan Hunt have observed, an ideology "always works to favor some and disadvantage others" and makes this disparity seem "natural."[76]

Natural, yes, but they still needed justifications. As historians like Yvette Huginnie and Linda Gordon have shown, defenders argued that Mexican workers had a lower standard of living than other workers. The seasonal migration patterns of Mexican immigrants that created high rates of turnover and a majority male population, their low wages, and thus dismal living conditions, all became fodder for arguments about their racial inferiority. One government investigator concluded in 1908 that "the wants of the Mexican peon are hardly more complex than those of the Indian from whom he is descended," and therefore low wages did not harm him.[77] White workers and managers interpreted circular migration and dismal living conditions of Mexican immigrants as racial characteristics that justified Mexicans' lower wages and their exclusion from skilled mining jobs. This reasoning's tautology did not diminish its power, nor did the failure to distinguish between recently arrived or migrant immigrants from Mexico and Mexican Americans rooted in the United States.

Nor did it give any pause to the Copper Queen's new owners. Although they did not invent the racial system, they did adopt it. Soon after Phelps Dodge took over, Mexican wages, but not white ones, declined.[78] Still, it is worth remembering that in Bisbee, home of Phelps Dodge's first mine, it was rough prospectors and early skilled miners, not New York managers, who first created the rules of racial division and social stratification. Phelps Dodge and other copper-mining corporations and sympathetic white workers preserved the dual-wage system until the 1950s, even in the face of strikes, federal investigations, and Supreme Court cases.

With its ardent opposition to unionization, Phelps Dodge acquiesced to and elaborated on the rules of the white man's camp in exchange for no labor trouble. The rules of the white man's camp constituted a kind of "gentlemen's agreement" between elite Western European miners and their corporate employers. When union organizers came to Bisbee in 1903 and 1907, they found a chilly—even chilling—reception. During an abortive strike in 1907, general manager Walter Douglas promised to shut down the mines if unions came to town.[79] By 1917, he and many others were willing to go farther still.

1917: A Turning Point

The year 1917 was a turning point not just for Bisbee but for Arizona. The brute force of the Bisbee Deportation—which involved perhaps one-fifth of the adult male population of the town—crushed an increasingly powerful labor movement in mining camps across Arizona. In the early twentieth century, many white unionists campaigned for laws that discriminated against immigrants' employment, but after several commanding strikes by Mexicans in other mining camps, white unionists grew more sympathetic to their once-maligned coworkers.

Yet this was a very controversial alliance. By 1917, Mexicans had long been second-class citizens in the white man's camp, and the decision of Mexican topmen to join the strike—and demand white men's wages—outraged many local residents. The Mexican Revolution, which prompted bloody skirmishes in the border towns of Naco and Agua Prieta near Bisbee in 1911, 1914, and 1915, only made local law enforcement officers and mining executives more hostile to Mexican immigrants. In early 1917, the revelation of the Zimmermann telegram, in which Germany promised to return the American Southwest to Mexico in exchange for its war support, had given border residents new reasons to fear the ongoing Mexican Revolution. Then in April, the United States officially entered World War I, three years after it began, amidst much domestic dissension and controversy. In 1917, the U.S. Congress implemented a literacy test for immigrants, although Mexicans were exempted through the course of the war,[80] and racial and labor conflicts like the East Saint Louis riots and thousands of strikes erupted across the United States.

The world had changed. But to understand the significance of 1917 as a local watershed requires an understanding of how Bisbee had changed since 1881. By 1917, Bisbee was a booming metropolis of perhaps twenty-five thousand people from at least thirty-four countries. This population—still predominantly male, but with thousands of women and families, too—was bursting at the seams in crowded rooming houses, at least twenty distinct neighborhoods, and in mine payrolls that numbered in the thousands. In response to the war effort, mine production was ramped up like never before, with shifts working around the clock.

Since 1881, the industry had changed, and the meanings of the white man's camp had changed alongside it. The exclusion of Chinese persisted, as did the relegation of Mexicans to low-paying jobs. But now Eastern and Southern European newcomers were also gathering by the hundreds in Bisbee. In May of 1903, the *Bisbee Daily Review* had reported, "a question of great moment is agitating the miners—that is, the American miners of Bisbee: viz., the employment of Italian and Slavonic [*sic*] workmen in some of the mines and the readiness with which they are employed by some of the foremen." Then the story invoked Bisbee's vaunted reputation: "The American miners contend that Bisbee has always been a 'White Man's Camp,' and much feeling is being manifested by the men who are, as they say, unable to secure employment by the influx of foreign labor." By 1903, in other words, "American miners" were using the ideology of the white man's camp not only to exclude the Chinese and segregate Mexicans, but also to lobby against the employment of Eastern and Southern European "foreigners." Their language betrayed the slippage between "white" and "American," and this could only be bad news for Mexicans in a town eight miles from the Mexico border. It put men from Eastern and Southern Europe in a strange, unsettled position, and revealed the growing fault lines between corporate managers and the white miners. One mine's general manager, John Merrill, insisted, "If Italian miners come, I will hire them, as I must have men to work."[81]

Bisbee's white workers opposed foreign labor by invoking the "American standard of living," a term that national trade unionists had been developing since the Jacksonian era.[82] Bisbee's white workers complained that "the foreign element can live on a mere pittance to what a white man can. . . . [N]orth of the Catholic church and in an oblong building [are] . . . a bunch of Italians living as no white man can." White versus foreign; an "oblong building," not a house; a "bunch of Italians," rather than a family.

As these dialectics reveal, the putative ideal was a married, white, "American" man in a single-family home full of children. Corporate policies encouraged this ideal. The mines kept married workers on during slow times and let single men go. Company managers funded schools and playgrounds in hopes of securing family workers. In 1907, the Copper Queen's first major competitor built an entire suburb and created generous home-financing plans for miners, because the company believed homeowners were less likely to strike.[83] The company's town site manager claimed to have "learned from experience that the robust American with a growing family is a better man for us than a man without these things."[84]

Ten years later, racialized assumptions about marriage, family, nation, and household saturated the rhetoric of the Bisbee Deportation. Sheriff Harry Wheeler, in particular, defended his role in the Deportation loudly and often by claiming his aim was to protect white (American) women. According to Wheeler, a group of female laundry workers "were so terrorized by visitations of a committee of Mexicans [to organize the laundry] . . . that the women one day left in a body in abject terror. Think of white women in an American town so terrorized by foreigners that they were compelled to quit work in terror of their lives."[85] In Wheeler's mind, protecting white womanhood was just as natural as self-defense; both actions were at the heart of his understanding of manhood and the defense of an American town.

The characteristics of the deputies and deportees also reflected the politics of race, nation, and family status. About 90 percent of the men rounded up on July 12 were immigrants. About half of these were Mexican or Slavic. Many were suspected sympathizers who were not even mine workers or strikers. The demographics of the deputies were the reverse. Ninety percent of the identifiable "deputies" were U.S. citizens, two-thirds of these native-born Americans. Only one in four deportees was married, compared to three out of four of the deputies. Twenty-eight percent of the deportees had children compared to 62 percent of the deputies (statistics on marriage and fatherhood were partly a function of age, as the deportees also tended to be younger).[86]

If the goal of the Bisbee Deportation was to purge foreigners and single men, then it was a resounding success. A large sample of deportees and deputies reveals that almost 40 percent (192 of 503 names) of the identifiable deputies from 1917 had stayed in Bisbee until 1920, despite a serious recession after the war ended. In contrast, the near-total erasure of the deportees is shocking. Just 6 percent of the deportees—61 of 1,003 identifiable names—were in a city directory published months after the Deportation. By 1920, only somewhere between 34 and 45 of that original 1,003 appeared in the local census.[87] Some men probably returned to town and changed their names to avoid blacklisting, but hardly enough to make a meaningful difference. As one deportee explained, "It is not that the men are determined to live in the town from which they were expelled. In fact, they appear without exception to realize that under any circumstances life would be made, in one way or another, unendurable for them in Bisbee, and it is altogether likely that even those with established homes would soon move away, rather than endure the persecution."[88] Another man recalled that "the [single] fellas moved out, and it became more of a family town after that."[89] An unsuccessful civil suit against the deputies contained only a handful of Mexican surnames among 500 plaintiffs; no doubt, they simply left the region, knowing they had little chance at justice.[90]

The effect of the Deportation on Bisbee's immigrant communities was dramatic. By the fall of 1917, the Calumet & Arizona (C&A) Company's underground workforce was over 70 percent American, compared to just under 50 percent a year earlier. The percentage of Serbs working there fell by more than half, from 3.4 to 1.5. The number of "Austrians," a category that was in fact heavily Slavic, fell by the largest percentage, from 14.7 to 3.8.[91] Six months after the Deportation, Bisbee's new city directory claimed that "no foreign labor is employed in the mines, thus making Bisbee stand out as the leading American industrial center of the Southwest."[92] By 1920, census figures suggest that perhaps half of Bisbee's large Slavic population, 20 percent of the Italians, and almost all of the Finns were gone.[93] The number of Mexican residents did not change as much as that of other ethnic groups, in part because they could be replenished from across the border. But they remained restricted to surface labor.

In 1918, Fred Sutter, a Bisbee attorney turned state senator, praised the deportation in a speech at the state capitol:

> And what are the results in Bisbee since the deportation? They are . . . a practically one hundred per cent American Camp. A foreigner to get a job there today has to give a pretty good account of himself; an increase of thirty-three percent in the number of children attending school; the erection of three new school buildings and the completion of over three hundred new dwelling houses. More miners own their homes . . . than in any other mining camp in the United States. The mines are today producing more copper than ever before and we are a quiet, peaceful, law-abiding community.[94]

The Deportation cast a long shadow. In later years, Bisbee was feted for avoiding "Mexicanization."[95] As late as 1929, a promotion in the *Arizona Labor Journal* boasted that Bisbee was the "last stand of the white miner."[96]

In the end, purging racially questionable foreigners increased the divide between Mexican and American. The white man's camp became known as the "American camp," with European immigrants counting as American. The Bisbee Deportation marked the death of racial subtleties, in part by literally removing many of the most racially ambiguous: radical Slavic, Italian, and Finnish immigrants. Those who chose to stay were in essence pronouncing their loyalty to the mining companies. A few Serbs and Finns even began buying homes in the American suburb. A new Catholic church and public schools segregated whites and Mexicans, but not foreigners.

Yet for all of this, even in 1917, the county still harbored multiple racial possibilities. Tres Alamos dwindled away, but a couple of other settlements snaked along the San Pedro River, where Mexican American families continued to homestead, ranch, and farm. They maintained their own schools and filled the newspaper social pages in the nearby railroad town of Benson.[97] In contrast, the *Bisbee Daily Review*, which was owned by Phelps-Dodge, rarely mentioned Mexicans outside of the crime reports. In Benson, Mexican Americans served on civic committees, were registered to vote in higher proportions than in Bisbee, and attended integrated schools. In 1917, less than two months before the Deportation, the son of pioneer San Pedro River homesteaders Francisco Soza was valedictorian of Benson High School.[98] Tucson's middle-class Mexican Americans, to whom the Tres Alamos homesteaders were closely related, opposed the Wobblies' strike in 1917 and carefully publicized their loyalty to the United States during World War I.[99] Shortly afterward, the Mexican American settlement of Cascabel fought off a challenge by Anglo newcomers to take over their school. The parents signed a petition to save the school in which they emphasized their landownership and rights as citizens: "We have maintained our homes here for many years. . . . As good citizens, we claim the right of tutelage for our children, and as reasonable persons," we want to keep the district out of "the hands of . . . those careless of our rights." The Anglo teacher they had hired concurred: "The people here own the land along the river," she wrote to the county superintendent. "[F]ew 'white people' would work so hard to maintain their land and raise their corn, beans, and hay and grain."[100]

Yet middle-class Mexican Americans' tiny base of power—based in landholding and mercantile interests—could hardly compete with the corporate juggernaut of the copper companies, and the decline in race relations would make this clear.

1934: New Deal Coda

A brief coda about where things stood by 1934 concludes the story of Cochise County's racial transformations. World War I turned out to have been the high point of the county's prosperity and political influence. Afterward, a mining recession and glutted agricultural markets devastated the county. The mining industry remained unsteady throughout the 1920s, and during the depression, mine and smelter payrolls fell by the thousands. From 1917 to 1940, the county's population fell by 30 percent, from around fifty thousand to around thirty-five thousand.[101] Bisbee lost a third of its population, while several rural settlements completely disappeared as prices for alfalfa hay and beef cattle fell by more than half from the 1920s to the 1930s.[102] In desperate times, Phelps Dodge gained power by buying out smaller, undercapitalized competitors.[103]

The ascendance of corporate control across the county unified the once-diverse local racial systems. By the 1930s, it was quite clear that Phelps Dodge called the shots in Cochise County, and that meant that the division between Mexican and white American became the operative racial system across the county. New Deal programs provided assistance to the needy, but their administration by local elites ensured that corporate mining's power would increase, and that the strict divisions between Mexican and white American enforced in mining wage scales would be instituted across the county in work and reform programs. White women reformers who represented what I call the "corporate maternalist" wing of the mining companies were hired to administer county New Deal programs and spread the inequalities and segregation of the dual-wage system across the county.

Of the years that organize this chapter, 1934 is admittedly the most arbitrary—a moment in a continuum rather than a landmark or watershed. Yet 1934 is a year that offers tidbits with great symbolic value. The most poignant is the 1934 yearbook of Bisbee High School (which, as the only public high school in town, had to admit Mexican Americans and African Americans, though lower grades were segregated). The senior pictures of a handful of Mexican American students and of two lonely African American young women occupy a separate page after the photo section for whites.[104]

Other 1934 anecdotes tell a similar story. In March of that year, the Arizona State Welfare Board—which distributed federal relief funds—reclassified relief wages based on local prevailing rates, which in Cochise County were of course created by Phelps Dodge. The mechanics of wage determination also weighed heavily in the mining industry's favor. Program rules required a county wage classification committee and grievance committee, in addition to the county board of welfare. The state board ruled, however, that the county public welfare boards could simply serve in all three capacities. In other words, the same committee set policy, distributed relief, and handled complaints.[105] Phelps Dodge partisans, including the superintendent of the Phelps Dodge smelter, dominated the board.[106] In the aftermath, Cochise County resident A. C. García wrote to Washington to complain about "gross irregularity on the distribution of relief work in this district." "Spanish-American citizens are being discriminated against, whether native born or naturalized," he explained. "This fact is shown on the posted lists and freely admitted by our relief boards." He went on: "We as Americans desire and demand this injustice be abolished."[107]

The copper fiefdoms of Bisbee and smelter town Douglas got the lion's share of county New Deal allocations, sometimes ten times as much. In April 1934, for instance, the Federal Emergency Relief Administration (FERA) funded twenty-eight projects in Cochise County. Eight projects, all in northern Cochise County, received just over $10,000. Nine others—totaling $176,148—were allotted to the Bisbee metropolitan area; one funded a golf course. Funds evened out slightly over time, but Bisbee and Douglas continued to monopolize federal work funds. When a Works Progress Administration (WPA) administrator mistakenly mentioned "Bisbee County" in official correspondence, it was a revealing slip.[108]

White women reformers were critical to New Deal programming, and they tended to replicate corporate inequalities. The popular Home Extension Service, a federal program for rural women that dated to the Progressive Era, had since 1917 retreated from work with Mexican American women. In 1934, home extension agent Bertha Virmond observed that "the 1918, 1919, and 1920 reports show much work with the Mexican girls and mothers in Douglas and Bisbee," but this trend, she noted, had not continued. WPA sewing rooms for women were segregated across the county, regardless of local race relations, and Mexican women were shunted into domestic aid programs to work for white volunteer employers. By focusing on Anglo women and segregating much of their programming, women reformers gave government sanction to deepening class, race, and religious divisions among women.[109]

The greatest injustice of the New Deal, though, was the policy that assigned explicitly lower relief funds and public works wages for Mexican Americans. In July 1934, a group calling itself the Latin-American Club of Cochise County complained to the State Board of Public Welfare about the "amount of relief given to Mexicans as compared to other families." One program gave Mexican and Indian families $3.66 per month, while whites received $6.69. The state board replied that "relief was given on the basis of need only."[110] This was a sly answer that did not deny the club's allegation—because state administrators widely agreed that Mexicans had less need than did whites, just as defenders of the companies' dual-wage system did.

Those few aid programs that did not discriminate annoyed white recipients and administrators, both of whom took the dual-wage economy's racial assumptions for granted. In the same month as the Latin-American Club's complaint, an Anglo resident of the county complained that funds distributed to family breadwinners based on the number of their dependents actually *favored* Mexican Americans, who tended to have larger families.[111] In 1934, State Board of Public Welfare secretary Florence Warner urged FERA's national director to increase the number of professional projects in Arizona. "It has been bitter for the educated people," she argued, "to have to see the peon type of Mexican receiving the same relief as they." Thousands of Mexican American workers, she explained, have a "standard of living [that] is very low but if they are citizens we are obliged to give them the same amount of relief as the people who have a high standard of living. Consequently, many American-Mexicans are living fatter than they have for a good many years. . . . On the other hand we have a group of people whose morale is almost at the breaking point."[112] She saw equal wages and relief not as simple justice but as a degradation of Anglos.

Countywide WPA programs, administered by mining company elites, overpowered local variations in race relations. On the one hand, some local racial integration persisted. While Mexican American students appeared on a separate page from white students (who included many Serbs) in Bisbee High's yearbook, Benson teenagers elected classmate William Molina to two different student council offices.[113] Benson also included Mexican Americans in its depression relief planning, while Bisbee did not. Benson's local National Recovery Administration (NRA) advisory committee included Paul Blanco, a Southern Pacific Railway employee with deep family roots in both Arizona and Mexico, and Ed Ohnesorgen, the grandson of German and Mexican pioneers at Tres Alamos. Both men represented Mexican mutual-aid societies.[114]

On the other hand, Benson got sucked into the same segregated New Deal orbit, whose center of gravity was the copper mines. In 1934, FERA (whose board was dominated by mining administrators) sponsored summer camps for children on relief rolls. Forty American children from the Benson area attended one week, with forty Spanish children to attend separately.[115] Which camp might the children of Benson's New Deal committee members have attended? If high school students attended, would William Molina have gone a different week from the rest of the student council? Though it was hardly the largest racial injustice in the county's history, the irony of William Molina's election as a class officer even as the New Deal brought segregation to his hometown seems especially bitter. It speaks volumes about the commitment of adults to maintaining social systems they insisted were natural in the face of contradictory evidence from their own children.

But there is hope in the year 1934 as well, and not just in the student council election. A nascent American Federation of Labor (AFL) local in Bisbee had begun organizing after the passage in 1933 of the National Industrial Recovery Act (NIRA), whose Section 7(a) guaranteed the right of collective bargaining.[116] By 1935, it would launch a strike that ended in a landmark antiblacklisting decision by the U.S. Supreme Court. Smelter workers challenged the dual-wage system again, and the federal Fair Employment Practices Commission (FEPC) investigated complaints about wage discrimination in 1942 and 1943. When one supervisor in the smelter town of Douglas told a Mexican American worker, "We have to save all of the best jobs for the Americans . . . that's the rule of the company," he meant that a Mexican (even if he was a native-born U.S. citizen) could not really be an American.[117] This was one of dozens of complaints filed with the FEPC.[118]

Although the FEPC complaints did not lead to sanctions against Phelps Dodge in the short term, they marked the beginning of the end for the dual-wage system. Mexican American workers, joined by a few Anglos belonging to International Union of Mine, Mill, and Smelter Workers (Mine-Mill) locals, began to push hard for its demise. These copper workers understood their battles were part of a broader attack on discrimination across the Southwest. The mining towns of Arizona would become bulwarks of Mexican American working-class political power; the sons and daughters of copper miners helped launch Arizona's Chicano/a movement in the early 1970s. One of them, Raúl Castro, became Arizona's first Mexican American governor; another, Ed Pastor, became its first Mexican American member of Congress (where he still serves).

These stories are not yet well known, but they are a triumphant rebuttal of the assumptions that guided the ordinary and elite men and women who created a world of two separate and unequal races—Mexican and white American—from a diverse set of nineteenth-century possibilities in

Cochise County and across the Southwest. It shows, as Ramón Gutiérrez' chapter reminds us, that we should continue to explore the persistent possibilities of MexAmerica.

Notes

The author would like to thank the members of the Americas Initiative, Georgetown University, and especially John Tutino, for their helpful readings and comments.

This chapter includes excerpted material from Benton-Cohen, *Borderline Americans*; idem, "Docile Children and Dangerous Revolutionaries," *Frontiers: A Journal of Women Studies* 24, nos. 2–3 (2003): 30–50; and idem, "Common Purposes, Worlds Apart," *Western Historical Quarterly* 36, no. 4 (Winter 2005): 429–452.

1. "Arizona Sheriff Ships 1,100 IWW's Out in Cattle Cars," *New York Times* (July 13, 1917): 1.

2. "Sheriff Wheeler's Statement on Strike," *Courtland Arizonan* (July 21, 1917): 2; Wheeler testimony in E. W. Powers, ed., "President's Mediation Commission Hearings at Bisbee, Arizona, November 5–11, 1917, U.S. Department of Labor, in *Papers of the Presidents' Mediation Commission, 1917–1919*, Melvyn Dubofsky, ed., rev. ed., microfilm (Frederick, Md., 1986) (hereafter PMC hearings), 154, 165, 140.

3. Jonathan Clark, "No Longer 'Ground Zero,'" *Sierra Vista Herald Review* (November 12, 2006), available at www.svherald.com (accessed December 8, 2007); Marc Cooper, "Last Exit to Tombstone," *Tucson Weekly* (March 29, 2005), www.tucsonweekly.com (accessed March 30, 2005); U.S. Rep. Gabrielle Giffords, Statement on Border Patrol Checkpoint, September 21, 2007, www .giffords.house.gov (accessed December 8, 2007); "Indiana Guard Has Big Impact on Border Mission," November 17, 2006, www.ngb.army.mil (accessed December 9, 2007).

4. See inter alia, Ruben Navarrette Jr., "Murder Conviction Serves Justice," CNN.com, February 16, 2011, http://edition.cnn.com/2011/OPINION/02/16 /navarrette.arizona.killing/# (last accessed February 21, 2011).

5. Most of the scholarly work on the region concerns the Apache Wars. See Karl Jacoby, *Shadows at Dawn* (New York: Penguin Press, 2008). The only book-length study of the Bisbee Deportation is James Byrkit, *Forging the Copper Collar* (Tucson: University of Arizona Press, 1982). Also see Samuel Truett, *Fugitive Landscapes* (New Haven: Yale University Press, 2006).

6. On *casta* and frontier racial systems, see note 40 below.

7. Linda Gordon, *The Great Arizona Orphan Abduction* (Cambridge: Harvard University Press, 1999).

8. Montejano, *Anglos and Mexicans*; Camarillo, *Chicanos in a Changing Society*; Mario T. García, *Desert Immigrants* (New Haven: Yale University Press, 1981); Tomás Almaguer, *Racial Fault Lines* (Berkeley: University of California Press, 1994); Armando C. Alonzo, *Tejano Legacy* (Albuquerque: University of New Mexico Press, 1998); Alonso, *Thread of Blood*; Brooks, *Captives and Cousins*.

9. See, e.g., Alonso, *Thread of Blood*; Brooks, *Captives and Cousins*; Barr, *Peace Came in the Form of a Woman*; Jacoby, *Shadows at Dawn*.

10. An exception is Tomás Almaguer's.

11. On the diversity of cross-border migration in this period, see Patrick Ettinger, *Imaginary Lines* (Austin: University of Texas Press, 2009).

12. Major studies of whiteness include Alexander Saxton, *The Rise and Fall of the White Republic* (London: Verso Books, 2003); David R. Roediger, *The Wages of Whiteness* (New York: Verso Books, 2007); idem, *Towards the Abolition of Whiteness* (New York, Verso Books, 1994); Matthew Jacobson, *Whiteness of a Different Color* (Cambridge: Harvard University Press, 1998); and George Lipsitz, *The Possessive Investment in Whiteness* (Philadelphia: Temple University Press, 1998). On the South, see especially Grace Elizabeth Hale, *Making Whiteness* (New York: Vintage Books, 1999). Critiques of whiteness studies include Peter Kolchin, "Whiteness Studies," *Journal of American History* 89 (June 2002): 154–173; Eric Arnesen, "Whiteness and the Historians' Imagination," *International Labor and Working-Class History* 60 (Fall 2001): 3–32; Barbara J. Fields, "Whiteness, Racism, and Identity," *International Labor and Working-Class History* 60 (Fall 2001): 48–56; Daniel Wickberg, "Heterosexual White Male," *Journal of American History* 92 (June 2005): 136–157; and Hasia Diner, "The World of Whiteness," *Historically Speaking* (September/October 2007): 20–22.

13. On Mexicans and whiteness, see Laura Gómez, *Manifest Destinies* (New York: New York University Press, 2007); Pablo Mitchell, *Coyote Nation* (Chicago: University of Chicago Press, 2005); and Carlos K. Blanton, "George I. Sánchez, Ideology, and Whiteness in the Making of the Mexican American Civil Rights Movement, 1930–1960," *Journal of Southern History* 72, no. 3 (August 2006). The rare examples of comparing Mexicans and Europeans include Gunther Peck, *Reinventing Free Labor* (New York: Cambridge University Press, 2000); Gordon, *Great Arizona Orphan Abduction*; and Foley, *White Scourge*. Mario T. García also makes some inroads on this question in *Desert Immigrants*. See also the literature on California listed below.

14. Although she did not go to California to "become white," Montgomery bus boycott organizer Jo Ann Robinson migrated west for racial freedom. See Virginia Scharff, *Twenty Thousand Roads* (Berkeley: University of California Press, 2003).

15. See Mark Wild, *Street Meeting* (Berkeley: University of California Press, 2005); Kevin Leonard, *The Battle for Los Angeles* (Albuquerque: University of New Mexico Press, 2006); Allison Varzally, *Making a Non-White America* (Berkeley: University of California Press, 2008); Natalia Molina, *Fit to Be Citizens?* (Berkeley: University of California Press, 2006). And see Scott Kurashige, *The Shifting Grounds of Race* (Princeton: Princeton University Press, 2008).

16. New Mexico has an extensive historiography, too large to detail here.

17. Katherine A. Benton-Cohen, "Docile Children and Dangerous Revolutionaries"; Susan L. Johnson, "'A Memory Sweet to Soldiers,'" *Western Historical Quarterly* 24, no. 3 (November 1993): 495. The pioneering work on gender in the borderlands is Gloria Anzaldúa, *Borderlands/La Frontera* (San Francisco: Aunt Lute Books, 2007). For a recent overview of the field, see Antonia Castañeda et al., eds., *Gender on the Borderlands* (Lincoln: University of Nebraska Press,

2007). Studies of gender in mining camps have transformed the field of western social history. Susan Johnson, *Roaring Camp*, and Matthew Basso, Laura McCall, Dee Garceau-Hagen, eds., *Across the Great Divide* (New York: Routledge, 2001), consider not just gender diversity in the camps, but the gender identities and anxieties of miners themselves.

18. See Erika Lee, *At America's Gates* (Chapel Hill: University of North Carolina Press, 2003); Grace Delgado, "In the Age of Exclusion," PhD dissertation, University of California–Los Angeles, 2000; Mae Ngai, *Impossible Subjects* (Princeton: Princeton University Press, 2004).

19. On Indian labor in Arizona and its relationship to racial hierarchies, see Eric Meeks, *Border Citizens* (Austin: University of Texas Press, 2007).

20. Here I reiterate my scholarly debt to David Montejano.

21. See Chapter 1 in this volume.

22. Henry F. Dobyns, Theodore Bundy, James E. Officer, and Richard W. Stoffle, *Los Tres Alamos del Rio San Pedro* (Tucson: Piñon Press, 1996), 41–42; Edward Soza, *Mexican Homesteaders in the San Pedro River Valley and the Homestead Act of 1862* (Altadena, Calif.: Published by author, 1993; rev. ed., 1994), 28; idem, *Hispanic Homesteaders in Arizona, 1870–1908 under the Homestead Act of May 20, 1862 and Other Public Land Laws* (Altadena, Calif.: Published by author, 1994), both available at http://parentseyes.arizona.edu (accessed February 8, 2011).

23. Many other Mexican farmers lived in the area and filed on public land but never received federal patents for it (figures based on Soza, *Mexican Homesteaders*).

24. Probate case of Antonio Grijalba, Cochise County Probate Court, Case No. 437, microfilm, Arizona State Library Archives, and Public Records, Phoenix (hereafter ASLAPR).

25. Conflicting evidence about the creation of the Tres Alamos District appears in Mary Belle (Mamie) Barnard Aguirre, "About My First School," typescript, Arizona Historical Society, Tucson (hereafter AHS); and Elsie Toles, "Rural and Small Town Schools of Cochise County" (1920?), Elsie Toles Collection, AHS, 3–4; Cochise County Probate Files, ASLAPR.

26. Grijalba et al. v. Dunbar et al., 1889, Cochise County District Court, 1st Judicial District, Case No. 1414, Film Files 90.6.2 and 90.6.3, ASLAPR, 410; Jay J. Wagoner, *Early Arizona* (Tucson: University of Arizona Press, 1975), 392–395; Edward Ellsworth, "Homesteaders in Tres Alamos Rio San Pedro, Pima County Arizona Territory, The Homestead Act of 1862," unpublished manuscript, 1998, 29, copy in possession of the author; correspondence with author from Edward Ellsworth, August 2001.

27. Aguirre, "About My First School"; idem, "Spanish Trader's Bride," typescript copy, AHS, 19–20.

28. "From San Pedro Valley," *Arizona Citizen* (August 10, 1872).

29. *Arizona Citizen* (May 17, 1873): 2.

30. Arlene Scadron, ed., *On Their Own* (Urbana: University of Illinois Press, 1988); and, for comparison, Carole Shammas, Marylynn Salmon, and Michael Dahlin, *Inheritance in America* (New Brunswick, N.J.: Rutgers University Press, 1987).

31. Examples in database of all Cochise County public land patents, compiled by Richard Selbach, Bureau of Land Management, Phoenix, Arizona, in posses-

sion of author (hereafter BLM database). See also Soza, *Hispanic Homesteaders and Mexican-American Homesteaders*.

32. BLM database; Ellsworth, *Homesteaders*, 76, and August 2001 Ellsworth letter; Katherine Mejía, oral history transcript, interviewed by Liz Brenner, April 18, 1997, San Pedro Valley Arts and Historical Museum, hereafter SPVAHM; and Jesús Maldonado, Probate Case No. 715, Cochise County Probate Court, microfilm, ASLAPR. (Likewise, Francisca Comadurán Díaz de Mejía, clearly a relative of Jesús, had a cash entry and a homestead claim in her own name that appears in Soza, *Hispanic Homesteaders*; *Grijalba v. Dunbar*.

33. Rudy Pacheco, "The Story of a Pioneer Family," manuscript in Pacheco Family File, AHS. On brands, see Bert Haskett, "Early History of the Cattle Industry in Arizona," *Arizona Historical Review* 6, no. 4 (October 1935): 3–42, especially 32.

34. Dobyns et al., *Los Tres Alamos*; Cochise County Superior Court Marriage Index No. 1, 1881–1963, microfilm file 90.5.69, ASLAPR.

35. Sheridan, *Los Tucsonenses* (Tucson: University of Arizona Press, 1986), 149; Donna J. Baldwin, "A Successful Search for Security," in Scadron, ed., *On Their Own*.

36. For more on the meanings of these marriages, see Deena González, *Refusing the Favor* (New York: Oxford University Press, 1999), especially 10, 107–122; but also see María Raquel Casas, *Married to a Daughter of the Land* (Las Vegas: University of Nevada Press, 2007); Miroslava Chávez-García, *Negotiating Conquest* (Tucson: University of Arizona Press, 2004); Paul R. Spickard, *Mixed Blood* (Madison: University of Wisconsin Press, 1989); Peggy Pascoe, "Race, Gender, and Intercultural Relations," *Frontiers* 12 (1991); Rebecca McDowell McCraver, *The Impact of Intimacy* (El Paso: Texas Western Press, 1982); Jane Dysart, "Mexican Women in San Antonio, 1830–1860," *WHQ* 7 (1976): 365–375; Darlis A. Miller, "Cross-Cultural Marriages in the Southwest," in Darlis A. Miller and Joan M. Jensen, eds., *New Mexico Women* (Albuquerque: University of New Mexico Press, 1986); Brading, *Miners and Merchants*, 21; Richard Boyer, *Lives of the Bigamists* (Albuquerque: University of New Mexico Press, 1995), 47; Diana Balmori, Stuart F. Voss, and Miles Wortman, *Notable Family Networks in Latin America* (Chicago: University of Chicago Press, 1984), 34–35, 101–102; John E. Kicza, "The Great Families of Mexico," *Hispanic American Historical Review* 62, no. 3 (August 1982): 429–457; and Reséndez, *Changing National Identities*, chap. 4.

37. Pascoe, "Race, Gender," 5–18. In 1865, the same year that the diverse Tucsonans settled in Tres Alamos, the Territorial Assembly passed a law outlawing marriage of whites to Indians, African Americans, or Asians; see Roger D. Hathaway, "Unlawful Love," *Journal of Arizona History* 27 (Winter 1986): 377–390.

38. Coles Bashford, comp., *The Compiled Laws of the Territory of Arizona from 1864–1871, Inclusive* (Albany, 1871), 231.

39. James M. Crane, "An Analysis of the Great Register of Cochise County, Arizona Territory, 1884," *Cochise Quarterly* 18 (1988): 5.

40. In one such Arizona case in 1921, a judge ruled that Mexicans belonged to the "Caucasian race" unless proven otherwise; cited in Peggy Pascoe, "Miscegenation Laws, Court Cases, and Ideologies of 'Race' in Twentieth-Century America," *Journal of American History* 83, no. 1 (June 1996): 51. See also Ian F.

Haney López, *White by Law* (New York: New York University Press, 1997); Neil Foley, "Becoming Hispanic," *Reflexiones: New Directions in Mexican American Studies* (1997): 53–70; Dara Orenstein, "Void for Vagueness," *Pacific Historical Review* 74, no. 3 (2005): 367–407; and *Law and History Review* 21, no. 1 (2003), passim. See also Crane, "Analysis of the Great Register," 3–9.

41. Gregory Rodríguez argues that this view increasingly shapes race relations in the contemporary United States; see *Mongrels, Bastards, Orphans, and Vagabonds* (New York: Vintage, 2007).

42. People who were as much as one-quarter Indian descent could safely consider themselves "real" Spaniards. Well into the American period, southern Arizonans distinguished between non-Christian Apaches (*indios bárbaros*) and the rest of the population, but even many Christianized Indians simply became part of the general mestizo population. On Arizona, see James Officer, *Hispanic Arizona, 1536–1856* (Tucson: University of Arizona Press, 1987), especially 41, 78; Martha Menchaca, *Recovering History, Constructing Race* (Austin: University of Texas Press, 2002). Discussion of *casta* and frontier racial systems is based on Magnus Mörner, *Race Mixture in the History of Latin America* (Boston: Little, Brown, 1967); José Cuello, "Racialized Hierarchies of Power in Colonial Mexican Society," in Jesús F. de la Teja and Ross Frank, eds., *Choice, Persuasion, and Coercion* (Albuquerque: University of New Mexico Press, 2005); Leo J. Garafolo and Rachel Sarah O'Toole, "Introduction: Constructing Difference in Colonial Latin America," *Journal of Colonialism and Colonial History* 7, no. 1 (2006), http://muse. jhu.edu (accessed May 13, 2008); Martin, *Governance and Society*; Tutino, *Making a New World*; and Radding, *Wandering Peoples*, especially 17, 111–115. On race mixing, see especially Alan Knight, "Racism, Revolution, and Indigenismo," in Richard Graham, ed., *The Idea of Race in Latin America, 1870–1940* (Austin: University of Texas Press, 1990); Menchaca, *Recovering History*; idem, "Chicano Indianism," *American Ethnologist* 20, no. 3 (1993): 583–603; Ramón A. Gutiérrez, *When Jesus Came*; John M. Nieto-Phillips, *The Language of Blood* (Albuquerque: University of New Mexico Press, 2004). On Sonora, see Miguel Tinker Salas, *In the Shadow of the Eagles* (Berkeley: University of California Press, 1997), especially 26–27.

43. Tombstone's history has long been blended with legend. I have found the following secondary sources relatively reliable: William B. Shillingberg, *Tombstone, A.T.* (Spokane, Wash.: Arthur H. Clark Company, 1999); Lynn R. Bailey, *Tombstone, Arizona "Too Tough to Die"* (Tucson: Westernlore Press, 2004); Truett, *Fugitive Landscapes*; Casey Tefertiller, *Wyatt Earp* (New York: John Wiley & Sons, 1997); Paula Mitchell Marks, *And Die in the West* (Norman: University of Oklahoma Press, 1996). For demographic statistics, see Eric L. Clements, *After the Boom in Tombstone and Jerome, Arizona* (Reno: University of Nevada Press, 2003), 31; and on mining methods and Mexicans in Tombstone, see James Officer, *Arizona's Hispanic Perspective* (Phoenix: Arizona Town Hall, 1981), 83–85; Truett, *Fugitive Landscapes*, 63; Castañeda Biofile, AHS; Clements, *After the Boom*, 315n29.

44. See Truett, *Fugitive Landscapes*; and David M. Pletcher, "Mexico Opens the Door to American Capital, 1877–1880," *The Americas* 16, no. 1 (July 1959): 1–14.

45. Quotations from Maj. James Biddle to [unnamed] Deputy U.S. Marshal, Tucson, June 11, 1881; James A. Zabriskie to Attorney General Benjamin Harris Brewster, January 22, 1885; both in Claire Prechtel-Kluskens and Sherman Lan-

dau, comps, Microcopy No. 2028, Records Relating to U.S. Marshal Crawley P. Duke, the Earp Brothers, and Lawlessness and "Cowboy Depredations" in Arizona, Territory, 1881–1885 (Washington, D.C.: National Archives and Records Administration, 1996), microfilm (hereafter MC 2028).

46. Arizona U.S. Attorney C. B. Pomroy, Tucson, to U.S. Attorney General Wayne MacVeagh, June 23, 1881, MC 2028; Lynn R. Bailey, ed., *Tombstone from a Woman's Point of View* (Tucson: Westernlore Press, 1998).

47. Torres to Evans, August 5, 1881, in Interior Department Territorial Papers Arizona 1868–1913, microcopy no. 429, roll 3, "Letters Received Relating to Disturbances along Mexican Border Dec. 13, 1878–January 25, 1884 and Miscellaneous Subjects February 14, 1868–January 24, 1888" (Washington, D.C.: National Archives and Record Administration, 1963, originally contained in RG 48, Records of the Office of the Secretary of the Interior) (hereafter MC 429).

48. Dake to MacVeagh, August 5, 1881, MC 2028.

49. Evans to Dake, June 15, August 4, 1881; Bowyer to Gosper, September 17, 1882; MacVeagh to Dake, August 5, 1881, all in MC 2028; Tefertiller, *Wyatt Earp*, 95–98.

50. Pomroy to MacVeagh, June 23, 1881, MC 2028.

51. Sherman to Brewster, April 12, 1882, MC 2028.

52. Dake to MacVeagh, August 5, 1881; Evans to Dake, August 10, 1881; Torres to Evans, June 24, 1881, all in MC 2028.

53. Gosper to Blaine, September 30, 1881, MC 2028.

54. Pomroy to MacVeagh, June 23, 1881, MC 2028.

55. Gosper to Acting Atty. General, December 8, 1881, MC 2028.

56. Copy of newspaper in Legation of Mexico (M. de Zamacona) to Blaine, April 13, 1881, MC 429.

57. *Arizona Star*, cited in Tefertiller, *Wyatt Earp*, 73.

58. Parsons and Brown, cited in ibid., 97–98.

59. See Ken Gonzales-Day, *Lynching in the West, 1850–1935* (Durham, N.C.: Duke University Press, 2006); Helen McLure, PhD dissertation, Southern Methodist University, in progress.

60. Pomroy to MacVeagh, June 23, 1881, MC 2028.

61. Sherman to Brewster, April 12, 1882, MS 2028.

62. Tritle, cited in Truett, *Fugitive Landscapes*, 65.

63. Though no comprehensive history of white man's camps exists, useful sources include Charles Howard Shinn, *Mining Camps* (New York, 1884, 1970); S. Johnson, *Roaring Camp*; Elizabeth Jameson, *All That Glitters* (Urbana: University of Illinois Press, 1998), especially 140–160; and Rodman Paul, *Mining Frontiers of the Far West, 1848–1890* (Albuquerque: University of New Mexico Press, 2001), especially 161–175. On Spanish/Mexican precedents for codes, see McWilliams, *North from Mexico*, 141.

64. Warren District Commercial Club, "Arizona's Treasure House "(Bisbee, 1913), 11; see also "Cochise Empire in Self," *Bisbee Daily Review*, 1915 mining edition.

65. Opie Rundle Burgess, *Bisbee Not So Long Ago* (San Antonio, Tex.: Naylor, 1967), 41.

66. The group named Horace Stillman secretary and specified fines and penalties for such crimes as stealing an "animal of draft or burden"; see Bailey, *Bisbee*, 53–55.

67. Thomas E. Sheridan, *Arizona* (Tucson: University of Arizona Press, 1995), 131, 151; Thomas E. Farish, *History of Arizona* (Phoenix, 1915), II: 303, 307, in http://southwest.library.arizona.edu/hav2/body.1_div.15.html (accessed April 4, 2007); Manuel P. Servín and Robert L. Spude, "Historical Conditions of Early Mexican Labor in the United States: Arizona—A Neglected Story," typescript, 99, 43–57; Rodolfo Acuña, *Occupied America* (New York: Longman, 1988), 81–82, 93–94; Yvette Huginnie, "Mexican Labour in a 'White Man's Town,'" in Peter Alexander and Rick Halpern, eds., *Racializing Class, Classifying Race* (New York: St. Martin's Press, 2000); and Clarence King, *The United States Mining Laws and Regulations Thereunder, and State and Territorial Mining Laws, to Which Are Appended Local Mining Rules and Regulations* (Washington, D.C., 1885), quotation on 254.

68. Bailey, *Bisbee*, 111–112; the *Bisbee Daily Review*, December 5, 1903, is quoted on 117; all cited in Tom Vaughan, "Everyday Life in a Copper Camp," in Carlos Schwantes, ed., *Bisbee* (Tucson: University of Arizona Press, 1992). And see James W. Loewen, *Sundown Towns* (New York: Touchstone Books, 2006).

69. Burgess, *Bisbee Not So Long Ago*, 128; see also Jane Eppinga, "Ethnic Diversity in Mining Camps," in J. Michael Canty and Michael N. Greeley, eds., *History of Mining in Arizona* (Tucson: Mining Club of the Southwest Foundation, 1991), vol. II; Juanita Tarin oral history transcript, interviewed by Roberta Vaughan, October 24, 1980, Bisbee Mining & Historical Museum.

70. Ibid.

71. On the dual-wage system, see especially Carl Strikwerda and Camille Guerin-Gonzales, "Labor, Migration, and Politics," in Camille Guerin-Gonzales and Carl Strikwerda, eds., *The Politics of Immigrant Workers* (New York: Holmes & Meier, 1993); and Camille Guerin-Gonzales, "The International Migration of Workers and Segmented Labor," in ibid. Also see M. García, *Desert Immigrants*; Joseph Park, "The History of Mexican Labor in Arizona during the Territorial Period," MA thesis, University of Arizona, 1961. Across Arizona, Mexicans doing the same work as other mine employees earned one-half to two-thirds of what their non-Mexican counterparts did, according to Park.

72. See Phelps Dodge Corporation Payroll Records, 1885, AHS; "March 13, 1923 Report re: wage scale for reduction works employees in Douglas," Copper Queen Mining Company Wage Scales, Phelps-Dodge Corporate Archives, Phoenix, Arizona.

73. Phelps Dodge Corporation Payroll Records, 1885, AHS.

74. Burgess, *Bisbee Not So Long Ago*, 43.

75. *El Fronterizo* (August 10, 1889): 2.

76. I am indebted here to Philip J. Deloria, *Indians in Unexpected Places* (Lawrence: University of Kansas Press, 2004); Trevor Purvis and Alan Hunt quoted on 10. And see Tomás Almaguer, *Racial Fault Lines* (Berkeley: University of California Press, 1994), 17–19.

77. Joseph Clark, cited in Dru McGinnis, "The Influence of Organized Labor

on the Making of the Arizona Constitution," MA thesis, University of Arizona, 1930, 18. On Anglo attitudes about Mexican wages, see, for example, Gordon, *Great Arizona Orphan Abduction*, 180.

78. Copper Queen Mining Company Wage Scales, 1885–1886, AHS.

79. James D. McBride, "Gaining a Foothold in the Paradise of Capitalism," *Journal of Arizona History* 23 (Autumn 1982): 303.

80. Ngai, *Impossible Subjects*, 64.

81. "No Foreign Labor Wanted," *Bisbee Daily Review* (May 27, 1903).

82. See Lawrence Glickman, "Inventing the 'American Standard of Living,'" *Labor History* 23, nos. 2–3 (1993). On the standard's relationship to the family wage, see Ron Rothbart, "'Homes Are What Any Strike Is About,'" *Journal of Social History* 23, no. 2 (1989): 267–284; and Martha May, "The Historical Problem of the Family Wage," *Feminist Studies* 8, no. 2 (Summer 1982).

83. C. d'Autremont Jr., to Charles Briggs, August 15, 1906, Calumet & Arizona Company, Phelps-Dodge Corporate Archives.

84. Cleveland Van Dyke Report to Kendric C. Babcock, president of the University of Arizona, December 16, 1907, Phelps-Dodge Corporate Archives, 8–9.

85. Wheeler testimony, PMC hearings, 253.

86. Unless otherwise noted, Bisbee Deportation statistics are from my database of deportees and deputies. The following sources provided data: on deportees, a census conducted by U.S. Army official Ben Dorcy at the Columbus deportation camp, contained in Hunt Papers, ASLAPR (also in PMC hearing reports); plaintiff list in Michael Simmons v. El Paso & Southwestern Railroad, Superior Court of Cochise County, AZ 114, Box 2, Folder 5, University of Arizona Special Collections (hereafter UASC); on deputies, I used Bisbee Deportation List of Gunmen and Witnesses, taken from Records of Cochise County, Arizona, microfilm, ASLAPR; for both, I used Walsh and Fitzgerald, comps., *Bisbee and Warren District Directory 1917–8* (Bisbee: Walsh & Fitzgerald, 1917); for 1920, I entered every name into the subscription genealogical database www.ancestry.com (last accessed December 8, 2007). The Bisbee Deportation database includes information on nationality, citizenship, address, occupation, home ownership, marital status, and parental status. This research was made possible through the research assistance of Sarah Lipscomb and Sara Hinsman, as well as the Louisiana State University Council-on-Research Summer Stipend Program for funding in 2004. The statistics on U.S. citizenship and nativity are lower than estimates based only on the Dorcy census, used by other researchers. Because we cannot trace every participant, the exact figures will never be known. See, for example, Colleen O'Neill, "Domesticity Deployed," *Labor History* 34, nos. 2–3 (Summer 1993): 256–273. The numbers on Mexicans and Slavs are 225 Mexicans out of a total of 894 with identifiable national origin; 227 Slavs/Eastern Europeans. I counted the following nationalities as Slavic/Eastern European: Austrian (these were largely what would become Yugoslavs), Bohemian, Bosnian, Bulgarian, Croat, Dalmatian, Hungarian, Lithuanian, Montenegrin, Polish, Russian, Serb, and Slav (as listed). On citizenship, the number is 223 out of 894.

87. A conspiracy theorist might argue that Fred McKinney, the compiler of the city directory, who was the editor of the *Daily Ore* and had served as a deputy, might have doctored the figures. But that would have required knowing the names

of almost all of the deportees, which is unlikely. Depending on how they were counted (being liberal about including people with common names or not), I found 34 or 45 of the original list of deportees in the 1920 census.

88. Frank J. Vaughan to George W. P. Hunt, July 25, 1917, Hunt Papers, ASLAPR.

89. Art Kent, Oral History, interviewed by James Houston, ca. 1970s, AHS.

90. Byrkit, *Forging the Copper Collar*, 285–294.

91. Employment figures reveal what had changed. From 1916 to October 1917, C&A's mine workforce (which excluded Mexicans and office staff) went from 49.3 percent American to 70.4 percent American; see PMC hearings, 427–428.

92. This statement was followed by a cheerful overview of Bisbee's pleasing climate; see Walsh and Fitzgerald, *Bisbee and Warren District Directory 1917–8.*

93. Between 1910 and 1920, the census changed the way it counted people from what became Yugoslavia; nonetheless, a total of nearly 800 Slavs had dwindled to 364 Yugoslavs by 1920. The number of Italians fell from 242 in 1910 to 200 in 1920; see U.S. Bureau of the Census, Thirteenth Census of the United States, 1910, vol. V, Population, Abstract with Supplement for Arizona (Washington, D.C.: GPO, 1912), 584; idem, Fourteenth Census of the United States, 1910, vol. III, Population (Washington, D.C.: GPO, 1911), 81; Art Kent Oral History, undated interview, c. 1970s, James Houston, interviewer, AHS.

94. "Address of Senator Sutter of Cochise County," June 4, 1918, Third Legislature, First Special Session, State of Arizona, 13, UASC.

95. Ralph Rollins, "Labor Situation in Arizona Points to Mexicanization," *Arizona Mining Journal* 4 (July 1920): 13–14.

96. "Bisbee, the Most Southern Mile-High City in North America," *Arizona Labor Journal* (May 31, 1929): 27.

97. For an example of inclusion of Mexican-origin people in the local newspaper, especially homesteading families, see *Benson Signal* (September 4, 1915), passim.

98. Soza also won the award for commercial work, two of the six prizes given out that year; see "Closing Exercises of the High School," *Benson Signal* (May 26, 1917).

99. Sheridan, *Los Tucsonenses*, 180.

100. First quotation from undated petition from Apodaca School District (sent May 30, 1918); second quotation from letters from Minnie K. Bisby to county school superintendent Elsie Toles, May 29, 1918, February 15, 1919, and May 27, 1918; MS 180, Cochise County School Superintendent Records, Arizona Historical Society, Tucson.

101. See U.S. Census Bureau's twelfth through fifteenth censuses.

102. U.S. Works Project Administration, *The Federal Civil Works Administration* (N.p., 1934), 7.

103. "Presbyterian Copper," *Fortune Magazine* (July 1932): 40–48, 104.

104. The following year the high school ceased the practice, but even one year is telling.

105. Such a system must have reminded many unemployed miners of Phelps Dodge's post-Deportation grievance committee, which excluded Mexican workers and over which company officials had absolute veto power; see minutes

of Arizona State Board of Welfare, March 14, 1934, Federal Emergency Relief Administration (FERA) Central Files, 1933–1936, State Series, March 1933–1936, B13, F Arizona Minutes, RG 69, Papers of the Works Progress Administration, National Archives II, College Park, Maryland (hereafter NACP).

106. William S. Collins, *The New Deal in Arizona* (Phoenix: Arizona State Parks Board, 1999), 58, 47; minutes of Arizona State Board of Welfare, March 14, 1934, FERA Central Files, 1933–1936, State Series, March 1933–1936, B13, F Arizona Minutes, RG 69, NACP.

107. A. C. Garcia, Douglas, Arizona, to U.S. Secretary of Labor Frances Perkins, Washington, D.C., March 28, 1935, RG 69, FERA Central Files, 1933–1936, State Series, March 1933–1936, B13, Folder 460, AZ Complaints A–F, NACP.

108. Some of the favoritism stemmed from an early rule that restricted certain kinds of relief to communities with populations of at least five thousand. As a result, rural areas were another group that got niggardly and demeaning direct relief; see minutes of Arizona State Board of Welfare, April 25, May 18, 1934; March 14, 1935, all in FERA Central Files, 1933–1936, State Series, March 1933–1936, B13, F Arizona Minutes, RG 69, NACP. Figures from "Report of Activities Cochise County Board of Public Welfare," May 1, 1934–August 1, 1935, ASLAPR, 53–62. I did not count local street improvements in the roadwork figures, only highway and county roads.

109. Laura Mae Seward, "Narrative Report for Cochise County," July 20, 1928–December 1, 1928, 32–33, UASC, 1920s and 1930s Reports, passim; Bertha Virmond, "Annual Report," 1934, A–C.

110. Minutes of Meeting of the Arizona Board of Public Welfare, Emergency Relief Administration (ERA), Phoenix, July 10, 1934, RG 69, FERA Central Files, 1933–1936, State Series, Arizona, 453 Chattel Mortgages, B13, NACP; Collins, New Deal in Arizona, 33.

111. S. C. Spencer, Cochise, Arizona, To Whom It May Concern, July 24, 1934, FERA Central Files, 1933–1936, State Series, March 1933–1936, Arizona Complaints, O–Z. See also J. E. Wilkie, Secretary, Arizona Peace Officers' Association, to Sen. Henry Ashurst, Washington, May 8, 1936, RG 69, B840 (690 AZ), NACP.

112. F. M. Warner, Secretary, to Arthur Goldschmidt, Acting Director of Professional Projects, FERA, September 9, 1934, FERA Central Files, 1933–1936, State Series, March 1933–1936, Alaska 401, Arizona 400, Arizona Official FERA, August, September 1934, RG 69, WPA, NACP.

113. Dobyns et al., *Los Tres Alamos*, 169.

114. Ibid., 174; Collins, *New Deal in Arizona*, 116–117.

115. Dobyns et al., *Los Tres Alamos*, 134–135.

116. Phelps Dodge v. National Labor Relations Board 313 U.S. 177 (1941). Also see Carlos Schwantes, *Vision & Enterprise* (Tucson: University of Arizona Press, 2000), 203.

117. Complaint of John B. Hart, Douglas, Arizona, August 17, 1942, Legal Div. Hearings 1941–1946, SW-(Mexicans) Folder: Entry 19, Box 340, Douglas, AZ (Phelps-Dodge Co.), RG 228, FEPC Papers, NACP.

118. This discussion collapses a complicated history of organizing and competition among AFL- and IWW-influenced mining unions and organizers, evi-

dent in the papers of the FEPC. See Cletus Daniel, *Chicano Workers and the Politics of Fairness* (Austin: University of Texas Press, 1991); Mario T. García, *Mexican Americans* (New Haven: Yale University Press, 1989), 175–198; and Zaragoza Vargas, *Labor Rights Are Civil Rights* (Princeton: Princeton University Press, 2004), especially 220–223; James C. Foster, ed., *American Labor in the Southwest* (Tucson: University of Arizona Press, 1982).

CHAPTER 6

Keeping Community, Challenging Boundaries: Indigenous Migrants, Internationalist Workers, and Mexican Revolutionaries, 1900–1920

DEVRA WEBER

Rosendo A. Dorame
1879–1932
Phoenix IWW Local 272
"An injury to one is an injury to all."
GRAVESTONE IN EVERGREEN CEMETERY, EAST LOS ANGELES

Since the 1980s, writers have noted that globalization has intensified international migration, and studies of Mexican migration have recorded the growing number of indigenous people from Mexico in the binational labor market. Scholars have documented how migration has altered communities and relations within and among them and has simultaneously changed and reinforced cultures. Analysts have explored how people are responding, adapting, manipulating, and shaping cultural tools within the frameworks of hegemonic and institutional structures. Others have discussed the impact of migration on binational social relations, and migrants' role in binational social organizations and movements. Yet indigenous migrations from Mexico, binational connections, manipulation of cultural signals and racial constructions, and the role of Mexican migrants in shaping binational social movements have deep historical roots in Mexico and the United States.

Mexican workers have been part of the making of the United States since, as the saying goes, the border crossed them, when the United States claimed half of Mexico at the conclusion to the War of 1848.[1] But it was the expanding industrial capitalism of the late nineteenth and early twentieth centuries that propelled an increasing number of Mexican migrants across the relocated border to work. Within Mexico and in the United States, the growth of mining, railroad, and agricultural industries and of cities and their infrastructures created a demand for workers often filled by Mexicans. Technological innovations in communication and transportation were accelerating the speed of movement and revolutionizing the relationship between time and space. The new conditions of modernity elicited new kinds of resistant social movements, which took the form of social revolution, internationalist unions, and local uprisings. Some responses were simultaneously local in their application and international in their influence and implications.

Yet a history of Mexican migrants constructed from their perspective is missing in accounts of the early twentieth century. There are understandable reasons. Documents on these earlier migrants are scant. An overreliance on English-language documents by U.S. historians and theoretical paradigms shaped by the narrow boundaries of the nation-state have truncated, or erased, any understanding of Mexican migrants of this period. Their absence in most U.S. histories has left us without historical perspective on current Mexican migrants and their diversity, often-binational community and social networks, and the social movements of which they are a part.

Early-twentieth-century Mexicans who migrated into the United States were diverse. Many were from indigenous communities, spoke indigenous languages, and were tied to families and social networks which still considered themselves indigenous. These social relations shaped migration and work and were cornerstones of developing communities. Mexicans were also part of an international group of workers laboring in the United States. Some Mexicans joined internationalist social movements such as the Partido Liberal Mexicano (PLM), which was organizing for a social revolution in Mexico. Others, usually members of the PLM, worked with the Industrial Workers of the World. Their members were often called Wobblies. Unlike the American Federation of Labor, the IWW was virtually the only major union which openly admitted Mexican workers. The Magonistas—so named after the PLM leader, Ricardo Flores Magón—helped shape Spanish-speaking locals of the IWW.

Mexican Magonistas who joined the IWW challenge the IWW historiography, which too often excludes these workers. Their participations suggest the need for multilingual research into workers whose communities and political concerns shaped local organizing. Much as indigenous people in the Ejército Zapatista de Liberación Nacional (EZLN) of Chiapas led the first uprising against NAFTA's neoliberal agenda in 1994, indigenous Mexicans were part of internationalist responses to the ravages of early-twentieth-century globalization.[2]

Mexican workers such as Rosendo Dorame, whose epitaph opens this chapter, are emblematic of Magonista Wobblies in the early twentieth century. Rosendo was born to a Mexican family from Sonora that had moved to Florence, Arizona.[3] He was possibly an Opata Indian. He found work where he could—as a barber, a miner, a carpenter, even serving a brief stint as an Arizona sheriff. Piecing together shards of information, we know he worked in Texas, found jobs across Arizona, in Colorado and California, and possibly labored in northern Mexico. Somewhere in these travels, he joined the Western Federation of Miners and participated in Colorado's Cripple Creek mining strike, which lasted from 1903 to 1905.[4]

He joined the IWW. Like many Mexicans, he worked with other organizations open to Mexicans and was a candidate on the Socialist Party ticket for its constitutional convention in 1910. This bilingual Mexican (for he was "Mexican" in the Southwest, regardless of his U.S. citizenship) also belonged to the Partido Liberal Mexicano.

In 1911, Dorame recruited Mexican men from mining camps across Arizona and led one arm of a coordinated invasion into Mexico that the PLM hoped would trigger a revolution.[5] He was arrested and, convicted of violating neutrality laws, spent a year in Leavenworth Prison. He organized an IWW strike in an El Paso smelter and in 1917 was part of organizing the Bisbee, Arizona, copper strike.[6]

Racial Categorizations and Mexican Migrants

Who were the early-twentieth-century Mexican migrants? Since the 1980s, scholarly and popular literature on migration has often focused on indigenous migrants. But is indigenous migration new, or does this attention reflect an increased visibility? Certainly, there is a growing migration from recognized indigenous areas such as Oaxaca in southern Mexico. Yet the visibility of indigenous peoples also stems from indigenous political changes. In 1992, panindigenous organizing across the Americas transformed a planned celebration of Columbus' "discovery" of the Americas into a public recognition of the five hundred years of genocide that followed his arrival. In 1994, the EZLN took the first shot at NAFTA's neoliberal policies, simultaneously asserting an indigenous presence on the international stage and joining local community demands with internationalist concerns about global economic and political policies. Growing numbers of Mexicans publicly identify as indigenous, and indigenous

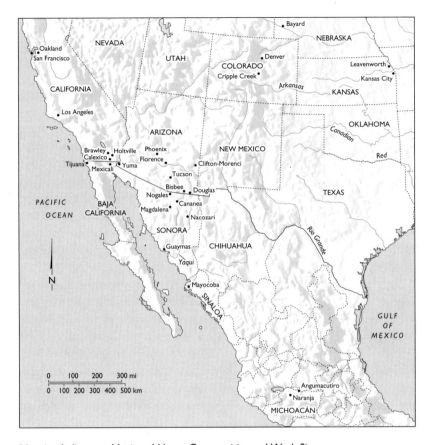

Map 6.1. Indigenous Mexicans' Home Communities and Work Sites

demands for political autonomy and economic self-determination have shifted political dialogue and public discourse in the Americas.

I first began thinking about historical indigenous migration in the 1980s after a conversation with Edward Banales. He had migrated to California in the early 1920s from Angumacutiro, Michoacán, in Mexico's central plateau. I had interviewed him several times before he mentioned, in passing, that his father was a Purépecha (Tarascan) from an "Indian town . . . just like all the other Mexicanos living here."[7] Over years of interviewing people in this California town, nobody had mentioned indigenous connections to me, and I had never asked. I returned to Mexico to visit Angumacutiro. Mexican academic friends insisted the town and its surroundings were mestizo. Historical documents agreed, and the 1940 census states, "The only racial group that exists in this municipality is the mestizo. There is only one pure blooded Indian."[8] However, people who lived in Angumacutiro in the 1980s (including the sizable Banales family) were clear that they, and their town, were Purépecha.

The relative paucity of historical works about indigenous roots of earlier migrants such as the Banales family stems in part from racial categorizations of both Mexico and the United States. In the early twentieth century, each country was articulating the nation-state in racial terms, albeit in very different ways. Racial categories contributed to disjunctures between imposed definitions, and more complex ways people identified themselves. Assumptions about race and the racialization of citizenship in each nation-state shaped historical records, popular perceptions, and written history in the twentieth century. As a result, historians—and I include myself—tended to homogenize "Mexican" in ways that obliterated the diverse ethnic and cultural connections of earlier migrants.

In Mexico, narrow definitions of "Indian" downplayed or erased indigenous roots. The term "Indian" itself homogenized diverse peoples, societies, and cultures into one category defined only in relation to the "European." The Spanish colonial *casta* system recognized mixture, or "mestizaje," and divided people into racial categories of Spaniard, Indian, African, and degrees of mixture. As racial categories became more fluid, increasingly defined by culture and class, people could and did change their racial classifications. External perceptions of Indian became dictated more by dress, language, the trappings of religion, and the appearance of class. Indians who adopted Spanish, Catholicism, and "non-Indian" manners and dress were considered mestizo, Hispanicized Indians, or "not Indian."[9]

The liberal project of the mid-nineteenth century, which ushered in Mexican independence and nationhood, also encouraged encroachment on Indian lands and limited indigenous peoples' citizenship in the conceptualization of the modern nation-state. By the 1920s, "indigenista" writers such as José Vasconcelos and Manuel Gamio celebrated the mestizo, born of Indian and European parents, as the quintessential Mexican. Living Indians were viewed as antithetical to the national project, while the Aztec and Mayan empires were elevated to iconic status. To be truly Mexican, living Indians had to disappear and become mestizo.[10] Indians who refused this Faustian bargain were regarded as backward, degenerate, and outside the modern Mexican state.[11]

Indians began to disappear through redefinition. By 1910, the Mexican census claimed that only a third of the population was indigenous, and by the 1920s, rural communities, hoping to present a "modern" face, began to make political demands on the state for land as campesinos, not Indians. By the late 1920s, the increase in campesino communities began to obscure that many were also indigenous, and by mid-century many communities classified as indigenous in the early twentieth century were considered mestizo and/or campesino.[12]

In the early twentieth century, the United States was also focusing on definitions of its citizenry and working to convert "foreign" immigrants into "Americans," a project that was both racial and national. The binary U.S. racial system recognized black and white but saw mixture—in the "one-drop rule"—as threatening "miscegenation" or "mongrelization." A more fluid system prevailed in the southwestern borderlands until the late nineteenth century; problems of water, land, and war overrode racial concerns.

Yet the coming of the railroad, large-scale capital interests, and a larger population changed communities by the 1880s. Racial categories shifted and hardened, and the terms "Mexican" and "American" obliterated more nuanced distinctions which had earlier existed among the indigenous population, mestizos, Mexican immigrants, Anglo-Americans, Europeans, Chinese, and other immigrants. In one area of Southern California, for example, Juaneños (Indians from Mission San Juan Capistrano), Californios (Mexicans with historical roots in California before U.S. annexation), and recent immigrants from Mexico were crammed into a homogenizing box as "Mexicans," a shift in racial categories articulated in the imposition of spatial segregation.

In Arizona mining areas, racial designations were also in flux. Although racial systems differed by community—Clifton-Morenci, for example, was different from nearby Bisbee—mining towns were moving toward a system in which Mexicans (legally defined as "white") were being redefined as both nonwhite and noncitizens, regardless of birth.[13]

Writers also tended to view Mexican migrants narrowly, usually in relation to specific economic or social concerns. In the United States, Mexicans were viewed through the lenses of industrial labor needs, potential for union activism, alleged social costs, and ongoing conflicts over race, legality, and restrictive immigration legislation. Writers in Mexico focused on emigration and how returning workers' experiences with industrial work and work habits could contribute to the growth of the Mexican nation. Certainly, reports by social workers, health inspectors, employers, and some journalists noted that some of these Mexicans were Indians. Yet increasingly, Mexican became understood as some kind of mixture, largely Indian. A Los Angeles doctor, discussing the high incidence of tuberculosis, blamed Mexicans' "extremely low racial immunity," due to their "large admixture of Indian blood," more than the wretched conditions of work and housing.[14]

In the 1970s, historians began to research women, workers, people of color, and others who had been ignored in written history. Oral histories began to explore peoples' perspectives on their own lives and the political and social context in which they lived. Chicano historians began to write the history of Mexicanos in the North and the development of Mexican communities which preceded the U.S. invasion. The history of Chicanos challenged the national U.S. narrative in important ways, and the questions these historians raised were shaped by long-standing problems with racism, ongoing violations of civil and other rights of Chicano communities, and pressing political and cultural issues.[15] Studies thus focused on recovering a Chicano history within the context of U.S. imperialism, U.S. relations with Mexico, and a long history of racism in the United States. Some poetically and analytically explored Chicano culture. While the Chicano movement recognized indigenous roots, activists focused on the iconic Aztecs. Within this political and culture framework, little attention was paid to the historical indigenous roots of migrants.

Yet many Mexican migrants of the early twentieth century were connected to indigenous communities, spoke an indigenous language, and considered themselves indigenous. How many were indigenous is unclear.[16] Anthropologist Manuel Gamio disagreed with the 1910 census, arguing that areas defined as mestizo—such as the populous central plateau—were indigenous, and that Indians were closer to two-thirds (and thus a majority) of Mexico's population. Furthermore, he argued that the largest numbers of migrants to the United States came from heavily indigenous areas and, he surmised, were a "large proportion" of immigrants.[17]

As Indians joined the industrial, mining, and agricultural workforces in the late nineteenth century, they had begun to shed visible markers by which Mexican society defined them as Indian. They exchanged huaraches for shoes, sombreros for workers' hats, and white pants for workers' overalls. Workers migrated to other parts of Mexico and the United States, learned Spanish, and met, worked with, and married people from other parts of Mexico. As a result, many Indians no longer conformed to Mexico's categorical definition of Indian.

Racism toward Indians, conflicts with the Mexican government, and attempts at regulating indigenous behavior contributed to some indigenous people's desire to be seen as non-Indian. Some denied they spoke an indigenous language, some parents encouraged children to speak Spanish, and some changed their name to sound "more Mexican." Repression and subterfuge made it difficult to distinguish between an appearance of acculturation as mestizo and the degree to which aspects of Western culture were actually adopted or adapted.[18]

Clearly, there was a disjuncture between externally imposed racial categories and how people thought of themselves and lived. Indians, like many Mexicans of the time, defined themselves "as belonging to an organized collectivity, a group, a society, a village . . . [whose] cultural heritage [had been] formed and transmitted through history by successive generations."[19] As Bartolomé argues, people were bound not so much by race as by ties of emotion, loyalty, and reciprocity created from participating in a mutually shared "moral universe."[20] Historically, these processes varied unevenly across Mexico, influenced by historical relations with the Spanish colonial power and, later, with the Mexican government, national cultural conflicts and changes, and the economic context. In the early twentieth century, there was only a nascent sense of a Mexican identity. Mexican migrants had stronger ties to community than to the nation-state, and some had conflictual relations with the Mexican as well as the U.S. nation-state. As David Gutiérrez suggests, they developed ideas of collective "identity and solidarity that were only tangentially related to broader notions of formal nationality or citizenship."[21]

Migration replicated aspects of home communities en route, at work sites, and in new communities where people settled. Many workers migrated at least part of the year and covered hundreds of miles. Some, such as the Yaquis, created broad transnational circuits, which, as Samuel Truett explains, stretched from the mines and smelters of Cananea and Nacozari to villages along the Yaqui River and into the copper towns on both sides of the border.[22] Migrants tended to travel with friends and family members, in effect reproducing social networks from home—and, over time, from migrations and work—which were crucial in deciding where and how people migrated, found jobs, learned skills, and negotiated life in new communities. Migrants gravitated to where they had family and friends, re-creating aspects of community in social and cultural enclaves.[23]

Thus the notion of community should be considered to encompass home communities, segments of community in the process of migration, and enclaves at work sites and in communities north of the border. Yaqui and Mayo workers, for example, lived in the labor camps of Chivatera and Buenavista in the copper-mining company town of Cananea, Mexico, where they shared a common language, Yoeme, migrated from neighboring areas of Sinaloa and Sonora, and shared similar histories not only as mine workers but as parts of indigenous societies. Refugio Savala's family migrated from Sonora to Tucson and Yuma, Arizona, then to California, their route following Yaqui enclaves at work sites, cotton fields, and the traveling work camps of the Southern Pacific Railway. Rosalío Moisés recalls that his home was "a meeting place for Yaquis," whether in Hermosillo or Colorada, Mexico; Arizona's multiethnic mining camps; or a multiethnic but Yaqui-dominated barrio of Tucson.[24]

People often migrated in ways which re-created aspects of layered social relations from home communities. Purépechas from Michoacán, for example, such as the Banales family, formed a chain of community enclaves as some settled in the Casa Blanca barrio in Riverside and in San Fernando, California. People originally from Angumacutiro living in Southern California formed labor crews and signed on with contractors they had known in Mexico to migrate to pick cotton in the San Joaquin Valley. Some contractors had been village leaders in Mexico who had marshaled people from their communities to work on Mexican haciendas. Thus the haciendas' hierarchical and paternalistic relations where transferred, in part, to the fields of California. Yet these relations were simultaneously modified by conceptions of communal labor, mutualism, and social relations which enhanced a contractor's ability to supply workers yet also engaged him in relations with his workers bounded by reciprocity and social obligations.[25]

While a broader discussion is outside the scope of this chapter, disparate views of history, space, and time coexisted for many indigenous workers, who maintained their cognitive systems and cultures even while simultaneously participating in and negotiating the social and cultural systems of the United States and Mexico. Refugio Savala (born in 1904 in Magdalena, Sonora), for example, worked the railroads and picked cotton in the southwestern United States. His *Autobiography of a Yaqui Poet* traces his cartography as Yaqui and worker, marking industry and work sites, paths of migration, and modern political borders through a particularly Yaqui lens. Savala seemed to move easily between different conceptions of time. As a railroad worker, he carried a pocket watch and timetable to accurately pinpoint arrivals and departures, yet he also participated in ceremonies based on cyclical conceptions of time that returned him to Yaqui communities and reasserted community-binding rituals.[26]

Social ties and emotional bonds stretched across the border, deep into Mexico, to hometowns and workplaces that dotted trails of migration. People sent home messages and money and returned periodically to their hometowns. They maintained a broad—if, for some, increasingly attenuated—relation to and sense of their home community. The disruption of the Mexican revolution of 1910–1920 would sunder these connections, sometimes permanently, but many maintained them. Purépechas in San Fernando, California, remained connected enough to Angumacutiro, Michoacán, that their marriages, births, and deaths were registered in the church there. In the 1980s, an elderly Banales in the Purépecha town remembered Edward Banales correctly as "the barber," although Edward had left sixty years before.

Indigenous collective interests could shape decisions about work, as most strikingly illustrated by Yaqui workers. Yaquis from the northern state of Sonora, despite a long history of interaction with Jesuit missions and work in silver mines, had maintained a strong sense of cultural identity and political independence. When Mexicans began to encroach on their lands in the mid-nineteenth century, Yaquis responded with a series of rebellions against the government which lasted into the twentieth century. Mexican troops attacked Yaqui communities, rounded up Yaqui workers on haciendas and mines, arrested and killed hundreds of Yaquis, and deported hundreds more to work as virtual slaves in the Yucatán. By the late nineteenth century, Yaquis, long regarded in Mexico as excellent workers and skilled miners, began to work in Arizona mines, on railroads, and in construction.

As Mexican attacks against Yaquis escalated, work in the United States became part of a larger strategy in the ongoing battle. Worried Mexican officials followed the movement of Yaquis, tracing links between Yaqui workers in Arizona and the ongoing guerrilla movement. Mine owners, concerned about an unsteady work force, were by the 1900s complaining that Yaquis worked the mines only long enough to raise money to buy guns, ammunition, and supplies for Yaqui guerrillas.[27] Mexican officials complained to their U.S. counterparts that Yaquis were buying guns in the United States to use against the Mexican government. Yaquis sidestepped the ban on selling guns to Indians, pointed out by the Arizona Republican, which warned in 1906 that "many of the Yaquis may be easily mistaken for Mexicans, [and will use this] in order to purchase guns."[28] Yaquis also established de facto panindigenous alliances with Tohono O'odham and Maricopa *rancherías* near the border, which offered Yaquis places to stay and cover from Mexican armies.

I make no case that Yaquis were typical. They were at war with the Mexican government and persecuted. Yet their relatively well documented decisions suggest how concerns of indigenous communities helped shape (in significant ways) patterns of migration and work in the United States.

Mexicans Reenvisioning the Industrial Workers of the World

Mexicans were a critical part of the workforce that built the expanding industrial United States, yet they were also an underrecognized part of organized efforts to improve working conditions through unions and social movements. Some Mexicans joined and organized with the IWW, which research connects directly to the Partido Liberal Mexicano. The PLM acted as a de facto recruiting tool for the IWW and "paved the way for the powerful IWW movement among the Mexican workers, both in America [sic] and Mexico," as a 1911 letter noted in the IWW newspaper, *The Industrial Worker*.[29] The Industrial Workers of the World, founded in 1905, was an industrial union open to all workers; it organized among workers excluded from the segregated trade unions.

Mexican participation in the PLM and the IWW illuminates a critical history of Mexicans in the United States and suggests the need to reexamine the history of the IWW.[30] Many studies have viewed the IWW through a paradigmatic lens of what it was not: a geographically rooted union, bounded by the U.S. nation-state, and composed of Anglo-Americans or immigrants in the process of "becoming American." Understandably, this lens has yielded an IWW that failed: failed to develop as a permanent union, failed to understand the nature of U.S. workers' "job consciousness," and failed to lastingly change the United States. This view, built on assumptions about unidirectional paths of migration and processes of "Americanization," ignores the messy multiethnic and linguistic reality of those who felt themselves part of "One Big Union." Stability-conscious paradigms dominated by questions of the "uprooted" perceived mobility and migration as only disruptive and ignored how migration expanded the spatial reach of groups and increased interaction among workers from disparate areas. This perspective also overlooks how the IWW worked in local areas, and how workers shaped the IWW for their own needs.

Migration is an important part of this story. This period was one of intense mobility, as the insecurity of jobs forced laborers to move in search of work. The IWW reflected the movement of workers and was as much in motion and en route as it was rooted in a factory town, rural area, or city. These movements were embodied in the IWW membership card, which became the de facto ticket to ride the rails: those without the card could be summarily removed from train cars by other Wobblies. The IWW traveled with workers and with traveling organizer-propagandists who carried the newspapers.

Through its newspaper, the *Industrial Worker*, the IWW could mobilize over large areas. The effect of this IWW in motion can be seen in actions such as the cry to join free-speech fights in western cities, which led to an influx of Wobblies. The IWW also traveled with workers across national boundaries. Italian and Swedish Wobblies returning home (for a visit or longer) formed grassroots internationalist ties. Among Mexicans, the experience with the PLM and the IWW, as they understood it, traveled back with some of them to villages, settlements, and work sites in Mexico.

Although unrecognized in most histories, Mexicans were a crucial part of building the IWW, especially in the Southwest. Within a year of the IWW's 1905 founding, Mexican organizers were working among Mexican laborers in the borderlands of northern Mexico and the southwestern United States. Rosendo Dorame and an Arizona-born blacksmith, Fernando Velarde, cofounded the Phoenix IWW Local 272 in 1906. Three years later, they started the first Spanish-language IWW newspaper, *La Unión Industrial*. Mexicans were among the Wobbly traveling organizers and propagandists, the lifeblood of the organization, who connected disparate groups of workers into an organizational network. For example, by 1905, Fernando Palomárez, a Mayo from Sinaloa, was organizing Mexican workers into the IWW in Arizona while meeting with Yaquis and Mayos in Cananea mining camps forty-some miles away.

Despite ongoing perceptions by Anglo workers, and many observers in the United States, that Mexican workers were peons untutored in organization, Mexicans joined the IWW and in some areas were a substantial part or majority of the membership. By 1909, "the bulk of [the Phoenix local's] membership was 'Spanish speaking.'"[31] In 1909 Los Angeles, the number of Mexican Wobblies had increased so much that the IWW local expected "to almost double our number" when it formed an all-Mexican branch.[32] While exact numbers are elusive, Mexican Wobblies were visible enough to inspire the *Los Angeles Times* (in hysteria-based inflation) to report that "15,000 Mexicans belong to this branch of this malcontent order," although more reliable sources put the number at about 500.[33]

In 1910, a labor march of 10,000 in the city sported a group of an estimated 2,000 "unskilled" men and women, mostly Mexican, who marched
under the banner of "Workers of the World Unite" along with Russian
workers.[34]

Yet Mexicans' work with, and support for, the IWW was part of other
strategies and concerns about Mexico. All Mexican Wobblies I have encountered in research were also members of the Partido Liberal Mexicano
and were often known as Magonistas, after the PLM leader and theore-
tician, Ricardo Flores Magón. The PLM had been founded in Mexico
in 1902 as part of the liberal opposition to Mexican president Porfirio
Díaz. Facing increasing repression in Mexico, the organization relocated
to the United States, eventually moving to Los Angeles. The PLM membership drew primarily from artisans, industrial workers, and a nascent
middle class in the United States and Mexico and had a substantial following north of the border, with strong enclaves in California, Texas, and
New Mexico. The circulation of its newspaper, *Regeneración*, was 30,000 in
1906, and in 1914, past the organization's heyday, the Los Angeles chapter's membership alone was 6,000.[35]

Through its newspaper, the PLM focused on abuses suffered by rural
and urban workers, attacked U.S. capitalist incursions in Mexico, defended indigenous rights to communal land, and called for a social revolution in Mexico. They found support among Anglos and left-wing organizations, among them the Western Federation of Miners and the Socialist
Party. From 1909 to 1911, the PLM was a popular cause of the left in the
United States, finding its staunchest allies in the IWW.

The PLM made several attempts to create revolts in Mexico, in 1906,
1908, and 1910–1911. Its continued attempts to foment a revolution in
Mexico were increasingly impeded by coordinated efforts of the U.S.
and Mexican governments, which worked to either incarcerate or assas-
sinate leading Magonistas. A number of Magonistas, including Ricardo
Flores Magón, were jailed by the U.S. government on charges of violating
neutrality laws. Flores Magón would die in Leavenworth Prison in 1920
under circumstances that led to widespread suspicion that he had been
murdered.[36]

Magonista-Wobblies shaped some locals into de facto syndicalist arms
of the PLM. They were ubiquitous enough that in Bisbee, Arizona, in
1917, where the head of the Mexican IWW local also sold *Regeneración*,
sheriffs used the terms "Magonistas" and "Mexican IWW" as substi-
tutes for each other.[37] Meeting places were used interchangeably, and a

meeting of one organization easily overlapped with a meeting focusing on concerns of the other. Arizona mining hubs such as Douglas, Clifton-Morenci, and Bisbee often held clandestine and open locals of both organizations, often with common members.

By 1909, the PLM had formed Grupo Regeneración, a network of small clubs established to raise money and increase sales for the PLM's newspaper and to spread PLM ideas. These clubs popped up in small towns as well as cities and formed de facto organizing foci for Magonistas. These small groups seem to have met regularly. Some appear to have formed discussion groups, which read *Regeneración* aloud, fueled petition campaigns, scrounged for arms, and in some areas, especially along the border, were part of ongoing battles. They also worked with IWW locals. In a number of cities and towns, women formed all-female branches.

Mexican women were among the Magonistas, although again documentation is relatively slim. It is unclear how many women actually joined the IWW, as did Isabel Fierro, a well-known IWW member in the California border town of Calexico, adjacent to Mexicali on the Mexican side. Fierro was a Magonista and member of the local Grupo Regeneración.[38]

Women who worked in the fields, ran boardinghouses, cooked, cleaned clothes, and raised children also supported workers' strikes and the PLM in various ways. Some made tamales and coffee and prepared food for fund-raisers, typed, sang, and passed out literature at rallies. They raised money. They smuggled letters in and out of jails and smuggled guns and ammunition across the border. They made flags, visited prisoners, and helped with plans for revolution. Activist partners of traveling organizer-propagandists continued political work while caring for children and households while their partners were away. Eloise Monreal Velarde, wife of Magonista Wobbly Fernando Velarde, hid organizers escaping the law in their California home, fed them, and organized a memorial in their home on the day the Swedish Wobbly Joe Hill was executed. Some probably read regular columns about women in *Regeneración*. Some fought. Margarita Ortega, a Magonista in Mexicali, fought against Mexican troops and in 1913 was captured, tortured, and killed by the Mexican militia. Some, such as María Talavera and Sara Estela Ramírez, were intellectuals who wrote and published articles in *Regeneración*. Teresa and Andrea Villareal published *La Mujer Moderna* in Texas.

As an organization, the PLM was more progressive than the IWW in its statements calling for women's liberation from bourgeois conceptualizations of gender relations. Magón's statement on women, "A la mujer," argued for the liberation of women. Yet most PLM pronouncements, similar to those of the IWW, implicitly or explicitly assumed a female "nature."[39]

Women's involvement in the PLM was reported in Magonista newspapers, but more research is needed to more thoroughly excavate political activities and familial dynamics of Magonista Wobblies. Politics was often a family affair. For example, Josefina Amador Fierro Arancibia, whose brother and father were Magonista Wobblies, sang Magonista songs at political rallies. She ran Winchester rifles across the border at Mexicali in a baby carriage. Another example is Basiliza Franco, the daughter of Magonista parents, who would marry another Magonista, Fernando Palomárez. Basiliza formed a support group for Magonista Wobblies imprisoned in Leavenworth Prison, among them her father, Efran Franco y Palomárez. Her mother, Josefa, was the group's treasurer. Basiliza made the red flags that Magonistas used in the subsequent "red flag revolt" of 1911 and led an all-female Grupo Regeneración in El Paso, Texas. She smuggled *Regeneración* and PLM literature across the border, and in 1914, Basiliza, with her infant, was arrested and held overnight during one of these forays. She may well have contributed to Fernando's organizing with the IWW in an El Paso smelter and his later work in Los Angeles with the PLM and the IWW.[40]

Mexicans published Spanish-language newspapers that were Wobbly papers which featured articles about PLM plans for revolution. Phoenix Local 272, under Fernando Velarde and Rosendo Dorame, published *La Unión Industrial*, which advertised itself as "the only Spanish paper in the United States teaching revolutionary industrial unionism." Mexican Wobblies in Los Angles published *Huelga General* between 1912 and 1914, and *El Rebelde*, which ran from 1915 to 1919.[41] The PLM newspaper *Regeneración* often ran news of IWW strikes and organizing, which helped build support for the union among Mexicans. The newspapers found a receptive audience, and an Anglo organizer in Arizona wrote, "Only a very limited number of them can read, but those that can sure can eat up the literature we can get to them in their own language."[42] Newspapers would be passed "from hand to hand and from one town to another until they fell to pieces from use. One man who could read would meet with others in a house or small hut, and there by the light of a candle, he would read the paper to them."[43] Newspapers were read aloud in homes, towns, public squares, and workplaces. A Mexican worker interviewed in the 1920s said he had picked up anarchism by listening to speakers in the old plaza of downtown Los Angeles, visiting the local hall of the

Spanish-language IWW (which sported a library of anarchist literature), and reading newspapers.[44]

Anglo-American workers, many employers, and observers appear to have been imbued with the racialized notion that most Mexican workers were peons, unlikely to organize. Yet among Mexican migrants moving north of the border were those who knew about or had been involved in the Liberal movement in Mexico, indigenous rebellions, and early labor organizing in Mexico. Some had been involved in strikes, such as mine workers who had been in the Cananea copper strike of 1906 in Sonora. Some Mexicans born north of the border knew about (and some may have participated in) organizing by the Knights of Labor (called Los Caballeros de Trabajo in Spanish) in the nineteenth century, who participated in limited binational organizing. Mexicans in the United States became involved in strikes in agriculture, the mines, the railroad, smelters, and other sites where they worked. Mexicans picking crops joined Japanese workers and went on strike in 1903 in Oxnard, California. Up to fourteen hundred Mexican track workers building the Los Angeles streetcar network went on a series of strikes from 1903 to 1911.[45] Mexican mine workers in the binational copper-mining triangle that spanned northern Mexico, Arizona, and New Mexico contested the dual-labor system that paid Mexicans half what their Anglo counterparts earned, and they were part of large and bitter strikes in 1903, 1906, 1907, 1909, 1915, and 1917, as well as of smaller work stoppages that became so frequent that they were dubbed "strikitos."[46] In 1907, an organizer in Clifton-Morenci, Arizona, remarked that Mexicans and Italians had a "strong sentiment for organization" and argued that those who "most require education along industrial lines are not wage workers of alien races but the so called 'intelligent American skilled workers.'"[47] Another wrote from California that "contrary to the accepted notion that Mexicans won't stick . . . the majority of [strikers] were Mexicans [and are] . . . setting a good example of solidarity."[48] The *Los Angeles Labor Press* said of the 1915 Arizona miners' strike that "everyone knows it was the Mexican miners that won the strike . . . by standing like a stone wall until the bosses came to terms."[49]

Magonista Wobblies circulated within a larger international grouping of workers and immigrants. Mexicans rubbed shoulders with Swedes, Lithuanians, Greeks, Russians, Italians, and workers from other backgrounds—at work, on the streets of cities such as Los Angeles, in towns, and on the road. *Regeneración* carried greetings of solidarity from Cuba, France, and Italy; printed news of the general strike in Sweden; and followed Yaqui battles against Mexican government troops. In downtown

Los Angeles multiethnic meetings were held in the old Los Angeles plaza, bounded by Chinatown on one side, Main Street on another—filled with bars, pool halls, and employment agencies—and the old plaza Catholic church. The Italian Hall, host to many multinational gatherings, was half a block away. This core of Los Angeles was a hub for international organizing for early-twentieth-century revolutions. By 1904, Sun Yat Sen was organizing Chinese in Los Angeles' Chinatown to join a revolution in China which would break out in 1911. A few years later, Magonista rallies called for the fall of Mexican president Díaz and a social revolution in Mexico. Similar rallies were held at the Italian Hall and nearby Burbank Hall, where meetings for the PLM boasted speakers in Spanish, Italian, "Hebrew" (probably Yiddish), and German.[50]

Smaller towns echoed this internationalism. In the dusty desert town of Holtville, in California's Imperial Valley near the Mexican border, *Regeneración* reported "real internationalism and solidarity" as French, Italian, Mexican, Argentinean, and North American Wobblies constructed a new labor temple in the agricultural town.[51]

Certainly, working together and living in proximity did not erase previous prejudices, animosities, and hostilities. Employers did successfully pit groups of workers against one another. Yet the conditions of work and migration encouraged a burgeoning sense of internationalism.

Fernando Palomárez: Leaving a "Trail of Powder"

Biography can trace the lives of Mexican organizers and suggest how working with the IWW was part of binational strategies. Mexican traveling organizer-propagandists were descendants of tramping artisans and the lifeblood of the PLM and the IWW. One of these, Fernando Palomárez, likened his work to "leaving a trail of powder," a reference to an incendiary mix of ideas, similar in effect to dynamite. Palomárez came from a Mayo Indian family near the small enclave of Mayocoba, Sinaloa. The trilingual Palomárez—he spoke Yoeme, Spanish, and English—joined the PLM in 1902. Sent by the PLM to the copper-mining town of Cananea in 1903, he worked with the liberal underground and organized miners, especially in Yaqui and Mayo labor camps. By 1905, he had joined the IWW and became a prominent traveling organizer and propagandist with both organizations. He was known as a Mayo, signing letters to Flores Magón with "el indio mayo."[52]

Palomárez, as one Anglo Wobbly wrote, was "well known to all California IWW men."[53] He served as a bridge between Magonistas and monolingual English-speaking allies. Palomárez was a dedicated IWW organizer, yet his primary loyalty was to the PLM and Flores Magón. In 1908, for example, Palomárez and Juan Olivares published a short-lived "independent liberal newspaper" in Los Angeles called *Libertad y Trabajo* for Spanish-speaking Wobblies and Magonistas. It included news of the IWW and noted that the local Club Tierra Igualdad y Justicia had cosponsored a ball with the IWW to raise money for the enterprise. *Libertad y Trabajo* "had quite a circulation, largely owing to the efforts of Local 12, IWW, of which Palomarez was a member."[54] Yet articles were more focused on the PLM, and many were penned, under pseudonyms, by Flores Magón and Magonistas. *Libertad y Trabajo* lasted a few months but was jettisoned when Palomárez and Olivares abruptly left to organize for a long-planned PLM revolutionary uprising in Mexico.[55]

Palomárez' departure marked the beginning of a trip that lasted from 1908 to 1910 and took him from Southern California, through northern and central Mexico, and back into the United States and across the Midwest, the Southwest, and the Pacific Northwest. This trip is the only journey of a traveling organizer of the time that is relatively well documented. It offers a window onto the scope of these travels, suggests how Magonista Wobblies combined work for both organizations, and suggests how indigenous tactics may have helped shape those of the PLM and the IWW.

The Mexican trip was a critical part of Flores Magón's plan for an uprising in Mexico in 1908. Flores Magón had appointed Palomárez as the designated delegate to work with Mayos and Yaquis in northern Mexico. In Mexico, Palomárez met with Magonista supporters organizing for the planned uprising. Walking some of the way, hopping trains when he could, he met with contacts, targeted workers in particular areas, distributed newspapers and literature—he carried copies of the PLM 1906 manifesto and *Regeneración*—and delivered clandestine plans and letters. Over four months, Palomárez made his way through northwest and central Mexico, speaking with workers, meeting with PLM cadres, and moving between safe houses, where he collected mail and money and wrote reports back to the PLM leadership. When the attempted revolution failed, he moved south, stopping at small settlements and staying among workers in factories, small towns, and larger cities.

Palomárez told the details of his trip to socialist ally and friend Ethel Duffy Turner, the wife of John Kenneth Turner, author of *Barbarous Mexico*. She was, for a short time, editor of the English page of *Regeneración*. Details of the trip suggest how indigenous activists used racialized assumptions about indigenous persons to their advantage and drew on tactics which the latter may have developed over years of dealing with Spanish and, later, Mexican authorities.

To avoid being captured by Mexican forces following him, Palomárez disguised himself as an Indian by changing into huaraches, white pants, a blanket, and a rosary, consciously using the social invisibility of Indians to hide in plain sight. His disguise worked. Although police arrested him for looking suspicious (they thought he was trying to rob a bank), it did not occur to them that this scruffy Indian could be the Magonista they were hunting. As a result, they did not search him, enabling Palomárez to destroy the documents tied to his leg that called for armed revolution. He was released before they realized, belatedly, who he was.

His network of political contacts in Mexico included PLM groups, but in Sinaloa, he relied on Mayo relatives. His family appeared to have been liberals. One uncle had fought for Mexican liberal and later president Benito Juárez against French invaders; he had taken Fernando to live and work with him at a nearby internationalist utopian colony. Another relative, Pedro Felician, became a PLM delegate for Sinaloa who may well have been in contact with Palomárez during this trip.[56] As Mexican soldiers followed him, Palomárez found refuge at the home of his uncle Hilario Felician. Felician hid the 5′8″ Palomárez in a pit dug under the floor of the main room, concealing him so well that he remained undetected. When Fernando departed, his uncle gave Palomárez sandals designed in such a way that the footprints they left would suggest to any tracker that the wearer was walking in the opposite direction.

These were not impromptu preparations. Deep pits and ingenious sandals suggest experience in tactics of hiding and evasion that were part of his uncle's (and possibly Mayo) "cultural baggage." These examples raise the probability that tactics developed by indigenous communities may have been reformulated and used by Magonista Wobblies north of the border.[57]

Although Duffy-Turner's account does not address the importance of language, Palomárez' use of Yoeme was critical for communication with Yoeme speakers, the Yaquis and Mayos, yet also signified shared bonds and reasserted aspects of culture and common understandings. A documented example of the underexplored importance of language is the multilingual Primo Tapia de la Cruz, a Purépecha Magonista Wobbly. One Purépecha remembered that Primo Tapia "always used to talk to us in [Purépecha]" and took time to carefully explain the precepts of anarcho-syndicalism and communism in the Purépecha language and within the context of a

Purépecha worldview. Indigenous languages could be used to communicate privately in the presence of Spanish and English speakers, be they employers, police, landlords, or others.[58]

When Palomárez crossed back into the United States, he first moved north across Texas, into Oklahoma, Kansas, Nebraska, then west into Wyoming, Colorado, Utah, and Nevada; north again into the mining areas of Montana, across into Washington, and then down into Oregon and California, where he crisscrossed between the interior and the coast. His itinerary was probably driven by prearranged meetings with groups of Magonistas and an interest in covering specific areas and industries where Mexicans worked, such as sugar beet farms, cotton farms, railroad camps, or mining camps. Some travel was dictated by specific tasks. In Denver, he served as an envoy of Flores Magón to formally thank Bill Haywood and Charles Moyer of the IWW for the support they extended to Cananea strikers in 1906 who were members of the Western Federation of Miners. His route into Washington and Montana suggests he may have been following IWW free-speech fights which were erupting in 1909; in Seattle he met with William Z. Foster, a leader in the Spokane free-speech fight. He may have met with Magonista Blas Lara, who worked at a coal mine near Seattle, or with Mexicans who surfaced in the Spokane free-speech fights in 1909, or some who were later among the fifteen hundred Mexicans who joined the Seattle general strike of 1919.[59]

Organizing for the PLM revolutionary efforts in Mexico coalesced in preparations for a 1910–1911 PLM/IWW invasion into Baja California. The focal points for organizing were the desert areas of the Imperial Valley of California and the adjacent Mexicali Valley of Baja California. By 1910, the valley was being transformed into a rich binational agricultural area dominated by U.S. investors and tended by a multinational workforce.[60] The Imperial Valley became the IWW's first foray into agricultural organizing in 1908. By late 1910, the multiethnic IWW Local 437 in the Imperial Valley town of Holtville had a Spanish-speaking organizer and was doing "great field work . . . among the Mexicans."[61] Yet Mexicans were clearly already organizing. *Regeneración* reported that PLM supporters in the area—numbering at least one hundred—all belonged to the IWW by 1911. Magonista-Wobbly organizers already in the valley, who would help organize the Baja invasion, were probably part of IWW organizing.[62]

Indigenous workers, and their knowledge of land, terrain, and people, are highlighted in preparation for this invasion. In 1910, Flores Magón delegated Fernando Palomárez, Camilo Jiménez, and Pedro Ramírez

Caule, who had organized with Palomárez in Cananea, to organize for the invasion, including mapping the terrain, obtaining arms, and recruiting Indians from both sides of the border.[63] Jiménez helped shape organizational strategies of the PLM. He was a Cocopah, an indigenous group that lives in the borderlands of northern Mexico, southern Arizona, and California. Jiménez lived in Holtville during agricultural seasons and returned to his Cocopah community when the season ended. He was an early member of the IWW whom Flores Magón called a connoisseur of the people, communities, land, roads, trails, water sources, and mountains of the border areas, and a "strategist, a master of geographic detail." Camilo recruited for the invasion, holding initial planning meetings in his Holtville home and, as the group grew, the newly constructed IWW hall. Working together, the group recruited indigenous people from the area, planned strategy based on Jiménez' knowledge, and, ultimately, Jiménez organized "a small cavalry" of about 350 Cocopahs, who formed what one writer estimated to be about a third of the expeditionary force in the immediate borderlands.[64]

At this same time, Palomárez was in San Diego organizing a Spanish-speaking IWW local.[65] Going by his pseudonym, Francisco Martínez, he had begun organizing in San Diego in 1910. One Wobbly noted appreciatively that "since Fellow Worker Martínez . . . came here, the local IWW movement is getting lively." According to *Regeneración*, night after night unnamed orators in San Diego were "instructing their brothers in their rights as the producing class" and through "their sincerity and truth of their words" maintained "the spirit of struggle." Palomárez led a multiethnic strike among the city's gas workers, doubling the size of the IWW and creating a Spanish-speaking public service workers' local of the IWW. This spirit was simultaneously directed toward organizing for the Baja invasion. An anonymous letter from the San Diego local pressed IWW leadership to support the revolution, pointing out that Mexican Wobblies were preparing to "cooperate with their fellow slaves in Mexico."[66] Tellingly, the union local abruptly dissolved itself in 1911: the reason for disbanding read simply, "Mexican Revolution."[67] Several other Magonistas were in charge of the overall invasion and led a multiethnic group into the fray. The attempt to take Baja California for the Revolution was ultimately a failure, yet these preparations provide a window onto Magonista Wobblies and the importance of indigenous organizers and workers in this period.

Indigenous Magonistas who returned to Mexico had a binational influence, although more research is needed. This influence was not unidirectional. One of the best examples is Primo Tapia de la Cruz, who embodied intertwined multidimensional influences on organizing in both the United States and Mexico. Tapia came from a family of prominent activists for indigenous rights and agrarian reform which had been active in Liberal clubs opposing Díaz. Tapia migrated to Los Angeles in 1907, worked as a bodyguard for Ricardo Flores Magón, and probably lived in the PLM house. He learned English and may well have participated in Spanish-language study groups reading Kropotkin and other anarchists. By 1911, he had joined the IWW. He translated IWW songs into Spanish, which he belted out while accompanying himself on the guitar. Tapia formed what he called a "revolutionary junta" of the IWW, which was composed of two cousins and a friend from his hometown of Naranja, Michoacán. This community-based group of Purépechas worked in beet fields, construction, and on the railroad of the Western and Rocky Mountain states.

By 1916, these Purépecha Magonista Wobblies were organizing among an international group of unskilled and migrant workers across the Rocky Mountain states and the wheat belt. The ties of family, community, shared experience, language, and shared understandings (and possibly conflicts as well) no doubt contributed to their ability to operate as a cohesive group. Yet Tapia was clearly concerned with communicating across linguistic boundaries. He learned English in the United States and reportedly was studying Russian to better communicate with Russian workers in Bayard, Nebraska, where his junta established an IWW local composed of five hundred Mexican, Greek, and Russian sugar beet workers.

Tapia's influence upon his return to Mexico suggests the influence of returning Mexican migrants. In 1921, he returned to his hometown and organized the largest campesino union to work with the fledgling Mexican Communist Party. The movement he led was pivotal to energizing agrarian reform in Purépecha regions of Michoacán before he was assassinated in 1926.[68] It is not beyond the realm of possibility that his cousins returned with him to Mexico and played a part in the union, as did one young nephew (who may have also joined the Mexican Communist Party).[69]

More research is needed on Mexican migrants' influence in shaping grassroots organizing in both the United States and Mexico. I want to stress that this influence was multidirectional. Mexican workers brought with them experience with struggles in Mexico which helped shape organizing north of the border, and those who returned helped develop responses to social change in Mexico. Tapia was not alone. A worker interviewed for Manuel Gamio's 1926 study on Mexican immigrants to the United States planned to return to Mexico in the 1920s as part of a colony. He remarked that among those returning were "a group of radicals who have the ideas of the anarchists that we all ought to work for each and each for all" and planned to apply these principles to the new colony in Mexico.[70]

Conclusion

As the chapters in this volume demonstrate, Mexican workers helped shape communities, culture, and politics in the United States as well as in Mexico. Indigenous workers have been a part of Mexican migration to the United States since at least the late nineteenth century. Many were not recognized as indigenous and fell between the conceptual cracks in both countries. Written history has not yet fully explored the people, indigenous and mestizo, who were part of this early emigration, and their social relations, histories, and cultures, their diverse ways of knowing, the cognitive systems they drew upon, as well as their participation in social movements on both sides of the border. Works about Chicano history have yet to be fully considered in rewriting older paradigms of United States history.

This returns us to the headstone of Rosendo Dorame. Gilbert Dorame, Rosendo's grandson and a union organizer, erected this headstone in the East Los Angeles cemetery. The headstone is indicative not just of history, but of persistent memories and influences of Magonista Wobblies among families and segments of Mexican origin. Magonista-Wobblies became a touchstone for a younger generation and influenced activists in the 1930s, who, in turn, educated activists of the 1960s. Some Mexican families boast multigenerational legacies of social activism: Magonista-Wobblies, members of the Communist Party, activists in the United Farm Workers, the Chicano movement, and in current immigration struggles. Josefina Amador Fierro Arancibia, for example, later joined the Communist Party of the USA, and her daughter, Josefina Fierro Bright, helped form the Spanish Speaking People's Congress in the late 1930s and 1940s. Fernando Velarde's son, Guillermo, helped form and lead the successful agricultural union, the Confederación de Uniones de Campesinos y Obreros Mexicanos (CUCOM), a union active in the 1930s in Southern California that eventually became part of the national CIO agricultural union.[71]

Magonista Wobblies provide a window into the diverse history of Mexicans who migrated to the United States and into the historical roots of many Chicano families and communities. They challenged economic structures and fought to launch a social revolution in Mexico. While their vision of revolution did not succeed in the way they envisioned, they are the familial and ideological links to earlier binational movements and provide historical perspectives and connections to binational visions and organizing for social change in the twenty-first century.

Notes

1. I want to thank Miguel Albert Bartolomé for his thoughtful comments on my initial presentation of this chapter, and comments by John Tutino, Laura Velasco-Ortiz, Juan Gómez-Quiñones, and Alice Wexler. Thanks also to Sharla Felt, Emily Able, Janet Brodie, Carla Bittel, and the University of California Riverside's Center for Ideas and Society. Some ideas contained here were originally published in "Un pasado no visto: Perspectivas históricas sobre la migración binacional de pueblos indígenas," in Laura Velasco Ortiz, *Migración, fronteras e identidades étnicas transnacionales* (Mexico City: El Colegio de la Frontera Norte and Miguel Ángel Porrúa, 2008), 119–139.

2. A number of historians have written about Mexican workers in the IWW, the unions, and the Communist Party of the United States of America (CPUSA). See D. Monroy, "Anarquismo y comunismo," *Labor History* 24, no. 1 (1983): 34–59; Zaragosa Vargas, *Proletarians of the North* (Berkeley: University of California Press, 1993); J. Gómez-Quiñones, *Mexican American Labor 1790–1990* (Albuquerque: University of New Mexico Press, 1994); G. González, *Labor and Community*; E. Zamora, *The World of the Mexican Worker in Texas* (College Station: Texas A&M University Press, 1993).

3. The *Los Angeles Times*, sure that Dorame was Indian but confused as to what kind, referred to him as "another California Mexican Indian"; see "Order IWW from El Paso," *Los Angeles Times* (April 24, 1913): 16. His family believes he was Opata or from a mixture of indigenous roots. Dorame is listed as Mexican on the census and Caucasian in his Leavenworth prison record.

4. *Regeneración* (March 23, 1912).

5. *Tucson Citizen* (October 31, 1911).

6. For a fuller account of the strike, see P. J. Mellinger, *Race and Labor in Western Copper* (Tucson: University of Arizona Press, 1995); Benton-Cohen, *Borderline Americans; The Pueblo Chieftain*, September 16, 1917; personal communication with Jo Dorame, February 4, 2009. See also file for Rosendo A. Dorame, Leavenworth Prison.

7. Interview by author with Edward Banales, Corcoran, California, May 1983.

8. Cited in José Antonio Figueroa Juárez, "Informe sanitario del municipio de Angumacutiro, Michoacan para obtener el título de médico cirjico [*sic*; cirúrgico]" (Mexico City: Universidad Nacional Autónoma de México, Facultad de

Medicina, 1944), located in Biblioteca Luis González y González, Colegio de Michoacán, unpaginated appendix, "Número de Habitantes."

9. M. A. Bartolomé, *Gente de costumbres y gente de razón* (Mexico City: Siglo Veintiuno, 1997), 53n16. At one point, the Mexican census defined as "Indian" anybody who wore huaraches. Bonfil-Batalla notes that there is no legal definition of Indian; see Bonfil-Batalla, *México Profundo: Reclaiming a Civilization*, 19.

10. Gamio, who had some appreciation of indigenous cultures, still reluctantly agreed that they had to be scuttled in the development of modern Mexico; see Gamio, *Forjando patria* (Mexico City: Editorial Porrúa, 1960).

11. Bartolomé, *Gente de costumbres*, note 4, 42–43; R. Bartra, *La jaula de la melancolía* (Mexico City: Grijalba, 1987).

12. Bonfil-Batalla, *México Profundo: Reclaiming a Civilization*, 4. As Boyer points out, campesino identity did not supplant ethnic or other identities but was an identity inflected with particular understandings of ethnicity and other markers; see C. R. Boyer, *Becoming Campesinos* (Stanford: Stanford University Press, 2003).

13. For an excellent discussion, see Benton-Cohen, *Borderline Americans*. Also see L. Haas, *Conquest and Historical Identities in California* (Berkeley: University of California Press, 1995); Gordon, *Great Arizona Orphan Abduction*.

14. Quoted in E. Abel, *Tuberculosis and the Politics of Exclusion* (New Brunswick, N.J.: Rutgers University Press, 2007), 68.

15. M. Gamio, *Mexican Immigration to the United States* (New York: Dover Press, 1971).

16. J. D. Cockcroft, *Intellectual Precursors of the Mexican Revolution, 1900–1913* (Austin: University of Texas Press, 1968), 29.

17. Most came from the central plateau states of Michoacán, Guanajuato, and Jalisco, with a lesser proportion from the northern plateau and northwestern coast and the states of Zacatecas, Durango, Sonora, Chihuahua, Coahuila, and Nuevo León; see Gamio, *Mexican Immigration*, 17–19.

18. Bonfil-Batalla, *México Profundo: Reclaiming a Civilization*, 21–22.

19. Ibid.

20. Bartolomé, *Gente de costumbres*, 48.

21. D. Gutiérrez, "Shifting Politics of Nationalism in Greater Mexico," *Journal of American History* 86, no. 2 (1999): 481–517.

22. Truett, *Fugitive Landscapes*, 118.

23. Ibid.

24. R. Savala, *The Autobiography of a Yaqui Poet* (Tucson: University of Arizona Press, 1980). Barrio Anita reportedly was populated by "Yaquis, Mexicans and Papago Indians"; see R. Moisés, *A Yaqui Life* (Lincoln: University of Nebraska Press, 1971), 24.

25. Devra Weber, *Dark Sweat, White Gold*, 57–72.

26. R. Savala, *The Autobiography of a Yaqui Poet*, 86–87. This was written by him, without the mediation of books which are "as told to" pieces.

27. Report from subsecretary, Mig. S. Machado, to the governor of the state of Hermosillo, Sonora, February 2, 1911, Archivo General de la Nación, Colección Manuel González Ramírez (hereafter AGN/MGR), vol. 55, p. 00067. Taken from vol. 2749, 1911, the General Government Archive of the State of Sonora, vol. 2749, 1911; telegram from Arizpe, June 11, 1902, AGN/MGR, vol. 14, p. 05142.

28. *Arizona Republican* (April 7, 1906).

29. Letter from Stanley M. Gue, Local 13, San Diego IWW, *Industrial Worker* (September 7, 1911).

30. M. Dubofsky, *We Shall Be All* (New York: Quadrangle Press, 1969). Among those who have discussed the need for revising the history of the IWW, see S. Salerno, *Red November Black November* (Albany: State University of New York Press, 1989); Mellinger, *Race and Labor*; idem, "How the IWW Lost Its Western Heartland," *Western Historical Quarterly* 27 (1996): 303–324.

31. *Industrial Worker* (May 20, 1909).

32. *Industrial Worker* (July 1, 1909).

33. *Los Angeles Times* (February 14, 1914). The lower estimate is from J. G. Monroy, *Ricardo Flores Magón y su actitud en la Baja California* (Mexico City: Editorial Academia Literaria, 1962), 109.

34. A. Lewis, "The Basis of Solidarity," *New Review* 3 (1915): 186; *Los Angeles Herald* (November 4, 1910); *Los Angeles Examiner* (November 4, 1910).

35. W. W. McEuen, "A Survey of the Mexicans in Los Angeles 1910–1914" (MA thesis, University of Southern California, 1914), 89.

36. For selected works on the PLM, see J. Gómez-Quiñones, *Sembradores* (Los Angeles: University of California—Los Angeles Chicano Studies Research Center Publications, 1982), 24; J. Torres-Pares, *La revolución sin frontera* (Mexico City: Universidad Nacional Autónoma de México, 1990); J. A. Sandos, *Rebellion in the Borderlands* (Norman: University of Oklahoma Press, 1992); A. T. Cienfuegos, *El magonismo en Sonora*.

37. Benton-Cohen, *Borderline Americans*, 210.

38. For Isabel Fierro, see *Regeneración* (November 24, December 12, 1911). She is also referred to as "a Mexican girl, a member of local 437" of the Calexico IWW; see *Industrial Worker* (December 7, 1911).

39. R. Flores-Magón, *A la mujer* (Oakland, Calif.: Prensa Sembradora, 1974); interview with Evelyn Velarde Benson by author, Los Angeles, California, May 4, 1971; E. Pérez, *The Decolonial Imaginary*.

40. Interview with Josefina Arancibia by author, Madera, California, 1982. For Basiliza, see *Regeneración* (July 29, December 6, 1911; January 11, 1913), Leavenworth Prison Fernando Palomares Files.

41. Mellinger claims it was put out by the Propaganda League of Mexicans in Los Angeles; see *Race and Labor*, 178.

42. Charles Clinton, IWW camp delegate, *Industrial Worker* (October 5, 1911).

43. Ethel Duffy Turner, "Fernando Palomarez," Bancroft Library, University of California, Berkeley.

44. "Guillermo Salorio," in Manuel Gamio, *The Life Story of the Mexican Immigrant* (Chicago: University of Chicago Press, 1930); W. Estrada, *The Los Angeles Plaza*.

45. Gómez-Quiñones, *Mexican American Labor 1790–1990*, 78.

46. Benton-Cohen, *Borderline Americans*, 203, see also Yvette Huginnie, 'Strikitos,'" PhD dissertation, Yale University, 1991, 380; Mellinger, *Race and Labor*, 178.

47. Letter from H. W. Kane, *Miners Magazine* (February 21, 1907).

48. *Industrial Worker* (October 15, 1911).

49. *Labor Press* (April 14, 1916), cited in Gómez-Quiñones, *Mexican American Labor 1790–1990*.

50. *Regeneración* (September 3, 1910; May 13, June 16, 1911; and other dates). See also Estrada, *The Los Angeles Plaza*, 134–138.

51. *Regeneración* (January 21, 1911).

52. See J. G. Monroy, *Ricardo Flores Magón*, 67; E. D. Turner, *Revolution in Baja California*, 60; P. L. Martínez, *A History of Lower California*, 467; J. B. Bassols, *Correspondencia* (Mexico City: Consejo Nacional para la Cultura y las Artes, 2001).

53. *Industrial Worker* (July 16, 1910).

54. *Regeneración* (March 6, 1912). All translations are mine unless otherwise noted.

55. Other articles, written by Magonistas such as Blas Lara, María Talavera, Lucie Norman (Talavera's daughter), and Teresa and Andrea Villarreal were prominently featured in the newspaper. *Libertad y Trabajo* ran from May 9 to June 13, 1908; held in UCLA Special Collections. Also see letter from Ricardo Flores Magón to Enrique Flores Magón, June 7, 1908, in Bassols, *Correspondencia*, I: 444–462, 699, concerning plans for the 1908 uprising. See also Gómez-Quiñones, *Sembradores*, 42. Palomárez wrote a letter to the editor of *Revolt* (March 6, 1912), concerning support of the IWW local; see also *Regeneración* (March 22, 1912).

56. Archivo General del Gobierno del Estado de Sonora, Vol. 2524, Year 1908, Exp. Rebelión Sonora y Chihuahua, AGN/MGR, 41.

57. The narrative of Palomárez' trip is contained in a short biography of him by Ethel Duffy Turner; see, for information on the family in Sinaloa, E. D. Turner, typewritten manuscript on Fernando Palomarez, Ethel Duffy Turner Collection, University of California at Berkeley. See also author's interviews with Bernabé Felician Castro, Jesús Felician Pinto, Mayocoba, Sinaloa, 2004.

58. Paul Friedrich, *The Princes of Naranja* (Austin: University of Texas Press, 1986), 6.

59. Ibid. Blas Lara-Cáceres wrote his autobiography under a pseudonym, Mariano Gómez-Gutiérrez, *La vida que yo viví* (Mexico City: N.p., 1954).

60. R. S. Street, *Beasts of the Field* (Stanford: Stanford University Press, 2004), 491.

61. Letter to *Industrial Worker* (December 1, 1910).

62. *Regeneración* (January 21, 1911); J. G. Monroy, *Ricardo Flores Magón*, 63.

63. G. Navarro, "¡Asalto a Baja California en 1910! No fue un movimiento filibustero, sino un ataque a Díaz." See also Turner, typewritten manuscript on Fernando Palomarez, Ethel Duffy Turner Collection, chap. 10.

64. Ironically, Camilo Jiménez also understood early-twentieth-century tourism and, playing off the popularity of all things "Indian," raised money for the invasion by "making moccasins and selling them to American tourists"; see *Regeneración* (April 29, 1911). See also Martínez, *A History of Lower California*; Monroy, *Ricardo Flores Magón*; E. D. Turner, *Revolution in Baja California*. On the Cocopahs, see Spicer, *Cycles of Conquest*, 25–45, 262–265.

65. L. L. Blaisdell, *The Desert Revolution* (Madison: University of Wisconsin Press, 1962), 156; *San Diego Union* (June 6, 1911); P. F. Brissenden, *The IWW* (New York: Columbia University Press, 1919), 156. For the strike, see *Industrial Worker*

(July 16, 1910); *Regeneración* (September 3, 1910). There was at least one report that a rally held at Germania Hall for the strikers was attended by a "mixed" gathering of 250, including Mexicans, "negroes and a number of Americans"; see *San Diego Union* (August 29, 1910).

66. Letter to *Industrial Worker* (November 2, 1910), from Local 13, San Diego. The writer, citing the large number of Mexican workers, also asked the IWW to fund a Spanish-speaking organizer for the southwestern states.

67. Brissenden, *The IWW*, 366.

68. The most detailed study of Primo Tapia, based on oral histories, is Paul Friedrich, *Agrarian Revolt in a Mexican Village* (Chicago: University of Chicago, 1977); see also idem, *The Princes of Naranja* (Austin: University of Texas, 1986); A. Martínez-Múgica, *Primo Tapia, semblanza de un revolucionario michoacano* (Mexico City: N.p., 1946); P. M. Anaya-Ibarra, *Precursores de la revolución mexicana* (Mexico City: Secretaría de Educación Pública, 1955); A. E. Osorio, *Primo Tapia: Cien años de su nacimiento* (Morelia, Mich.: Coordinación de la Investigación Científica, Departamento de Historia, 1987), 154; G.L.-y.-R. Alicia Castellanos-Guerrero, *Primo Tapia de la Cruz, un hijo del pueblo* (Mexico City: Centro de Estudios Históricos del Agrarismo en México, 1991); M. Becker, *Setting the Virgin on Fire* (Berkeley: University of California Press, 1995); P. Ignacio-Taibo, *Bolshevikis* (Mexico City: Editorial Joaquín Mortiz, 1986).

69. Friedrich, *Agrarian Revolt*, 68–69; Ignacio-Taibo, *Bolshevikis*, 189–192.

70. Gamio, *Mexican Immigration*, 128–130.

71. Devra Weber, *Dark Sweat, White Gold*, 85, 159–160.

CHAPTER 7

Transnational Triangulation: Mexico, the United States, and the Emergence of a Mexican American Middle Class

JOSÉ E. LIMÓN

During and since the election of Barack Obama to the presidency, the American middle class has been at the center of a wrenching national debate relative to the economy in general and taxation policy in particular. All political figures, pundit commentary, and tavern debates sooner or later make reference to the well-being of the "middle class" as the objective of any particular view or position in these debates.

Such a recurring and almost venerating reference clearly suggests something that we have always known, namely, that this is the largest and most politically active class in our polity even as it is also its economic, social, and even cultural bedrock, or in anthropologist Sherry Ortner's definition, "simply all those Americans who have signed up for the American dream, who believe in a kind of decent life of work and family, in the worth of the 'individual' and the importance of 'freedom,' and who strive for a moderate amount of material success. It is everybody except the very rich and the very poor."[1] Later, we shall flesh out this general definition with more substantive data.

However, it also seems to be the case that this American and largely white middle class is also the target audience for another wrenching national debate, that concerning undocumented immigration, largely from Mexico, which is of course intimately linked to the first—that of the economy. In 2011, as unemployment remains high and governmental entities are experiencing severe budget shortfalls, such immigrants are accused of taking American jobs and draining governmental resources especially in health care and education. Beyond such possibly quantifiable measures, for some, possibly many, white middle-class Americans, there is also the more emotionally subjective cultural anxiety created by more dark people entering their environment, people also speaking a foreign language.

In what follows, I want to propose that this binary between the American middle class—at the heart of the United States—and immigration—largely from a socially fraught Mexico—needs to be *triangulated* to take account of another distinctive set of players, namely, Mexican Americans—U.S. citizens—many over several generations, many themselves members of the middle class. Their real and potential role in the immigration debate but also in a whole host of social issues before us merits a more careful attention to this class formation than has been offered in the past.

Erasing the Middle Class

For indeed, it is interesting in and of itself how little sustained attention has been paid to the Mexican American middle class. In large part this inattention has much to do with what one senses is a general antipathy that many intellectuals and artists feel toward the middle class, especially within those disciplines and discourses that today are loosely grouped under the rubric of "cultural studies" rather than, let us say, sociology or economics, which almost by necessity must always at least posit the category of the middle class. It is from cultural studies, then, that the middle class remains largely omitted, although when it is recognized, it is usually as a negative phenomenon. This omission/negation has its own history in the West.

Though neither of them specifically used the term "middle class," the nineteenth century thinkers Matthew Arnold and Karl Marx, writing at about the same moment and generally in the same place, offer the first sustained but vexed recognition and characterization of such a class. For both it is a negatively valenced formation. For Arnold, such a class is one of the sites of what he calls "philistine" culture, with its inferior or nonexistent tastes in the arts and learning.[2] Marx and Engels also lent support to such a characterization, but for them, the middle-class petty bourgeoisie also takes on an additional negative valence, namely, its ambivalent relation to the emerging revolutionary working class, and the possible propensity of this petty bourgeoisie to ally itself with those in true and full control of the means of production.[3]

These disparaging left and right perspectives continue at the heart of much cultural commentary into the twentieth century; on the right one need only recall the Englishman F. R. Leavis, the American T. S. Eliot, and the Spaniard Ortega y Gasset, and much of leftist European modernism through the Frankfurt School. Indeed, Ortega y Gasset drew a correlation between Nazism and the German middle class.[4]

From these principal and European origin points (although no doubt with antecedents as far back as the early modern period), the intellectually/artistically maligned middle class made its way to our shores. But even as this class began to form in the United States, it did so in a continuing state of intellectual and artistic repression save for parody, satire, or sarcasm, whether at the hands of Mark Twain in *Huckleberry Finn*, Sinclair Lewis by way of *Main Street*, Andy Warhol by way of Campbell soup (after all, the mainstay dietary fuel of the American middle class), or the New York intellectuals associated with the *Partisan Review*.

Many of us in academia and the arts have inherited this disparaging legacy, which is to say, we—most of us—simply do not like the middle class and can speak its name only with a slight sneer. Yet, in spite of these continuing repressions and evasions by and from cultural elites (save perhaps Norman Rockwell), the American middle class was expanding apace especially after the end of World War II. As with all such proposals, there are interesting exceptions but principally from social scientists. One thinks in the past of Lynd's *Middletown* and, later, the work of Herbert Gans.[5] Here we see again sociologists in action although engaged in more qualitative research. More recently, we can also note a plethora of work—empirical, historical, and theoretical—on the middle class, again, principally from sociologists and anthropologists, and I shall draw on these in my final section.

A Further Erasure

Unfortunately, Mexican American cultural studies has also inherited this bias against the middle class within Mexican American society. The most coherent and abundant such work, encompassing both scholarship and the arts, began in the 1960s and did so under the impetus of the Chicano movement of those years, the political effort to seek redress for the marginalized state of Mexicans in the United States at that moment and to assert their cultural presence. But as productive as this movement was in these terms, it generated a less-than-comprehensive, less-than-complex view of Mexican America as it largely overlooked the middle class. Moreover, current postmovement activity, for all of its theoretical sophistication, continues to have this skewed vision, all of which is to say that the broader Western intellectual legacy of maligning the middle class has also been true of the Chicano/Chicana intelligentsia of Mexican America, which is to say, people like myself.

Elsewhere I have closely examined the manner in which much Chicano movement–inspired scholarship and cultural expression avoid the middle class in marked favor of two principal subjects and sets of imagery: the urban barrio dweller, more specifically, the character of the street-gang adolescent—the *pachuco*; and that of the farmworker.[6] Such scholarship included the field of social history where labor and union activity were the dominant subjects.[7] We, too, have not particularly liked our middle class, and we can speak its name only with some contempt and derision. At a West Los Angeles, West Austin, or Berkeley cocktail party, many of us who are Mexican American might proudly claim that our parents or grandparents were farmworkers; however, precious few might admit to a now possibly larger reality, namely, that our mom or dad sold insurance for State Farm.

To be sure, the middle class was somewhat noted during the Chicano movement and still is today, but, as I say, usually as an elitist and retrograde force. Such notice occurred principally in political histories that, negatively and critically, identified a small, allegedly middle-class and allegedly assimilationist grouping called the League of United Latin American Citizens (LULAC).[8]

Other kinds of studies also exhibit this attitude even as they grudgingly admit to the existence of such a growing class formation. For example, an ethnomusicological study by Manuel Peña focuses on a particular popular musical aggregation and style, an ensemble consisting of accordion, rhythm, and guitars predominantly playing fast-tempo polka music based on northern Mexican music.[9] It is a music closely identified with the Mexican American working class in the twentieth century, particularly in Texas. However, to make his affirmative, admiring case on behalf of *conjunto*, Peña feels obligated both to identify and to attack another musical style, one based on an American-style big band ensemble, and which he identifies with an assimilative Mexican American middle class. One can debate the merits of his argument, but what I find germane to my present purpose is, first, that he even identifies a middle class at all, and then that he thinks it sufficiently cohesive and developed to have its own musical style.

However, within early Chicano studies, the middle class could not be wholly evaded or criticized. Three other important books deal with the middle class in more affirmative tones. Richard García explores the identity features of this class in detail and argues for its importance to the de-

Table 7.I. Occupational Distribution of Spanish-Origin Population in Texas, 1930, 1950, 1970, and 1980

	Spanish-Origin Population			
Occupation	% 1930*	% 1950	% 1970	% 1980
White collar				
Professional/technical	1.4	2.2	7.6	8.0
Proprietor/manager	16.4	8.7	5.8	5.4
Clerical/sales	4.2	10.2	19.3	22.4
Skilled				
Craftsman/foreman	6.7	10.2	15.0	17.1
Operative	5.8	17.7	21.5	18.2
Unskilled				
Service worker/laborer	32.0	27.8	25.0	25.2
Farmworker	33.6	23.2	5.8	3.8

*Includes a small number of Native Americans and Asian Americans.
Source: Montejano, *Anglos and Mexicans*, based on U.S. Department of Commerce, Bureau of the Census, Fifteenth, Seventeenth, Nineteenth, Twentieth Censuses of the United States: 1930, 1950, 1970, 1980.

velopment of its Mexican American community of San Antonio, Texas.[10] However, García stresses the leadership of this class, as does Mario García for the Southwest in general.[11] Largely missing here, however, is a more sociological, economic, or anthropological assessment of the worldview and activities of such a class. Closer to this mark is David Montejano's now-classic *Anglos and Mexicans in the Making of Texas, 1836–1986*, a historical study, but one written by a sociologist. I am particularly interested in his closing chapter, where he offers a relatively optimistic rendering of the future of Mexican American social mobility in Texas, an assessment based on a reading of economic census data from 1930 through 1980 (see Table 7.1).

Says Montejano: "By 1950 the effects of war-related industrialization in increasing the ranks of skilled and semiskilled laborers as well as of clerical workers were evident. The skilled and professional workers accounted for nearly half of the Texas Mexican work force, while the unskilled made up the other half." By 1970, the occupational distribution of 1930 had been reversed. The unskilled category of farmworkers and service workers-laborers made up slightly less than a third (30.8 percent) of the workforce, while the skilled and professional workers made up slightly more than two-thirds (69.2 percent). This occupational division of thirds is evident in the 1980 data, but with a further weakening of the unskilled categories and a strengthening of the white-collar categories. In 1980, 35.8 percent of Texas Mexicans had white-collar occupations; 35.3 percent had skilled occupations; and the number with unskilled jobs had dropped to 29 percent.[12]

Montejano summarizes his findings thusly: "The importance of these occupational changes for Mexican-Anglo relations cannot be overstated. The general effect of an expanding white collar and skilled strata within the Mexican American community was the attainment of a measure of economic stability."[13]

In large part, Montejano explains the social origins of this "expanding white collar and skilled strata within the Mexican American community" with reference to "war-related industries," although he specifically names employment at the several military bases created in Texas during World War II but maintained during the long period of the Cold War.[14] Large numbers of Mexican Americans—many of these veterans—were able to secure dependable, relatively well paying civilian employment under federal jurisdiction and thus relatively free from the local racism that affected hiring and mobility in the private and local governmental sectors. Growing up in South Texas at this time, I heard the expression "*la base*" (the base) uttered as an almost religious mantra of achievement and success. If only dad, but also mom, could secure employment there, life could change dramatically. Even today for a young Mexican American, the road from, let us say, San Antonio, to, let us say, Georgetown University or the University of Notre Dame may have its beginnings at Kelly Air Force Base in San Antonio in some previous generation.

The mobility effect of the military base complex was augmented by other, related, factors. Large numbers of Mexican Americans served in World War II, and those who survived were exposed to a wider range of American and also international cultural experience, but perhaps most decisively, to greater fluency in the English language. As Eric Ávila has noted of Los Angeles, "Clearly, the experience of Mexican American soldiers during the war effort heightened a sense of patriotic nationalism in the Chicano community and inculcated a sense of entitlement to the good life that burgeoned in suburban Southern California. Neighborhoods in the San Gabriel Valley such as Pico Rivera cradled a Chicano middle class during the postwar period."[15] Some of these returning veterans also took advantage of the GI Bill for postsecondary education of various kinds.[16] Attendance at research universities was probably minimal though not wholly absent, but the effect of local community and state colleges on such mobility remains greatly underresearched, especially but not exclusively in their production of K–12 educational personnel now to be seen as educators and as stable governmentally employed income earners.[17]

Yet another unexplored factor follows upon education and also upon a continuing bilingualism, especially along the border, namely, the increasing movement of Mexican Americans into the governmental and economic structures dealing with the Republic of Mexico, from Border Patrol agents to Ambassador Tony Garza.

Montejano's findings for 1930–1980 can be updated to the present. In 2001, the authoritative Tomás Rivera Policy Center issued a quantitative study of 1990 census data called *The Latino Middle Class: Myth, Reality and Potential*. Its conclusions attest far more to a reality and a potential than to a myth. Based on a close examination of income, education, and housing variables but primarily resting its case on regionally adjusted annual incomes of $40,000 or more, the authors conclude that "frequent depictions of Latinos as predominantly foreign-born, uneducated, and poor have caused many observers to overlook appreciable gains in Latino economic status in recent years. In fact, a substantial and prosperous Latino middle class has emerged" (1). They note more specifically that "41 percent of Mexican origin . . . had reached middle class status by 1998."[18]

These findings are borne out by others such as the Pew Hispanic Center's statistical compilations of "Hispanic" for 2005.[19] By these data on income distribution, one can see that some 32.6 percent of native-born Hispanics are earning $56,606 or more annually as against 43.8 percent of white earners, a disparity indeed (but not as large as might be expected), but also a finding that still speaks to a significant basis for a middle-class existence to which one might add the upper rungs of the third quintile. These figures also appear to correlate with occupational categories for Hispanics (Table 7.2).

If, in the ranking of occupations, we establish a "middle-class" cutoff point at and including "Healthcare practitioners & technical," that is, physicians, registered nurses, skilled medical technicians, then it would appear that close to 2.5 million out of some 10.5 million total population of native-born Hispanics are employed in these "upper" categories. There are other additional middle-class possibilities in the "lower" levels, such as long-term, well-paid employees in "office & administrative support" (for example, the senior administrative associate for the Center for Mexican American Studies at my former university), highly skilled and possibly unionized workers in "construction trades" (foremen, electricians,

Table 7.2. Household Income Distribution by Race and Ethnicity, 2005

	Income					
Race/Ethnic Category	1st Quintile $0–$18,999	2nd Quintile $19,000–35,999	3rd Quintile $36,000–56,499	4th Quintile $57,500–89,599	5th Quintile $89,600+	Total
Hispanic	3,029,753	3,210,650	2,702,402	2,147,974	1,411,737	12,502,516
Native-born	1,402,924	1,287,358	1,194,363	1,086,825	795,390	5,766,860
Foreign-born	1,626,829	1,923,292	1,508,039	1,061,149	616,347	6,735,656
White alone, not Hispanic	14,016,496	15,648,752	16,599,086	17,450,080	18,614,093	82,328,509
Black alone, not Hispanic	4,422,219	3,194,377	2,490,796	2,055,232	1,316,776	13,479,402
Asian alone, not Hispanic	695,419	620,797	724,938	896,496	1,297,449	4,235,099
Other, not Hispanic	578,385	473,129	433,212	396,497	313,094	2,194,317
Total	22,742,272	23,147,705	22,950,436	22,946,279	22,953,151	114,739,843
	% Distribution					
Hispanic	24.2	25.7	21.6	17.2	11.3	100.0
Native-born	24.3	22.3	20.7	18.8	13.8	100.0
Foreign-born	24.2	28.6	22.4	15.8	9.2	100.0
White alone, not Hispanic	17.0	19.0	20.2	21.2	22.6	100.0
Black alone, not Hispanic	32.8	23.7	18.5	15.2	9.8	100.0
Asian alone, not Hispanic	16.4	14.7	17.1	21.2	30.6	100.0
Other, not Hispanic	26.4	21.6	19.7	18.1	14.3	100.0
Total	19.8	20.2	20.0	20.0	20.0	100.0

Note: Quantities are based on 2005 total household income distribution. Figures based on reported incomes, not adjusted incomes. Percentages may not add to 100 because of rounding.
Source: Pew Hispanic Center tabulations of 2005 American Community Survey; Pew Hispanic Center, A Statistical Portrait of Hispanics at Mid-Decade.

etc.), and Hispanics serving in the officer corps of the "military" category (see Table 7.3). We also need to recall that today's norm is the two-salary family, a shared double income within one residential unit not reflected in the Pew reports.

Taken together, all of these additional factors would likely raise the middle-class figure of 2.5 million perhaps to as much as half of the total native-born population of 10.5 million. One might further infer that higher education is also a characteristic of this middle class. Other sources do not disagree with this emerging portrait of the middle class: "Hispanic households earning between $40,000 and $140,000 annually reached 2.5 million in 1999, or about one-third of all Hispanic households nationwide . . . 64 percent of middle-class Hispanic households either owned or were buying a home, and 20 percent were headed by someone with a bachelor's or advanced degree."[20]

Perhaps more than any other urban concentration, it is Southern California that always evokes a predominant imagery of a wholly socially beleaguered and besieged Mexican-origin population. And, while there is some considerable truth to that imaginary, sociologist Jody Agius Vallejo's extensive fieldwork observation and interviews clearly show that "a Mexican middle class is thriving in Southern California and that this population defies the range of predicted outcomes for the children of Mexican immigrants."[21]

In offering these data, my focus is indeed largely on U.S. native-born second-generation and after subjects. They also offer compelling evidence and analysis concerning those who have *not* reached middle-class status, who are at some far distance from it. These people, not too surprisingly, are predominantly recent Mexican immigrants. According to the Tomás Rivera report, beginning in 1979, "the number of poor foreign-born Latino households increased almost three-fold, from less than 600,000 to over 1.6 million households, with most of the increase occurring during the 1990s."[22] For their part, the Pew tables noted above clearly indicate that foreign-born "Hispanics" predominantly occupy the lowest rungs of the income and occupational ladders.[23] As noted earlier, we are only too familiar with the major national debate concerning such immigration and the deep ambivalence of the American public toward immigration, an ambivalence fostered indeed by commentators like Lou Dobbs but also by the marked anti-immigration sentiment within the Republican Party. But what is the role of the native-born, largely Mexican American, middle class as we currently know it in these debates and others?[24]

Current theoretical and empirical social science scholarship on the cul-

ture and politics of the middle class in the West may be useful in addressing this question. Such middle-class existences are worth examining if
only because they constitute a large part of human existence in the West.
More important, such formations offer particularly interesting sites in
which to examine the ambivalent and paradoxical play of culture in relation to economics and politics. Moreover, within the contradictory space
of neoliberal democracy, it is largely from this class and its cultural configuration that the most promising social leadership is likely to emerge on
behalf of those structurally below them. Sociologists continue to debate
the Marxist-inspired legacy of the middle class under the rubric of the
"new middle class" in our contemporary late-capitalist culture and political economy, a class now defined substantially by its higher education in
the new postindustrial economy of our time.[25] In more contemporary
language and with more nuanced analyses, the debate continues to focus
on the role of this new middle class in the West, but, more specifically,
in the United States, in a progressive/liberal versus reactionary/conser-
vative opposition or, perhaps worse yet, a co-opted consumerist quies-
cence. While there is no dominant consensus on this question, Glassman
et al. offer the most persuasive view, namely, that "the new middle class,
in its short history, has already exhibited forms of social action that call
into question the extremely pessimistic view that sees only co-optation
and self-centered withdrawal . . . members of the new middle class are
quite active politically. . . . However, as a class it has no distinctive political orientation, being instead torn between sectors aligned to the political left and those on the right."[26] However, these debates largely assume
a predominantly white and long-term native middle class. Does this lack
of a "distinctive political orientation" change when race, ethnicity, and/
or recent immigration into the United States are introduced into the
assessment?

Keya Ganguly ethnographically examines legalized immigrants from
India in New Jersey who have made it into the middle class, a formation
that she theorizes in surprising, critical Marxist terms not to damn it but
to quietly admire its everyday practices, such as Indian food and popular film. She sees not "resistance" but moments of potential postcolonial
ethnic and political solidarity and efficacy in a still-alienating racialized
American world even as immigrants succeed socioeconomically within it.
She offers no evidence that such a stance translates into anything resem-
bling a practical politics.[27]

My own ongoing ethnographic work in South Texas among the Mexican American middle class is yielding similar cultural findings supported

Table 7.3. Occupation by Race and Ethnicity, 2005

Occupation	Hispanic			Non-Hispanic				Total
	Total	Native-Born	Foreign-Born	White Alone	Black Alone	Asian Alone	Other	
Management	1,046,092	611,209	434,883	12,070,602	960,837	633,230	243,830	14,954,591
Business operations	237,483	162,178	75,305	2,414,520	301,905	143,051	58,018	3,154,977
Financial	251,340	168,658	82,682	2,790,598	306,557	295,990	57,305	3,701,790
Computer & math	185,521	122,442	63,079	2,544,747	251,151	568,901	60,757	3,611,077
Architecture & engineering	187,073	113,385	73,688	2,412,537	155,331	303,793	48,449	3,107,183
Life, physical & social sciences	87,062	53,380	33,682	1,117,717	88,428	167,757	28,636	1,489,600
Community & social services	222,833	155,442	67,391	1,732,233	454,139	76,297	64,594	2,550,096
Legal	111,068	84,674	26,394	1,477,445	104,160	61,917	30,670	1,785,260
Education, training & library	741,261	505,397	235,664	7,691,727	928,337	392,308	174,214	9,927,847
Arts, design, sports, entertainment, media	267,220	156,076	111,144	2,643,588	201,290	161,284	66,565	3,339,947
Health practitioners & technical	419,437	283,278	136,159	5,873,802	786,050	594,008	125,743	7,799,040
Health-care support	461,392	281,353	180,039	2,169,630	980,642	156,543	102,258	3,623,116

Protective services	373,604	291,008	82,596	2,416,767	666,428	67,004	99,293	3,870,465
Food prep & serving	1,816,504	656,712	1,159,792	6,072,824	1,210,545	486,554	271,996	9,858,423
Building & grounds cleaning and maint.	2,045,248	486,632	1,558,616	3,565,221	1,129,947	172,524	164,243	7,097,183
Personal care & services	779,486	378,759	400,727	3,745,520	862,394	333,901	159,620	5,880,921
Sales	2,186,754	1,315,563	871,191	15,062,476	1,985,108	915,410	410,318	20,560,066
Office & admin. support	2,871,203	1,911,782	959,421	18,040,686	3,181,115	949,484	537,989	25,580,477
Farming, fishing & forestry	569,010	79,279	489,731	690,827	71,025	16,615	24,931	1,372,408
Construction trades	2,609,482	639,985	1,969,497	7,061,465	737,776	113,725	253,628	10,776,076
Extraction workers	24,649	14,098	10,751	144,864	9,691	212	6,298	185,914
Install., maint. & repair workers	779,168	359,886	419,282	4,405,062	498,285	152,578	108,596	5,943,689
Production	2,409,744	705,293	1,704,451	7,560,154	1,497,180	604,061	233,562	12,304,701
Transport & material moving	1,885,300	767,057	1,118,243	6,882,116	1,771,322	232,292	245,058	11,016,088
Military	40,385	32,455	7,930	312,567	69,901	14,639	12,612	450,104
Unemployed	303,246	159,301	143,945	542,223	337,820	63,546	48,562	1,295,397
Total	22,911,765	10,495,282	12,416,483	121,441,938	19,547,364	7,677,624	3,657,745	175,236,436

Note. Universe: Household population 16 and older that worked in the past five years.
Source: Pew Hispanic Center, A Statistical Portrait of Hispanics at Mid-Decade.

by other ethnographic scholarship. In this region, a Mexican American, largely Democratic Party, aggressive politics is evident and decisive everywhere, one still keyed on a sense of an ongoing "war of position" within an Anglo-dominant Texas.[28] Such a perception is consistent with another Pew report, *Hispanics in the 2008 Election*, clearly demonstrating that in the 2008 national elections, Hispanics reasserted their decisive historical allegiance to the Democratic Party after some Republican gains in the 1990s: "Some 57% of registered Hispanic voters now call themselves Democrats or say they lean to the Democratic Party while just 23% align with the Republican Party—meaning there is now a 34 percentage point gap in partisan affiliation among registered Latinos. In July, 2006, the same gap was just 21 percentage points—whereas back in 1999, it had been 33 percentage points."[29] However, it is also the case that the marked difference in such party identification does drop to 21 percentage points (56 percent Democrat, 35 percent Republican) among households with $50,000 or above annual income. Even there the difference is still decisive. Generally, middle-class status correlates effectively with Democratic Party participation.

This participation is keyed to a variety of specific issues, among them the question of Mexican immigration. Here, anthropological work on another middle-class ethnic group may be comparatively useful. Sherry Ortner's work on her own native, socially mobile Jewish community in New Jersey suggests that African Americans have a complicated contrapuntal role to Jewish Americans, serving as a kind of social foil for Jewish social mobility though not without great ambivalence and a sense of obligation toward marginalized African Americans manifested in a variety of social actions.[30] On the other hand, it is also clear that we must now recognize the emergence of an African American middle class in terms much like those that I am setting out here for Mexican Americans.[31] But, if Jewish Americans project difference, ambivalence, yet support onto African Americans, for Mexican Americans there has been increasingly available since the 1970s a possibly similar site of ambivalence—the recent immigrant Mexican. Yet here—and probably because there is no marked racial difference and there are shared cultural practices—there appears to be much less ambivalence and a higher degree of affinity. Another recent Pew report tells us that

> Hispanics are feeling a range of negative effects from the increased public attention and stepped up enforcement measures that have accompanied the growing national debate over illegal immigration. Just over half

of Hispanics worry that they or someone close to them could be deported. Nearly two-thirds say the failure of Congress to enact an immigration reform bill has made life more difficult for all Latinos. And about half of all Hispanics report a specific negative impact on them personally as a result of heightened attention to the immigration issue. They oppose—often by lopsided margins—many of the new enforcement measures being pursued by federal and state authorities. The report finds Hispanics generally see illegal immigrants as a plus—both for the Latino community itself and for the U.S. economy in general. Foreign-born Latinos are significantly more positive than the native born in their views about the effects of illegal immigrants, but even the native born are more positive than negative.[32]

Often this support for Mexican immigrants is articulated along kinship networks, as Vallejo demonstrates for Southern California, but she also provides ample evidence of "how a civically active group of Latino professionals mobilize ethnic resources to promote the mobility of co-ethnics and to combat the immigrant shadow that follows them despite their class status."[33] This support for Mexican immigrants has reached dramatic proportions in the very recent and ongoing struggles of middle-class Mexican American organizations and leaders opposing the construction of a fence along the U.S.-Mexico border.[34]

From all of the foregoing, we can question any simple perception of the Mexican American middle class as embarked on a unilinear life passage from some traditional "Mexican" ethnic but also working-class background to some relatively new "Anglo" middle-class existence. This rising class does *not* appear to be following a simple unidirectional mobility path toward a full cultural assimilation into American society and into a right-of-center politics. Both history and contemporary analyses would suggest a more complex picture in which interpretation is never crystal clear or singular. Contrary to the modernist leftist dismissal of the American middle class noted at the beginning, some of its regional sectors have demonstrated a progressive presence historically.[35] Among Mexican Americans, historically there is ample evidence of such a class engaging in a left-of-center and progressive organizational politics on issues affecting the larger Mexican-origin community, including recent immigrants—"en defensa de mi raza," in the words of one such major figure, Alonso Perales—even as they also voiced some ambivalence toward such immigrants.[36] With new scholarship and more nuanced interpretation, we can also now see that, rather than assimilationist, such efforts also correlated with a much closer adherence to a pro–Mexican American cultural practice in the United States than we had previously thought.[37]

The contemporary Mexican American middle class that I am just beginning to examine has become such a class—most often through its own initiative—but also without relinquishing many aspects of its ethnic cultural experience, indeed, often creating new forms of itself consistent with its middle-class style. As I have also tried to suggest, it also continues to exert a progressive left-liberal pressure on the issues of the day.

While I have lent some emphasis to immigration in these remarks, other issues actually appear to be of greater importance to the Hispanic middle-class registered voter. The aforecited Pew report by Taylor and Frye on the 2008 election offers this ranking order: education (94 percent), health care (91 percent), the economy and jobs (91 percent), crime (84 percent), immigration (79 percent), the war in Iraq (70 percent), although most if not all of these are deeply influenced by immigration.[38]

Indeed, if it is the case—and I think it is—that Mexican American U.S. citizens are becoming a large, viable, and socially effective middle class, it may be also the case that over the short and long terms, they may be joined by Mexican immigrants to the degree that the latter can stabilize their presence in this country. The latter are often represented as "un-American" and marginal to the economy by people like Lou Dobbs and, increasingly, the Republican Party as a whole.[39] Anthropologist Leo Chávez has done extensive fieldwork within this population and offers a distinctive and refreshing portrayal: "Another major theme in the reasons given for leaving Mexico is what I call 'the immigrant's dream' which is similar to 'the American dream.' Undocumented immigrants view the United States as the land of opportunity, where the streets are paved with gold, and where hard work and sacrifice can earn them upward mobility, at least for their children if not for themselves." "Such ideas" he continues, "pervaded the discussions and interviews I had with undocumented immigrants."[40] And if some think such views to be some species of fantasy or false consciousness, Chávez provides telling evidence of concrete achievement against the odds.[41]

We can now imagine a contemporary Mexican immigrant contribution to an expanding middle class within the total Mexican-origin community in the United States. But I reiterate, this social achievement occurs and has always occurred in a continuing context of racialized adversity and is substantially to the credit of this total community and its social abilities and ambitions. In 2008, the *Los Angeles Times* reported on the efforts of NALEO, the National Association of Latino Elected and Appointed

Officials, to naturalize undocumented Latinos so that they might gain the right to vote. Undoubtedly launched by middle-class Latinos, NALEO's efforts were mounted against a perceived effort on the part of the Bush administration to slow down the process. Citizenship could come soon enough for Mrs. Julia Moreno: "It's a long wait. Mrs. Clinton needs my vote. Maybe my vote will put her in the White House."[42] Yet other Latinos grounded in the middle class have actively participated in shaping national policy on immigration and other issues as well, among them Henry Cisneros, Gov. Bill Richardson, Amb. Tony Garza, Sec. Hilda Solís, Mayor Julián Castro, and Gen. Ricardo Sánchez.

While these remarks have been offered on the economic and political side of things, elsewhere and at length I have explored the manner in which this Mexican American middle-class existence has recently begun to appear in Mexican American cultural expression, especially literature and film.[43] I begin to close here by bridging this disciplinary divide through one of the best-known Mexican American middle-class figures in the United States—Richard Rodríguez.

Rodríguez is the well-known journalist, lecturer, and essayist-author of three books.[44] He has also been a frequent commentator on the PBS nightly *News Hour* with Jim Lehrer. Mexican American cultural studies intellectuals severely criticized his first book, *Hunger of Memory*, a lyrical autobiography, largely for Rodríguez' seemingly conservative criticism of bilingualism, affirmative action, and Mexican American studies and his also seeming advocacy of cultural assimilation. Yet I have often wondered if they were not also reacting to the very title of his first chapter, "Middle-class Pastoral," and its opening passage: "I have taken Caliban's advice. I have stolen their books. I will have some run of this isle. Once upon a time, I was a 'socially disadvantaged' child. An enchanted happy child. Mine was a childhood of intense family closeness. And extreme public alienation. Thirty years later I write this book as a middle-class American. Assimilated. Dark-skinned. To be seen at a Belgravia dinner party. Or in New York. Exotic in a tuxedo."[45]

For many such critics, the passage and the rest of the book were but the words of a dissembling, modernist poseur in cool advocacy of the assimilation that would begin with the learned canonical reference to Shakespeare's *The Tempest* and the stealing of the colonizing Prospero's books, that is, absorbing Anglo-American culture, but eventually ending as a middle-class American enjoying the material and psychological reward of assimilation—New York, tuxedos, dinner parties, and so on—with his Mexican culture left far behind.[46] Elsewhere, I have criticized this criticism to suggest that Rodriguez was actually taking a critical, if discerning and ambivalent, stance toward Anglo-American society even in these early pages.[47]

Yet, whatever his original stance, the same critics now see a "new" Richard Rodríguez in his last two books, one now more explicitly critical of the United States and more affirmative of his Mexicanness, including a position of proimmigrant advocacy.[48]

For my purposes here, I only wish to underscore the original middle-class self-definition of this most important of our Mexican American social critics, an enabling middle-class status not of his own making but, rather, one forged by his hard-working Mexican immigrant parents, focused on their children's achievements in this country.

In the aforementioned book, with its intriguing title, *For Democracy: The Noble Character and Tragic Flaw of the Middle Class*, Glassman, Swatos, and Kivisto have traced the presence and politics of the middle class from the Greeks to the present. They argue that indeed the middle class can have a tragic flaw, namely, its susceptibility to bureaucratization and conservative conformity and consumerism, especially in the current moment. On the other hand, it can also partake of and fashion a "noble character," by which they mean a willingness to participate in the Aristotelian polis as active agents of change and sociocultural creativity. As I have argued here, too many of us are too willing to consign the middle class to the former and not grant it the possibility of the latter. These authors clearly see the possibilities for the latter, especially to the degree that the middle class is increasingly college educated.

Such I think is the more likely possibility for the Mexican American middle class increasingly in possession of higher education and with another asset not typically associated with the larger and white American middle class: its recent memory of poverty, racism, and also the presence of Mexican immigrants as a very visible reminder of that past and therefore possibly an arena of social obligation on the basis of that memory and of continuing cultural kinship. I for one—and I may be the only one—do not think it advisable to continue to dismiss this class with the facile adjective "assimilationist" in favor of our now too dominant, ironically hegemonic, historical Mexican American studies images of farmworkers and barrio gangs. Rather than disparage middle-class achievement from the sometimes elitist vantage point of the university, I think that it is time to seriously examine the consciousness and the emergent formation of such a class.

I am proposing that we take up the complicated analytical challenge that would serve to more adequately understand the Mexican American attorneys, journalists, businesspeople, law enforcement personnel, pharmacists, teachers, nurses, accountants, dentists, salaried skilled workers at local military bases—and social critics. We should think of them, indeed, of ourselves, as victors in the still-continuing struggle and not foreclose their (our) productive and progressive possibilities in the interests of a better Mexican America, especially with respect to their (our) kindred immigrant community.

Finally, as the economy and immigration continue to be at the center of a heated national debate, the United States as a whole needs to be reminded that many such successful middle-class Mexican Americans are often the children and grandchildren of poor and often undocumented Mexican immigrants who, largely through their own efforts and often against the American grain, have now become economically and socially productive citizens of the United States. A continued attack on newly arriving immigrants will be taken by such middle-class subjects as an attack on those ancestral origins and memories, and there will be political consequences as this middle class continually expands in size and electoral influence. Consequences in other realms such as culture and the arts are less clear but will no doubt be fascinating to watch. We can already see some evidence, for example, that one highly desirable by-product of this class formation, especially at its upper levels, is support for Latino arts and the development of a museum culture.[49]

The eminent historian, the late Tony Judt, wrote that "the first task of radical dissenters today is to remind their audience of the achievements of the twentieth century . . . the left, to be quite blunt about it, has something to conserve. It is the *right* that has inherited the ambitious modernist urge to destroy and innovate in the name of a universal project." He continued: "Social democrats, characteristically modest in style and ambition, need to speak more assertively of past gains. The rise of the social service state, the century-long construction of a public sector whose goods and services illustrate and promote our collective identity and common purposes, the institution of welfare as a matter of right and its provision as a social duty: these were no mean accomplishments."[50]

Within this world of social accomplishment, both as beneficiaries and contributors, I would add the Mexican American middle class. I would not blame any who would want yet more, and I would, indeed, support that group. I write these words in California in 2011 as, for example, working-class Mexican American access to the California State University System is being effectively and severely curtailed. We must, said Judt, also protect what we have achieved: "That these accomplishments were no more than partial should not trouble us . . . others have spent the last three decades methodically unraveling and destabilizing those same improvements: this should make us much angrier than we are. . . . To abandon the labors of a century is to betray those who come before us as well as generations yet to come."[51]

Notes

A version of this chapter was presented as a public lecture in the American Initiatives Program at Georgetown University on October 18, 2007.

1. Sherry B. Ortner, *New Jersey Dreaming* (Durham, N.C.: Duke University Press, 2003), 8.

2. David J. DeLaura, *Hebrew and Hellene in Victorian England* (Austin: University of Texas Press, 1969), chap. 3, "The Onslaught of the Philistines."

3. There is much commentary on this issue in Marxism, but see, for example, Martin Nicolaus, "Proletariat and Middle Class in Marx," *Studies on the Left* 7 (1967): 12–27.

4. Val Burris, "The Discovery of the New Middle Classes," in Arthur J. Vidich, ed., *The New Middle Classes* (New York: New York University Press, 1995).

5. Robert Staughton Lynd, *Middletown* (New York: Harcourt, Brace, 1929); Herbert Gans, *The Levittowners* (New York: Pantheon, 1967).

6. José E. Limón, *Hispanic Self-Fashioning: The Making of a Mexican-American Middle Class Identity*, chap. 1: "Wild Man and Noble Savage," in progress. For a continuation of such themes in more contemporary scholarship, see Chad Richardson, *Batos, Bolillos, Pochos, and Pelados* (Austin: University of Texas Press, 1999).

7. See, for example, the special issue on Chicano labor history: *Aztlán* 6, no. 2 (1975). For the continuing influence of this labor emphasis, see Zamora, *The World of the Mexican Worker*.

8. See, for example, my own such early assessment, José E. Limón, "El Primer Congreso Mexicanista de 1911: A Precursor to Contemporary Chicanismo," *Aztlán* 5 (1974): 85–118.

9. Manuel H. Peña, *The Texas-Mexican Conjunto* (Austin: University of Texas Press, 1985).

10. Richard García, *The Rise of the Mexican-American Middle Class, San Antonio, 1929–1941* (College Station: Texas A&M University Press, 1991).

11. Mario García, *Mexican Americans*.

12. Montejano, *Anglos and Mexicans*, 298.

13. Ibid., 299.

14. Ibid., 298.

15. Eric Ávila, *Popular Culture in the Age of White Flight* (Berkeley: University of California Press, 2004), 52.

16. Maggie Rivas-Rodríguez, ed., *Mexican Americans and World War II* (Austin: University of Texas Press), 2005.

17. I am thinking of institutions such as the former Texas A&I University (now Texas A&M) in Kingsville, in the middle of predominantly Mexican American South Texas; Cal State–Los Angeles; and New Mexico State University in Las Cruces.

18. Frank D. Bean, Stephen J. Trejo, Randy Capps, and Michael Tyler, *The Latino Middle Class* (Claremont: Tomás Rivera Policy Institute, 2001), 1.

19. Pew Hispanic Center, *A Statistical Portrait of Hispanics at Mid-Decade* (Washington, D.C., January 2008).

20. Robert R. Brischetto, "The Hispanic Middle Class Comes of Age," *Hispanic Business* (December 2001): 21–32.

21. Jody Agius Vallejo, *The Mexican Origin Middle Class in Los Angeles* (Los Angeles: Center for the Study of Immigrant Integration, University of Southern California, 2009), 4.

22. Pew Hispanic Center, *A Statistical Portrait*, 1.

23. We should never forget that these data also show us that there is a large segment of the native-born population that is still in a working-class status and in social marginality, although one suspects that these are largely second- and third-generation "native"-born, though of relatively recent immigrant parentage.

24. The astute observer of such data will no doubt note that the categories of "Hispanic" and "Latino" are not broken down by national origin in these surveys. However, the one national group that could skew these figures in an upward direction and thus offer a misleading portrait of overall success is probably the Cuban community for a complexity of reasons that cannot be explained here. On the other hand, this is a relatively small community (3.5 percent) in comparison to the very large Mexican-origin group (61 percent) that is my focus in these remarks. The next largest group is, of course, Puerto Ricans, at 9 percent (Pew Hispanic Center, *A Statistical Portrait*, table 3).

25. Ronald Glassman, William H. Swatos Jr., and Peter Kivisto, *For Democracy* (Westport, Conn.: Greenwood Press, 1993).

26. Ibid., 142–143.

27. Keya Ganguly, *States of Exception* (Minneapolis: University of Minnesota Press, 2001).

28. Margaret E. Dorsey, *Pachangas* (Austin: University of Texas Press, 2006).

29. Paul Taylor and Richard Fry, *Hispanics and the 2008 Election* (Washington, D.C.: Pew Hispanic Center, 2007), 1.

30. Ortner, *New Jersey Dreaming*, 68–69.

31. Joe R. Feagin and Melvin P. Sikes, *Living with Racism* (Boston: Beacon Press, 1994).

32. Pew Hispanic Center, *2007 National Survey of Latinos* (Washington, D.C., 2007), 1.

33. Vallejo, *The Mexican Origin Middle Class*, 5.

34. These efforts, especially in the Lower Rio Grande Valley of Texas, are continually being reported in a remarkable online newspaper begun in 2005, the *Rio Grande Guardian* (www.riograndeguardian.com), published by Melinda Barrera,

and itself a product of a middle-class Mexican American active and progressive participation in civic and political affairs.

35. Robert D. Johnston, *The Radical Middle Class* (Princeton: Princeton University Press, 2003).

36. R. García, *The Rise of the Mexican-American Middle Class*; D. Gutiérrez, *Walls and Mirrors*; Benjamin H. Johnson, *Revolution in Texas* (New Haven: Yale University Press, 2003).

37. John M. González, *Border Renaissance* (Austin: University of Texas Press, 2009).

38. Taylor and Frye, *Hispanics and the 2008 Election*, 10.

39. Ryan Lizza, "Return of the Nativist," *New Yorker* (December 17, 2007): 46–51.

40. Leo R. Chávez, *Shadowed Lives* (Fort Worth, Tex.: Harcourt, Brace, 1992), 33.

41. Ibid., 200.

42. Anna Gorman, "Eager to Vote but Stuck in the Citizenship Process," *Los Angeles Times* (January 2, 2008): B-1.

43. José E. Limón, "'Midway to the Second Floor': The Literary Self-Fashioning of a Mexican-American Middle Class Identity," the Distinguished Matthews Lecture, Department of Spanish, University of California–Los Angeles, spring 2001.

44. Richard Rodríguez, *Hunger of Memory* (Boston: David R. Godine, 1982); idem, *Days of Obligation* (New York: Penguin Books, 1992); idem, *Brown* (New York: Penguin Books, 2002).

45. R. Rodríguez, *Hunger of Memory*, 3.

46. José D. Saldívar, *The Dialectics of Our America* (Durham, N.C.: Duke University Press, 1991), 136–138.

47. Limón, "Midway to the Second Floor," 2001.

48. José D. Saldívar, *Border Matters* (Berkeley: University of California Press, 1997), 146–151.

49. Teresa McKenna, "Collecting against Forgetting," in Richard Meyer, ed., *Representing the Passions* (Los Angeles: Getty Research Institute, 2003).

50. Tony Judt, "What Is Living and What Is Dead in Social Democracy?" *New York Review of Books* 57 (December 17, 2009): 86–96.

51. Ibid., 96.

CHAPTER 8

New Mexico, Mestizaje, and the Transnations of North America

RAMÓN A. GUTIÉRREZ

How has New Mexico shaped North America? As the northernmost out-post of New Spain, from the late sixteenth to the mid-nineteenth centuries, New Mexico was ruled by men who saw themselves as Spaniards. They conquered and colonized the Pueblo Indians in 1598, lived side by side, often mixing biologically with them, and were sustained by the tribute they paid in labor, food, and handicrafts. Both the Spanish colonists and the Pueblo Indians were themselves surrounded by nomadic peoples known as the Utes, Navajos, Apaches, and Comanches. Spaniards presumed to rule; Pueblos sometimes adapted and sometimes resisted—often mixing both; and Spaniards and Pueblos, together and separately, faced enduring combinations of war and trade, conflict and integration. Historically, New Mexico has been a place where people have faced enduring paradoxes shaped by sharpening differences and ongoing integrations.

New Mexico has long been a marginal, out-of-the-way place in the popular imagination. When children in central New Spain (what became Mexico) were deemed particularly unruly in the sixteenth and seventeenth centuries, parents often warned that if they continued to misbehave they would be shipped to the Apachería, to the land of the wild Apache Indians in the Kingdom of New Mexico. Though no child that I know of was ever banished to this remote spot, there were plenty of convicts, misfits, rebels, and adventurers who were exiled to, or sought refuge in, New Mexico to escape state surveillance. Crypto Jews and wayward philandering friars are but two of the most immediate examples that come to mind.

Under Mexican and American rule New Mexico fared no better. A poor province with few resources other than salt, wool, and clay for making pottery, Mexico's central authorities were rarely concerned about and even less frequently interfered in the business affairs of the area's merchants and first families. Indeed, the popular mythology about New Mexico's American conquest in 1846 was that Gen. Stephen Watts Kearny, the commander of the U.S. Army of the West, simply marched into Santa Fe and staged a bloodless conquest, having first bribed Gov. Manuel Armijo to abandon his post. A land of milk and honey, of abundant cheap land, of a salubrious arid climate, of low taxes and little government regulation is how the American territorial governors advertised New Mexico to attract Anglo-American settlers between 1848 and 1912. In the 1920s, New Mexico became a refuge from modernity and the machine age, as artists, writers, intellectuals, and dropouts left New York and the industrial Northeast yearning for a simpler, more primal connection to a primitive American place. This was indeed the "Land of Enchantment" that was created for tourists; the slogan still brings them to the state.

New Mexico's place in Spain's historical imagination is tied primarily to the grand expeditions of exploration, conquest, and settlement. The account of Alvar Núñez Cabeza de Vaca's 1528 shipwreck and trek through Texas and New Mexico in the 1530s, and the 1540 journal of Francisco Vásquez de Coronado's gold-seeking journey through New Mexico, Oklahoma, and Kansas are both in all the large documentary publications chronicling Spain's presence in America. There the interest seems to end, with one exception. Spanish linguists in the 1920s began to marvel at the archaic Spanish lexicon still utilized in the isolated villages of northern New Mexico and have studied language persistence and change there ever since.

For Mexico, New Mexico is primarily about humiliation, loss, and nostalgia. "El México perdido," that part of Mexico lost during the Mexican American War in 1846–1848, still stings national pride. Since the early 1920s, numerous attempts have been made by Mexican presidents to recuperate this lost terrain, if only culturally, by promoting Mexican national celebrations, constructing Mexican cultural centers, maintaining robust consular offices and staffs, even forming in the 1960s a ministerial post devoted to *los mexicanos en el exterior*, or Mexicans outside Mexico. Mexico has done everything in its capacity to cultivate a sense of national belonging among its emigrants to assure monetary remittances, even fostering dual citizenship and hometown associations to assure that *mexicanos* do not forget *la patria*, or the homeland.

The triumphal narratives of the origins and growth of the United States of America which historians have written usually start with the formation of Jamestown in 1607, proceed to Plymouth Plantation in 1620, to the witchcraft craze at Salem, to colonial independence in 1776, to westward expansion, industrialization, and America's expansionist wars across the Pacific. If historians want their books to be seriously considered for adoption in the American Southwest, where the architecture, the language, and bodies constantly serve as reminders of Spain and Mexico's long cultural influence, the narrative begins with Christopher Columbus, mentions Hernán Cortés' conquest of the Aztecs in tones still reminiscent of the Black Legend, and note the expeditions of Coronado into New Mexico and of De Soto into Florida. Of course, this is all necessary background to later explain the dense concentration of Hispanics in Florida, Texas, New Mexico, and California post-1965. If specific mention is made of New Mexico, it is usually as the birthplace of the nuclear age, when the Manhattan Project was located in Los Alamos in 1942.

So what can New Mexico teach us about the development of North America? And why, given the centuries of neglect and marginality, is this important now? The why now I suspect is easily answered by turning to the popular press. On July 12, 1999, Newsweek magazine devoted its cover story and in-depth reporting to "Latin U.S.A." "On the last Independence Day of the millennium, a new nation is being born," the issue announced. Never mind that the Fourth of July had already passed, since the beginning of a millennium had not, Newsweek offered some apocalyptic prophesies about this Latino "new nation." The year 2000 would bring a Latino population explosion, "ground zero for a demographic upheaval," the magazine warned. Chronicling transformations wrought by immigration and high reproductive rates, Newsweek described a national geometry of culture, politics, and money radiating from Miami, Los Angeles, and Chicago, from Santa Fe, San Jose, and New York. "By 2005, Latinos will be the largest U.S. minority; they're already shaping pop culture and presidential politics. The Latin wave will change how the country looks—and how it looks at itself." As a diasporic nation, diverse and dispersed, "Latino America" was not neatly bounded territorially, with multiple population hubs, extensive networks, and switching points. Calling the residents of "Latino U.S.A." Hispanics and Latinos interchangeably, Newsweek proclaimed, "Hispanics are hip, hot and making history."

Since 1965, large numbers of immigrants, mostly from Mexico, but also from Central America, the Dominican Republic, and Cuba, have entered the United States, affecting schools, housing, labor, business, and politics in complicated ways. Today there are 42.7 million Hispanics in the United States, or more than the total number of Canadians in Canada.

Hispanics constitute roughly 13 percent of the total population. Through high rates of natural growth they are projected to represent 18 percent of the population by 2020, 25 percent by 2050. Already in states like New Mexico, California, Texas, and Florida, which historically had initial Hispanic settlements and later became major destinations for Latin American immigrants, the Hispanic proportion of the total population is much higher. In 2000, Hispanics accounted for 42 percent of New Mexico's population, 31 percent of California's, 30 percent of Texas', and 15 percent of Florida's. The population in the first three of these states is largely of Mexican origin, while Cubans and Puerto Ricans constitute the majority in Florida. These proportions are even higher in specific metropolitan areas. El Paso, Texas, in 1997 had a population that was 75 percent Hispanic; San Antonio, Texas, 53 percent; Fresno, California, 42 percent; Albuquerque, New Mexico, 39 percent; Los Angeles, California, 39 percent; Miami–Fort Lauderdale, Florida, 37 percent.

If the proportion of the minority population (that is, blacks, Asian-Pacific Islanders, American Indians, and Hispanics) in each of these states is aggregated, the impact of the racial transformation under way is even more profound. Minorities—what really are majorities in some places and emerging majorities in others—represent 55 percent in New Mexico, 51 percent in California, 45 percent in Texas, and 32 percent in Florida. Similar calculations by city produce even more startling results. El Paso in 1997 had a population that was 80 percent minority; San Antonio, 62 percent; Fresno, 58 percent; Albuquerque, 50 percent; Los Angeles 59, percent; and Miami–Fort Lauderdale, 59 percent.[1]

These changing demographic realities and the social and cultural changes they portend have provoked contemporary Hispanophobic responses akin to those recorded in the remote and recent past. Nativists railing against Mexican immigrants have used racist arguments and incendiary words to voice their opposition to the "browning" of America. Peter Brimelow's rhetoric in *Alien Nation* is rather typical of anti-Mexican sentiment:

> There is a sense in which current immigration policy is Adolf Hitler's posthumous revenge on America. The U.S. political elite emerged from the war passionately concerned to cleanse itself from all taints of racism or xenophobia. Eventually, it enacted the epochal Immigration Act (technically, the Immigration and Nationality Act Amendments) of 1965. And this, quite accidentally, triggered a renewed mass immigration, so huge and so systematically different from anything that had gone before as to

transform—and ultimately, perhaps even destroy—the one unquestioned victor of World War II: the American nation, as it had evolved by the middle of the twentieth century.[2]

"The American nation has always had a specific core," Brimelow asserts. "And that core has been white." Americans, he says, have a right to demand that their government stop shifting the nation's racial balance. "Indeed, it seems to me that they have a right to insist that it be shifted back."[3]

Brimelow's words, though particularly incendiary, capture the tenor and tone of the anti-Mexican rants expressed by others such as Lawrence Auster in *The Path to National Suicide: An Essay on Immigration and Multiculturalism* (1990), and Richard D. Lamm and Gary Imhoff in *The Immigration Time Bomb* (1985). The natural result of such thinking was the reemergence in the 1990s of scientific racist ideas about the relationship between race and intelligence, dismissed a century ago. Mexican immigrants, claim Richard J. Hernstein and Charles Murray in *The Bell Curve*, on average, score 9 percent lower than whites on IQ tests. Such disparity, they claim, would lower the overall intelligence of the United States and ultimately lead to higher crime rates, increasing female dependence on welfare, and single female–headed households.[4]

One naturally would expect such words to hail from the conservative political right, but even academic liberals have expressed similar concerns about America's changing racial composition. The late Arthur Schlesinger Jr., in 1992, decried how particularistic immigrant loyalties (read Mexicans) in the United States were leading to "the disuniting of America" and held the potential to create a separatist nationalism among Mexicans seeking independence for the American Southwest comparable to the long-standing movement among the Quebecois. Harvard professor Samuel P. Huntington, the highly venerated but now deceased political theorist who in 1996 anticipated the clash of civilizations in the Middle East, in 2004 drew attention to the Hispanic immigrant problem in a book titled *Who Are We? The Challenges to America's National Identity*. There Huntington argues that the cultural division between Hispanics and Anglos will soon replace the racial division between blacks and whites as the most potentially incendiary cleavage in U.S. society. The vast majority of Hispanics, as Huntington explains, are of Mexican descent. Many entered the country illegally and are reproducing much more rapidly than whites or blacks, by a ratio of about 5 to 1. They keep speaking Spanish in their homes and at work, refuse to learn English, are leading highly segregated lives among their own, and are largely confined in society's lowest economic rungs. These facts portend anarchy, racial war, and separatist possibilities, Huntington warns.

Already, nativist whites have responded in California by approving punitive electoral initiatives (Propositions 187 and 209) against government benefits for illegal immigrants, affirmative action, and bilingual education. Some whites, like the Minutemen militia, are taking up arms to protect the republic from southern assault. They warn that Mexicans will retaliate, undoubtedly aiming to retake the southwestern states they lost in 1848 at the end of the U.S. Mexican War, plunging the nation into an unprecedented racial war. Patriots will, of course, fight to protect Anglo-Protestant culture and the English language from barbaric Mexican assault.

The continuing arrival of large numbers of Hispanic immigrants in the United States and their high reproductive rates clearly have transformed American cities and what Carey McWilliams once called the "factories in the fields." Look at the people on the streets of any major city, the children in the schools, the nationalities of the stockholders of major American companies, and the number of languages you can hear on the streets of Albuquerque, Los Angeles, or Dallas. The old America of memory and nostalgia is being remade. America is quickly becoming AmeRíca.

"AmeRíca! AmeRíca!" the Nuyorican poet Tato Laviera sings of his native Puerto Rico, a home he will not leave behind, a home he always carries on his lips and in his mind, while seeking his fortunes in New York. In Tato Laviera's Latinization, accentuation, and syncopation of the English word "America" as AmeRíca is embedded the painful history of Puerto Rico's colonial and neocolonial past, yearning for nationhood, yet denied even statehood. In AmeRíca's disruption of America, Tato Laviera draws our attention to AmeRíca's pervasive and ongoing miscegenation, to its hybridity and increasing heterogeneity created by movement and mixing. AmeRíca is complex. AmeRíca is centerless. The various parts that now make up AmeRíca are increasingly unstable.[5]

What Tato Laviera describes so lyrically in poetry, Arjun Appadurai discusses analytically when he tells us that America has become a series of nodes in a postnational network of population movements. America is "a diasporic switching point for the world's population. Where once the melting pot putatively turned immigrants into Americans through assimilation, now immigrants living in the United States tenaciously cling to their places of origin through strong ideological and technological ties. While living in the United States they form themselves into numerous delocalized transnations, which no existing conception of Americanness can possibly contain."[6]

The process of globalization at the beginning of the twenty-first century has spawned a proliferation of different and conflicting ideological and economic maps of the new world order. The North American Free Trade Agreement, the European Community, the Pacific Rim, queer nationality, Islamic fundamentalism, the war on terror are but a few. The old Cold War division of the globe into East and West, symbolic of the cosmic struggle between capitalism and communism, in rubble rests, and the warriors who concocted such spaces in mausoleums slumber. The globe divided into three—a First, a Second, and a Third World—has been replaced by different world orderings, prompting Robert B. Reich, the former U.S. secretary of labor, to ask rhetorically in 1990, "Who Is Us?"[7] Posing the same question Samuel Huntington asked above, Reich's answer focuses on the dynamism and innovation immigration and globalization bring to the natural and ever-changing transformation of nations and states.

In the *Nine Nations of North America*, Joel Garreau asks us to question the very logic of North America and to interrogate what states and regions mean today. "Forget the pious wisdom you've been handed about North America," Garreau enjoins:

> Forget about the borders dividing the United States, Canada, and Mexico, those pale barriers so thoroughly porous to money, immigrants, and ideas. Forget the bilge we taught you in sixth-grade geography about East and West, North and South, faint echoes of glorious pasts that never really existed save in sanitized textbooks. Forget the maze of states and provincial boundaries, those historical accidents and surveyors. Mistakes . . . Consider, instead the way North America really works. It is Nine Nations. Each has a capital and a distinctive web of power and influence . . . Each has a peculiar economy, each commands a certain emotional allegiance from its citizens. These nations look different, feel different, and sound different from each other, and few of their boundaries match the political lines drawn on current maps.[8]

With Garreau's injunctive in mind, let us consider New Mexico's place in the development of how North America really works. From my vantage as a historian of colonial America, what New Mexico bequeathed to the continent over the *longue durée* was a very different way of understanding race. Quite early in the development of the English colonies into the United States, a binary opposition, was used to divide the population of into black and white and, later, particularly with the arrival of Asian immigrants, into whites and nonwhites. In Spain's colonial empire, in places like New Mexico, a very different interval assessment of legal color based on ancestry and appearance held sway. Known as "mestizaje," a word that poorly translates as miscegenation, this racial classification system was no less hierarchical or oppressive than what developed in the United States. But the color intervals assumed social mobility, that subject populations would gradually whiten and eventually enjoy fuller integration into the body politic. The racial binary system of classification in the United States did not allow for this possibility. A person with "one drop" of black blood was considered black even though the other 99 percent was white, thus continually augmenting the number of persons classified as inferior on the basis of color.

In what follows I argue that New Mexico's contribution to the making of North America is its theory and practice of mestizaje, which still operates today among many of the Latin American immigrants who enter the United States. The theory of mestizaje more recently has also inspired a host of scholarly studies that use the concept as a cultural aesthetic for the hybridity and mixing that inspires writing, music, performance, even the writing of history in liminal zones and borderlands. To understand the uniqueness of mestizaje, I will briefly describe three contemporary and vibrant postnational spaces and then explicate how race operates in each.[9] The first of these three I call the Eastern Atlantic Seaboard. The second has been variously called "MexAmerica" (Langley), "TexMex" (Patterson), "Hispanic Nation" (Fox), and "Aztlán" (Acuña).[10] Finally, there is the Pacific Northwest, referred to by some writers as "Ecotopia," "Cascadia," "Pacifica," and the "Northeast Pacific Rim" (Schell and Hamer).[11]

The Eastern Atlantic Seaboard is one of the most important transnations of our age. It ties the eastern shore of the United States with Caribbean states and the republics of northern South America. Since about 1980, this area has been transformed by massive flows of capital, people, and ideas moving in both directions. New York City and Miami are now the major transfer nodes in this space. Forty percent of all Jamaicans, 50 percent of all Puerto Ricans, and half of all working adults of the Eastern Caribbean states live in the United States in communities dependent on the economies of New York and Miami, selling skilled and unskilled labor, moving legal and illegal capital within a larger area that includes much of the Caribbean. Moving as immigrants and workers back and forth, the residents of this transnation practice voodoo in Saint Petersburg, play cricket in Kingston, and teach white kids in Florida to wear dreadlocks, even to celebrate West Indian carnival in New York. Because of the development of this transnation, the social and political boundaries that separate the United States and Jamaica, Puerto Rico, the Dominican Republic, and Barbados have little meaning—as perhaps will be the case for Cuba and Haiti soon.[12]

Traditionally in the mainland regions of this area, race was defined in strict binary terms, as black and white. It was here that the one-drop rule was invented. The one-drop rule meant that a single drop of "black blood" made one black, assigning the person the status of the subordinate and inferior group. This descent rule is unique to the United States and, paradoxically, has defined millions of people who are more European than African as black in law and in public opinion.[13]

The one-drop rule appeared in the late 1600s and eventually became the dominant understanding of racial descent. With the end of slavery and the beginning of Jim Crow segregation laws, a strict separation between the races was deemed necessary. A racial taxonomy that did not recognize intermediate hues was put in place and enforced through the prohibition of miscegenation. The function of antimiscegenation laws was to maintain the putative purity of the white race by prohibiting interracial unions and by defining sex between members of different races as a crime. Though upholding such laws required tortured legal definitions of who was black and who was not, sixteen states continued to ban interracial marriage until 1967, when the U.S. Supreme Court struck down such laws.

In Louisiana, this binary system of racial classification continued, nevertheless, ordering that anyone with a "trace" of black ancestry be classed as black. As part of a "humane" reform undertaken by the state in 1970, Louisiana enacted the "one-thirty-second rule," by which anyone with a single black great-great-great-great-grandparent and thirty-one white great-great-great-great-grandparents was legally black. This regulation went unchallenged until Susie Guillory Phipps, the wife of a wealthy seafood importer who had always considered herself white, obtained a copy of her birth certificate for a passport application. The state had classified her as black. Phipps sued in 1982. Louisiana hired a genealogist to investigate her background and discovered that Phipps' great-great-great-great-grandmother had been the free black mistress of an Alabama plantation owner in 1760. Susie Phipps was thus three-thirty-seconds black, or black by law. In 1983, the law was repealed, though not without the state of Louisiana appealing the ruling all the way to the Supreme Court.[14]

In *Who Is Black?* F. James Davis argues that, paradoxically, the rigidity and continued vitality of the one-drop rule in popular thinking can, at least since the 1960s, be traced to the growth of black pride, black beauty, black achievement, black history, and the use of the term "black" rather than Negro. Whereas previous generations had placed a high value on whitening the race, in the 1960s, African Americans increasingly valorized dark skin colors as emblems of pride and discouraged blacks from seeking closer contacts with whites. The fear that the Black Power movement provoked among whites further reinforced the binary color line.[15]

How this black-white color line lives on and yet how it is significantly influenced by the forces of globalization was evident at Augusta, Georgia, on April 13, 1997. On that day Tiger Woods won the Masters' championship at the Augusta National Golf course. The major television sports commentators immediately hailed the victory as the end of segregation in golf. Tiger Woods was the greatest black golfer ever, and his achievement was equal to Jackie Robinson's shattering of the color barrier in baseball, or so they said. The owners of many golf courses previously had denied Tiger Woods playing rights because they deemed him black. The sport's spectators saw him as a black. Even American blacks claimed Tiger as one of their own.

Then came Oprah Winfrey. She asked Tiger Woods in an interview on her nationally televised show if it bothered him that he was being described as black. "It does," he replied. "Growing up, I came up with this name: I'm a 'Cablinasian.'" Woods explained that because he was one-eighth Caucasian, one-fourth black, one-eighth American Indian, one-fourth Thai, and one-fourth Chinese, he had taken the first two letters of these identities to fashion an acronym for the identity that best described his racial past.[16] Oprah Winfrey responded positively and with understanding as Tiger Woods described how he felt it necessary to honor his Thai Buddhist immigrant mother's ancestry as well as his father's.[17]

Prominent American blacks were not so kind. When Colin Powell was asked in an ABC television interview by Sam Donaldson what he thought of Tiger Woods' Cablinasian identity, Powell retorted: "Look at him. He's black. People who look like him are black, in my book." Kweisi Mfume, the president of the National Association for the Advancement of Colored People (NAACP), recited the absurd history of how blackness had been defined under the one-drop rule and urged Tiger Woods and all African Americans of mixed race not to forget that society sees things "in very narrow boxes. We are either Black or White." Jesse Jackson likewise deemed Tiger Woods black "because he's been called n——r, because he's been the object of race-bait jokes." Leonard Dunston, the president of the National Association of Black Social Workers, added that "race is a political category defined by those who are numerically in power. By definition, then, Tiger Woods is viewed as an African American, whether he chooses to accept this or not." Actress Salli Richardson summed up in altruistic terms the racial essentialism others had expressed when she chimed in on Tiger Woods' mixed identity: "That whole mixed-race category issue separates us more when we need to be coming together more."[18]

Interestingly enough, Asian Americans claimed Tiger Woods as Asian, but with a perverse twist. He was acknowledged as a bright, family-centered, and community-minded man who knew his history. These characteristics were attributed primarily to his Asian ancestry. "Yes, he does seem intelligent. But remember that his mother is Asian." "Yes, it does seem like he cares about his parents. But that is an Asian tradition." "Yes, he does pay tribute to Lee Elders and others who paved his way, but remember he is Asian and Asians are respectful." Writing in the Boston Globe, columnist Martin Nolan noted that an Asian American golfer he knew well had told him: "Tiger gets his determination from his father. Ahh, but his finesse comes from his Asian mother."[19]

One can only speculate about why the thinking behind the one-drop rule reemerged so forcefully at the end of the twentieth century as a new racial essentialism, only fourteen years after the last legal remnants of the rule were dismantled. The year 2000 ushered in not only a new millennium, but also the first population count of the century. Preceding the count there were fierce debates in Congress about how multiracial individuals should be enumerated, particularly whether they merited a separate category. Arthur Fletcher, an African American member of the U.S. Commission on Civil Rights worried in 1993 about the appearance of a multiracial category on the census: "I can see a whole host of light-skinned black Americans running for the door the minute they have another choice. All of a sudden they have a way of saying, 'In this discriminatory culture of ours, I am something other than black.'"[20]

In the days of slavery, the one-drop rule separated masters from slaves and kept the number of slaves and those physically marked by the stigma of slavery rising. Today, despite the extensive hybridity that exists among many blacks, I suspect that they proclaim a racial purity to expand their ranks in a similar fashion. Increased numbers translate into political clout and economic resources. How the government draws the racial boundaries for the census has profound consequences. Clearly, the Hispanic and Asian populations of the United States have expanded tremendously since 1965, both numerically and proportionately. In comparison to these two groups, and by these measures, blacks are rapidly losing numerical ground.[21] Already Hispanics have overtaken blacks as the largest minority group in the United States. The moment to gain racial justice and to erase the stigma of color that blacks have endured since the sixteenth century seems to be slipping away.[22] Thus many who can, pass, and those who are light-skinned and multiracial are seen as a threat by many blacks.[23] The parallel to the 1870s, when those who could pass as white were so threatening to the fiction of white racial purity, is clear—if inverted.

How the flow of immigrants into the United States has influenced the impact of the black/white binary is illustrated in the book *Black Identities: West Indian Immigrant Dreams and American Realities*, by sociologist Mary Waters, on the racialization of black West Indian immigrants in New York. Waters focuses on people who in the West Indies are not classified primarily by race but in the United States are seen only as blacks by most Americans. Fearing that as blacks they will be mistaken for African Americans, these immigrants go to great pains to emphasize their immigrant origins and their ethnic identities as Jamaicans, Haitians, and Trinidadians—a reaction to the overwhelming way they are viewed in the United States as blacks, pure and simple. Because they are "invisible immigrants" in relation to African Americans, they go to great lengths to make their ethnicity visible and audible, wearing ethnic insignias and dress, emphasizing their "British" Creole accents, and constantly mentioning their immigrant origin when interacting with whites.[24]

In New York, Waters found long-standing tensions between newly arrived West Indians and African Americans. The immigrants saw themselves as hardworking, ambitious, militant about their ethnic identity but not oversensitive or obsessed by race, and committed to education and family. They saw African Americans as lazy, disorganized, obsessed with racial slights and barriers, with a disorganized and laissez-faire attitude toward family life and child rearing. African Americans described the immigrants as arrogant, selfish, exploited in the workplace, oblivious to racial tensions and politics, and unfriendly and unwilling to have relations with black Americans. From the perspective of West Indian immigrants, they perceived that their status was superior to that of African Americans and that their chances for upward mobility rested on their distinctive community resources and their heightened ethnicity. The minute second-generation West Indians in New York abandoned their ethnic culture, their insignias, dress, hairdos, and accents, they experienced downward mobility and were viewed and treated as African Americans by the dominant society.[25] If the black-white binary of Eastern Atlantic America was rooted in slavery and the Jim Crow era it spawned, the polarity has persisted among many whites and in the solidarity of blacks who see their shared racial identity as the essential basis for the continued pursuit of rights in a globalizing world now complicated by accelerating immigration from a Caribbean with distinct, more graded racial patterns.

Unlike the binary system of racial classification that developed and operates in the Eastern Atlantic Seaboard, an interval, polychromatic system operates in MexAmerica, which is densely populated by Hispanics and ethnic Mexicans. With capitals in Houston and Los Angeles, San Antonio, Phoenix, and San Francisco, it encompasses northern Mexico, the U.S. Southwest, and the American West. The postnational network centered here is based on commerce, a trade in labor, skills, and culture that routinely brings together Latin, Asian, Native, African, and European Americans. This area has often been described as America's melting pot and as a mosaic of diverse nationalities. But in recent times the area has been more of a simmering cauldron that has occasionally boiled over, as was the case during the Los Angeles upheaval of 1992, and with the white nativist militias that "patrol" the U.S.-Mexico border today.

Roughly two-thirds of the 42.7 million Hispanics in the United States today are concentrated in this transnation. As noted above, the demographic and racial transformation under way in MexAmerica is profound. The Hispanic presence in what is now the United States dates from the original Spanish settlement of St. Augustine, Florida, in 1565. Colonists shortly thereafter ventured into New Mexico in 1598, forming the most densely populated province of frontier New Spain in the colonial period. Today the offspring of these original settlers call themselves Hispanos and, over the centuries, have been joined by millions of Mexicanos who have traveled northward first within New Spain and then Mexico, later into lands claimed by the United States, to settle and find work, legally and illegally. To this mix one must add immigrants from other nations in Central America and South America who continue to arrive.

The Hispanic residents of MexAmerica, whether from Mexico or Guatemala, have lives and ties to their places of origin that daily are renewed through communication, through telephones and fax machines, through e-mail, and through monetary remittances. Hispanics, whether living in Santa Fe or Chihuahua, do not have to forget or to homogenize their culture in either place. For many of these residents the logic of global capitalism defines their possibilities in Mexico, Puerto Rico, Costa Rica, and the United States. And it is that same logic that keeps them actively engaged in hometown associations, ever informed of events and politics in their countries of origin through the evening Spanish-language television networks.

The racial system that operates in MexAmerica is quite distinct from that found in other parts of the United States and particularly from the one depicted by the national media as hegemonic. Race in MexAmerica separates the population into many distinct groups measured by gradations and intervals. This polychromatic system establishes race by assessing the level of mixing (or mestizaje) among Europeans, Africans, and Indians. During the colonial period, legal taxonomies based on ancestry were established to putatively measure every conceivable mix. Though the legal codes created more categories than were visually perceivable, at the popular level determinations of race were understood as distinct phenotypes. These types spawned numerous other caricatures and stereotypes that endured with lives of their own in legal, learned, and popular discourses about racial mixing.

Mestizaje as a process of biological mixing dates to 1492 in the Americas. When Christopher Columbus and the compatriots that followed conquered and colonized Mexico and Peru, they claimed that their intention was to win souls, but what they most wanted was gold, silver, and other sources of profit. What they mostly begot was children of mixed ancestry, born often of violent acts of assault. The Spanish conquest of the Americas was certainly won with guns, with horses, with dogs, and with smallpox. But it was also through the sexual conquest of Indian women that the legacy of Spanish colonialism vibrantly lives on.

The year 1492 began a massive process of biological and cultural mixing, of exchanges and population changes that produced in the Americas something quite new. When Europeans, Africans, and Amerindians procreated and genetically mixed, they gave birth to the mestizo, to mixed-breeds who blended cultures, languages, traditions, and worldviews.

This biological mixing emerged from relationships between Spanish men and Indian and African slave women, and between African men and Indian women. Mestizaje occurred for a simple demographic reason. Most of the Spanish men who participated in the conquest and colonization of Spanish America were single; most of the African slaves brought to New Spain (and they far outnumbered Spaniards) were also single men. As is common in war, unmarried conquering soldiers took for their pleasure the bodies of native women through acts of violence. Indeed, some historians maintain that the conquest of America was a "sexual conquest" of Indian women and the sexual exploitation of African slaves.[26] To curtail the high levels of sexual violence against indigenous women, the Catholic clergy urged conquerors and other Spaniards to take Indian brides in sacramental marriage. Some did. Others established sexual liaisons with Indian women through concubinage and cohabitation, especially with domestic servants and African slaves. Casual encounters, promiscuity, and rapes, taken together with stable unions, greatly expanded the number of persons of mixed ancestry during the seventeenth and eighteenth centuries. So did the growing numbers of relationships, also mixing conquests, liaisons, and enduring unions, between men of African ancestry escaping slavery and Indian women in the regions stretching from Guanajuato to Chihuahua.[27]

From roughly 1521 to the early 1700s, the Spanish Crown tolerated unions between Indian women and Spanish men as a necessary evil it hoped would stabilize colonial society, improve trade and tributary relations with the Indians, cement military alliances, and promote the extension of missionary work. The authorities resisted unions between people of African and indigenous ancestry, but could never block them in the vast spaces of New Spain's north. But prejudice against such mixed unions, and particularly against children of mixed ancestry, was always present in law and in elite culture and only intensified in the late eighteenth century as French-inspired Enlightenment ideas about social hierarchies diffused from Spain into the colonies.[28]

In early colonial society, children of mixed ancestry were despised as vibrant symbols of defilement and were often treated as outcasts by Spaniards, Indians, and Africans alike. Most were born or presumed to have been born of sinful relationships and illicit liaisons between Spaniard men and Indian and African women. Simply put, mixed children were bastards of illegitimate birth and so regarded in law. The Spanish legal theorist Juan de Solórzano Pereira, writing on mestizos and mulattoes in 1542, noted that "generally they are born in adultery and other ugly and illicit unions, because there are few Spaniards of honor who marry Indians or Negroes. This defect of their birth makes them infamous to which are added the stain of different color and other vices." For Solórzano, racial mixing was synonymous with illegitimacy and infamy.[29]

Such negative views of miscegenation held strong in Spain. The first edition of the Diccionario de la Academia Española (1737) defines the word "raza" (race) to mean "caste or racial status of origin." The dictionary adds: "When speaking of persons, it usually means illegitimacy. Also, stain or dishonor of the lineage." The physical signs of mixed ancestry were still equated with illegitimate birth and, by implication, with illicit sexual unions. This was the stigma that Spaniards placed on mestizos, mulattoes, and others of mixed ancestry. As groups, they were often generically referred to as *castas*, drawing the name and inspiration from the caste system in India.

From 1521 to roughly 1700, many *castas* in Spanish America seem to have been amalgamated into their mothers' indigenous communities. Many offspring of Spanish masters and African slave mothers remained slaves in the households or enterprises of their master-fathers. Over time, and especially in northern New Spain, growing numbers, especially the offspring of African fathers and Indian mothers (definitionally free, as were their mixed children), moved into the open spaces of Spanish colonial society as marginals or dependent workers—often in the mines. Of these persons of mixed ancestry—even as they became key mine workers in Guanajuato and Chihuahua—little good was ever said by those who gained by their labors—until centuries later when Mexico declared the hybrid mestizo a symbol of national unity to challenge the dominance of pure racial types.

The persistent denigration of the expanding populations of *castas* was rooted in medieval Spain. Noble families had guarded with great care their *limpieza de sangre*, or blood purity, determined to avoid mixture with Jews and Moors. In Spanish America, families of aristocratic pretense similarly aimed to protect their bloodlines against pollution by Indians, mulattoes, *castas*, and persons of despicable birth. They closely monitored the behavior of their sons and daughters, prohibiting unequal mixed marriages and frowning on cohabitation and its issue.

Mestizaje nevertheless became the norm between the dominant Spaniards and Indians and Africans, slave and free, resulting in high levels of illegitimacy particularly throughout the eighteenth century—and notably in the expansive commercial societies driving north to eventually engage New Mexico after 1750. The regime, the church, and those who claimed the benefits of Spanish privilege aimed to classify the children born of interracial unions and liaisons in hierarchical ranks according to the degree of putative mixing between the races. A Spaniard and an Amerindian mother engendered a mestizo. A Spaniard and a black woman begot a mulatto. A mestizo and a Spanish woman produced a *castizo*. A Spaniard and a mulatto woman produced a *morisco*. A Spaniard and a *morisco* woman produced an *albino*, and so on and so on. Precise legal categories existed for most known combinations among Spaniards, Amerindians, and Africans. Yet in the north of New Spain, everyday practice and prejudice reduced most people to three primary groups—Spaniards, Indians, and negros (blacks)—and their growing numbers of mixed offspring to two—mestizos (favoring indigenous ancestry) and mulattoes (showing signs of African ancestry). In sharp contrast to official presumptions and prescriptions, most mulattoes in northern New Spain mixed African and indigenous ancestry. And in the north, especially in times of boom on the frontiers, a few mestizos and mulattoes acquired the wealth and local respect to assert Spanish status.

Rising levels of miscegenation and presumed illegitimacy in the 1700s were met with pronounced levels of racial prejudice emanating from Enlightenment Europe against persons of mixed ancestry. In the eighteenth century, "pure" Spaniards forcefully articulated elaborate explanations of their own superiority and, conversely, of the inferiority of *castas*. To guarantee that such notions were enforced through law, whenever a person stood before a civil or ecclesiastical court, his or her *calidad*, literally "quality" or social standing, was one of the first facts that had to be entered into the record. A person's *calidad* usually began with the individual's age, sex, and place of residence, followed by race and whether of legitimate or illegitimate birth. The type and extent of punishment one could possibly receive was based on this information. Spaniards could not be given vile forms of punishment. Indians, by virtue of their presumed childishness and irrationality, could not be held accountable for certain acts, particularly for heresy. Mestizos and persons of mixed ancestry, while prohibited from ostentatious displays of pomp or wealth, were exempt from certain forms of tribute and work.

Still, across Spanish America and especially in northern New Spain, legal prescriptions could not constrain high levels of miscegenation and illegitimacy during the eighteenth century. Phenotypic and physical color distinctions in the population rapidly began to blur, allowing individuals to pass for members of higher and lower castes, depending on their wealth, social role—whatever was most in their favor. As populations grew in the eighteenth century and people moved about more freely, prestige hierarchies, at least those based on color, became much more difficult to maintain and even more difficult to enforce. The Crown and local authorities responded by reinforcing legal color distinctions, demanding their mention in all legal proceedings and promulgating a number of laws strengthening the power of parents over their children, particularly in the selection of marriage partners. The state reasoned that if parents con-

trolled the selection of marital partners for their children, social hierarchies would be maintained and the racial integrity of elite families would
be saved. But simultaneously a Crown strapped for cash resorted to selling
titles and certificates that whitened stained lineages. For decades money
had made Spaniards of the most fortunate of mixed peoples; the Crown,
unable to prevent the process, late in the colonial era capitulated, cashed
in, and consolidated that route to legitimate favor.[30] By the early 1800s,
the biological mixing that had taken place was so extensive that legal color
codes were impossible to enforce, much less to recognize as distinct types
in the population. As one Latin American republic after another declared
its independence from Spain between 1810 and 1821, legal color categories
were abolished, but color consciousness as measured through intervals remained intact.

New Mexico lived a unique local variant of mestizaje. Long at the
northern limit of Spanish North America, in New Mexico Spaniards had
ruled settled Pueblo Indians and together they both fought and traded
with independent warring peoples all around. The "standard" processes
of mixing in which Spaniards first imposed themselves on Pueblo women
and then joined in diverse relations ranging from rape to brief liaisons to
enduring unions led to mixing were common enough within New Mexico.
Among the offspring, some took places on the margins of Spanish society; many remained "Indians" within Pueblo communities.

Simultaneously, centuries-long conflicts between Spaniards, their
Pueblo dependents, and Apaches, Comanches, Navajos, and other independent peoples led to practices of taking captives—sometimes men,
often women and children. Spaniards "adopted" captive Indian women,
incorporated them into their households, and produced children with
them. Independent natives "adopted" captive Spanish and Pueblo women,
kept them in their households, and generated children with them, too.
In New Mexico, through long colonial centuries, the brief Mexican era,
and into time of U.S rule, miscegenation persisted with levels of coercion
most common in conquest times across Spanish America. At the frontier,
conquest seemed a continuing process, slow to give way to less violent
ways of ethnic mixing.[31]

We do not know very much about how Mexicans incorporated into
Texas in 1836, and those who became de jure citizens of the United States
with the Treaty of Guadalupe Hidalgo in 1848 continued to think or talk
about race among themselves. What is clear from the historical literature is that, in the aftermath of territorial conquest, Anglo-Americans
sooner or later used their system of binary classification to describe Mexi-

cans, deeming them in some instances as whites and in others as non-whites. Tomás Almaguer argues in *Racial Fault Lines: The Historical Origins of White Supremacy in California* (1994) that Mexicans were located in an intermediate space in the American racial order, the bottom of which was occupied by Indians, Asians, and blacks. By virtue of Spanish origin, Mexicans could legitimately claim a European genealogy, a Latin-derived language, belief in a Christian God, and thus Caucasian and white status. Neil Foley's study *The White Scourge: Mexicans, Blacks, and Poor Whites in Texas Cotton Culture* (1997) paints a much more ambiguous picture. Though Mexicans in Texas were considered legally white, in practice they were treated as nonwhites, a fact they constantly contested until in the 1960s Chicano/a nationalism began to celebrate their mestizo roots and to denigrate their white European ancestry.[32] The racial structure of domination David Montejano documents in *Anglos and Mexicans in the Making of Texas, 1836–1986* (1987), leaves little ambiguity. Mexicans were classified as inferior, nonwhites, ranked as low as blacks and exploitable as such. Katherine Benton-Cohen, in *Borderline Americans: Racial Division and Labor War in the Arizona Borderlands* (2009) and her chapter in this volume, details how in southern Arizona Mexican fluidities and amalgamations persisted into the late nineteenth century, and how the coming of the U.S.-dominated mining economy turned "Mexican" into the polarized "other" of the early twentieth century. While more research will illuminate our understanding of the racial dynamics of the U.S. conquest of the Southwest, and perhaps settle this debate, it is clear that by the turn of the twentieth century "Mexican" in popular usage in the United States was becoming a stigmatized nonwhite racial status associated with social, political, and mental inferiority. The point was clearly underscored in 1930, when the U.S. census listed Mexicans as a separate race.

Research shows that in the contemporary United States, skin color still carries significant weight in the social outcomes among Hispanics, particularly those of Mexican origin. Edward Telles and Edward Murguía tested the widely reported observation that darker-skinned Chicanos were economically disadvantaged in the United States.[33] Using the 1979 Chicano National Sample drawn from the Southwest, they asked whether those individuals rated as light-skinned by interviewers had higher average earnings than those who were darker. Since the light-skinned group was too small for sound statistical comparisons, it was merged with a group judged to be of medium skin color, and a comparison was then made with the darkest group. The researchers found a strong tendency for the lighter group to earn more than the darker one; they argued that this could not be explained in terms of educational differences, for the two groups had similar levels of education. Carlos Arce, Edward Murguía, and W. Parker Frisbie similarly concluded that phenotype—defined as dark skin and Indian facial features—correlated closely with socioeconomic status among Chicanos, a result sociologist Clara Rodríguez also found among Puerto Ricans with dark skin and "African" features in the United States.[34]

Zweigenhaft and Domhoff tested a similar hypothesis about the relationship between color and class among Hispanics by using two samples composed mainly of elites.[35] The first sample consisted of photographs of Hispanic directors of Fortune 500 companies. The second sample was photos of the 188 individuals that Hispanic Business identified in its magazine as the "top influential" Hispanics in 1993 and 1994. Two independent panels of reviewers concluded that the Fortune 500 Hispanic directors were overwhelmingly "white" or "Anglo." About 50 percent of the influential Hispanics were deemed "white," the rest readily identified as "Hispanic." One reader of Hispanic Business intuitively drew the same conclusion. Writing to the editor about the November 1996 picture survey of "top influentials," Gustavo E. Gonzales complained that the magazine had "failed to include a single dark face." The editor of Hispanic Business replied that their list contained Hispanics of "African ancestry" and that one should avoid conclusions based on "visual evidence alone."[36]

Social scientists have also found that the residential segregation of Hispanics in the United States is significantly dependent on skin color. Denton and Massey discovered housing discrimination and limited residential mobility to be most pronounced among Puerto Ricans who were dark-skinned and had phenotypic African features.[37] It is clear that the "racial" polarities at the core of the Atlantic Seaboard/Caribbean transnation exerted profound influence on the life prospects and Anglo perceptions of the Hispanic peoples incorporated by conquest into the United States in the MexAmerica transnation. Yet while facing those polarities, have MexAmericans retained some of the openness to amalgamation, to mestizaje, rooted in their Hispanic (and often mixed) ancestry?

I turn finally and only briefly to the third transnation I want to discuss, in the Pacific Northwest, with its dendritic hubs centered in Vancouver, Seattle, and Portland. This area integrates the Canadian state of British Columbia with East Asia and the U.S. Northwest and produces the most advanced economic activity in computer hardware and software, in bio- and environmental technologies, and in the in aerospace industry. As the region of North America closest to China, Hong Kong, and Japan, Ecotopia's ports are among the busiest in the world, rapidly mixing Asian immigrants with European and African Americans.

Since the 1970s, large numbers of immigrants have settled in this transnation from China, Japan, Korea, India, and Vietnam. We know that these immigrants come from home countries in which there are powerful myths of origin. In each of these countries, identity has been constructed through ideologies of blood and biological descent that have produced notions of racial hierarchy. Racial identities have been particularly important since the rise of nationalist movements in the late nineteenth century. The primacy of blood and kinship in creating a sense of national belonging has long been as important to Asians as it has been to Europeans and to residents of the United States.[38]

We know, for example, that the Chinese have long thought of themselves in exclusivist terms as superior to barbarian outsiders, and that by the nineteenth century they had begun ordering the world's races in hierarchical fashion, vaunting how the yellow and white races were the two most superior in the world.[39] While the Chinese have thought of themselves as the "yellow race" since at least the seventeenth century and have placed a high symbolic value on this color, no such idea is indigenous to Japan. The Japanese began referring to themselves as members of the "yellow race" only as a result of their contact with China and the West during the late nineteenth century. Scholars maintain that because of Japan's long history of island isolation and a relatively homogeneous population, no native vocabulary for skin color other than black and white ever developed. If discrimination exists in Japan against the Burakumin, the Ainu, and Okinawans, a fact contested by the state and scholars alike, it is not based on genetic or physiological traits generally associated with race. Rather, it is rooted in an essential and exclusive national identity that fiercely protects against outsiders and denies those who are not Japanese the right to assimilate or even to belong to the body politic.[40] The case of the Nikkeijin, Japanese persons who initially migrated to Brazil and Peru but who have returned to Japan in search of work, is particularly interesting. By "blood" they are putatively members of the Japanese "family," but culturally and linguistically they have been treated as outsiders and discriminated against.

How do these values and attitudes translate in the United States? In a set of interviews conducted with Japanese college students attending the University of California, Berkeley in the late 1960s, social psychologist Hiroshi Wagatsuma found that many of the students knew intellectually that they should not discriminate against blacks. In open-ended discussions they would always begin by disavowing any personal prejudice. But when questioned more closely they would explain that they actually avoided contact with blacks: "I feel resistance to coming closer to them"; "It's almost a physical reaction and has nothing to do with my thinking"; "It's almost like a biological repulsion"; "It's the feeling of uneasiness and something uncanny."[41] Wagatsuma discovered that while Japanese students initially thought of themselves as white when they first arrived in the United States, gradually that too changed. As a result of living here, students expanded their color consciousness and embraced the dominant stereotype of their color as yellow.

How should we imagine the racial sensitivities of South Asians who migrate to the Pacific Northwest? In any white-majority context, the dark-skinned South Asians are identified as black. But South Asians, regardless of their national origin on the subcontinent, cling to a belief that they are "Aryans."[42] To this day, upper-caste Hindus in India maintain that they are of Aryan descent, a belief also currently expounded by the Sinhala majority in Sri Lanka, despite considerable contradictory archaeological evidence.

In the United States since as early as 1907, South Asians have resisted racial classification as black or nonwhite, asserting that they are Aryans and thus entitled to citizenship status as white. From 1907 to 1923, American courts agreed, granting seventy South Asians citizenship as members of the Aryan race and as such white and Caucasian. All this changed in 1923, when the U.S. Supreme Court asserted in the case of Bhagat Singh Thind that although South Asians might be Aryan, they were not white as was commonly understood in the "language of the common man."[43]

Indians see themselves as Aryan and Caucasian. Whatever discrimination they may experience and share with other Asians in the United States, they feel no affinity toward other Asians. There are Indians in the United States, notes Harold Isaacs,

> who really think of themselves as more "white" than the "whites," indeed, as descendants from that "pure Aryan family" of prehistoric time. This endows them with a sort of Mayflower status in relation to "whiteness" or "Aryanism" which they deny to many of their own darker-skinned countrymen. This Indian . . . is not challenging the white man's racism as such. He is crying: "How dare you assume your air of Aryan superiority over me when I am just as Aryan as you, even more so!" This was the

substance of the Indian claim in that 1923 court case . . . and it is still the substance of many an Indian response to American racism.[44]

We know relatively little about how Asian racial ideologies are experienced and articulated by Asian immigrants in the United States. In Japan, the Japanese clearly have a binary color consciousness, while the Chinese and East Asians articulate interval, hierarchically ranked notions of race. The scholarly challenge before us is to explore how immigrants, particularly in the second generation, fuse and make sense of several models of race. When contemplating assimilation and integration, how are dominant and subordinate understandings of race dynamically employed in Ecotopia in the face of encounters with Eastern Seaboard polarities and MexAmerican openness to amalgamations, as more Mexicans and other Hispanics migrate to the Northwest? We simply do not know.

This discussion of the history of racial meanings, understandings, and identities among residents of three emerging postnational spaces helps us explore the ways in which New Mexico helped shape North America. Mestizaje continues to forge North America's self-consciousness about its self as a unique place in a number of complicated ways. In *The Matachines Dance: Ritual Symbolism and Interethnic Relations in the Upper Rio Grande Valley* (1996), anthropologist Sylvia Rodríguez documents a dance drama that originated during the Spanish conquest of the area and is still performed yearly in the towns all along the Upper Rio Grande drainage. The four persons most prominent in the Matachines dance are Malinche (the mistress and confidant of Hernán Cortés who historically is depicted as the first convert to Spanish Catholicism and the woman who gave birth to the first mestizo), Montezuma (the last Aztec king), and two *abuelos* (grandparents). In the formal steps of the dance, Malinche, dressed as a bride, engages Montezuma and gradually converts him to Catholicism and leads him into the church. From the margins of the dance field, the *abuelos* constantly taunt, mock, and ridicule the official dancers and even scandalously copulate and give birth to a child.

Rodríguez perceptively notes that two narratives and two sets of characters enact the dance drama. The official ecclesiastical narrative is that of sacramental marriage between Spaniards and Indians and the conversion of the latter, as depicted by Malinche, Montezuma, and their retinues. The other text, the subversive text of the dance, is performed by the *abuelos*, who accurately depict the history of consensual unions, mestizaje, and illicit mixing which have long been the realities of life along the Rio Grande.

For another legacy of mestizaje, travel to New Mexico and carefully survey the items for sale in tourist shops. There you will find many coyote figurines, in every size and color, howling at the moon. To understand how coyotes relate to mestizaje, bear in mind that while the Régimen de Castas legally assigned race by putative degrees of blood mixture, popular forms of racial classification often predominated. I noted earlier that in popular parlance people were often racially classified not by legal categories but by physical appearance. Half-breeds were widely referred to by animal names, the most frequent being coyote and *lobo*. To this day in MexAmerica, persons of mixed descent call themselves, or are referred to by others, as coyotes. The coyote in American Indian folklore is a trickster, an animal that constantly crosses borders, surviving at the margins, consuming both animal and vegetable matter, foodstuffs that are both living and dead. The mestizos' existence was likened to that of a coyote in the popular imagination because they were born of two cultures but are members of neither and, like coyotes, exist at the margins of society. Not so coincidentally, the person who helps Mexican migrants cross illegally into the United States is called a coyote.

In recent Chicana/o cultural studies, inspired by the late Gloria Anzaldúa's highly influential book *Borderlands/La Frontera: The New Mestiza* (2007), the mestiza has emerged as a metaphor for a host of personal identities and psychological states of mind born of life along the U.S.-Mexico border. The mestiza is "cradled in one culture, sandwiched between two cultures, straddling all three cultures and their value systems, la mestiza undergoes a struggle of flesh, a struggle of border, an inner war . . . a cultural collision." For Anzaldúa, the mestiza is the hybrid woman born of the history of conflict along the U.S.-Mexico border. This mestiza is a creature of plural selves, selves that allow her to challenge dualistic thinking and vulgar dichotomies generated by life along the border. "To live in the Borderlands," Anzaldúa explains, "means you are neither hispana india negra española ni gabacha, eres mestiza, mulato, half-breed caught in the crossfire between camps while carrying all five races on your back not knowing which side to turn to, run from . . . To live in the Borderlands means to put chile in the borscht, eat whole wheat tortillas, speak Tex-Mex with a Brooklyn accent; be stopped by la migra at the border checkpoints. . . . To survive the Borderlands you must live sin fronteras be a crossroads."[45]

Performance artist Guillermo Gómez-Peña similarly asks us to imagine a new cartography of North American possibilities in his book *The New World Border: Prophecies, Poems & Locuras for the End of the Century.*[46] A single modernist map of sealed territorial boundaries, each with a discrete center and margins that meet at borders, does not fit the reality of existence at the end of the twentieth century. One now needs "a more complex system of overlapping, interlocking, and overlaid maps," he explains, a cartography of hybridity based on the experiences of individuals who experience dominant culture from the margins and from the outside, persons who are members of multiple communities, intercultural translators, political tricksters, and nomadic chroniclers who "trespass, bridge, interconnect, reinterpret, remap, and redefine."[47]

Tato Laviera, Guillermo Gómez-Peña, and Gloria Anzaldúa's writings have had broad influence in the humanities and social sciences in North America, prompting a reexamination of modernist assumptions about the unity of nation-states, the coherence of national languages, the consistency of communities and of subjectivities. This still-emerging set of ideas has taken the border that currently divides MexAmerica as a place of mestizaje, as a liminal zone, as a space of cultural hybridity and transculturation, where peoples, cultures, and ideas can move in complicated ways, defying linearity, indeed, mirroring the very logic of the new global economy.

My conclusion must be a question: As racial polarities persist among peoples rooted in the Eastern Atlantic Seaboard transnation, will such sharp dualities find reinforcement among Asian immigrants to the northwestern Ecotopia and elsewhere or will they be eroded, perhaps challenged, by the openness to mestizaje, even its celebration, that persists among the growing numbers of peoples rooted in MexAmerica and spreading across North America?

Notes

1. U.S. Department of Commerce, *Statistical Abstract of the United States* (Washington, D.C.: GPO, 1999), 34.

2. Peter Brimelow, *Alien Nation* (New York: Random House, 1995), xv.

3. Ibid., 10, 265.

4. Richard J. Hernstein and Charles Murray, *The Bell Curve* (New York: Free Press, 1994), 362–365.

5. Tato Laviera, *AmeRícan* (Houston, Tex.: Arte Público Press, 1985).

6. Arjun Appadurai, "Patriotism and Its Futures," *Public Culture* 5, no. 3 (1993): 411–429.

7. Robert B. Reich, "Who Is Us?" *Harvard Business Review* 68, no. 1 (1990): 53–63.

8. Joel Garreau, *The Nine Nations of North America* (Boston: Houghton Mifflin, 1981), 1.

9. This chapter was inspired by the literature on racial formations, which posits that different regions and nations often have distinct histories and thus very different understandings of race. I was particularly inspired by the work of Orlando Patterson, "Cultural Transmission and the American Cosmos," in Robert S. Leiken, ed., *A New Moment in the Americas* (New Brunswick, N.J.: Transaction Publishers, 1994); Michael Omi and Howard Winant, *Racial Formations in the United States, from the 1960s to the 1990s* (New York: Routledge, 1994); and, David Theo Goldberg, *The Threat of Race* (Malden, Mass.: Blackwell, 2009). Goldberg's categories—racial Americanization, racial Palestinianization, racial Europeanization, racial Southafricanization, racial Neoliberalism—were particularly generative in my thinking.

10. Lester D. Langley, *MexAmerica* (New York: Crown Publishers, 1988); Patterson, "Cultural Transmission"; Geoffrey E. Fox, *Hispanic Nation* (New York: Carol Publications, 1996); Rodolfo Acuña, *Occupied America* (New York: Harper and Row, 1981).

11. Paul Schell and John Hamer, "Cascadia," in Robert L. Earle and John D. Wirth, eds., *Identities in North America* (Stanford: Stanford University Press, 1995).

12. Orlando Patterson, "The Emerging West Atlantic System," in William Alonso, ed., *Population in an Interacting World* (Cambridge: Harvard University Press, 1987); idem, "Cultural Transmission and the American Cosmos."

13. Audrey Smedley, *Race in North America* (Boulder, Colo.: Westview Press, 1993); C. Vann Woodward, *The Strange Career of Jim Crow* (New York: Oxford University Press, 1966); John Hope Franklin, *The Color Line* (Columbia: University of Missouri Press, 1993).

14. López, *White by Law*.

15. F. James Davis, *Who Is Black?* (University Park: Pennsylvania State Press, 1991), 123–139.

16. J. E. White, "I'm Just Who I Am" *Time* (May 5, 1997): 32–36.

17. Ibid.; and John Kuntz, "The Young Master," *Newsweek* (April 28, 1997): 58–62.

18. "Black America and Tiger's Dilemma," *Ebony Magazine* (July 1997): 28–34, 138.

19. R. E. Lapchick, "Lessons of Tiger Woods Will Not Be Easy Ones," *New York Times* (May 18, 1997): S9; Henry Yu, "How Tiger Woods Lost His Stripes," in John C. Rowe, ed., *Post-National American Studies* (Berkeley: University of California Press, 2000).

20. White, "I'm Just Who I Am," 34.

21. Dale Maharidge, *The Coming White Minority* (New York: Vintage, 1996).

22. Georgia A. Pearson, *Race and Representation* (New Brunswick, N.J.: Transaction Publishers, 1997).

23. Jon Michael Spencer, *The New Colored People* (New York: New York University Press, 1997).

24. Mary C. Waters, *Black Identities* (Cambridge: Harvard University Press, 1999).

25. Mary C. Waters, "Ethnic and Racial Identities of Second-Generation Black Immigrants in New York City," in Alejandro Portes, ed., *The New Second Generation* (New York: Russell Sage, 1996).

26. Mörner, *Race Mixture*; Herbert H. Klein, *African Slavery in Latin America and the Caribbean* (New York: Oxford University Press, 1986).

27. Martin, *Governance and Society*; María Guevara Sanginés, *Guanajuato diverso* (Guanajuato: Ediciones La Rana, 2001); Tutino, *Making a New World*.

28. Claudio Esteva-Fabregat, *Mestizaje in Ibero-America* (Tucson: University of Arizona Press, 1995); Winthrop R. Wright, *Café Con Leche* (Austin: University of Texas Press, 1990).

29. Mauricio Solaún and Sidney Kronus, *Discrimination without Violence* (New York: Wiley, 1973).

30. Ann Twinam, *Public Lives, Private Secrets* (Stanford: Stanford University Press, 1999).

31. R. Gutiérrez, *When Jesus Came*; Brooks, *Captives and Cousins*.

32. Foley, "Becoming Hispanic."

33. Edward Telles and Edward Murguía, "Phenotypic Discrimination and Income Differences among Mexican Americans," *Social Science Quarterly* 71 (1990): 682–696.

34. Carlos Arce, Edward Murguía, and W. Parker Frisbie, "Phenotype and Life Chances among Chicanos," *Hispanic Journal of Behavioral Sciences* 9 (1987): 19–32; Clara Rodríguez, "Racial Classification among Puerto Rican Men and Women in New York," *Hispanic Journal of Behavioral Sciences* 12 (1990): 366–380; idem, "The Effect of Race on Puerto Rican Wages," in Edwin Meléndez, Clara Rodríguez, and Janis Barry, eds., *Hispanics in the Labor Force* (New York: Plenum Press, 1991).

35. Richard L. Zweigenhaft and G. William Domhoff, *Diversity in the Power Elite* (New Haven: Yale University Press, 1998).

36. Gustavo E. Gonzales, "Are Black Hispanics Being Ignored?" *Hispanic Business* (November 1996): 6.

37. Nancy Denton and Douglas Massey, "Residential Segregation of Blacks, Hispanics, and Asians by Socioeconomic Status and Generation," *Social Science Quarterly* 69 (1988): 797–817; idem, "Racial Identity among Caribbean Hispanics," *American Sociological Review* 54 (1989): 790–808.

38. Frank Dikötter, "Group Definition and the Idea of 'Race' in Modern China (1793–1949)," *Ethnic and Racial Studies* 13, no. 3 (1990): 421–432; idem, "Racial Identities in China," *China Quarterly* 138 (1994): 404–412.

39. Frank Dikötter, *The Discourse of Race in Modern China* (Stanford: Stanford University Press, 1992).

40. D. M. Potter, and P. Knepper, "Comparing Official Definitions of Race in Japan and the United States," in Joan Ferrante and Prince Brown, eds., *The Social Construction of Race and Ethnicity in the United States* (New York: Longman, 1998).

41. Hiroshi Wagatsuma, "The Social Perception of Skin Color in Japan," in John Hope Franklin, ed., *Color and Race* (Boston: Houghton Mifflin, 1968), quotations on 149.

42. A. Béteille, "Race and Descent as Social Categories in India," in John Hope Franklin, ed., *Color and Race* (Boston: Houghton Mifflin, 1968).

43. Sucheta Mazumdar, "Race and Racism," in Gail M. Nomura, Russell Endo, Stephan H. Sumida, and Russell C. Leong, eds., *Frontiers of Asian American Studies* (Pullman: Washington State University Press, 1989); López, *White by Law*.

44. Harold Isaacs, *Images of Asia* (New York: Harper and Row, 1972), 290.

45. Anzaldúa, *Borderlands/La Frontera*, 78, 194.

46. Guillermo Gómez-Peña, *The New World Border* (San Francisco: City Lights, 1996).

47. Ibid., 6, 12.

Bibliography

Abel, E. *Tuberculosis and the Politics of Exclusion: A History of Public Health and Migration to Los Angeles.* New Brunswick, N.J.: Rutgers University Press, 2007.

Acuña, Rodolfo. *Occupied America: A History of Chicanos.* 7th ed. Englewood Cliffs, N.J.: Prentice Hall, 2010; New York: Longman, 1988; New York: Harper and Row, 1981.

Alcaraz, Ramón. *Apuntes para la historia de la guerra entre México y los Estados Unidos.* Mexico City: Tip. de M. Payno (hijo) 1848.

———, et al. *The Other Side; or, Notes for the History of the War between Mexico and the United States* (1850). Trans. Albert C. Ramsey. New York: Burt Franklin, 1970.

Alemán, Jesse. "The Other Country: Mexico, the United States, and the Gothic History of Conquest." *American Literary History* 18, no. 3 (Fall 2006): 406–426.

———, and Shelley Streeby, eds. *Empire and the Literature of Sensation: An Anthology of Nineteenth-Century Popular Fiction.* New Brunswick, N.J.: Rutgers University Press, 2007.

Alexander, Peter, and Rick Halpern. *Racializing Class, Classifying Race: Labour and Difference in Britain, the USA, and Africa.* New York: St. Martin's Press, 2000.

Allen, Robert C. *Enclosure and the Yeoman.* London: Clarendon, 1992.

Almaguer, Tomás. *Racial Fault Lines: The Historical Origins of White Supremacy in California.* Berkeley: University of California Press, 1994.

Alonso, Ana María. *Thread of Blood: Colonialism, Revolution, and Gender on Mexico's Northern Frontier.* Tucson: University of Arizona Press, 1995.

Alonzo, Armando C. *Tejano Legacy: Rancheros and Settlers in South Texas, 1734–1900.* Albuquerque: University of New Mexico Press, 1998.

Anderson, Virginia DeJohn. *Creatures of Empire: How Domestic Animals Transformed Early America.* New York: Oxford University Press, 2004.

Andrews, Tracy J. "Ecological and Historical Perspectives on Navajo Land Use and Settlement Patterns in Canyons de Chelly and del Muerto." *Journal of Anthropological Research* 47 (Spring 1991): 39–67.

Anna, Timothy. *Forging Mexico, 1821–1835.* Lincoln: University of Nebraska Press, 1998.

Annino, Antonio. "El Jano bifronte: Los pueblos y los orígenes del liberalismo en México." In Leticia Reina and Elisa Servín, eds., *Crisis, reforma y revolución.* Mexico City: Taurus, 2002.

Anzaldúa, Gloria. *Borderlands/La Frontera: The New Mestiza* (1987). 3rd ed. San Francisco: Aunt Lute Books, 2007.

Appadurai, Arjun. "Patriotism and Its Futures." *Public Culture* 5, no. 3 (1993): 411–429.

Arce, Carlos, Edward Murguía, and W. Parker Frisbie. "Phenotype and Life Chances among Chicanos." *Hispanic Journal of Behavioral Sciences* 9 (1987): 19–32.

Arnesen, Eric. "Whiteness and the Historians' Imagination." *International Labor and Working-Class History* 60 (Fall 2001): 3–32.

Aron, Stephen. "Lessons in Conquest: Towards a Greater Western History." *Pacific Historical Review* 63 (1994): 125–147.

Ashworth, John. *Slavery, Capitalism, and Politics in the Antebellum Republic.* Cambridge: Cambridge University Press, 1995.

Ávila, Alfredo. *En nombre de la nación.* Mexico City: Taurus, 2002.

Ávila, Eric. *Popular Culture in the Age of White Flight: Fear and Fantasy in Suburban Los Angeles.* Berkeley: University of California Press, 2004.

Bailey, Lynn R. *If You Take My Sheep: The Evolution and Conflicts of Navajo Pastoralism, 1630–1868.* Pasadena, Calif.: Westernlore, 1980.

———. *Bisbee: Queen of the Copper Camps.* 2nd ed. Tucson: Westernlore Press, 2002.

———. *Tombstone, Arizona "Too Tough To Die": The Rise, Fall, and Resurrection of a Silver Camp; 1878–1990.* Tucson: Westernlore Press, 2004.

———, ed. *Tombstone from a Woman's Point of View: The Correspondence of Clara Spalding Brown, July 7, 1880 to November 14, 1882.* Tucson: Westernlore Press, 1998.

Bakewell, Peter J. *Silver Mining and Society in Colonial Mexico: Zacatecas, 1546–1700.* Cambridge: Cambridge University Press, 1971.

Bakker, Elna. *An Island Called California: An Ecological Introduction to Its Natural Communities.* 2nd ed. Berkeley: University of California Press, 1984.

Balderrama, Francisco, and Raymond Rodríguez. *Decade of Betrayal.* Albuquerque: University of New Mexico Press, 1995.

Ballentine, George. *Autobiography of an English Soldier in the United States Army.* New York: Stringer and Townsend, 1853.

Balmori, Diana, Stuart F. Voss, and Miles Wortman. *Notable Family Networks in Latin America.* Chicago: University of Chicago Press, 1984.

Barr, Juliana. *Peace Came in the Form of a Woman: Indians and Spaniards in the Texas Borderlands.* Chapel Hill: University of North Carolina Press, 2007.

Bartolomé, M. A. *Gente de costumbres y gente de razón: Las identidades étnicas en México.* Mexico City: Siglo Veintiuno, 1997.

Bartra, R. *La jaula de la melancolía: Identidad y metamórfosis del mexicano.* Mexico City: Grijalba, 1987.

Bashford, Coles, comp. *The Compiled Laws of the Territory of Arizona from 1864–1871, inclusive.* Albany, N.Y.: N.p., 1871.

Basso, Matthew, Laura McCall, and Dee Garceau-Hagen, eds. *Across the Great Divide: Cultures of Manhood in the U.S. West*. New York: Routledge, 2001.

Bassols, J. B. *Correspondencia: Obras completas Ricardo Flores-Magón*. 2 vols. Mexico City: Consejo Nacional para la Cultura y las Artes, 2001.

Bean, Frank D., Stephen J. Trejo, Randy Capps, and Michael Tyler. *The Latino Middle Class: Myth, Reality and Potential*. Claremont, Calif.: Tomás Rivera Policy Institute, 2001.

Beckwith, Martha Warren. "Mythology of the Oglala Sioux." *Journal of American Folklore* 43 (October–December 1930): 339–442.

Belsky, A. Joy, and Dana M. Blumenthal. "Effects of Livestock Grazing on Stand Dynamics and Soils in Upland Forests of the Interior West." *Conservation Biology* 11 (April 1997): 315–327.

Bender, Thomas. *A Nation among Nations*. New York: Hill and Wang, 2006.

Benson, Todd. "The Consequences of Reservation Life: Native Californians on the Round Valley Reservation, 1871-1884." *Pacific Historical Review* 60 (May 1991): 221–244.

Benton-Cohen, Katherine. "Docile Children and Dangerous Revolutionaries: The Racial Hierarchy of Manliness and the Bisbee Deportation of 1917." *Frontiers: A Journal of Women Studies* 24, nos. 2–3 (2003): 30–50.

———. "Common Purposes, Worlds Apart: Mexican-American, Mormon and Midwestern Women Homesteaders in Cochise County, Arizona." *Western Historical Quarterly* 36, no. 4 (Winter 2005): 429–452.

———. *Borderline Americans: Racial Division and Labor War in the Arizona Borderlands*. Cambridge: Harvard University Press, 2009.

Berneker, Walther. *De agiotistas a empresarios: En torno a la temprana industrialización mexicana, siglo XIX*. Mexico City: Universidad Iberoamericana, 1992.

Berthrong, Donald J. *The Southern Cheyennes*. Norman: University of Oklahoma Press, 1963.

Béteille, A. "Race and Descent as Social Categories in India." In John Hope Franklin, ed., *Color and Race*. Boston: Houghton Mifflin, 1968.

Billington, Ray Allen. "The American Frontier Thesis." *Huntington Library Quarterly* 23, no. 3 (May 1960): 201–216.

Bird, Robert Montgomery. *Calavar; or the Knight of the Conquest. A Romance of Mexico*. Philadelphia: Carey, Lea, and Blanchard, 1834.

———. *The Infidel; or the Fall of Mexico. A Romance*. Philadelphia: Carey, Lea, and Blanchard, 1835.

"Black America and Tiger's Dilemma: National Leaders Praise Golfer's Accomplishments and Debate Controversial 'Mixed Race' Issue." *Ebony Magazine* (July 1997): 28–34, 138.

Blaisdell, L. L. *The Desert Revolution: Baja, California, 1911*. Madison: University of Wisconsin Press, 1962.

Blanton, Carlos K. "George I. Sánchez, Ideology, and Whiteness in the Making of the Mexican American Civil Rights Movement, 1930–1960." *Journal of Southern History* 72, no. 3 (August 2006): 569–604.

Bogue, Allan G. "An Agricultural Empire." In Clyde A. Milner II, Carol A. O'Connor, and Martha Sandweiss, eds., *The Oxford History of the American West*. New York: Oxford University Press, 1994.

Bonfil-Batalla, Guillermo. *México Profundo*. Mexico City: Grijalbo, 1994.
———. *México Profundo: Reclaiming a Civilization*. Austin: University of Texas Press, Institute of Latin American Studies, 1996.
Boyer, C. R. *Becoming Campesinos: Politics, Identity and Agrarian Struggle in Post-revolutionary Michoacán, 1920–1935*. Stanford: Stanford University Press, 2003.
Boyer, Richard. *Lives of the Bigamists: Marriage, Family, and Community in Colonial Mexico*. Albuquerque: University of New Mexico Press, 1995.
Brading, D. A. *Miners and Merchants in Bourbon Mexico 1763–1810*. Cambridge: Cambridge University Press, 1971.
———. *The First America*. Cambridge: Cambridge University Press, 1991.
Brickhouse, Anna. *Transamerican Literary Relations and the Nineteenth-Century Public Sphere*. Cambridge: Cambridge University Press, 2004.
Brimelow, Peter. *Alien Nation: Common Sense about America's Immigration Disaster*. New York: Random House, 1995.
Brischetto, Robert R. "The Hispanic Middle Class Comes of Age." *Hispanic Business* (December 2001): 21–32.
Brissenden, P. F. *The IWW: A Study of American Syndicalism*. New York: Columbia University Press, 1919.
Brooks, James F. *Captives and Cousins: Slavery, Kinship, and Community in the Southwest Borderlands*. Chapel Hill: University of North Carolina Press, 2002.
Brown, Lauren. *Grasslands*. New York: Knopf, 1985.
Brown, Richard Maxwell. "Violence." In Clyde A. Milner II, Carol A. O'Connor, and Martha Sandweiss, eds., *The Oxford History of the American West*. New York: Oxford University Press, 1994.
Buntline, Ned. *Magdalena the Beautiful Mexican Maid: A Story of Buena Vista* (1847). In Jesse Alemán and Shelley Streeby, *Empire and the Literature of Sensation: An Anthology of Nineteenth-Century Popular Fiction*. New Brunswick, N.J.: Rutgers University Press, 2007.
———. *The Volunteer; or, The Maid of Monterey*. A Tale of the Mexican War. Boston: F. Gleason, 1847.
Burgess, Opie Rundle. *Bisbee Not So Long Ago*. San Antonio, Tex.: Naylor, 1967.
Burris, Val. "The Discovery of the New Middle Classes." In Arthur J. Vidich, ed., *The New Middle Classes: Life Styles, Status Claims and Political Orientations*. New York: New York University Press, 1995.
Byrkit, James. *Forging the Copper Collar: Arizona's Labor-Management War of 1901–1921*. Tucson: University of Arizona Press, 1982.
Camarillo, Albert. *Chicanos in a Changing Society: From Mexican Pueblos to American Barrios in Santa Barbara and Southern California, 1848–1930*. Cambridge: Harvard University Press, 1979.
Campbell, Randolph. *An Empire for Slavery*. Baton Rouge: Louisiana State University Press, 1989.
Campbell, Robert B. "Newlands, Old Lands: Native American Labor, Agrarian Ideology, and the Progressive-Era State in the Making of the Newlands Reclamation Project, 1902–1926." *Pacific Historical Review* 71 (May 2002): 203–238.
Cañizares-Esquerra, Jorge. *Puritan Conquistadores*. Stanford: Stanford University Press, 2006.
Caplan, Karen. *Indigenous Liberalisms*. Stanford: Stanford University Press, 2009.

Carr, David Charles Wright. *La conquista del Bajío y los orígenes de San Miguel de Allende*. Mexico City: Fondo de Cultura Económica, 1998.

Carrico, Richard L., and Florence C. Shipek. "Indian Labor in San Diego County, 1850–1900." In Alice Littlefield and Martha Knack, eds., *Native Americans and Wage Labor: Ethnohistorical Perspectives*. Norman: University of Oklahoma Press, 1996.

Carroll, Patrick. *Felix Longoria's Wake: Bereavement, Racism, and the Rise of Mexican American Activism*. Austin: University of Texas Press, 2003.

Casas, María Raquel. *Married to a Daughter of the Land: Interethnic Marriages in California, 1820–1880*. Las Vegas: University of Nevada Press, 2007.

Castañeda, Antonia, et al., eds. *Gender on the Borderlands: The Frontiers Reader*. Lincoln: University of Nebraska Press, 2007.

Castillo-Feliú, Guillermo I. *Xicoténcatl: An Anonymous Historical Novel about the Events Leading Up to the Conquest of the Aztec Empire*. Austin: University of Texas Press, 1999.

Castro Gutiérrez, Felipe. *Movimientos populares en Nueva España. 1766–67*. Mexico City: Universidad Nacional Autónoma de México, 1990.

———. *Nueva ley y nuevo rey: Reformas borbónicas y rebelión popular en Nueva España*. Zamora: Colegio de Michoacán, 1996.

Cayton, Andrew R. L., ed. *Contact Points: American Frontiers from the Mohawk Valley to the Mississippi, 1750–1830*. Chapel Hill: University of North Carolina Press, 1998.

Cerutti, Mario. *Propietarios, empresarios y empresa en el norte de México: Monterrey de 1848 a la globalización*. Mexico City: Siglo Veintiuno, 2000.

Chávez, Leo R. *Shadowed Lives: Undocumented Immigrants in American Society*. Fort Worth, Tex.: Harcourt, Brace, 1992.

Chávez-García, Miroslava. *Negotiating Conquest: Gender and Power in California, 1770s to 1880s*. Tucson: University of Arizona Press, 2004.

Chavis, Ben. "All-Indian Rodeo: A Transformation of Western Apache Tribal Warfare and Culture." *Wicazo Sa Review* 9 (Spring 1993): 4–11.

Chevalier, François. *Land and Society in Colonial Mexico: The Great Hacienda*. Trans. Alvin Eustis, ed. Lesley Bird Simpson. Berkeley: University of California Press, 1963.

Cienfuegos, A. T. *El magonismo en Sonora: Historia de una persecución*. Hermosillo: Universidad de Sonora, 2003.

Clements, Eric L. *After the Boom in Tombstone and Jerome, Arizona*. Reno: University of Nevada Press, 2003.

Cockcroft, J. D. *Intellectual Precursors of the Mexican Revolution, 1900–1913*. Austin: University of Texas Press, 1968.

Collins, William S. *The New Deal in Arizona*. Phoenix: Arizona State Parks Board, 1999.

Countryman, Edward. *The American Revolution*. New York: Hill and Wang, 2003.

Crane, James M. "An Analysis of the Great Register of Cochise County, Arizona Territory, 1884." *Cochise Quarterly* 18 (1988): 5.

Cronon, William. *Nature's Metropolis: Chicago and the Great West*. New York: Norton, 1991.

Crosby, Alfred W. *The Columbian Exchange: Biological and Cultural Consequences of 1492.* Westport, Conn.: Greenwood, 1972.

———. *Ecological Imperialism: The Biological Expansion of Europe, 900–1900.* New York: Cambridge University Press, 1986.

Cuello, José. "Racialized Hierarchies of Power in Colonial Mexican Society: The Sistema de Castas as a form of Social Control in Saltillo." In Jesús F. de la Teja and Ross Frank, eds., *Choice, Persuasion, and Coercion: Social Control on Spain's North American Frontiers.* Albuquerque: University of New Mexico Press, 2005.

Dallam, James. *The Lone Star: A Tale of Texas, Founded upon Incidents in the History of Texas.* New York: E. Ferret, 1845.

Daniel, Cletus. *Chicano Workers and the Politics of Fairness: The FEPC in the Southwest, 1941–1945.* Austin: University of Texas Press, 1991.

Davis, F. James. *Who Is Black?: One Nation's Definition.* University Park: Pennsylvania State University Press, 1991.

Davis, Mike. *Ecology of Fear: Los Angeles and the Imagination of Disaster.* New York: Vintage, 1998.

deBuys, William. *Enchantment and Exploitation: The Life and Hard Times of a New Mexico Mountain Range.* Albuquerque: University of New Mexico Press, 1985.

Deeds, Susan. *Defiance and Deference in Mexico's Colonial North.* Austin: University of Texas Press, 2003.

Degler, Carl. *Neither Black nor White.* New York: MacMillan, 1971.

DeGuzmán, María. *Spain's Long Shadow: The Black Legend, Off-Whiteness, and Anglo-American Empire.* Minneapolis: University of Minnesota Press, 2005.

de la Teja, Jesús F. *San Antonio de Béjar.* Albuquerque: University of New Mexico Press, 1995.

———, and Ross Frank. *Choice, Persuasion, and Coercion: Social Control on Spain's North American Frontiers.* Albuquerque: University of New Mexico Press, 2005.

DeLaura, David J. *Hebrew and Hellene in Victorian England: Newman, Arnold and Pater.* Austin: University of Texas Press, 1969.

DeLay, Brian. *War of a Thousand Deserts: Indian Raids and the U.S.-Mexican War.* New Haven: Yale University Press, 2009.

De León, Arnoldo, and Kenneth L. Stewart. *Tejanos and the Numbers Game.* Albuquerque: University of New Mexico Press, 1989.

Delgado, Grace. "In the Age of Exclusion: Race, Religion, and Chinese Identity in the Making of the Arizona-Sonora Borderlands, 1863–1943." PhD dissertation, University of California–Los Angeles, 2000.

Deloria, Philip J. *Indians in Unexpected Places.* Lawrence: University of Kansas Press, 2004.

Denevan, William. "Livestock Numbers in Nineteenth-Century New Mexico, and the Problem of Gullying in the Southwest." *Annals of the Association of American Geographers* 57, no. 4 (December 1967): 691–703.

Denton, Nancy, and Douglas Massey. "Residential Segregation of Blacks, Hispanics, and Asians by Socioeconomic Status and Generation." *Social Science Quarterly* 69 (1988): 797–817.

———. "Racial Identity among Caribbean Hispanics: The Effects of Double

Minority Status on Residential Segregation." *American Sociological Review* 54 (1989): 790–808.

Diamond, Jared. *Guns, Germs, and Steel: The Fates of Human Societies*. New York: Norton, 1997.

Dikötter, Frank. "Group Definition and the Idea of 'Race' in Modern China (1793–1949)." *Ethnic and Racial Studies* 13, no. 3 (1990): 421–432.

———. *The Discourse of Race in Modern China*. Stanford: Stanford University Press, 1992.

———. "Racial Identities in China: Context and Meaning." *China Quarterly* 138 (1994): 404–412.

Dillehay, Tom D. "Late Quaternary Bison Population Changes in the Southern Plains." *Plains Anthropologist* 19 (August 1974): 180–196.

Diner, Hasia. "The World of Whiteness." *Historically Speaking* (2007): 20–22.

Dobyns, Henry F., Theodore Bundy, James E. Officer, and Richard W. Stoffle. *Los Tres Alamos del Rio San Pedro: The Peculiar Persistence of a Place Name*. Tucson: Piñon Press, 1996.

Dorsey, Margaret E. *Pachangas: Borderlands Music, U.S. Politics, and Transnational Marketing*. Austin: University of Texas Press, 2006.

Dubofsky, M. *We Shall Be All: A History of the IWW*. New York: Quadrangle Press, 1969.

Duganne, A.J.H. *The Peon Prince; or the Yankee Knight Errant, a Tale of Modern Mexico*. New York: Beadle, 1861.

———. *Putnam Pomfret's War; or, a Vermonter's Adventures in Mexico*. New York: 1861.

Duncan, Silvio R., and John Markoff. "Civilization and Barbarism: Cattle Frontiers in Latin America." *Comparative Studies in Society and History* 20, no. 4 (October 1978): 587–620.

Dunlay, Tom. *Kit Carson and the Indians*. Lincoln: University of Nebraska Press, 2000.

Dunmire, William W. *Gardens of New Spain: How Mediterranean Plants and Foods Changed America*. Austin: University of Texas Press, 2004.

Dunn, Richard. *Sugar and Slaves*. Chapel Hill: University of North Carolina Press, 1972.

Durand, Jorge. *Más allá de la línea*. Mexico City: Consejo Nacional para la Cultura y las Artes, 1994.

———, ed. *Braceros*. Mexico City: Miguel Ángel Porrúa, 2007.

Dysart, Jane. "Mexican Women in San Antonio, 1830–1860: The Assimilation Process." *WHQ* 7 (1976): 365–375.

Eccles, W. J. "The Frontiers of New France." In George Wolfskill and Stanley Palmer, eds., *Essays on Frontiers in World History*. College Station: Texas A&M University Press, 1983.

Edmunds, R. David. "Native Americans and the United States, Canada, and Mexico." In Philip J. Deloria and Neal Salisbury, eds., *A Companion to Native American History*. Malden, Mass.: Blackwell, 2002.

Elliott, J. H. *Atlantic Empires*. New Haven: Yale University Press, 2006.

Elton, Charles. *The Ecology of Invasions by Plants and Animals*. London: Chapman and Hall, 1958.

Emerald, John. *The Crested Serpent; or the White Tiger of the Tropics*. New York: Beadle, 1874.

Emmons, David M. "Constructed Province: History and the Making of the Last American West." *Western Historical Quarterly* 25 (1994): 437–459.

Eppinga, Jane. "Ethnic Diversity in Mining Camps." In J. Michael Canty and Michael N. Greeley, eds., *History of Mining in Arizona*. Vol. II. Tucson: Mining Club of the Southwest Foundation, 1991.

Escalante Gonzalbo, Fernando. *Ciudadanos imaginarios*. Mexico City: El Colegio de México, 1992.

Espinosa, Víctor. *El dilema del retorno*. Zamora: El Colegio de Michoacán, 1998.

Esteva-Fabregat, Claudio. *Mestizaje in Ibero-America*. Tucson: University of Arizona Press, 1995.

Estrada, William. *The Los Angeles Plaza: Sacred and Contested Space*. Austin: University of Texas Press, 2008.

Ettinger, Patrick. *Imaginary Lines: Border Enforcement and the Origins of Undocumented Immigration, 1882–1930*. Austin: University of Texas Press, 2009.

Feagin, Joe R., and Melvin P. Sikes. *Living with Racism: The Black Middle Class Experience*. Boston: Beacon Press, 1994.

Field, Joseph. *Three Years in Texas Including a View of the Texas Revolution, and an Account of the Principal Battles; Together with Descriptions of the Soil, Commercial and Agricultural Advantages, &c.* Greenfield, Mass.: J. Jones, 1836.

Fields, Barbara J. "Whiteness, Racism, and Identity." *International Labor and Working-Class History* 60 (Fall 2001): 48–56.

Fischer, David Hackett. *The Great Wave: Price Revolutions and the Rhythm of History*. New York: Oxford University Press, 1996.

Flint, Timothy. *Francis Berrian; or, The Mexican Patriot*. Boston: Cummings, Hilliard & Co., 1826.

———. *Biographical Memoir of Daniel Boone, the First Settler of Kentucky; Interspersed with Incidents in the Early Annals of the Country*. Cincinnati: N. and G. Guilford, 1833.

———. *Indian Wars of the West: Containing Biographical Sketches of Those Pioneers Who Headed the Western Settlers in Repelling the Attacks of the Savages, Together with a View of the Character, Manners, Monuments, and Antiquities of the Western Indians*. Cincinnati: E. H. Flint, 1833.

Flores, Dan. "Bison Ecology and Bison Diplomacy: The Southern Plains from 1800 to 1860." *Journal of American History* 78 (September 1991): 465–485.

Flores-Magón, R. *A la mujer*. Oakland, Calif.: Prensa Sembradora, 1974.

Florescano, Enrique. *Etnia, estado y nación*. Mexico City: Taurus, 1997.

———. *National Narratives in Mexico: A History*. Trans. Nancy Hancock. Norman: University of Oklahoma Press, 2006.

Flynn, Dennis, and Arturo Giráldez. "Born with a 'Silver Spoon': The Origins of World Trade in 1571." *Journal of World History* 6, no. 2 (1995): 201–221.

———. "Cycles of Silver: Global Economic Unity through the Mid-Eighteenth Century." *Journal of World History* 13, no. 2 (2002): 391–427.

Foley, Neil. "Becoming Hispanic: Mexican Americans and the Faustian Pact with Whiteness." In Foley, ed., *Reflexiones: New Directions in Mexican American Studies* (1997).

———. *The White Scourge: Mexicans, Blacks, and Poor Whites in Texas Cotton Culture.* Berkeley: University of California Press, 1997.

Foner, Eric. *The Story of American Freedom.* New York: Norton, 1999.

Foster, James C., ed. *American Labor in the Southwest: The First Hundred Years.* Tucson: University of Arizona Press, 1982.

Fox, Geoffrey E. *Hispanic Nation: Culture, Politics, and the Constructing of Identity.* New York: Carol Publications, 1996.

Franklin, John Hope. *The Color Line: Legacy for the Twenty-First Century.* Columbia: University of Missouri Press, 1993.

Friedrich, Paul. *Agrarian Revolt in a Mexican Village.* Chicago: University of Chicago Press, 1977.

———. *The Princes of Naranja: An Essay in Anthrohistorical Method.* Austin: University of Texas Press, 1986.

Fritz, Henry E. *The Movement for Indian Assimilation, 1860–1890.* Philadelphia: University of Pennsylvania Press, 1963.

Frost, John. *Pictorial History of Mexico and the Mexican War.* Philadelphia: Thomas, Cowperthwait and Co., 1848.

Gallay, Alan. *The Indian Slave Trade: The Rise of the British Empire in the American South, 1670–1717.* New Haven: Yale University Press, 2003.

Gálvez, José de. *Informe sobre las rebeliones populares de 1767.* Mexico City: Universidad Nacional Autónoma de México, 1990.

Gamio, Manuel. *Forjando patria.* Mexico City: Editorial Porrúa, 1960.

———. *Mexican Immigration to the United States: A Study of Human Migration and Adjustment.* New York, Dover Press, 1971.

———. *The Life Story of the Mexican Immigrant: Autobiographic Documents Collected by Manuel Gamio.* Chicago: University of Chicago Press 1930. Reprint: New York: Dover Publications, 1972.

Ganguly, Keya. *States of Exception: Everyday Life and Postcolonial Identity.* Minneapolis: University of Minnesota Press, 2001.

Ganilh, Anthony. *Mexico versus Texas.* Philadelphia: Siegfried, 1838.

Gans, Herbert. *The Levittowners: Ways of Life and Politics in New Suburban Community.* New York: Pantheon, 1967.

———. *Middle American Individualism: The Future of Liberal Democracy.* New York: Free Press, 1988.

García, Mario T. *Desert Immigrants: The Mexicans of El Paso, 1880–1920.* New Haven: Yale University Press, 1981.

———. *Mexican Americans: Leadership, Ideology, and Identity, 1930–1960.* New Haven: Yale University Press, 1989.

García, Richard. *The Rise of the Mexican-American Middle Class, San Antonio, 1929–1941.* College Station: Texas A&M University Press, 1991.

Garreau, Joel. *The Nine Nations of North America.* Boston: Houghton Mifflin, 1981.

Gates, Paul Wallace. *California Ranchos and Farms, 1846–1862.* Madison: State Historical Society of Wisconsin, 1967.

———. *Land and Law in California: Essays on Land Policies.* Ames: Iowa State University Press, 1991.

Gereffi, Gary. *The Mexican Pharmaceutical Industry.* Durham, N.C.: Duke University Press, 1983.

Gibson, Charles. *The Aztecs under Spanish Rule*. Stanford: Stanford University Press, 1964.

Gilly, Adolfo. *El Cardenismo: Una utopia mexicana*. Mexico City: Cal y Arena, 1993.

Glassman, Ronald, William H. Swatos Jr., and Peter Kivisto. *For Democracy: The Noble Character and Tragic Flaw of the Middle Class*. Westport, Conn.: Greenwood Press, 1993.

Glickman, Lawrence. "Inventing the 'American Standard of Living': Gender, Race and Working-Class Identity, 1880–1925." *Labor History* 23, nos. 2–3 (1993): 221–235.

Goldberg, David Theo. *The Threat of Race: Reflections on Racial Neoliberalism*. Malden, Mass.: Blackwell, 2009.

Gómez, Laura. *Manifest Destinies: The Making of the Mexican American Race*. New York: New York University Press, 2007.

Gómez-Galvariato, Aurora, ed. *La industria textil en México*. Mexico City: Instituto Mora, 1999.

Gómez-Gutiérrez, Mariano. *La vida que yo viví: Novela histórico-liberal de la revolución mexicana*. Mexico City: N.p., 1954.

Gómez-Peña, Guillermo. *The New World Border: Prophecies, Poems & Locuras for the End of the Century*. San Francisco: City Lights, 1996.

Gómez-Quiñones, J. *Sembradores: Ricardo Flores Magón y el Partido Mexicano*. Los Angeles: University of California–Los Angeles Chicano Studies Research Center Publications, 1982.

———. *Mexican American Labor 1790–1990*. Albuquerque: University of New Mexico Press, 1994.

Gonner, Edward C. K. *Common Land and Inclosure*. London: Macmillan, 1912.

Gonzales-Day, Ken. *Lynching in the West, 1850–1935*. Durham, N.C.: Duke University Press, 2006.

González, Deena. *Refusing the Favor: The Spanish-Mexican Women of Santa Fe, 1820–1880*. New York: Oxford University Press, 1999.

González, Gilbert. *Labor and Community: Mexican Citrus Worker Villages in a Southern California County, 1900–1950*. Urbana: University of Illinois Press, 1994.

González, John M. *Border Renaissance: The Texas Centennial and the Emergence of Mexican American Literature*. Austin: University of Texas Press, 2009.

González Quiroga, Miguel. "Mexicanos in Texas during the Civil War." In Emilio Zamora, Cynthia Orozco, and Rodolfo Rocha, eds., *Mexican Americans in Texas History*. Austin: Texas State Historical Association, 2000.

González y González, Luis. *San José de Gracia: Mexican Village in Transition*. Trans. of *Pueblo en vilo* by John Upton. Austin: University of Texas Press, [1974].

Gordon, Linda. *The Great Arizona Orphan Abduction*. Cambridge: Harvard University Press, 1999.

Graf, LeRoy P. "The Economic History of the Lower Rio Grande Valley, 1820–1875." PhD dissertation, Harvard University, 1942.

Granados, Luis. *Sueñan las piedras*. Mexico City: Ediciones Era, 2003.

Greene, Jack. *Pursuits of Happiness: The Social Development of Early Modern British*

Colonies and the Formation of American Culture. Chapel Hill: University of North Carolina Press, 1988.

Greenwood, Grace. "The Volunteer." In *Greenwood Leaves: A Collection of Sketches and Letters*, 2nd series. Boston: Ticknor, Reed, and Fields, 1852.

Griswald del Castillo, Richard. *The Los Angeles Barrio, 1850–1890: A Social History*. Berkeley: University of California Press, 1979.

———. *The Treaty of Guadalupe Hidalgo*. Norman: University of Oklahoma Press, 1992.

Gruesz, Kirsten Silva. *Ambassadors of Culture: The Transamerican Origins of Latino Culture*. Princeton: Princeton University Press, 2002.

Guardino, Peter. *Peasants, Politics, and the Formation of the Mexican National State: Guerrero, 1800–1855*. Stanford: Stanford University Press, 1996.

———. *In the Time of Liberty*. Durham, N.C.: Duke University Press, 2005.

Guarisco, Claudia. *Los indios del Valle de México y la construcción de una nueva sociabilidad política, 1770–1835*. Zinacatepec: El Colegio Mexiquense, 2003.

Guerin-Gonzales, Camille. "The International Migration of Workers and Segmented Labor: Mexican Immigrant Workers in California Industrial Agriculture, 1900–1940." In Camille Guerin-Gonzales and Carl Strikwerda, eds., *The Politics of Immigrant Workers: Labor Activism and Migration in the World Economy since 1830*. New York: Holmes & Meier, 1993.

Guerra, François-Xavier. *Modernidades e independencias*. Mexico City: Fondo de Cultura Económica, 1993.

Guevara Sanginés, María. *Guanajuato diverso: Sabores y sinsabores de su ser mestizo*. Guanajuato: Ediciones La Rana, 2001.

Gump, James. *The Dust Rose Like Smoke: The Subjugation of the Zulu and the Sioux*. Lincoln: University of Nebraska Press, 1994.

Gutiérrez, David. *Walls and Mirrors: Mexican Americans, Mexican Immigrants, and the Politics of Ethnicity*. Berkeley: University of California Press, 1995.

———. "Shifting Politics of Nationalism in Greater Mexico." *Journal of American History* 86, no. 2 (1999): 481–517.

Gutiérrez, Ramón A. *When Jesus Came the Corn Mothers Went Away*. Stanford: Stanford University Press, 1991.

Gutmann, Matthew. *The Meanings of Macho*. 2nd ed. Berkeley: University of California Press, 2006.

Guy, Donna, and Thomas E. Sheridan, eds. *Contested Ground: Comparative Frontiers on the Northern and Southern Edges of the Spanish Empire*. Tucson: University of Arizona Press, 1998.

Haas, L. *Conquest and Historical Identities in California*. Berkeley: University of California Press, 1995.

Haber, Stephen, Armando Razo, and Noel Maurer. *The Politics of Property Rights: Political Instability, Credible Commitments, and Economic Growth in Mexico, 1876–1929*. Cambridge: Cambridge University Press, 2003.

Hackel, Steven. "Land, Labor, and Production: The Colonial Economy of Spanish and Mexican California." In Ramón A. Gutiérrez and Richard J. Orsi, eds., *Contested Eden: California before the Gold Rush*. Berkeley: University of California Press, 1998.

———. *Children of Coyote, Missionaries of Saint Francis: Indian-Spanish Relations in Colonial California, 1769–1850*. Chapel Hill: University of North Carolina Press, 2005.

Hagan, William T. "Adjusting to the Opening of the Kiowa, Comanche, and Kiowa-Apache Reservation." In Peter Iverson, ed., *The Plains Indians of the Twentieth Century*. Norman: University of Oklahoma Press, 1985.

Hale, Grace Elizabeth. *Making Whiteness: The Culture of Segregation in the South, 1890–1940*. New York: Vintage Books, 1999.

Hall, William Jared. *The Slave Sculptor; or, The Prophetess of the Secret Chamber. A Tale of Mexico at the Period of the Conquest*. New York: Beadle, 1860.

Hämäläinen, Pekka. *The Comanche Empire*. New Haven: Yale University Press, 2009.

Hamill, Hugh. *The Hidalgo Revolt*. Gainesville: University of Florida Press, 1966.

Hamilton, Nora. *The Limits of State Autonomy: Post-Revolutionary Mexico*. Princeton: Princeton University Press, 1982.

Hammond, J. L., and B. Hammond. *The Village Labourer, 1760–1832: A Study in the Government of England before the Reform Bill*. London: Longman's, 1912.

Hamnet, Brian. *Roots of Insurgency: Mexican Regions, 1750–1825*. Cambridge: Cambridge University Press, 1986.

Haney López, Ian F. *White by Law: The Legal Construction of Race*. New York: New York University Press, 1997.

Hart, John. *Empire and Revolution*. Berkeley: University of California Press, 2002.

Haskett, Bert. "Early History of the Cattle Industry in Arizona." *Arizona Historical Review* 6, no. 4 (October 1935): 3–42.

Hathaway, Roger D. "Unlawful Love: A History of Arizona's Miscegenation Law." *Journal of Arizona History* 27 (Winter 1986): 377–390.

Hennessy, Charles. *The Frontier in Latin American History*. Albuquerque: University of New Mexico Press, 1978.

Hernstein, Richard J., and Charles Murray. *The Bell Curve: Intelligence and Class Structure in American Life*. New York: Free Press, 1994.

Herrejón Peredo, Carlos. *Hidalgo*. Mexico City: Secretaría de Educación Pública, 1986.

Hewitt de Alcántara, Cynthia. *Modernizing Mexican Agriculture*. Geneva: United Nations, 1976.

Hinderaker, Eric, and Peter C. Mancall, eds. *At the Edge of Empire: The Backcountry in British North America*. Baltimore: Johns Hopkins University Press, 2003.

Hoebel, E. Adamson. *The Cheyennes: Indians of the Great Plains*. 2nd ed. Fort Worth, Tex.: Holt, Rinehart, and Winston, 1978.

Holden, Robert H. "Priorities of the State in the Survey of the Public Lands in Mexico, 1876–1911." *Hispanic American Historical Review* 70 (November 1990): 579–608.

Holt, Michael. *The Rise and Fall of the American Whig Party*. New York: Oxford University Press, 1999.

———. *The Fate of Their Country: Politicians, Slavery Extension, and the Coming of the Civil War*. New York: Hill and Wang, 2005.

Hondagneu-Sotelo, Pierrette. *Gendered Transitions*. Berkeley: University of California Press, 1994.

————, ed. *Gender and U.S. Immigration*. Berkeley: University of California Press, 2003.

Hornbeck, David. "Land Tenure and Rancho Expansion in Alta California, 1784–1846." *Journal of Historical Geography* 4 (1978): 371–390.

Horsman, Reginald. *Race and Manifest Destiny: The Origins of American Racial Anglo-Saxonism*. Cambridge: Harvard University Press, 1981.

Howe, Carolyn. *Political Ideology and Class Formation: A Study of the Middle Class*. Westport, Conn.: Praeger, 1992.

Hu-DeHart, Evelyn. *Yaqui Resistance and Survival: The Struggle for Land and Autonomy, 1821–1910*. Madison: University of Wisconsin Press, 1984.

Huginnie, Yvette. "'Strikitos': Race, Class and Work in the Arizona Copper Industry, 1870–1920." PhD dissertation, Yale University, 1991.

————. "Mexican Labour in a 'White Man's Town': Racialism, Imperialism, and Industrialization in the Making of Arizona, 1840–1905." In Peter Alexander and Rick Halpern, eds., *Racializing Class, Classifying Race: Labour and Difference in Britain, the USA, and Africa*. New York: St. Martin's Press, 2000.

Hurtado, Albert L. *Indian Survival on the California Frontier*. New Haven: Yale University Press, 1988.

————. "California Indians and the Workaday West: Labor, Assimilation, and Survival." *California History* (1990): 2–11.

————. *Intimate Frontiers: Sex, Gender, and Culture in Old California*. Albuquerque: University of New Mexico Press, 1999.

Ibarra Bellón, Araceli. *El comercio y el poder en México, 1821–1864*. Mexico City: Fondo de Cultura Económica, 1998.

Ignacio-Taibo, P. *Bolshevikis*. Mexico City: Editorial Joaquín Mortiz, 1986.

Ingold, Tim. *Hunters, Pastoralists, and Ranchers: Reindeer Economies and Their Transformations*. Cambridge: Cambridge University Press, 1980.

Ingraham, J. H. *Montezuma the Serf; or the Revolt of the Mexitili. A Tale of the Last Days of the Aztec Dynasty*. Boston: H. L. Williams, 1845.

Irby, James A. *Backdoor at Bagdad: The Civil War on the Rio Grande*. El Paso: Texas Western Press, 1977.

Isaacs, Harold. *Images of Asia*. New York: Harper and Row, 1972.

Isenberg, Andrew. *The Destruction of the Bison: An Environmental History, 1750–1920*. New York: Cambridge University Press, 2000, 2001.

————. "The Wild and the Tamed: Indians, Euroamericans, and the Destruction of the Bison." In Mary Henninger-Voss, ed., *Animals in Human Histories*. Rochester, N.Y.: University of Rochester Press, 2002.

————. "'To See Inside of an Indian': Missionaries and Dakotas in the Minnesota Borderlands." In Kenneth Mills and Anthony Grafton, eds., *Conversion: Old Worlds and New*. Rochester, N.Y.: University of Rochester Press, 2003.

————. *Mining California: An Ecological History*. New York: Hill and Wang, 2006.

Iverson, Peter. *When Indians Became Cowboys: Native Peoples and Cattle Ranching in the American West*. Norman: University of Oklahoma Press, 1994.

Jacobsen, Cardell. "Internal Colonialism and Native Americans: Indian Labor in the United States from 1871 to WWII." *Social Science Quarterly* 65, no. 1 (March 1984): 158–171.

Jacobson, Matthew F. *Whiteness of a Different Color: European Immigrants and the Alchemy of Race*. Cambridge: Harvard University Press, 1998.

Jacoby, Karl. *Shadows at Dawn: The Camp Grant Massacre and the Borderlands of History*. New York: Penguin Press, 2008.

Jameson, Elizabeth. *All That Glitters: Class, Conflict, and Community in Cripple Creek*. Urbana: University of Illinois, 1998.

Jiménez, Tomás. *Replenished Ethnicity: Mexican Americans, Immigration, and Identity*. Berkeley: University of California Press, 2010.

Johannsen, Robert. *To the Halls of the Montezumas: The Mexican War in the American Imagination*. New York: Oxford University Press, 1985.

Johnsen, Thomas N. "One-Seed Juniper Invasion of Northern Arizona Grasslands." *Ecological Monographs* 32 (Summer 1962): 187–207.

Johnson, Arthur H. *The Disappearance of the Small Landowner*. London: Oxford University Press, 1963.

Johnson, Benjamin H. *Revolution in Texas: How a Forgotten Rebellion and Its Bloody Suppression Turned Mexicans into Americans*. New Haven: Yale University Press, 2003.

Johnson, Susan. "'A Memory Sweet to Soldiers': The Significance of Gender in the American West." *Western Historical Quarterly* 24, no. 3 (November 1993): 495.

———. *Roaring Camp: The Social World of the California Gold Rush*. New York: Norton, 2000, 2002.

Johnston, Robert D. *The Radical Middle Class: Populist Democracy and the Question of Capitalism in Progressive Era Portland, Oregon*. Princeton: Princeton University Press. 2003.

Jones, Kristine L. "Comparative Raiding Economies: North and South." In Donna Guy and Thomas E. Sheridan, eds., *Contested Ground: Comparative Frontiers on the Northern and Southern Edges of the Spanish Empire*. Tucson: University of Arizona Press, 1998.

Jordan, Terry. *North American Cattle-Ranching Frontiers: Origins, Diffusion, Differentiation*. Albuquerque: University of New Mexico Press, 1993.

Judt, Tony. "What Is Living and What Is Dead in Social Democracy?" *New York Review of Books* 57 (December 17, 2009): 86–96.

Kamen, Henry. *Empire*. New York: HarperCollins, 2003.

Kearney, Michael, *Reconceptualizing the Peasantry*. Boulder, Colo.: Westview Press, 1996.

Kelly, Lawrence C., ed. *Navajo Roundup: Selected Correspondence of Kit Carson's Expedition against the Navajo, 1863–1865*. Boulder, Colo.: Pruett, 1970.

Kerby, Robert L. *Kirby Smith's Confederacy: The Trans-Mississippi South, 1863–1865*. Tuscaloosa: University of Alabama Press, 1972.

Kicza, John E. "The Great Families of Mexico: Elite Maintenance and Business Practices in Late Colonial Mexico City." *Hispanic American Historical Review* 62, no. 3 (August 1982): 429–457.

King, Clarence. *The United States Mining Laws and Regulations Thereunder, and State and Territorial Mining Laws, to Which Are Appended Local Mining Rules and Regulations*. Washington, D.C., 1885.

Klein, Alan. "The Political Economy of Gender: A 19th-Century Plains Indian

Case Study." In Patricia Albers and Beatrice Medicine, eds., *The Hidden Half: Studies of Plains Indian Women.* Washington, D.C.: University Press of America, 1983.

Klein, Herbert H. *African Slavery in Latin America and the Caribbean.* New York: Oxford University Press, 1986.

Knack, Martha C. "Nineteenth-Century Great Basin Indian Wage Labor." In Alice Littlefield and Martha Knack, eds., *Native Americans and Wage Labor: Ethnohistorical Perspectives.* Norman: University of Oklahoma Press, 1996.

Knight, Alan. "Racism, Revolution, and *Indigenismo*: Mexico, 1910–1940." In Richard Graham, ed., *The Idea of Race in Latin America, 1870–1940.* Austin: University of Texas Press, 1990.

Knight, Larry. "The Cart War: Defining American in San Antonio in the 1850s." *Southwestern Historical Quarterly* 109, no. 3 (January 2006).

Kolchin, Peter. "Whiteness Studies: The New History of Race in America." *Journal of American History* 89 (June 2002): 154–173.

Kraenzel, Friedrich. *The Great Plains in Transition.* Norman: University of Oklahoma Press, 1955.

Kuntz, John. "The Young Master." *Newsweek* (April 28, 1997): 58–62.

Kurashige, Scott. *The Shifting Grounds of Race: Black and Japanese Americans in the Making of Multiethnic Los Angeles.* Princeton: Princeton University Press, 2008.

Lack, Paul. *The Texas Revolutionary Experience.* College Station: Texas A&M University Press, 1992.

Ladd, Doris. *The Making of a Strike: Mexican Silver Worker's Struggles in Real del Monte, 1766–1767.* Lincoln: University of Nebraska Press, 1988.

Lamar, Howard. "From Bondage to Contract: Ethnic Labor in the American West, 1600–1890." In Stephen Hahn and Jonathan Prude, eds., *The Countryside in the Age of Capitalist Transformation: Essays in the Social History of Rural America.* Chapel Hill: University of North Carolina Press, 1985.

———. *The Far Southwest, 1846–1912: A Territorial History.* Rev. ed. Albuquerque: University of New Mexico Press, 2000.

———, and Leonard Thompson. "The North American and Southern African Frontiers." In *The Frontier in History: North American and Southern Africa Compared.* New Haven: Yale University Press, 1981.

Landrum, Francis S., ed. *Guardhouse, Gallows, and Graves: The Trial and Execution of Indian Prisoners of the Modoc Indian War by the U.S. Army.* Klamath Falls, Ore.: Klamath County Museum, 1988.

Langley, Lester D. *MexAmerica: Two Countries, One Future.* New York: Crown Publishers, 1988.

Langston, Nancy. *Forest Dreams, Forest Nightmares: The Paradox of Old Growth in the Inland West.* Seattle: University of Washington Press, 1995.

Lapchick, R. E. "Lessons of Tiger Woods Will Not Be Easy Ones: Floodgates May Not Open, but Perhaps Minds Will." *New York Times* (May 18, 1997): S9.

Lara Cisneros, Gerardo. *El cristianismo en el espejo indígena.* Mexico City: Archivo General de la Nación, 2002.

Laviera, Tato. *AmeRícan.* Houston, Tex.: Arte Público Press, 1985.

Lazo, Rodrigo. *Writing to Cuba: Filibustering and Cuban Exiles in the United States.* Chapel Hill: University of North Carolina Press, 2005.

Lee, Erika. *At America's Gates: Chinese Immigration during the Exclusion Era, 1882–1943*. Chapel Hill: University of North Carolina Press, 2003.

Lee, Richard B. "What Hunters Do for a Living, or, How to Make Out on Scarce Resources." In Richard B. Lee and Irven DeVore, eds., *Man the Hunter*. Chicago: Aldine, 1968.

Leiken, Robert S. *A New Moment in the Americas*. New Brunswick, N.J.: Transaction Publishers, 1994.

Leonard, Kevin. *The Battle for Los Angeles: Racial Ideology and World War II*. Albuquerque: University of New Mexico Press, 2006.

Lerner, Jesse. "Imported Nationalism." *Evil Winter* 5 (2001–2002).

Lewis, A. "The Basis of Solidarity." *New Review* 3 (1915): 186.

Limerick, Patricia Nelson. *The Legacy of Conquest*. New York: Norton, 1987.

———, Clyde A. Milner II, and Charles E. Rankin, eds. *Trails: Toward a New Western History*. Lawrence: University Press of Kansas, 1991.

Limón, José E. "El Primer Congreso Mexicanista: de 1911: A Precursor to Contemporary Chicanismo." *Aztlán* 5 (1974): 85–118.

———. *American Encounters*. Boston: Beacon Press, 1998.

Lippard, George. *Legends of Mexico*. Philadelphia: T. B. Peterson, 1847.

———. "'Bel of Prairie Eden: A Romance of Mexico" (1848). In Jesse Alemán and Shelley Streeby, *Empire and the Literature of Sensation: An Anthology of Nineteenth-Century Popular Fiction*. New Brunswick, N.J.: Rutgers University Press, 2007.

Lipsitz, George. *The Possessive Investment in Whiteness: How White People Profit from Identity Politics*. Philadelphia: Temple University Press, 1998.

Littlefield, Alice, and Martha Knack, eds. *Native Americans and Wage Labor: Ethnohistorical Perspectives*. Norman: University of Oklahoma Press, 1996.

Lizza, Ryan. "Return of the Nativist: Behind the Republicans' Anti-Immigration Frenzy." *New Yorker* (December 17, 2007): 46–51.

Loewen, James W. *Sundown Towns: A Hidden Dimension of American Racism*. New York: Touchstone Books, 2006.

López Austin, Alfredo, and Leonardo López Luján. *El pasado indígena*. Rev. ed. Mexico City: Fondo de Cultura Económica, 2001.

Lowell, James Russell. *Biglow Papers*. Ed. Thomas Wortham. DeKalb: Northern Illinois University Press, 1977. (1st series, 1848.)

Lynd, Robert Staughton. *Middletown: A Study in American Culture*. New York: Harcourt, Brace, 1929.

MacCameron, Robert. "Environmental Change in Colonial New Mexico." *Environmental History Review* 18 (1994): 17–39.

Maharidge, Dale. *The Coming White Minority: California's Eruptions and America's Future*. New York: Vintage, 1996.

Mallon, Florencia. *Peasant and Nation: The Making of Post-Colonial Mexico and Peru*. Berkeley: University of California Press, 1995.

Marichal, Carlos. *La bancarrota del virreinato*. Mexico City: Fondo de Cultura Económica, 1999.

Marks, Paula Mitchell. *And Die in the West: The Story of the O.K. Corral Gunfight*. Reprint. Norman: University of Oklahoma Press, 1996.

Martin, Cheryl English. *Rural Society in Colonial Morelos.* Albuquerque: University of New Mexico Press, 1985.

———. *Governance and Society in Colonial Mexico: Chihuahua in the Eighteenth Century.* Stanford: Stanford University Press, 1996.

Martínez, P. L. *A History of Lower California.* Mexico City: Editorial Baja California, 1960.

Massey, Douglas, et al. *Return to Aztlán.* Berkeley: University of California Press, 1985.

———. *Beyond Smoke and Mirrors.* Albany, N.Y.: Russell Sage Foundation, 2003.

Matovina, Timothy. *The Alamo Remembered: Tejano Accounts and Perspectives.* Austin: University of Texas Press, 1995.

Maturin, Edward. *Montezuma, the Last of the Aztecs. A Romance.* New York: Paine and Burgess, 1845.

May, Martha. "The Historical Problem of the Family Wage: The Ford Motor Company and the Five Dollar Day." *Feminist Studies* 8, no. 2 (Summer 1982): 399–424.

Mayer, Brantz. *Mexico: Aztec, Spanish, and Republican.* Hartford, Conn.: S. Drake, 1850.

Mazumdar, Sucheta. "Race and Racism: South Asians in the United States." In Gail M. Nomura, Russell Endo, Stephan H. Sumida, and Russell C. Leong, eds., *Frontiers of Asian American Studies: Writing, Research and Commentary.* Pullman: Washington State University Press, 1989.

McBride, James D. "Gaining a Foothold in the Paradise of Capitalism: The Western Federation of Miners and the Unionization of Bisbee." *Journal of Arizona History* 23 (Autumn 1982): 299–316.

McCraver, Rebecca McDowell. *The Impact of Intimacy: Mexican-Anglo Intermarriage in New Mexico, 1821–1846.* El Paso: Texas Western Press, 1982.

McCusker, John, and Russell Menard. *The Economy of British America, 1607–1789.* Chapel Hill: University of North Carolina Press, 1985.

McEuen, W. W. "A Survey of the Mexicans in Los Angeles 1910–1914." MA thesis, University of Southern California, 1914.

McGinnis, Dru. "The Influence of Organized Labor on the Making of the Arizona Constitution." MA thesis, University of Arizona, 1930.

McKenna, Teresa. "Collecting against Forgetting: East of the River: Chicano Art Collectors Anonymous." In Richard Meyer, ed., *Representing the Passions: Histories, Bodies, Visions.* Los Angeles: Getty Research Institute, 2003.

McNeill, Williams. *Plagues and Peoples.* New York: Anchor, 1976.

McWilliams, Carey. *North from Mexico: The Spanish-Speaking People of the United States.* Reprint. New York: Praeger, 1990.

Meeks, Eric V. "The Tohono O'Odham, Wage Labor, and Resistant Adaptation, 1900–1930." *Western Historical Quarterly* 30 (Winter 1999): 449–473.

———. *Border Citizens: The Making of Indians, Mexicans, and Anglos in Arizona.* Austin: University of Texas Press, 2007.

Mellinger, P. J. *Race and Labor in Western Copper: The Fight for Equality, 1896–1918.* Tucson: University of Arizona Press, 1995.

———. "How the IWW Lost Its Western Heartland: Western Labor History Revisited." *Western Historical Quarterly* 27 (1996): 303–324.

Melville, Elinor G. K. *A Plague of Sheep: Environmental Consequences of the Conquest of Mexico*. New York: Cambridge University Press, 1997.

Menchaca, Martha. "Chicano Indianism: A Historical Account of Racial Repression in the United States." *American Ethnologist* 20, no. 3 (1993): 583-603.

————. *Recovering History, Constructing Race: The Indian, Black, and White Roots of Mexican Americans*. Austin: University of Texas Press, 2002.

Miller, Crane S., and Richard S. Hyslop. *California: The Geography of Diversity*. Mountain View, Calif.: Mayfield Publishing, 1983.

Miller, Darlis A. "Cross-Cultural Marriages in the Southwest: The New Mexico Experience, 1846-1900." In Darlis A. Miller and Joan M. Jensen, eds., *New Mexico Women: Intercultural Perspectives*. Albuquerque: University of New Mexico Press, 1986.

————, and Joan M. Jensen, eds. *New Mexico Women: Intercultural Perspectives*. Albuquerque: University of New Mexico Press, 1986.

Milner, Clyde A., II. "National Initiatives." In Clyde A. Milner, Carol A. O'Connor, and Martha Sandweiss, eds., *The Oxford History of the American West*. New York: Oxford University Press, 1994.

Mingay, G. E. *Parliamentary Enclosure in England: An Introduction to its Causes, Incidence, and Impact 1750-1850*. London: Longman, 1997.

Mishkin, Bernard. *Rank and Warfare among the Plains Indians*. Lincoln: University of Nebraska Press, 1992.

Mitchell, Pablo. *Coyote Nation: Sexuality, Race, and Conquest in Modernizing New Mexico, 1880-1920*. Chicago: University of Chicago Press, 2005.

Moises, R. *A Yaqui Life: The Personal Chronicle of a Yaqui Indian*. Lincoln: University of Nebraska Press, 1971.

Molina, Natalia. *Fit to Be Citizens?: Public Health and Race in Los Angeles, 1879-1939*. Berkeley: University of California Press, 2006.

Monroy, D. "Anarquismo y Comunismo: Mexican Radicalism and the Communist Party in Los Angeles during the 1930s." *Labor History* 24, no. 1 (1983): 34-59.

Monroy, J. G. *Ricardo Flores Magón y su actitud en la Baja California*. Mexico City: Editorial Academia Literaria, 1962.

Montejano, David. *Anglos and Mexicans in the Making of Texas, 1836-1986*. Austin: University of Texas Press, 1986.

————. *Quixote's Soldiers: A Local History of the Chicano Movement, 1966-1981*. Austin: University of Texas Press, 2010.

Montoya, María E. *Translating Property: The Maxwell Land Grant and Conflict over Land in the American West, 1840-1900*. Berkeley: University of California Press, 2002.

Morgan, Edmund, and Helen Morgan. *The Stamp Act Crisis*. Chapel Hill: University of North Carolina Press, 1995.

Mörner, Magnus. *Race Mixture in the History of Latin America*. Boston: Little Brown, 1967.

————. "The Spanish American Hacienda: A Survey of Recent Research and Debate." *Hispanic American Historical Review* 53 (May 1973): 183-216.

Morrison, Michael. *Slavery and the American West*. Chapel Hill: University of North Carolina Press, 1999.

Murphy, Gretchen. *Hemispheric Imaginings: The Monroe Doctrine and Narratives of U.S. Empire*. Durham, N.C.: Duke University Press, 2005.

Neeson, J. M. *Commoners: Common Right, Enclosure, and Social Change in England, 1700–1820*. Cambridge: Cambridge University Press, 1993.

Ngai, Mae. *Impossible Subjects: Illegal Aliens and the Making of Modern America*. Princeton: Princeton University Press, 2004.

Nicolaus, Martin. "Proletariat and Middle Class in Marx: Hegelian Choreography and the Capitalist Dialectic." *Studies on the Left* 7 (1967): 12–27.

Nieto-Phillips, John M. *The Language of Blood: The Making of Spanish-American Identity in New Mexico, 1880s–1930s*. Albuquerque: University of New Mexico Press, 2004.

Nudelman, Franny. *John Brown's Body: Slavery, Violence, and the Culture of War*. Chapel Hill: University of North Carolina Press, 2004.

Officer, James. *Arizona's Hispanic Perspective: A Research Report*. Phoenix: Arizona Town Hall, 1981.

———. *Hispanic Arizona, 1536–1856*. Tucson: University of Arizona Press, 1987.

Olmstead, Frederick Law. *A Journey through Texas; or, a Saddle-Trip on the Southwestern Frontier*. New York: Dix, Edwards & Co., 1857. Reprint: Austin: University of Texas Press, 1978.

Omi, Michael, and Howard Winant. *Racial Formations in the United States, from the 1960s to the 1990s*. New York: Routledge, 1994.

O'Neill, Colleen. "Domesticity Deployed: Gender, Race, and the Construction of Class Struggle in the Bisbee Deportation." *Labor History* 34, nos. 2–3 (Summer 1993): 256–273.

Orenstein, Dara. "Void for Vagueness: Mexicans and the Collapse of Miscegenation Law in California." *Pacific Historical Review* 74, no. 3 (2005): 367–407.

Ortega Soto, Martha. *Alta California: Una frontera olvidada del noroeste de México, 1769–1846*. Mexico City: Universidad Autónoma Metropolitana, 2001.

Ortiz Escamilla, Juan. *Guerra y gobierno: Los pueblos y la independencia de México*. Seville: Universidad de Sevilla, 1997.

Ortner, Sherry B. *New Jersey Dreaming: Capital, Culture, and the Class of '58*. Durham, N.C.: Duke University Press, 2003.

Otto, J. S., and N. E. Anderson. "Cattle Ranching in the Venezuelan Llanos and the Florida Flatwoods." *Comparative Studies in Society and History* 28 (October 1986): 672–683.

Owensby, Brian. *Empire of Law and Indian Justice in Colonial Mexico*. Stanford: Stanford University Press, 2008.

Padilla, Genaro. *"My History, Not Yours": The Formation of Mexican American Autobiography*. Madison: University of Wisconsin Press, 1993.

Park, Joseph. "The History of Mexican Labor in Arizona during the Territorial Period." MA thesis, University of Arizona, 1961.

Parker, Theodore. *Sermons on War* (1847). Ed. Francis Cobbe. New York: Garland Publishing, 1973.

Pascoe, Peggy. "Race, Gender, and Intercultural Relations: The Case of Interracial Marriage." *Frontiers* 12 (1991): 5–18.

———. "Miscegenation Laws, Court Cases, and Ideologies of 'Race' in Twentieth-Century America." *Journal of American History* 83, no. 1 (June 1996): 44–69.

Patterson, Orlando. "The Emerging West Atlantic System: Migration, Culture, and Underdevelopment in the United States and the Circum-Caribbean Region." In William Alonso, ed., *Population in an Interacting World*. Cambridge: Harvard University Press, 1987.

———. "Cultural Transmission and the American Cosmos." In Robert S. Leiken, ed., *A New Moment in the Americas*. New Brunswick, N.J.: Transaction Publishers, 1994.

Paul, Rodman. *Mining Frontiers of the Far West, 1848–1890*. Rev. and exp. Elliott West. Albuquerque: University of New Mexico Press, 2001.

Pawel, Miriam. *The Union of Their Dreams: Power, Hope, and Struggle in Cesar Chavez's Farm Worker Movement*. New York: Bloomsbury Press, 2009.

Paz, Octavio. *The Labyrinth of Solitude*. New York: Grove Press, 1961.

Pearson, Georgia A. *Race and Representation*. New Brunswick, N.J.: Transaction Publishers, 1997.

Peck, Gunther. *Reinventing Free Labor: Padrones and Immigrant Workers in the North American West, 1880–1930*. New York: Cambridge University Press, 2000.

Peña, Manuel H. *The Texas-Mexican Conjunto: History of a Working Class Music*. Austin: University of Texas Press, 1985.

Pérez, E. *The Decolonial Imaginary: Writing Chicanas into History*. Bloomington: Indiana University Press, 1999.

Pérez Rosales, Laura. *Minería y sociedad en Taxco durante el siglo XVIII*. Mexico City: Universidad Iberoamericana, 1996.

Perkin, Harold. *Origins of Modern English Society*. London: Routledge, 1969.

Pew Hispanic Center. *2007 National Survey of Latinos: As Illegal Immigration Issue Heats Up, Hispanics Feel a Chill*. Washington, D.C., 2007.

———. *A Statistical Portrait of Hispanics at Mid-Decade*. Washington, D.C., 2008.

Pitt, Leonard. *Decline of the Californios: A Social History of Spanish-Speaking California, 1846–1890*. Berkeley: University of California Press, 1966. Rev. ed., Berkeley: University of California Press, 1999.

Pletcher, David. *Rails, Mines, and Progress*. Ithaca, N.Y.: Cornell University Press, 1958.

———. "Mexico Opens the Door to American Capital, 1877–1880." *The Americas* 16, no. 1 (July 1959): 1–14.

Portes, Alejandro, ed. *The New Second Generation*. New York: Russell Sage, 1996.

Potash, Robert. *El Banco de Avío de México: El fomento de la industria, 1821–1846*. Mexico City: Fondo de Cultura Económica, 1959.

Potter, D. M., and P. Knepper. "Comparing Official Definitions of Race in Japan and the United States." In Joan Ferrante and Prince Brown, eds., *The Social Construction of Race and Ethnicity in the United States*. New York: Longman, 1998.

Powell, Philip. *Mexico's Miguel Caldera: The Taming of America's First Frontier*. Tucson: University of Arizona Press, 1977.

———. *La guerra chichimeca, 1550–1600*. Trans. Juan José Utrilla. Mexico City: Fondo de Cultura Económica, 1994.

Powers, Stephen. "A Pony Ride on Pit River." *Overland Monthly* 13 (October 1874): 347.

Prescott, W. H. *History of the Conquest of Mexico* (1843). New York: Modern Library, 1998.

Pulling, Hazel Adele. "A History of California's Range-Cattle Industry, 1770–1912." PhD dissertation, University of Southern California, 1944.

Purnell, Jennie. "With All Due Respect: Popular Resistance to the Privatization of Communal Lands in Nineteenth-Century Michoacán." *Latin American Research Review* 34 (1999): 85–121.

Radding, Cynthia. *Wandering Peoples: Colonialism, Ethnic Spaces, and Ecological Frontiers in Northwestern Mexico, 1700–1850.* Durham, N.C.: Duke University Press, 1997.

Ramos, Raúl. *Beyond the Alamo: Forging Mexican American Ethnicity in San Antonio, 1821–1861.* Chapel Hill: University of North Carolina Press, 2008.

Ramos, Samuel. *Profile of Man and Culture in Mexico.* Austin: University of Texas Press, 1962.

Reed, Nelson. *The Caste War of Yucatán.* Stanford: Stanford University Press, 1964.

Reich, Robert B. "Who Is Us?" *Harvard Business Review* 68, no. 1 (1990): 53–63.

Reina, Leticia. "The Sierra Gorda Peasant Rebellion, 1847–1850." In Friedrich Katz, ed., *Riot, Rebellion, and Revolution: Rural Social Conflict in Mexico.* Princeton: Princeton University Press, 1988.

Reisler, Mark. *By the Sweat of Their Brow.* Westport, Conn.: Greenwood Press, 1977.

Reséndez, Andrés. *Changing National Identities at the Frontier: Texas and New Mexico, 1800–1850.* Cambridge: Cambridge University Press, 2004, 2006.

Richardson, Chad. *Batos, Bolillos, Pochos, and Pelados: Class and Culture on the South Texas Border.* Austin: University of Texas Press, 1999.

Richter, Daniel. *Facing East from Indian Country: A Native History of Early America.* Cambridge: Harvard University Press, 2001.

Ricklis, Robert. *The Karankawa Indians of Texas.* Austin: University of Texas Press, 1996.

Ríos-Bustamente, Antonio. *Los Ángeles: Pueblo y región, 1769–1846.* Mexico City: Instituto Nacional de Antropología e Historia, 1991.

Rivas-Rodríguez, Maggie, ed. *Mexican Americans and World War II.* Austin: University of Texas Press, 2005.

Robinett, Dan. "Tohono O'odham Range History." *Rangelands* 12 (December 1990): 296–300.

Rodríguez, Clara. "Racial Classification among Puerto Rican Men and Women in New York." *Hispanic Journal of Behavioral Sciences* 12 (1990): 366–380.

———. "The Effect of Race on Puerto Rican Wages." In Edwin Meléndez, Clara Rodríguez, and Janis Barry, eds., *Hispanics in the Labor Force: Issues and Policies.* New York: Plenum Press, 1991.

Rodríguez, Gregory. *Mongrels, Bastards, Orphans, and Vagabonds: Mexican Immigration and the Future of Race in America.* New York: Vintage, 2007.

Rodríguez, Richard. *Hunger of Memory: The Education of Richard Rodríguez.* Boston: David R. Godine, 1982.

———. *Days of Obligation: An Argument with My Mexican Father.* New York: Penguin Books, 1992.

———. *Brown: The Last Discovery of America.* New York: Penguin Books, 2002.

Rodríguez, Sylvia. *The Matachines Dance: Ritual Symbolism and Interethnic Relations in the Upper Rio Grande Valley.* Albuquerque: University of New Mexico Press, 1996.

Roediger, David R. *Towards the Abolition of Whiteness: Essays on Race, Politics, and Working Class History.* New York, Verso Books, 1994.

———. *The Wages of Whiteness: Race and the Making of the American Working Class.* 2nd ed. New York: Verso Books, 2007.

Rolle, Andrew. *The Lost Cause: The Confederate Exodus to Mexico.* Norman: University of Oklahoma Press, 1992.

Rollins, Ralph. "Labor Situation in Arizona Points to Mexicanization." *Arizona Mining Journal* 4 (July 1920): 13–14.

Rosenbaum, Robert J. *Mexicano Resistance in the Southwest.* Dallas, Tex.: Southern Methodist University Press, 1998.

Rothbart, Ron. "'Homes Are What Any Strike Is About': Immigrant Labor and the Family Wage." *Journal of Social History* 23, no. 2 (1989): 267–284.

Rugeley, Terry. *Yucatan's Maya Peasantry and the Origins of the Caste War.* Austin: University of Texas Press, 1996.

Ruiz, Vicki. *Out of the Shadows.* New York: Oxford University Press, 1998.

Salas, Miguel Tinker. *In the Shadow of the Eagles: Sonora and the Transformation of the Border during the Porfiriato.* Berkeley: University of California Press, 1997.

Saldívar, José David. *The Dialectics of Our America: Genealogy, Cultural Critique, and Literary History.* Durham, N.C.: Duke University Press, 1991.

———. *Border Matters: Remapping American Cultural Studies.* Berkeley: University of California Press, 1997.

Salerno, S. *Red November Black November: Culture and Community in the Industrial Workers of the World.* Albany: State University of New York Press, 1989.

Salvatore, Ricardo D. "Modes of Labor Control in Cattle—Ranching Economies: California, Southern Brazil, and Argentina, 1820–1860." *Journal of Economic History* 51, no. 2 (June 1991): 441–451.

Sánchez, Rosaura. *Telling Identities: The Californio Testimonios.* Minneapolis: University of Minnesota Press, 1995.

Sandos, J. A. *Rebellion in the Borderlands: Anarchism and the Plan of San Diego, 1904–1923.* Norman: University of Oklahoma Press, 1992.

Sandweiss, Martha A. *Eyewitness to War: Prints and Daguerreotypes of the Mexican War, 1846–1848.* Fort Worth, Tex.: Amon Carter Museum, 1989.

Savage, Melissa, and Thomas W. Sweetnam. "Early 19th-Century Fire Decline Following Sheep Pasturing in a Navajo Ponderosa Pine Forest." *Ecology* 71 (December 1990), 2374–2378.

Savala, R. *The Autobiography of a Yaqui Poet.* Tucson: University of Arizona Press, 1980.

Saxton, Alexander, with David Roediger. *The Rise and Fall of the White Republic: Class Politics and Mass Culture in Nineteenth-Century America.* 2nd ed. London: Verso Books, 2003.

Scadron, Arlene, ed. *On Their Own: Widows and Widowhood in the American Southwest, 1848–1939.* Urbana: University of Illinois Press, 1988.

Scharff, Virginia. *Twenty Thousand Roads: Women, Movement, and the West.* Berkeley: University of California Press, 2003.

Schell, Paul, and John Hamer. "Cascadia: The New Binationalism of Western Canada and the U.S. Pacific Northwest." In Robert L. Earle and John D. Wirth, eds., *Identities in North America: The Search for Community*. Stanford: Stanford University Press, 1995.

Schoenherr, Allan A. *A Natural History of California*. Berkeley: University of California Press, 1992.

Schryer, Frans J. "A Ranchero Economy in Northeastern Hidalgo, 1880–1920." *Hispanic American Historical Review* 59 (August 1979): 418–443.

———. *Ethnicity and Class Conflict in Rural Mexico*. Princeton: Princeton University Press, 1990.

Schwantes, Carlos. *Bisbee: Urban Outpost on the Frontier*. Tucson: University of Arizona Press, 1992.

———. *Vision & Enterprise: Exploring the History of Phelps Dodge Corporation*. Tucson: University of Arizona, 2000.

Schwartz, Stuart, ed. *Tropical Babylons: Sugar and the Making of the Atlantic World, 1450–1680*. Chapel Hill: University of North Carolina Press, 2004.

Sears, Paul. *Lands beyond the Forest*. Englewood Cliffs, N.J.: Prentice—Hall, 1969.

Servín, Elisa, Leticia Reina, and John Tutino, eds. *Cycles of Conflict, Centuries of Change*. Durham, N.C.: Duke University Press, 2007.

Shammas, Carole, Marylynn Salmon, and Michael Dahlin. *Inheritance in America: From Colonial Times to the Present*. New Brunswick, N.J.: Rutgers University Press, 1987.

Sheridan, Thomas E. *Arizona: A History*. Tucson: University of Arizona Press, 1995.

———. *Los Tucsonenses: The Mexican Community in Tucson, 1854–1941*. Tucson: University of Arizona Press, 2001.

Sherman, Rachel Thorndike, ed. *The Sherman Letters: Correspondence between General and Senator Sherman from 1837 to 1891*. New York: Scribner's, 1894.

Shillingberg, William B. *Tombstone, A.T.: A History of Early Mining, Milling, and Mayhem*. Spokane, Wash.: Arthur H. Clark Co., 1999.

Shinn, Charles Howard. *Mining Camps: A Study in American Frontier Government*. New York: N.p., 1884; reprint 1970.

Siddons, Leonora. *The Female Warrior: An Interesting Narrative of the Sufferings and Singular and Surprising Adventures of Miss Leonora Siddons* (1843). In Jesse Alemán and Shelley Streeby, *Empire and the Literature of Sensation: An Anthology of Nineteenth-Century Popular Fiction*. New Brunswick, N.J.: Rutgers University Press, 2007.

Simmons, Marc. "New Mexico's Smallpox Epidemic of 1780–81." *New Mexico Historical Review* 41 (October 1966): 319–326.

Slater, Gilbert. *The English Peasantry and the Enclosure of Common Fields*. London: Constable, 1907.

Slatta, Richard W. "Spanish Colonial Military Strategy and Ideology." In Donna Guy and Thomas E. Sheridan, eds., *Contested Ground: Comparative Frontiers on the Northern and Southern Edges of the Spanish Empire*. Tucson: University of Arizona Press, 1998.

Smedley, Audrey. *Race in North America: Origins and Evolution of a World View*. Boulder, Colo.: Westview Press, 1993.

Smith, Robert. *Mexican New York*. Berkeley: University of California Press, 2005.

Solaún, Mauricio, and Sidney Kronus. *Discrimination without Violence: Miscegenation and Racial Conflict in Latin America*. New York: Wiley, 1973.

Sommer, Doris. *Foundational Fictions: The National Romances of Latin America*. Berkeley: University of California Press, 1991.

Soto Laveaga, Gabriela. *Jungle Laboratories*. Durham, N.C.: Duke University Press, 2009.

Soza, Edward. *Mexican Homesteaders in the San Pedro River Valley and the Homestead Act of 1862: 1870–1908*. Altadena, Calif.: Published by author, 1993; rev. ed. 1994.

———. *Hispanic Homesteaders in Arizona, 1870–1908 under the Homestead Act of May 20, 1862 and Other Public Land Laws*. Altadena, Calif.: Published by author, 1994.

Spencer, Jon Michael. *The New Colored People: The Mixed-Race Movement in America*. New York: New York University Press, 1997.

Spicer, Edward H. *Cycles of Conquest: The Impact of Spain, Mexico, and the United States on the Indians of the Southwest, 1533–1960*. Tucson: University of Arizona Press, 1962.

Spickard, Paul R. *Mixed Blood: Intermarriage and Ethnic Identity in Twentieth-Century America*. Madison: University of Wisconsin Press, 1989.

Stein, Stanley, and Barbara Stein. *Silver, War, and Trade*. Baltimore: Johns Hopkins University Press, 2000.

Stern, Steve. *The Secret History of Gender*. Chapel Hill: University of North Carolina Press, 1995.

Stewart, Rick. "Artists and Printmakers of the Mexican War." In *Eyewitness to War: Prints and Daguerreotypes of the Mexican War, 1846–1848*, ed. Martha A. Sandweiss et al. Fort Worth, Tex.: Amon Carter Museum, 1989.

Stimson, Frederick S. "'Francis Berrian: Hispanic Influence on American Romanticism.'" *Hispania* 42, no. 4 (1959): 511–516.

Streeby, Shelley. *American Sensations: Class, Empire, and the Production of Popular Culture*. Berkeley: University of California Press, 2002.

Street, R. S. *Beasts of the Field: A Narrative History of California Farmworkers, 1769–1913*. Stanford: Stanford University Press, 2004.

Strikwerda, Carl, and Camille Guerin-Gonzales. "Labor, Migration, and Politics." In Camille Guerin-Gonzales and Carl Strikwerda, eds., *The Politics of Immigrant Workers: Labor Activism and Migration in the World Economy since 1830*. New York: Holmes & Meier, 1993.

Swann, Michael. *Tierra Adentro: Settlement and Society in Colonial Durango*. Boulder, Colo.: Westview Press, 1982.

Tanck de Estrada, Dorothy. *Los pueblos de indios y la educación en la Nueva España*. Mexico City: El Colegio de México, 1999.

Taylor, Paul, and Richard Fry. *Hispanics and the 2008 Election: A Swing Vote?* Washington, D.C.: Pew Hispanic Center, 2007.

Taylor, William. *Drinking, Homicide, and Rebellion in Colonial Mexican Villages*. Stanford: Stanford University Press, 1979.

———. *Magistrates of the Sacred*. Stanford: Stanford University Press, 1996.

Tefertiller, Casey. *Wyatt Earp: The Life behind the Legend*. New York: John Wiley & Sons, 1997.

Telles, Edward, and Edward Murguía. "Phenotypic Discrimination and Income Differences among Mexican Americans." *Social Science Quarterly* 71 (1990): 682–696.

Thompson, E. P. *The Making of the English Working Class*. New York: Vintage, 1963.

Thompson, Jerry, *Vaqueros in Blue and Gray*. Austin, Tex.: Presidial Press, 1976.

Thoreau, Henry David. "Resistance to Civil Government" (1849). Reprinted in Henry David Thoreau, *Reform Papers*, ed. Wendell Glick. Princeton: Princeton University Press, 1973.

Tijerina, Andrés. *Tejanos and Texas under the Mexican Flag, 1821–1836*. College Station: Texas A&M University Press, 1994.

Tinnemeyer, Andrea. "Enlightenment Ideology and the Crisis of Whiteness in Francis Berrian and Caballero." *Western American Literature* 35, no. 1 (Spring 2000): 21–32.

Torres-Pares, J. *La revolución sin frontera: El Partido Liberal Mexicano y las relaciones entre el movimiento obrero de México y de los Estados Unidos 1900–1923*. Mexico City: Universidad Nacional Autónoma de México, 1990.

Trafzer, Clifford E. *The Kit Carson Campaign: The Last Great Navajo War*. Norman: University of Oklahoma Press, 1982.

Trennert, Robert A. "Educating Indian Girls at Non-Reservation Boarding Schools, 1878–1920." *Western Historical Quarterly* 13 (July 1982): 271–290.

Truett, Samuel. *Fugitive Landscapes: The Forgotten History of the U.S.-Mexico Borderlands*. New Haven: Yale University Press, 2006.

Turner, Ethel Duffy. *Revolution in Baja California: Ricardo Flores Magon's High Noon*. Detroit: Blaine Ethridge Books, 1981.

Turner, Frederick Jackson. "The Significance of the Frontier in American History." *American Historical Association Annual Report* (1893): 199–227.

Turner, Michael. *Enclosures in Britain, 1750–1830*. London: Macmillan, 1984.

Tutino, John. "Life and Labor on North Mexican Haciendas." In Elsa Cecilia Frost et al., eds., *El trabajo y los trabajadores en la historia de México*. Mexico City: El Colegio de México, 1979.

———. *From Insurrection to Revolution in Mexico: Social Bases of Agrarian Violence, 1750–1940*. Princeton: Princeton University Press, 1986.

———. "Urban Power and Agrarian Society: Mexico City and Its Hinterland in the Colonial Era." In *La ciudad, el campo y la frontera en la historia de México*. Mexico City: Universidad Nacional Autónoma de México, 1992.

———. "The Revolution in Mexican Independence." *Hispanic American Historical Review* 78, no. 3 (1998): 367–418.

———. "Buscando independencias populares." In José Antonio Serrano and Marta Terán, eds., *El tiempo de las independencias en la América Española*. Zamora: El Colegio de Michoacán, 2002.

———. "From Involution to Revolution in Mexico: Liberal Development, Patriarchy, and Social Violence in the Central Highlands, 1870–1915." *History Compass* 6 (May 2008): 796–842.

————. *Making a New World: Founding Capitalism in the Bajío and Spanish North America.* Durham, N.C.: Duke University Press, 2011.

Twinam, Ann. *Public Lives, Private Secrets: Gender, Honor, Sexuality and Illegitimacy in Latin America.* Stanford: Stanford University Press, 1999.

Vale, Thomas P. "Forest Changes in the Warner Mountains, California." *Annals of the Association of American Geographers* 67 (March 1977): 28–45.

Vallejo, Jody Agius. *The Mexican Origin Middle Class in Los Angeles.* Los Angeles: Center for the Study of Immigrant Integration, University of Southern California, 2009.

Van Young, Eric. *The Other Rebellion.* Stanford: Stanford University Press, 2003.

Vargas, Zaragosa. *Proletarians of the North: A History of Mexican Industrial Workers in Detroit and the Midwest, 1917–1933.* Berkeley: University of California Press, 1993.

————. *Labor Rights Are Civil Rights: Mexican American Workers in Twentieth-Century America.* Princeton: Princeton University Press, 2004.

Varzally, Allison. *Making a Non-White America: Californians Coloring Outside Ethnic Lines, 1925–1955.* Berkeley: University of California Press, 2008.

Vasconcelos, J. *Ulises criollo.* Mexico City: Fondo de Cultura Económica, 1982.

Vaughan, Tom. "Everyday Life in a Copper Camp." In Carlos Schwantes, ed., *Bisbee: Urban Outpost on the Frontier.* Tucson: University of Arizona Press, 1992.

Vázquez, Josefina, ed. *México al tiempo de su guerra con Estados Unidos, 1846–1848.* Mexico City: Fondo de Cultura Económica, 1997.

Velasco Ortiz, Laura. *Migración, fronteras e identidades étnicas transnacionales.* Mexico City: El Colegio de la Frontera Norte and Miguel Ángel Porrúa, 2008.

Vidich, Arthur J., ed. *The New Middle Classes: Life Styles, Status Claims and Political Orientations.* New York: New York University Press, 1995.

Wagatsuma, Hiroshi. "The Social Perception of Skin Color in Japan." In John Hope Franklin, ed., *Color and Race.* Boston: Houghton Mifflin, 1968.

Wagoner, Jay J. *Early Arizona: Prehistory to Civil War.* Tucson: University of Arizona Press, 1975.

Walsh and Fitzgerald, comps. *Bisbee and Warren District Directory 1917–8.* Bisbee, Ariz.: Walsh & Fitzgerald, 1917.

Walton, John. *Western Times and Water Wars: State, Culture, and Rebellion in California.* Berkeley: University of California Press, 1992.

————. *Storied Land: Community and Memory in Monterey.* Berkeley: University of California Press, 2003.

Warner, Michael. *Letters of the Republic: Publication and the Public Sphere in Eighteenth-Century America.* Cambridge: Harvard University Press, 1992.

Waters, Mary C. "Ethnic and Racial Identities of Second-Generation Black Immigrants in New York City." In Alejandro Portes, ed., *The New Second Generation.* New York: Russell Sage, 1996.

————. *Black Identities: West Indian Immigrant Dreams and American Realities.* Cambridge: Harvard University Press, 1999.

Weber, David. *The Mexican Frontier, 1821–1846: The American Southwest under Mexico.* Albuquerque: University of New Mexico Press, 1982.

————. *The Spanish Frontier in North America.* New Haven: Yale University Press, 1992.

———. *Bárbaros: Spaniards and Their Savages in the Age of Enlightenment.* New Haven: Yale University Press, 2006.

Weber, Devra. *Dark Sweat, White Gold: California Farm Workers, Cotton and the New Deal.* Berkeley: University of California Press, 1994.

West, Elliott. *The Way to the West: Essays on the Central Plains.* Albuquerque: University of New Mexico Press, 1997.

West, Robert. *The Mining Community in Northern New Spain: The Parral Mining District.* Berkeley: University of California Press, 1949.

White, J. E. "I'm Just Who I Am: Race Is No Longer as Simple as Black or White. So, What Does This Mean for America?" *Time* (May 5, 1997): 32–36.

White, Richard. "The Winning of the West: The Expansion of the Western Sioux in the Eighteenth and Nineteenth Centuries." *Journal of American History* 65 (September 1978): 319–343.

———. *The Roots of Dependency: Subsistence, Environment, and Social Change among the Choctaws, Pawnees, and Navajos.* Lincoln: University of Nebraska Press, 1983.

———. *The Middle Ground: Indians, Empires, and Republics in the Great Lakes Region, 1650–1815.* Cambridge: Cambridge University Press, 1991.

———. "Animals and Enterprise." In Clyde A. Milner II, Carol A. O'Connor, and Martha Sandweiss, eds., *The Oxford History of the American West.* New York: Oxford University Press, 1994.

Wickberg, Daniel. "Heterosexual White Male: Some Recent Inversions in American Cultural History." *Journal of American History* 92 (June 2005): 136–157.

Wild, Mark. *Street Meeting: Multi-Ethnic Neighborhoods in Early Twentieth-Century Los Angeles.* Berkeley: University of California Press, 2005.

Williams, Jon Hoyt. "Black Labor and State Ranches: The Tabapi Experience in Paraguay." *Journal of Negro History* 62 (October 1977): 378–789.

Witherspoon, Gary. "Sheep in Navajo Culture and Social Organization." *American Anthropologist* 75 (October 1973): 1441–1447.

Woodward, C. Vann. *The Strange Career of Jim Crow.* New York: Oxford University Press, 1966.

Wright, Angus. *The Death of Ramón González.* Austin: University of Texas Press, 1990.

Wright, Winthrop R. *Café con Leche: Race, Class, and National Image in Venezuela.* Austin: University of Texas Press, 1990.

Wrightson, Keith. *Earthly Necessities: Economic Lives in Early Modern Britain.* New Haven: Yale University Press, 2000.

Xicoténcatl: An Anonymous Historical Novel about the Events Leading Up to the Conquest of the Aztec Empire. Trans. Guillermo I. Castillo-Feliú. Austin: University of Texas Press, 1999. The first, Spanish-language, version of the novel is *Jicoténcal.* Philadelphia: William Stavely, 1826.

Yelling, J. A. *Common Field and Enclosure in England, 1450–1850.* London: Macmillan, 1977.

Yturria, Frank Daniel. *The Patriarch: The Remarkable Life and Extraordinary Times of Francisco Yturria.* Brownsville: University of Texas at Brownsville, 2006.

Yu, Henry. "How Tiger Woods Lost His Stripes: Post-National American Studies as a History of Race, Migration and the Commodification of Culture." In John C. Rowe, ed., *Post-National American Studies*. Berkeley: University of California Press, 2000.

Zamora, Emilio. *The World of the Mexican Worker in Texas*. College Station: Texas A&M University Press, 1993.

Zweigenhaft, Richard L., and G. William Domhoff. *Diversity in the Power Elite: How It Happened, Why It Matters*. New Haven: Yale University Press, 1998.

Contributors

KATHERINE BENTON-COHEN is Associate Professor of History at Georgetown University. She is author of *Borderline Americans: Racial Division and Labor War in the Arizona Borderlands* (Harvard University Press, 2009). Her current project focuses on immigration and immigration policy in the United States in the early twentieth century.

RAMÓN A. GUTIÉRREZ is Morton Distinguished Service Professor of American History at the University of Chicago. He is author of *When Jesus Came, the Corn Mothers Went Away: Marriage, Sexuality, and Power in New Mexico, 1500–1846* (Stanford University Press, 1991) and co-editor of *Contested Eden: California before the Gold Rush* (University of California Press, 1998).

ANDREW C. ISENBERG is Professor of History at Temple University. He is author of *The Destruction of the Bison: An Environmental History, 1750–1920* (Cambridge University Press, 2000) and *Mining California: An Ecological History* (Hill and Wang, 2005).

JOSÉ E. LIMÓN serves as Notre Dame Professor of American Literature and Professor of American Studies at Notre Dame University. He has written *Mexican Ballads, Chicano Poems: History and Influence in Mexican-American Social Poetry* (University of California Press, 1992), *Dancing with the Devil: Society and Cultural Poetics in Mexican-American South Texas* (University of Wisconsin Press, 1994), and *American Encounters: Greater Mexico, the United States, and the Erotics of Culture* (Beacon Press, 1998).

DAVID MONTEJANO is Professor in the Ethnic Studies Department of the University of California, Berkeley. He is author of *Anglos and Mexicans in the Making of Texas, 1836–1986* (University of Texas Press, 1987), and *Quixote's Soldiers: A Local History of the Chicano Movement, 1966–1981* (University of Texas Press, 2010).

SHELLEY STREEBY is Associate Professor in the Department of Literature at the University of California, San Diego. She is author of *American Sensations: Class, Empire, and the Production of Popular Culture* (University of California Press, 2002) and co-editor of *Empire and the Literature of Sensation: An Anthology of Nineteenth-Century Popular Fiction* (Rutgers University Press, 2007).

JOHN TUTINO is Professor in the History Department and School of Foreign Service at Georgetown University. He is author of *From Insurrection to Revolution in Mexico: Social Bases of Agrarian Violence, 1750–1940* (Princeton University Press, 1986) and *Making a New World: Founding Capitalism in the Bajío and Spanish North America* (Duke University Press, 2011).

DEVRA WEBER is Associate Professor of History at the University of California, Riverside. Author of *Dark Sweat, White Gold: California Farmworkers and the New Deal, 1919–1939* (University of California Press, 1994), she is currently completing a history of the participation of indigenous Mexicans in the U.S. labor movement in the early twentieth century.

Index

Page numbers in italics refer to illustrations.